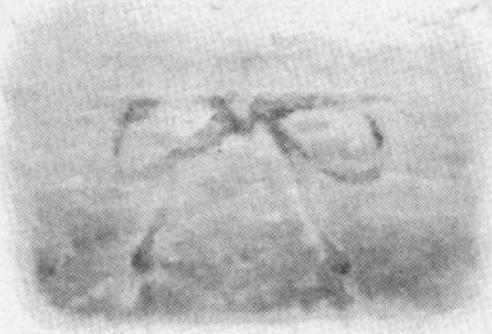

久保帯人

I've recently learned to tie almost perfect butterfly knots, something I've never been able to do and had almost given up on. Life is a daily learning process. So now, whenever someone asks me, "What's your hobby?" it's my policy to respond: "Butterfly knots." This is a limited-time offer, so act soon.
Tite Kubo

Bleach is author Tite Kubo's second title. Kubo made his debut with *Zombie Powder*, a four-volume series for *Weekly Shonen Jump*. To date, *Bleach* has been translated into numerous languages and has also inspired an animated TV series that began airing in Japan in 2004. Beginning its serialization in 2001, *Bleach* is still a mainstay in the pages of *Weekly Shonen Jump*. In 2005, *Bleach* was awarded the prestigious Shogakukan Manga Award in the *shonen* (boys) category.

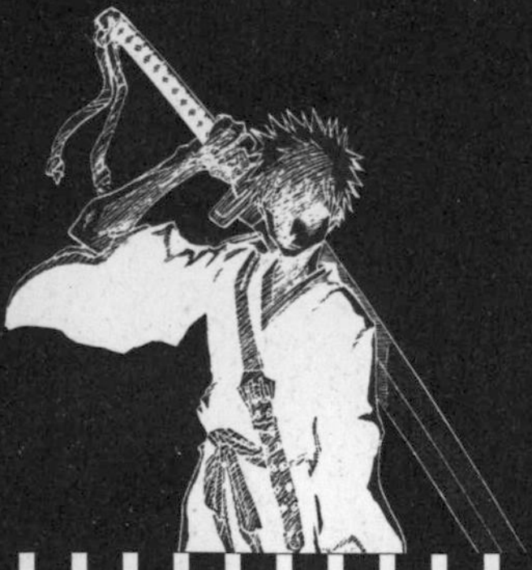

BLEACH
Vol. 10: TATTOO ON THE SKY
The SHONEN JUMP Manga Edition

STORY AND ART BY
TITE KUBO

English Adaptation/Lance Caselman
Translation/Joe Yamazaki
Touch-Up Art & Lettering/Andy Ristaino
Design/Sean Lee
Editor/Kit Fox

Editor in Chief, Books/Alvin Lu
Editor in Chief, Magazines/Marc Weidenbaum
VP of Publishing Licensing/Rika Inouye
VP of Sales/Gonzalo Ferreyra
Sr. VP of Marketing/Liza Coppola
Publisher/Hyoe Narita

Printed in the U.S.A.

Published by VIZ Media, LLC
P.O. Box 77010
San Francisco, CA 94107

SHONEN JUMP Manga Edition
10 9 8 7 6 5
First printing, November 2005
Fifth printing, May 2008

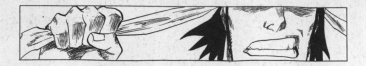

We reach out with our hands
Brush away the clouds and pierce the sky
To grab the moon and Mars
But we still can't reach the truth

BLEACH 10

TATTOO ON THE SKY

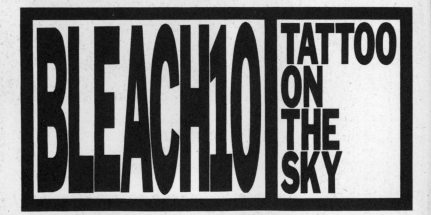

Shonen Jump Manga

STARS AND

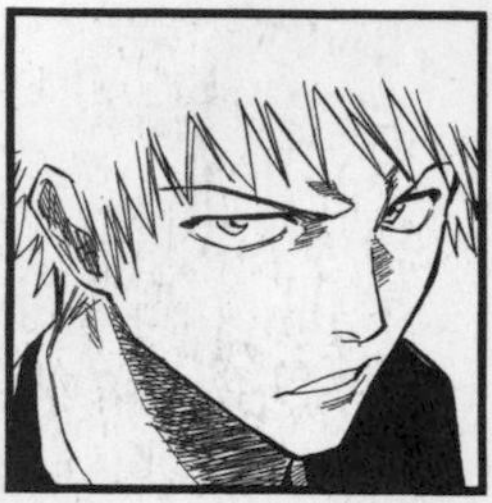

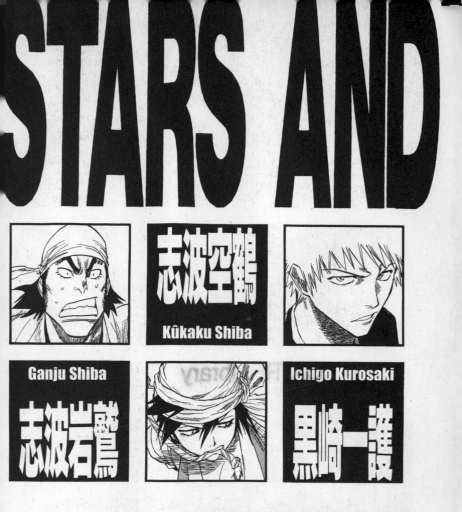

志波空鶴
Kûkaku Shiba

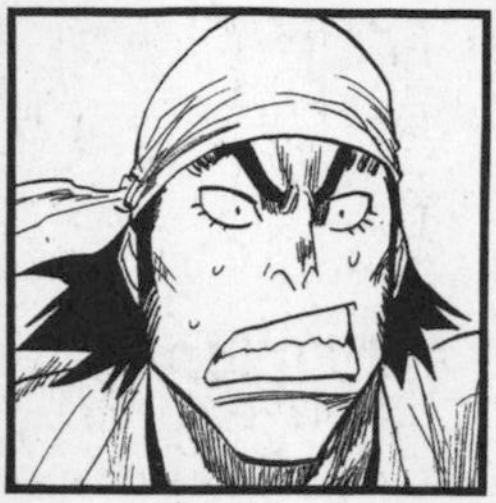

Ichigo Kurosaki
黒崎一護

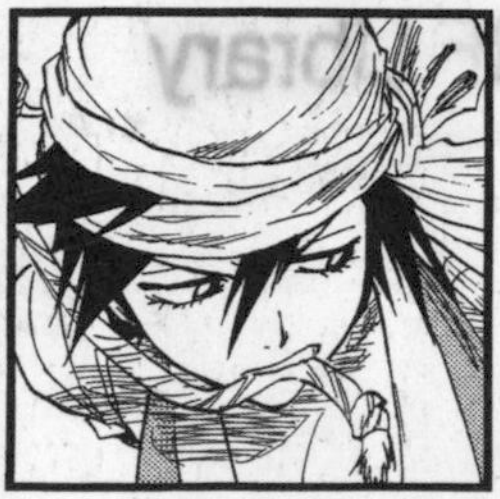

Ganju Shiba
志波岩鷲

plot

One fateful night, Ichigo Kurosaki encounters Soul Reaper Rukia Kuchiki and ends up helping her do her job—which is cleansing lost souls, called Hollows, and guiding them to the Soul Society. But when Rukia is arrested and taken back to the Soul Society to be executed, Ichigo vows to save her. He and a band of friends make the dangerous journey to the other world. There they attempt to infiltrate the Seireitei, the abode of the Soul Reapers, only to be thwarted by Gin Ichimaru. With time running out, Yoruichi turns for help to Kûkaku Shiba, Rukongai's premier fireworks technician!!

BLEACH ALL STORIES

藍染惣右介
Sôsuke Aizen

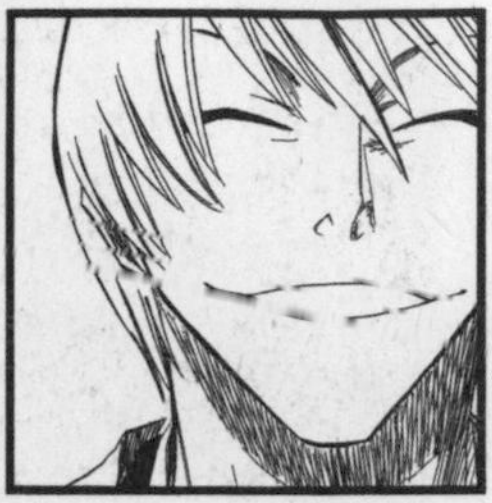

斑目一角
Ikkaku Madarame

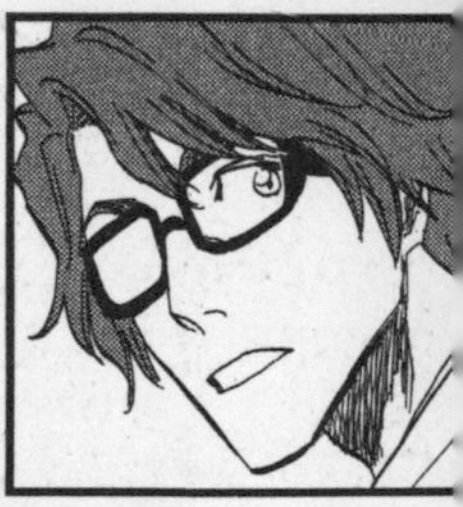

Gin Ichimaru
市丸ギン

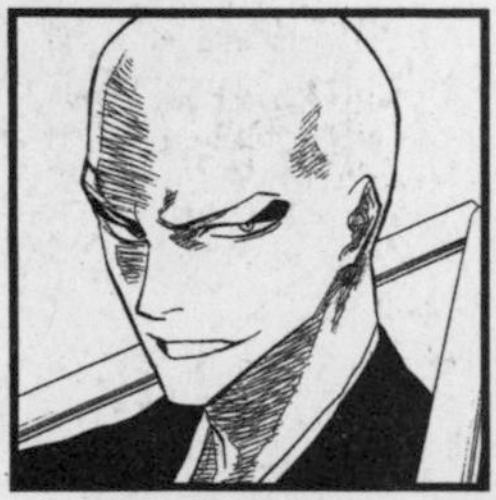

BLEACH 10

TATTOO ON THE SKY

Contents

80. The Shooting Star Project

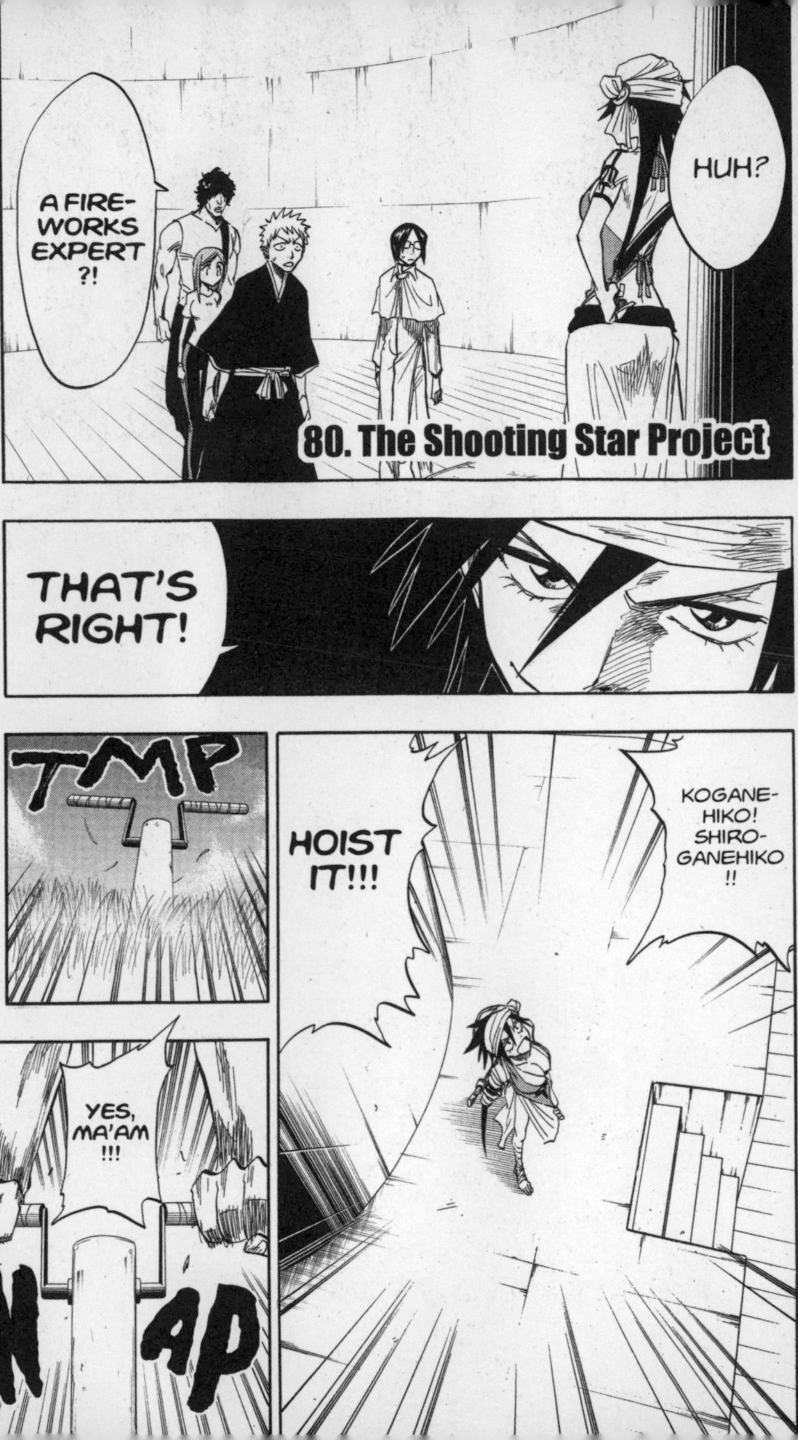
HUH?
A FIRE-WORKS EXPERT?!
THAT'S RIGHT!
KOGANE-HIKO! SHIRO-GANEHIKO!!
HOIST IT!!!
TMP
YES, MA'AM!!!
WAP

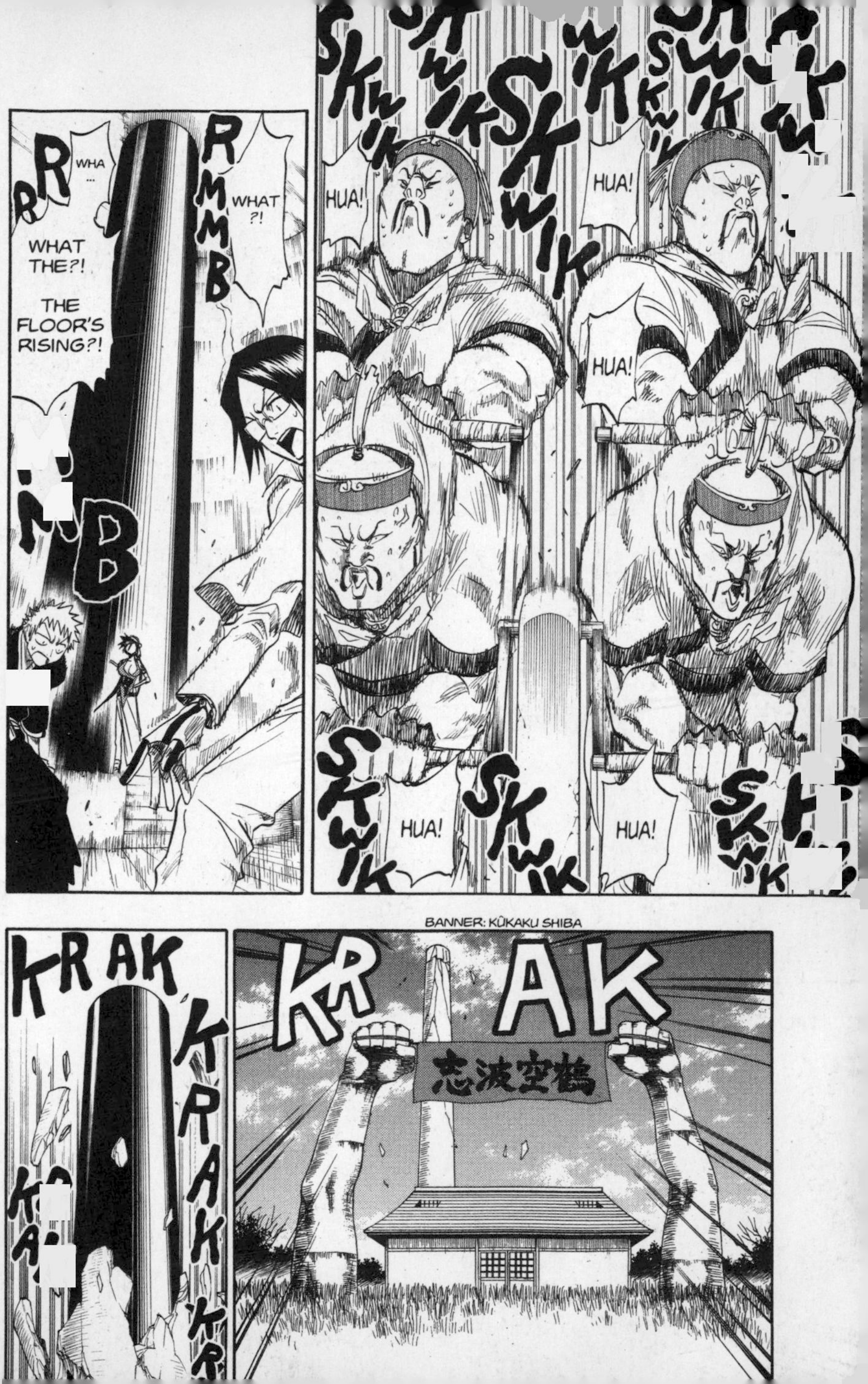
SHWIK SHWIK SHWIK
HUA!
HUA!
HUA!
HUA!
HUA!
HUA!
SKWIK SKWIK
RRRMMMB
WHA ...
WHAT ?!
WHAT THE?!
THE FLOOR'S RISING?!
BANNER: KŪKAKU SHIBA
KR AK
志波空鶴
KRAK KRAK
KRAK

READ THIS WAY

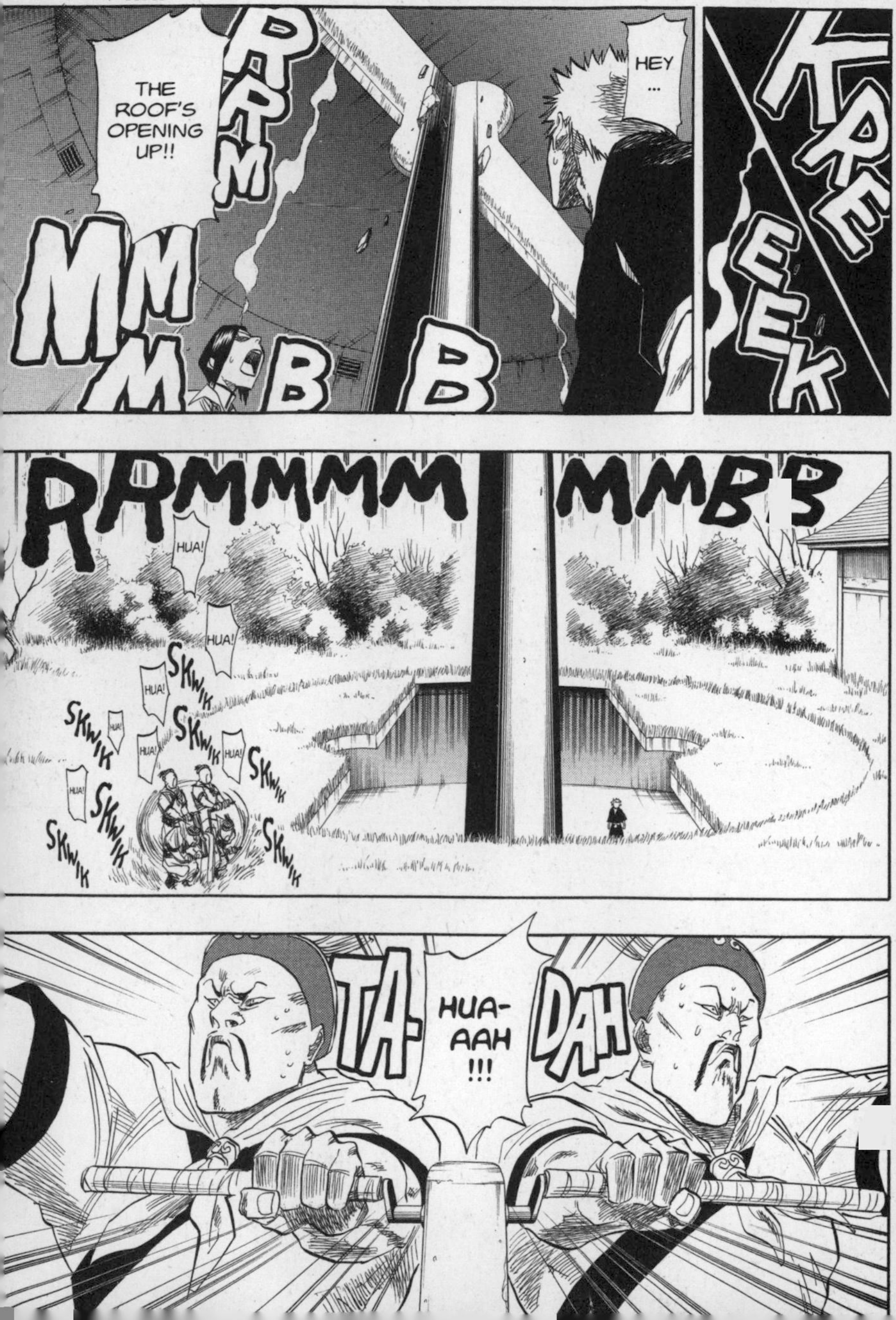
KREEEK
HEY ...
RRMMMMMBB
THE ROOF'S OPENING UP!!
RRMMMMMMMMMBB
HUA!
HUA!
HUA!
HUA!
HUA!
HUA!
HUA!
SKWIK
SKWIK
SKWIK
SKWIK
SKWIK
SKWIK
SKWIK
TA-DAH
HUA-AAH!!!

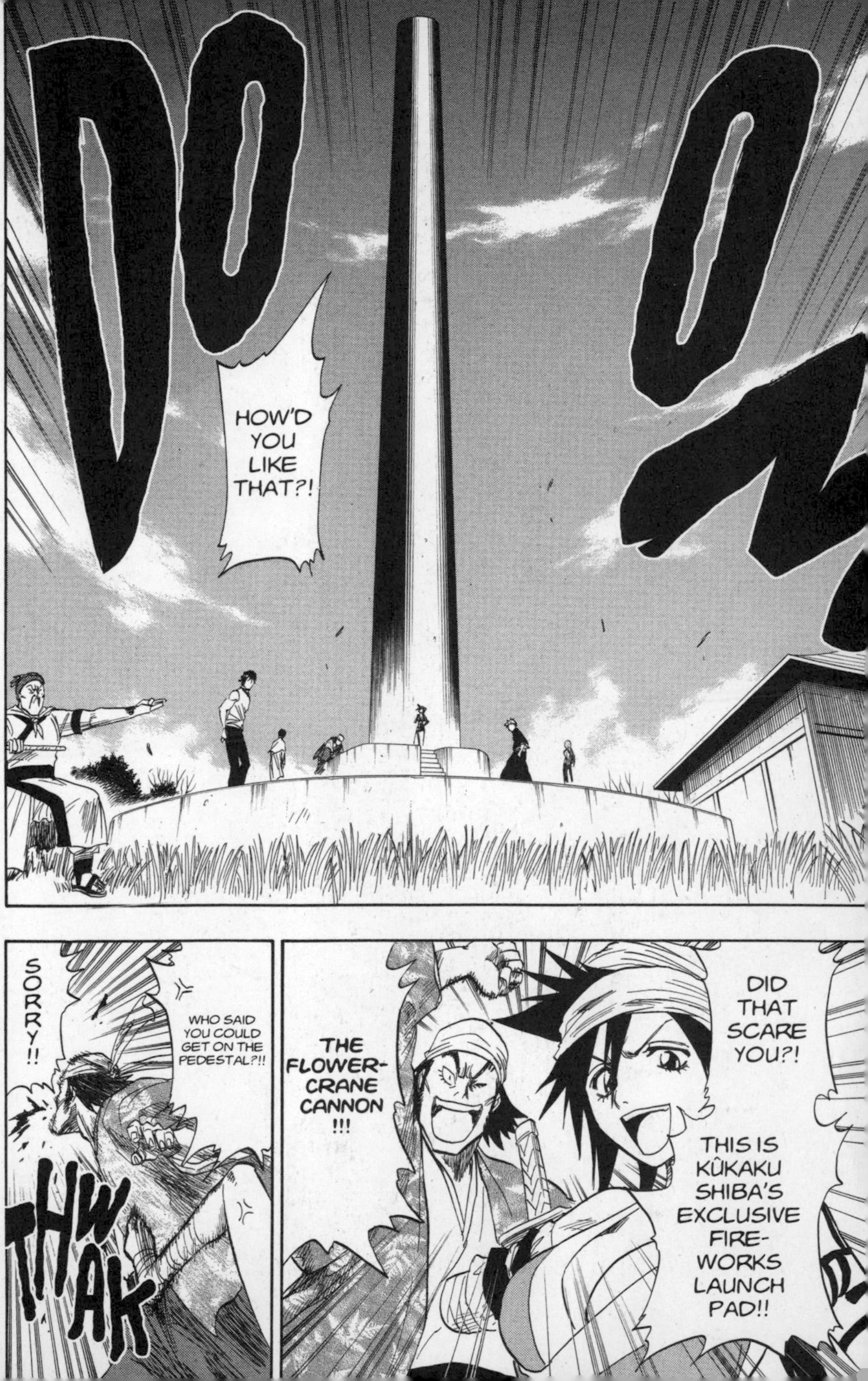
DOON
HOW'D YOU LIKE THAT?!
DID THAT SCARE YOU?!
THIS IS KÛKAKU SHIBA'S EXCLUSIVE FIRE-WORKS LAUNCH PAD!!
THE FLOWER-CRANE CANNON !!!
WHO SAID YOU COULD GET ON THE PEDESTAL?!!
SORRY!!
THWAK

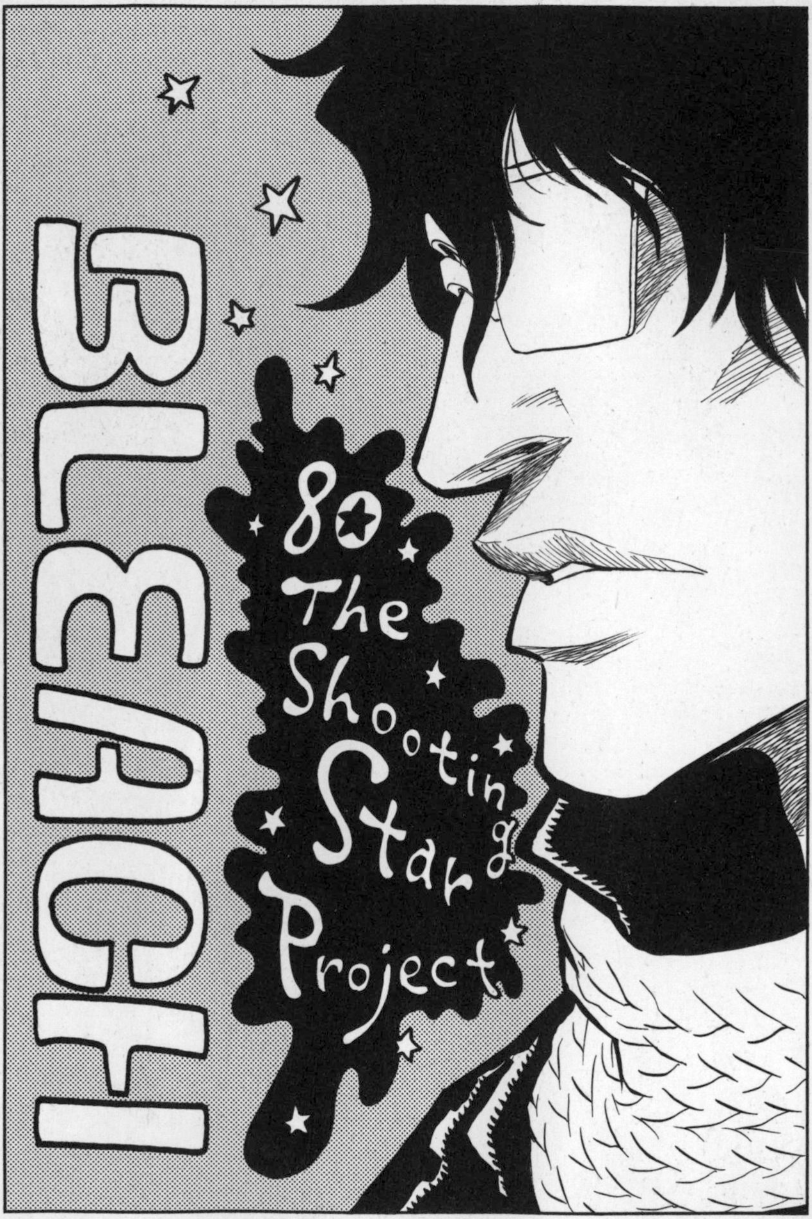
BLEACH
80 The Shooting Star Project

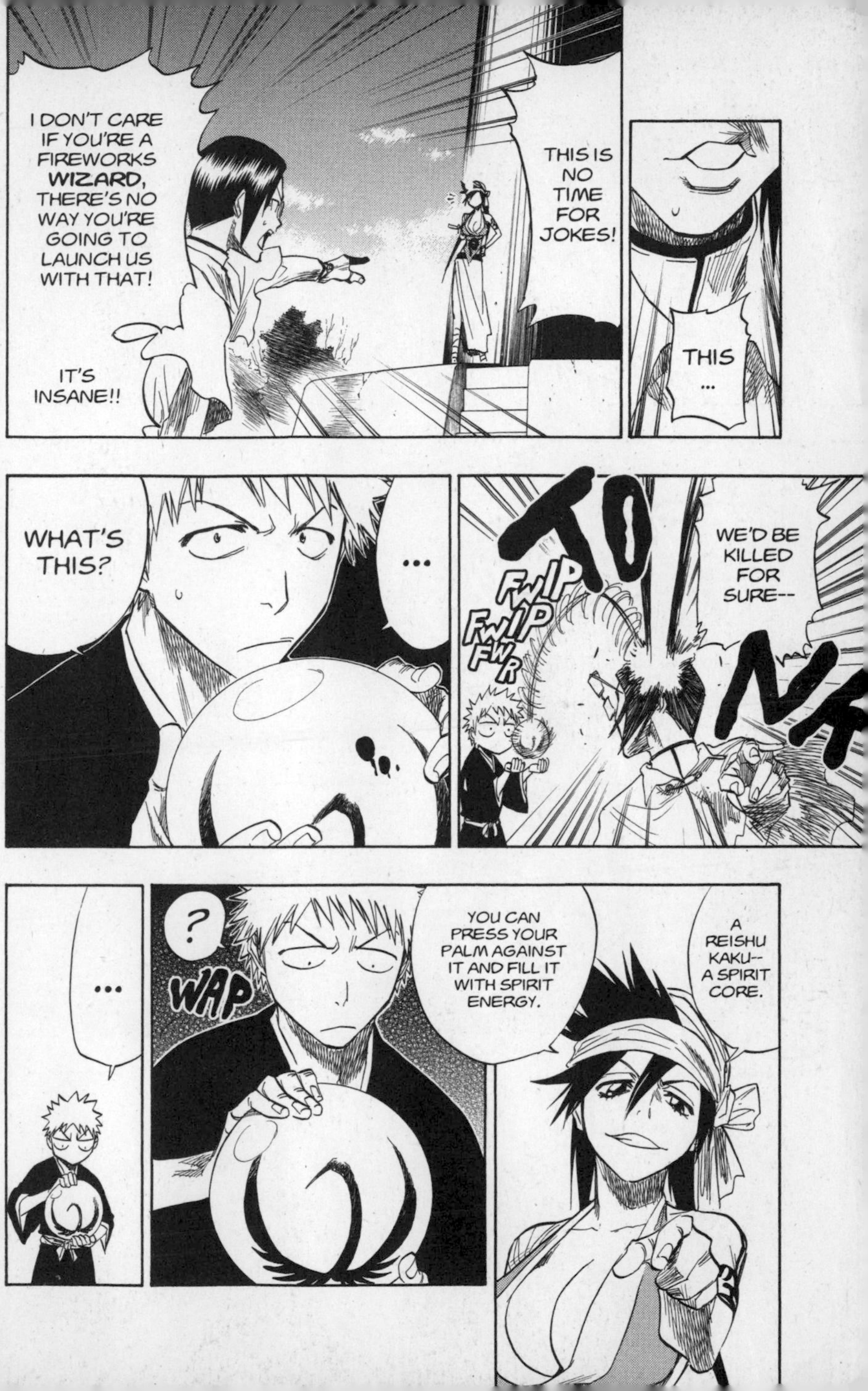
THIS ...
THIS IS NO TIME FOR JOKES!
I DON'T CARE IF YOU'RE A FIREWORKS WIZARD, THERE'S NO WAY YOU'RE GOING TO LAUNCH US WITH THAT!
IT'S INSANE!!
TO
WE'D BE KILLED FOR SURE--
N
FWIP FWIP FWR
...
WHAT'S THIS?
A REISHU KAKU-- A SPIRIT CORE.
YOU CAN PRESS YOUR PALM AGAINST IT AND FILL IT WITH SPIRIT ENERGY.
?
WAP
...

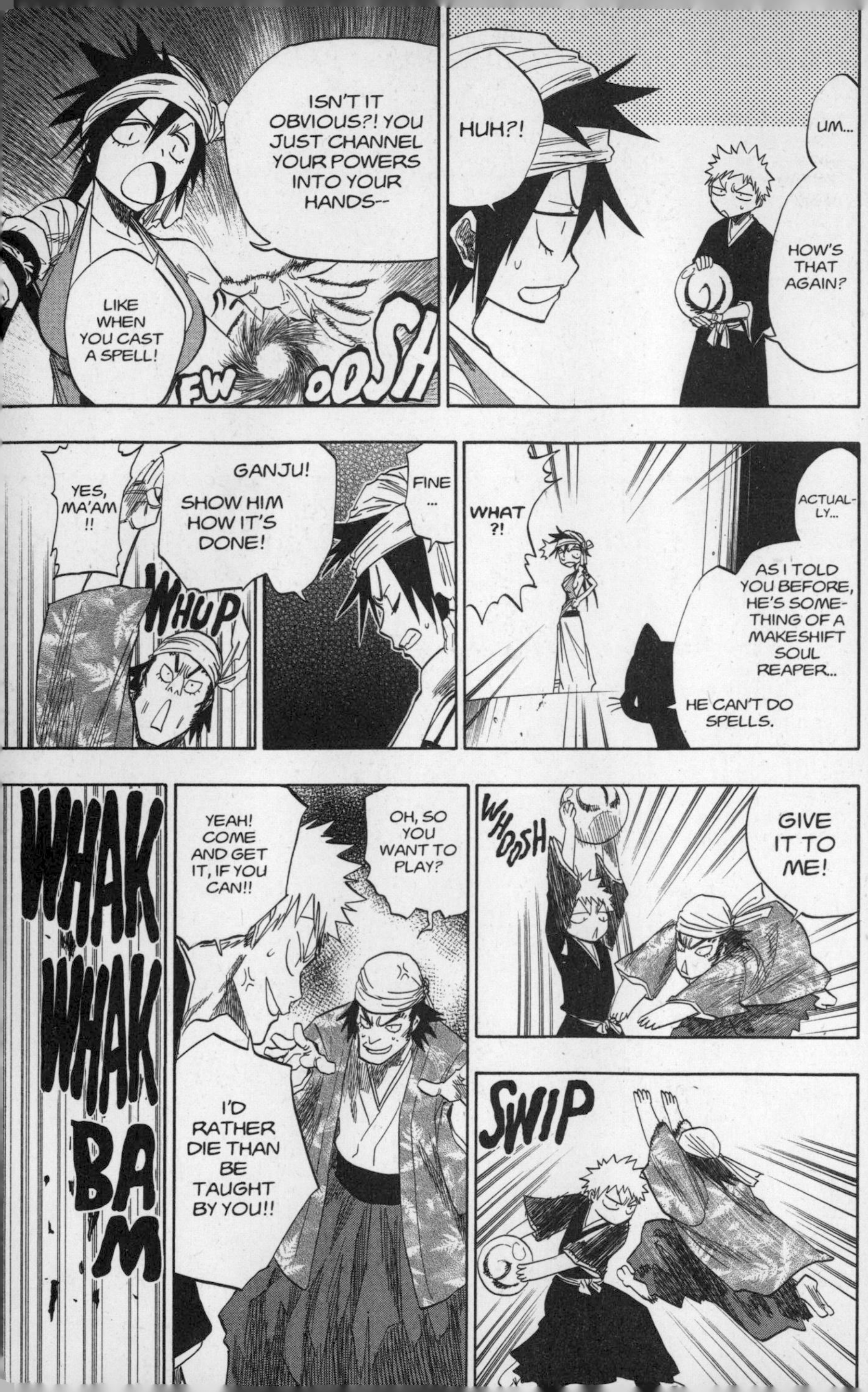
UM...
HUH?!
HOW'S THAT AGAIN?
ISN'T IT OBVIOUS?! YOU JUST CHANNEL YOUR POWERS INTO YOUR HANDS--
LIKE WHEN YOU CAST A SPELL!
FWOOSH
ACTUAL-LY...
AS I TOLD YOU BEFORE, HE'S SOME-THING OF A MAKESHIFT SOUL REAPER...
HE CAN'T DO SPELLS.
WHAT?!
FINE...
GANJU!
SHOW HIM HOW IT'S DONE!
YES, MA'AM!!
WHUP
GIVE IT TO ME!
WHOOSH
SWIP
OH, SO YOU WANT TO PLAY?
YEAH! COME AND GET IT, IF YOU CAN!!
I'D RATHER DIE THAN BE TAUGHT BY YOU!!
WHAK
WHAK
BAM

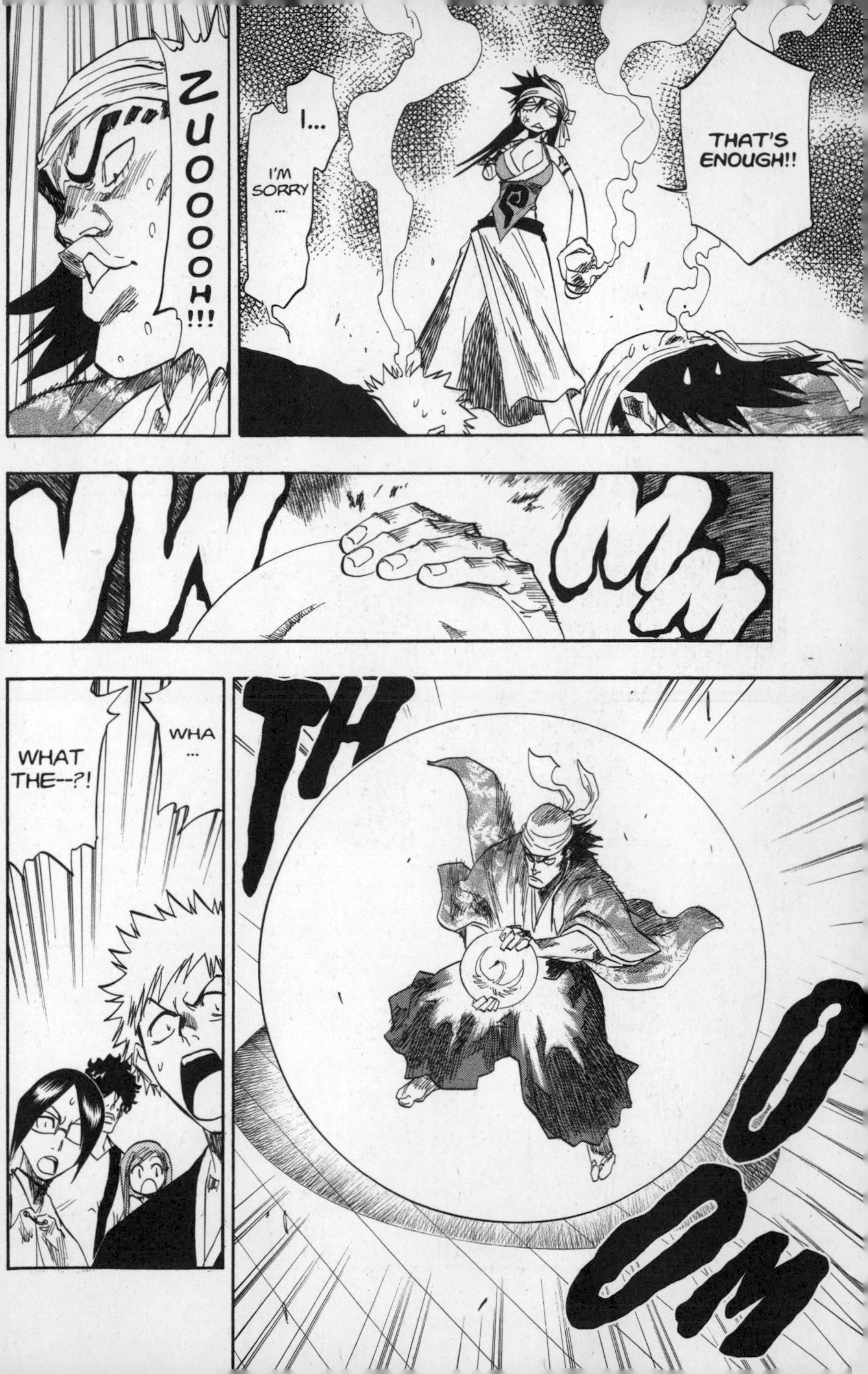
THAT'S ENOUGH!!
I...
I'M SORRY...
ZUOOOOOH!!!
VWMM
THOOM
WHA...
WHAT THE--?!

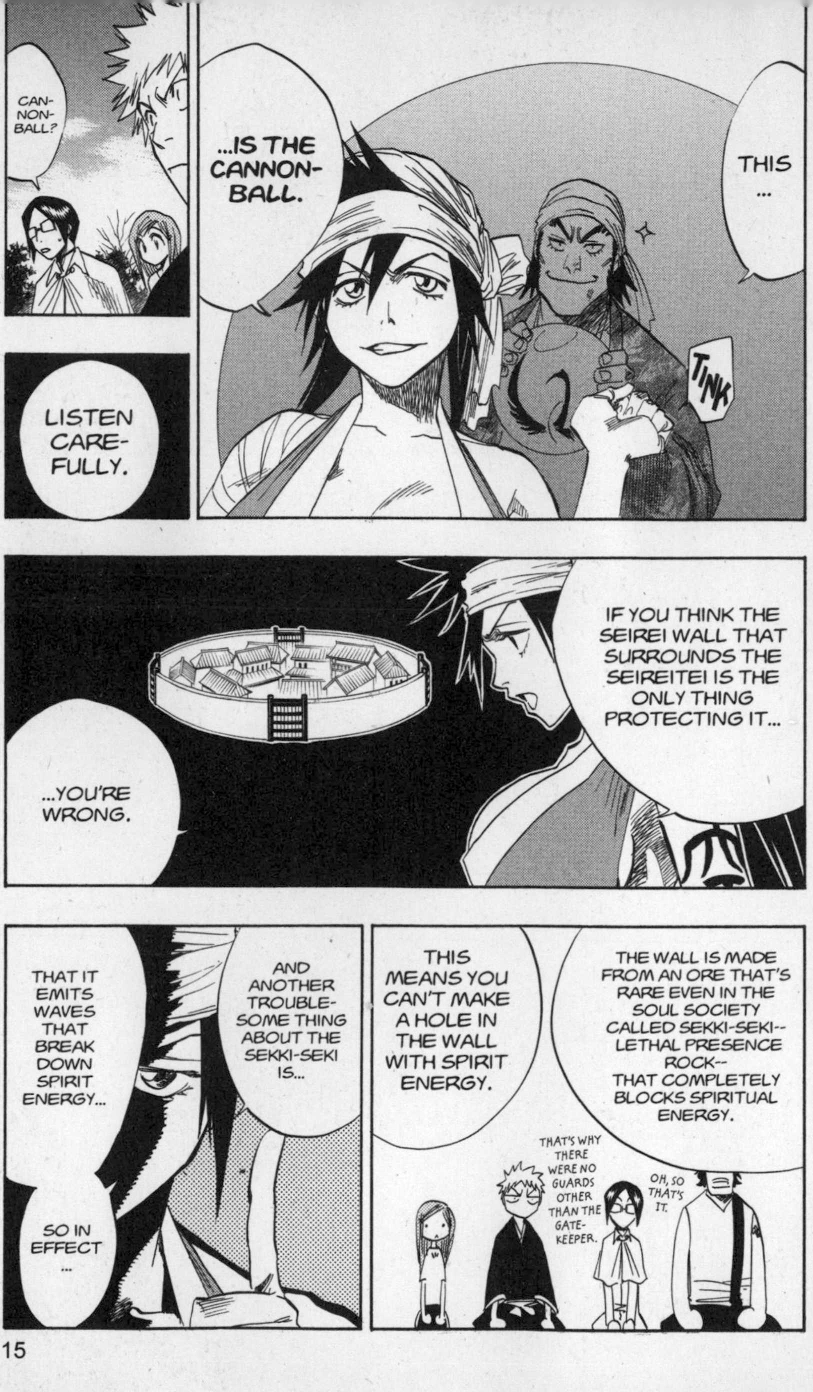
THIS ...
...IS THE CANNON-BALL.
TINK
CAN-NON-BALL?
LISTEN CARE-FULLY.
IF YOU THINK THE SEIREI WALL THAT SURROUNDS THE SEIREITEI IS THE ONLY THING PROTECTING IT...
...YOU'RE WRONG.
THE WALL IS MADE FROM AN ORE THAT'S RARE EVEN IN THE SOUL SOCIETY CALLED SEKKI-SEKI-- LETHAL PRESENCE ROCK-- THAT COMPLETELY BLOCKS SPIRITUAL ENERGY.
THIS MEANS YOU CAN'T MAKE A HOLE IN THE WALL WITH SPIRIT ENERGY.
THAT'S WHY THERE WERE NO GUARDS OTHER THAN THE GATE-KEEPER.
OH, SO THAT'S IT.
AND ANOTHER TROUBLE-SOME THING ABOUT THE SEKKI-SEKI IS...
THAT IT EMITS WAVES THAT BREAK DOWN SPIRIT ENERGY...
SO IN EFFECT ...

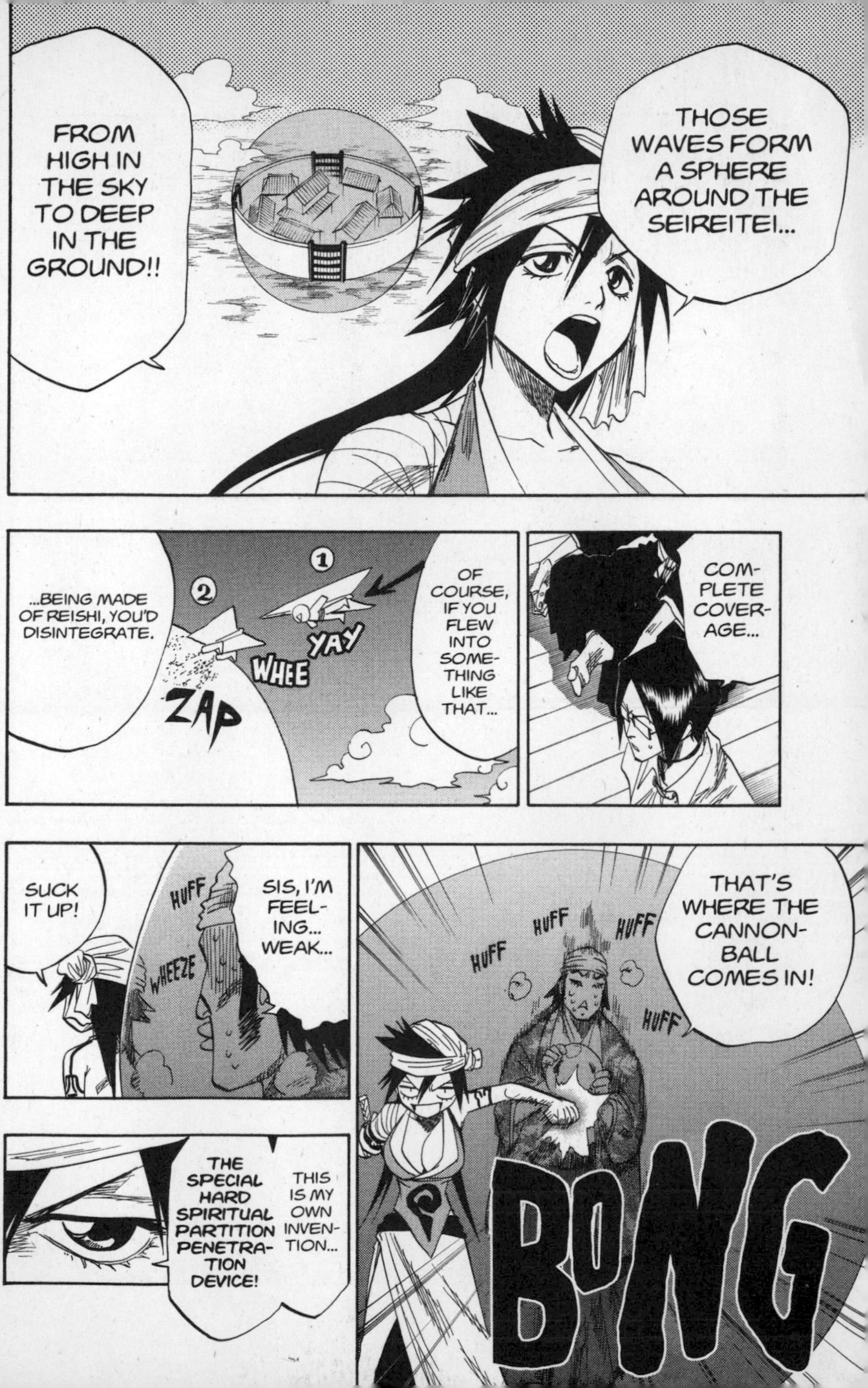
THOSE WAVES FORM A SPHERE AROUND THE SEIREITEI...
FROM HIGH IN THE SKY TO DEEP IN THE GROUND!!
COMPLETE COVERAGE...
OF COURSE, IF YOU FLEW INTO SOMETHING LIKE THAT...
1
YAY
2
WHEE
ZAP
...BEING MADE OF REISHI, YOU'D DISINTEGRATE.
THAT'S WHERE THE CANNONBALL COMES IN!
HUFF
HUFF
HUFF
HUFF
BONG
SIS, I'M FEELING... WEAK...
HUFF
WHEEZE
SUCK IT UP!
THIS IS MY OWN INVENTION...
THE SPECIAL HARD SPIRITUAL PARTITION PENETRATION DEVICE!

READ THIS WAY

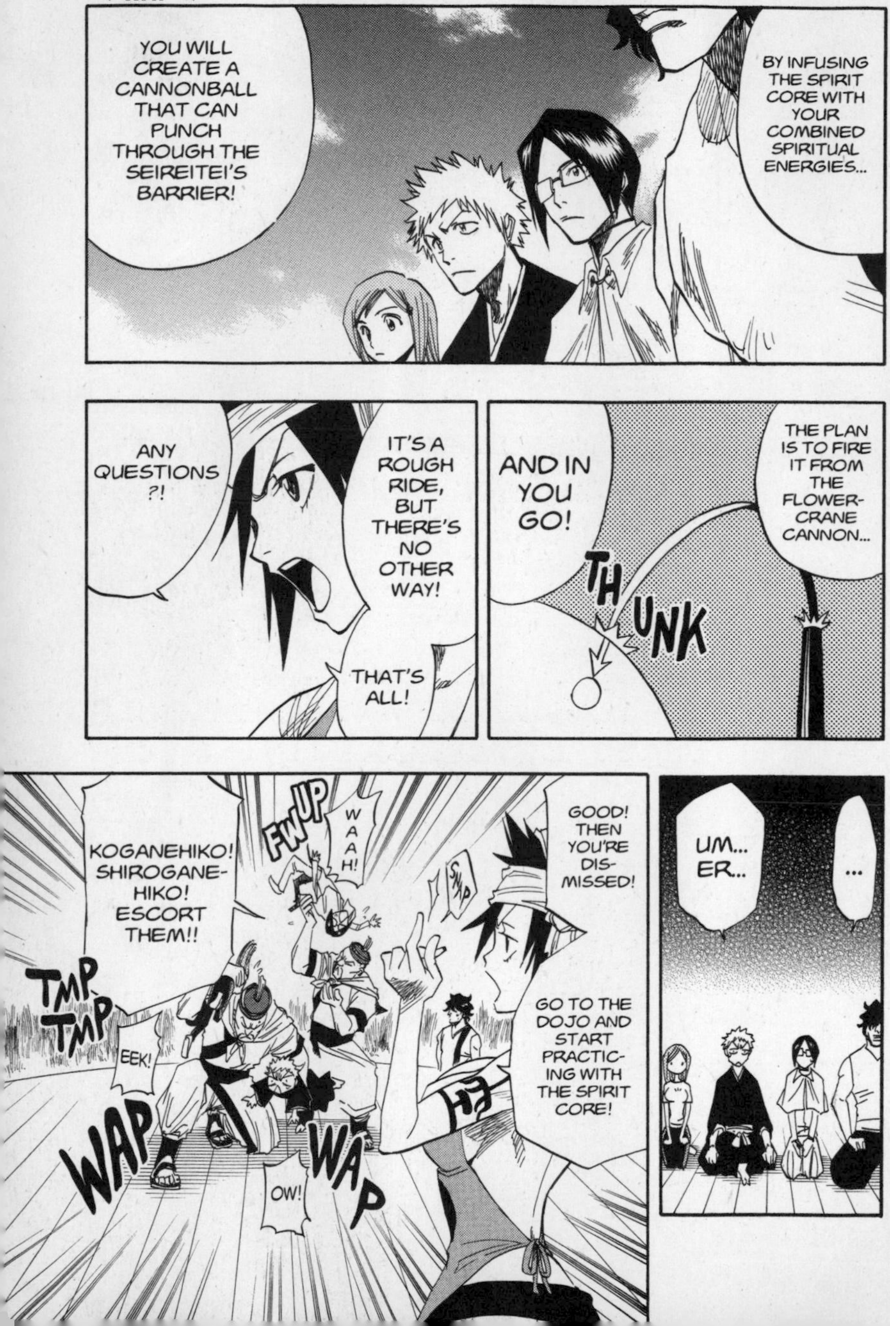
BY INFUSING THE SPIRIT CORE WITH YOUR COMBINED SPIRITUAL ENERGIES...
YOU WILL CREATE A CANNONBALL THAT CAN PUNCH THROUGH THE SEIREITEI'S BARRIER!
THE PLAN IS TO FIRE IT FROM THE FLOWER-CRANE CANNON...
AND IN YOU GO!
THUNK
IT'S A ROUGH RIDE, BUT THERE'S NO OTHER WAY!
ANY QUESTIONS?!
THAT'S ALL!
...
UM... ER...
GOOD! THEN YOU'RE DISMISSED!
GO TO THE DOJO AND START PRACTICING WITH THE SPIRIT CORE!
SNAP
WAAAH!
FWUP
KOGANEHIKO! SHIROGANEHIKO! ESCORT THEM!!
TMP TMP
EEK!
WAP
OW!
WAP

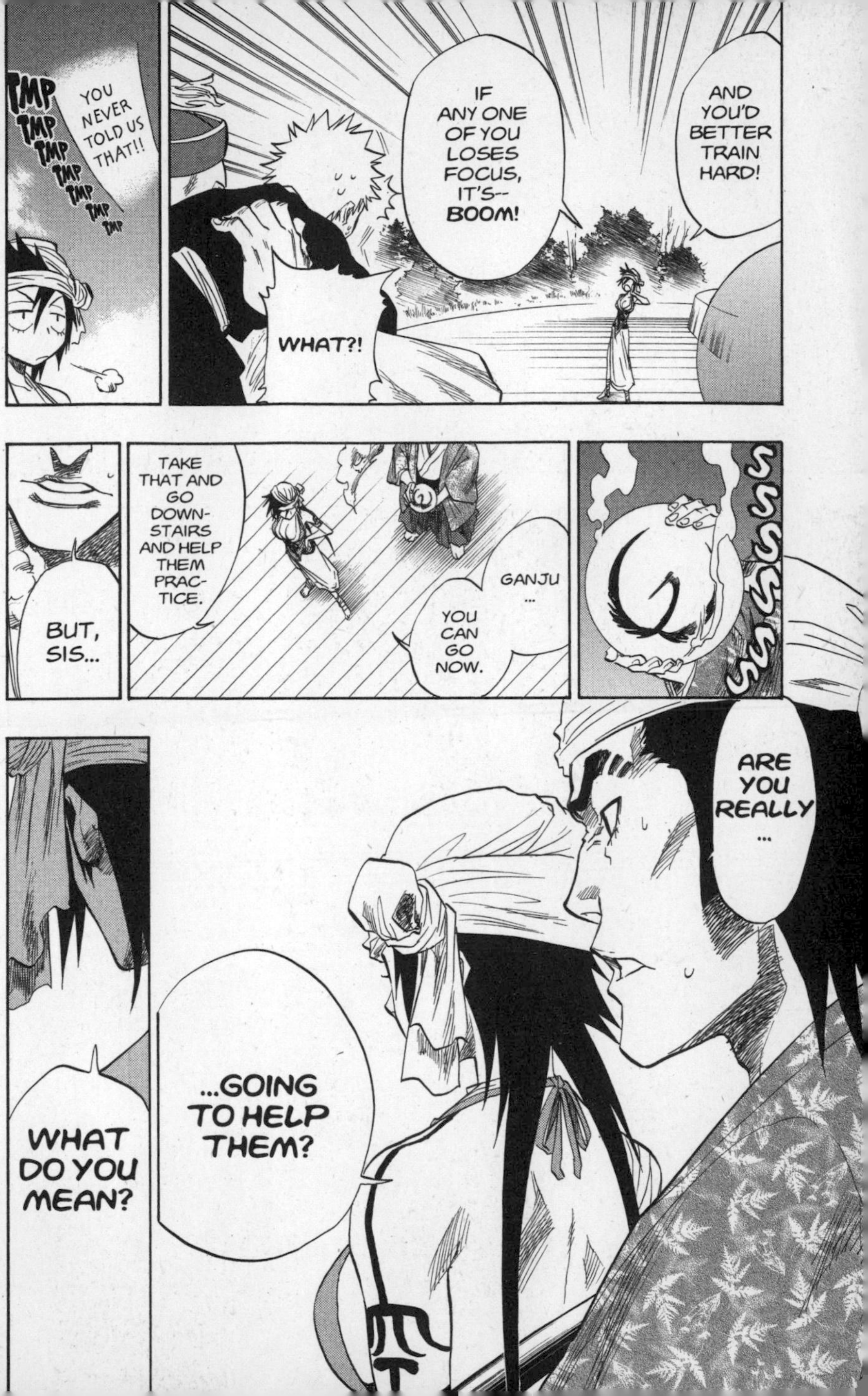
IF ANY ONE OF YOU LOSES FOCUS, IT'S-- BOOM!
AND YOU'D BETTER TRAIN HARD!
WHAT?!
TMP TMP TMP TMP TMP TMP TMP
YOU NEVER TOLD US THAT!!
SSSSSSS
GANJU ...
YOU CAN GO NOW.
TAKE THAT AND GO DOWN-STAIRS AND HELP THEM PRAC-TICE.
BUT, SIS...
ARE YOU REALLY ...
...GOING TO HELP THEM?
WHAT DO YOU MEAN?

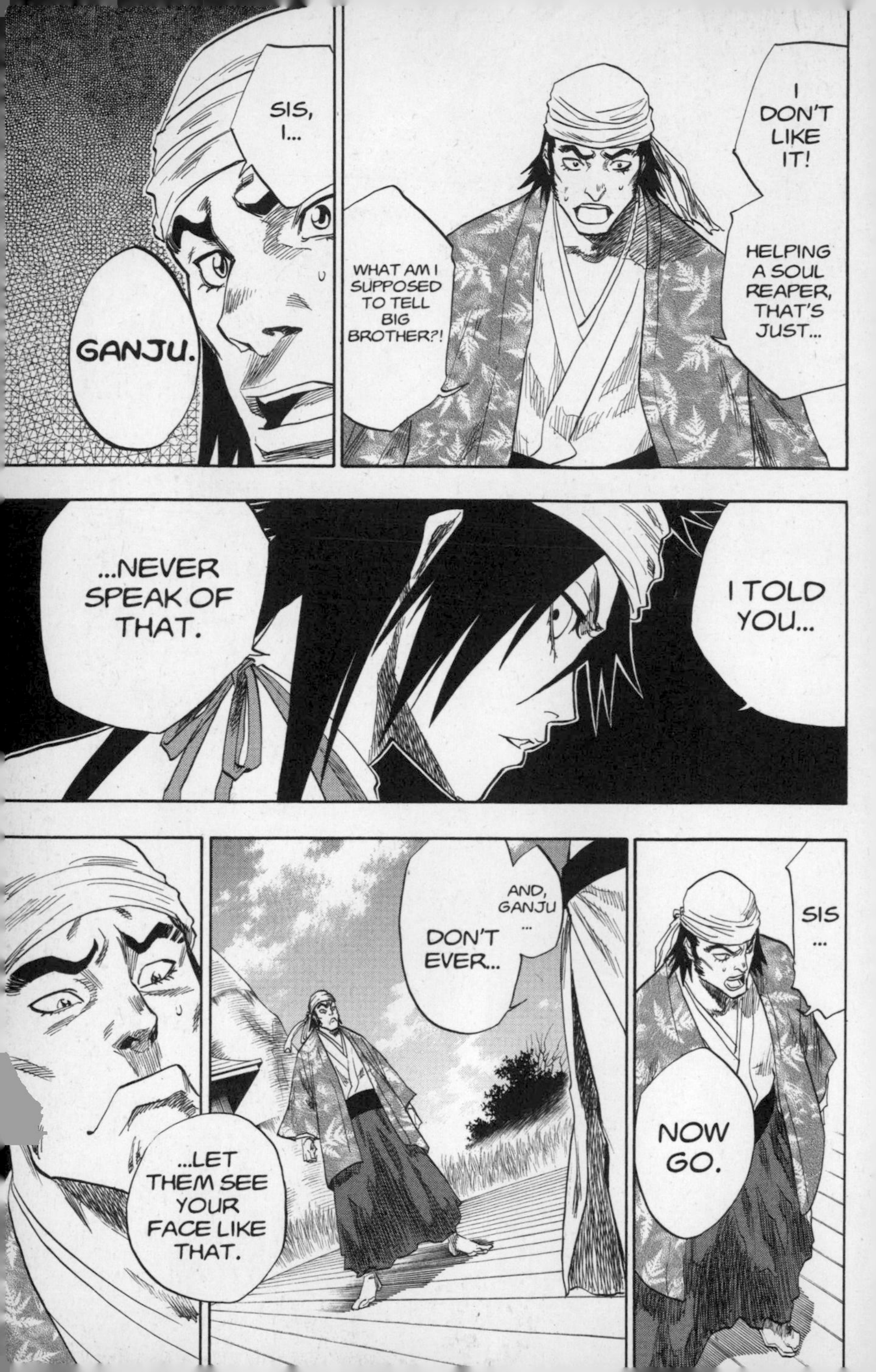
I DON'T LIKE IT!
HELPING A SOUL REAPER, THAT'S JUST...
WHAT AM I SUPPOSED TO TELL BIG BROTHER?!
SIS, I...
GANJU.
I TOLD YOU...
...NEVER SPEAK OF THAT.
SIS...
NOW GO.
AND, GANJU...
DON'T EVER...
...LET THEM SEE YOUR FACE LIKE THAT.

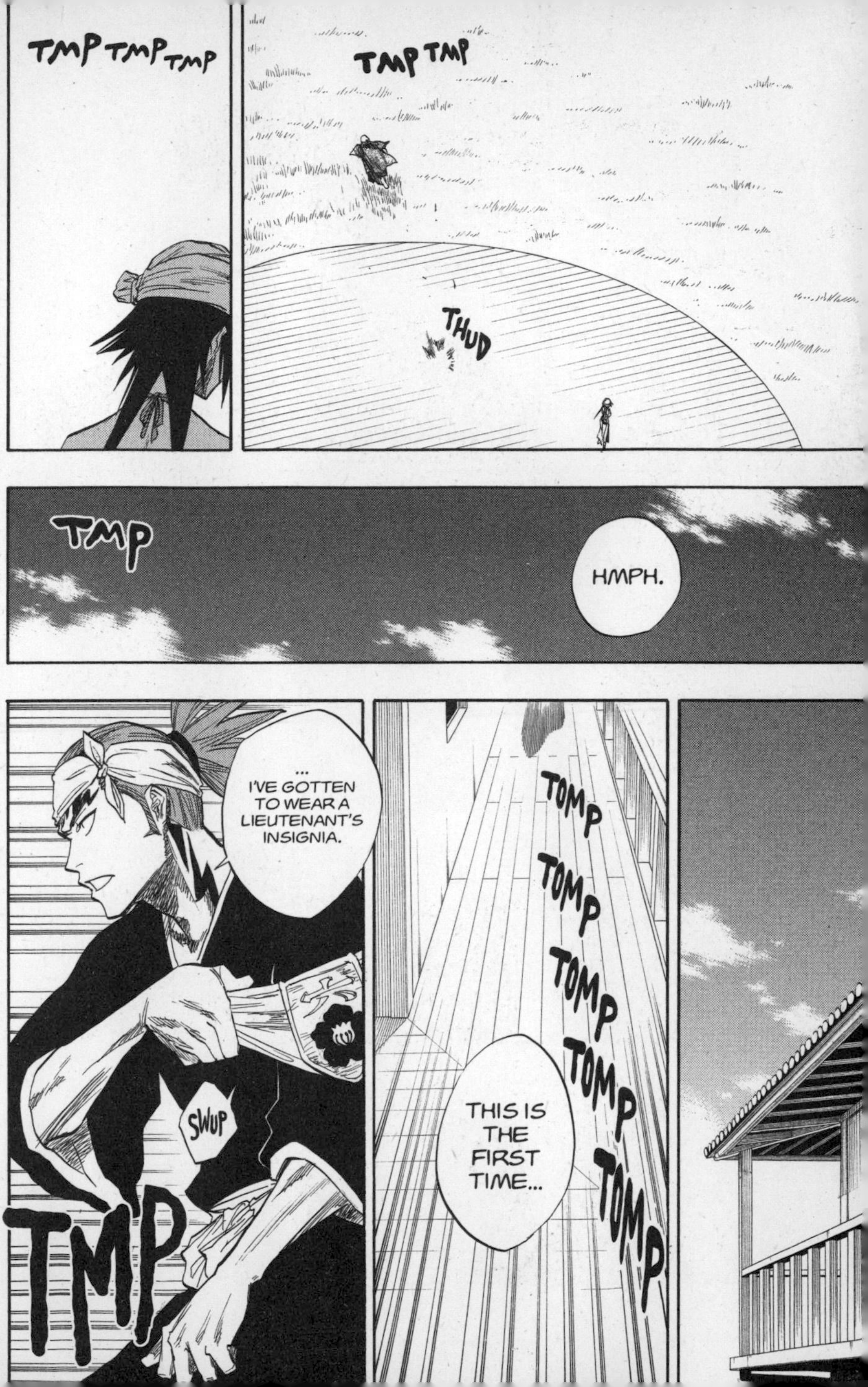
TMP TMP
THUD
TMP TMP TMP
HMPH.
TMP
TOMP TOMP TOMP TOMP TOMP TOMP
THIS IS THE FIRST TIME...
... I'VE GOTTEN TO WEAR A LIEUTENANT'S INSIGNIA.
SWUP
TMP

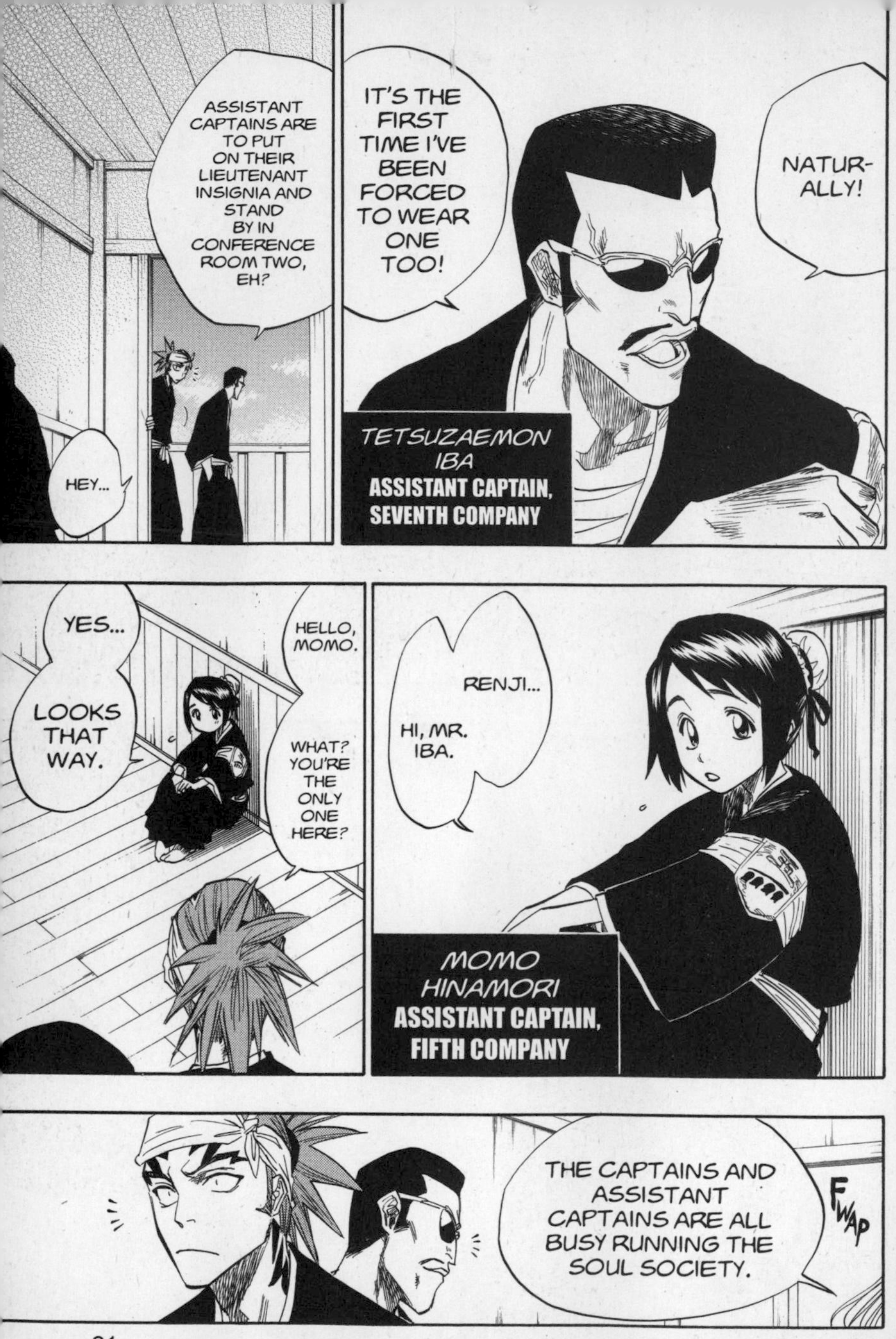
NATUR-ALLY!
IT'S THE FIRST TIME I'VE BEEN FORCED TO WEAR ONE TOO!
TETSUZAEMON IBA
ASSISTANT CAPTAIN, SEVENTH COMPANY
ASSISTANT CAPTAINS ARE TO PUT ON THEIR LIEUTENANT INSIGNIA AND STAND BY IN CONFERENCE ROOM TWO, EH?
HEY...
RENJI...
HI, MR. IBA.
MOMO HINAMORI
ASSISTANT CAPTAIN, FIFTH COMPANY
HELLO, MOMO.
WHAT? YOU'RE THE ONLY ONE HERE?
YES...
LOOKS THAT WAY.
FWAP
THE CAPTAINS AND ASSISTANT CAPTAINS ARE ALL BUSY RUNNING THE SOUL SOCIETY.

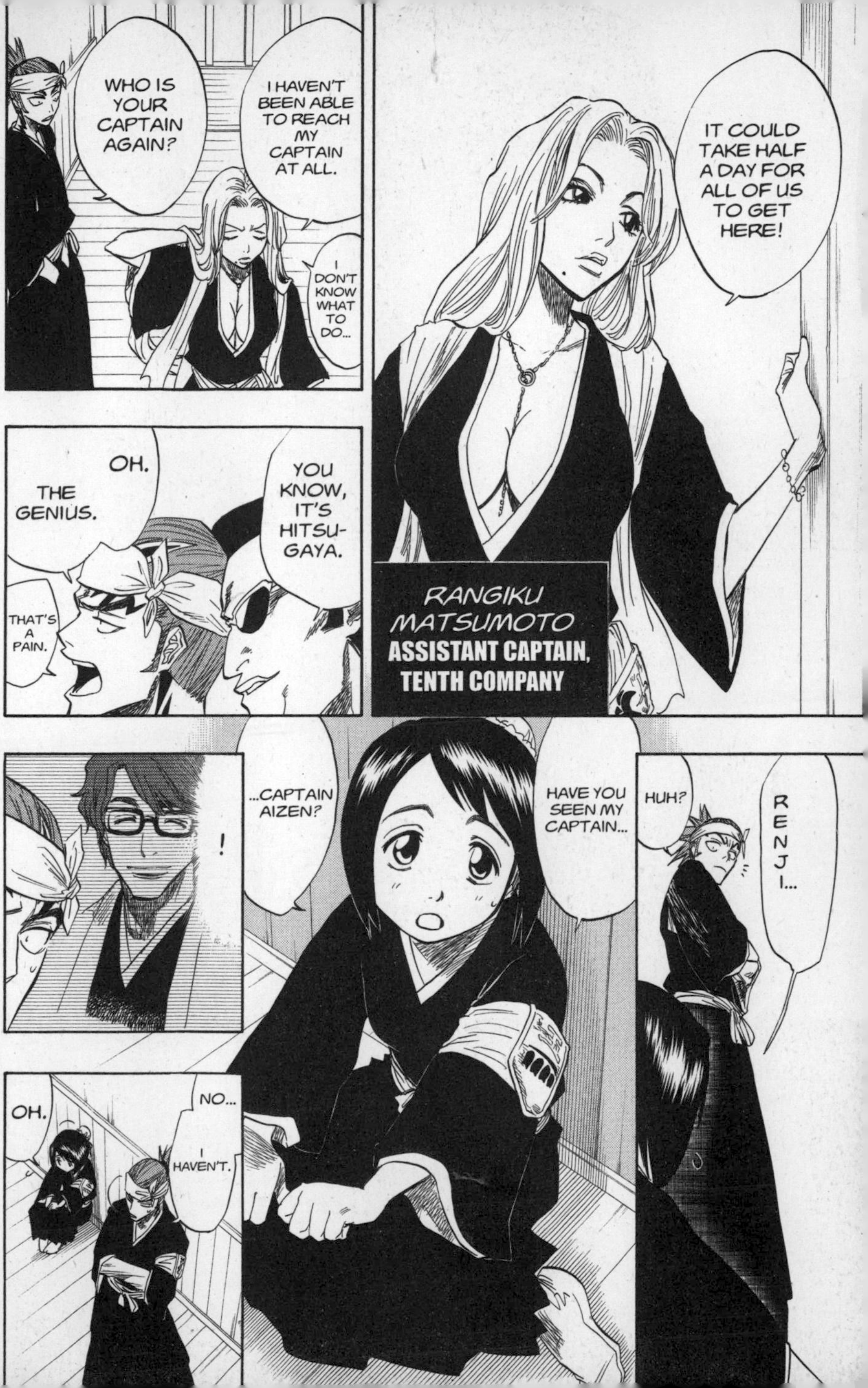
IT COULD TAKE HALF A DAY FOR ALL OF US TO GET HERE!
RANGIKU MATSUMOTO
ASSISTANT CAPTAIN, TENTH COMPANY
I HAVEN'T BEEN ABLE TO REACH MY CAPTAIN AT ALL.
I DON'T KNOW WHAT TO DO...
WHO IS YOUR CAPTAIN AGAIN?
YOU KNOW, IT'S HITSU-GAYA.
OH.
THE GENIUS.
THAT'S A PAIN.
RENJI...
HUH?
HAVE YOU SEEN MY CAPTAIN...
...CAPTAIN AIZEN?
!
NO...
I HAVEN'T.
OH.

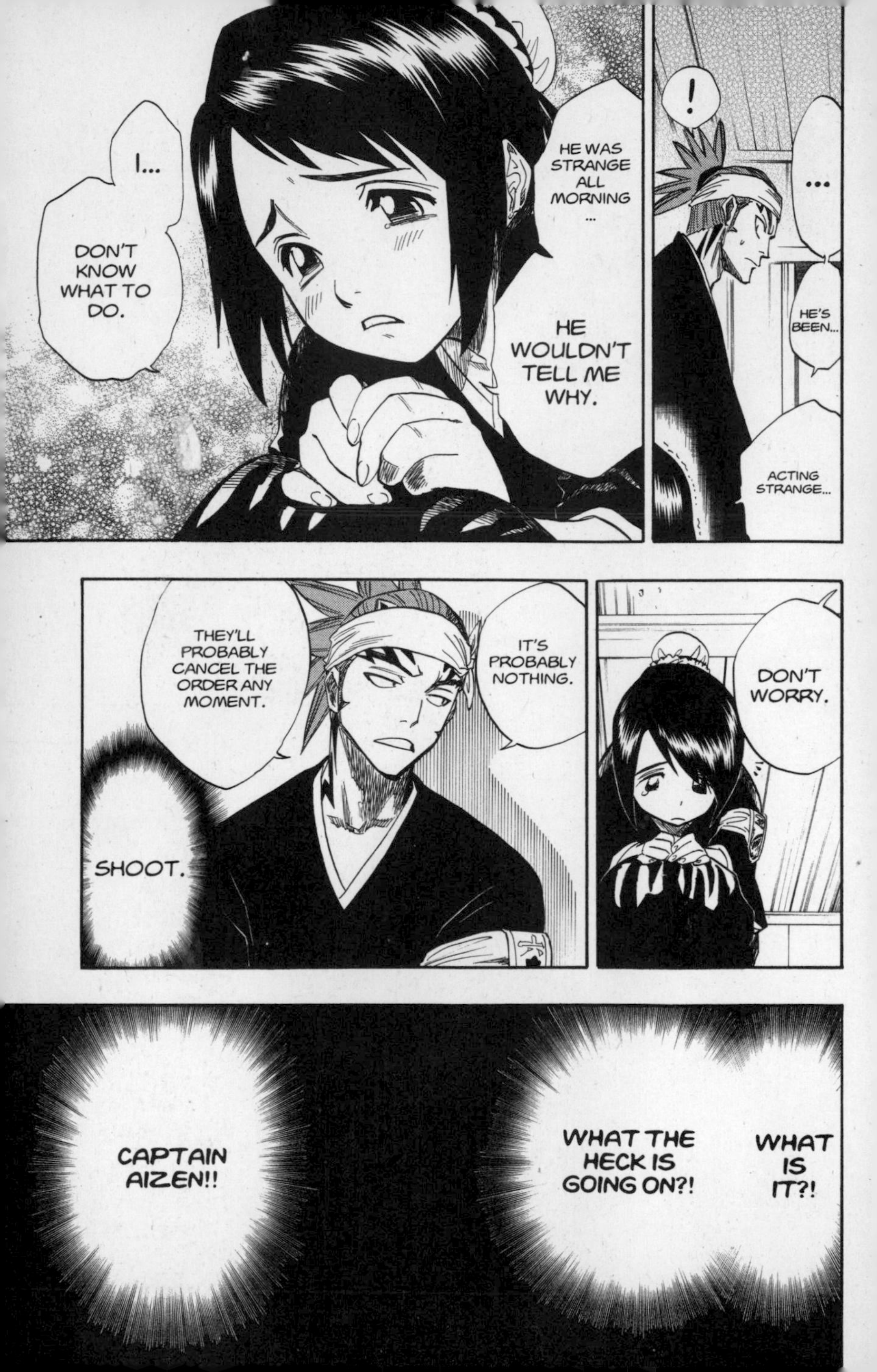
!
...
HE'S BEEN...
ACTING STRANGE...
HE WAS STRANGE ALL MORNING ...
HE WOULDN'T TELL ME WHY.
I...
DON'T KNOW WHAT TO DO.
DON'T WORRY.
IT'S PROBABLY NOTHING.
THEY'LL PROBABLY CANCEL THE ORDER ANY MOMENT.
SHOOT.
WHAT IS IT?!
WHAT THE HECK IS GOING ON?!
CAPTAIN AIZEN!!

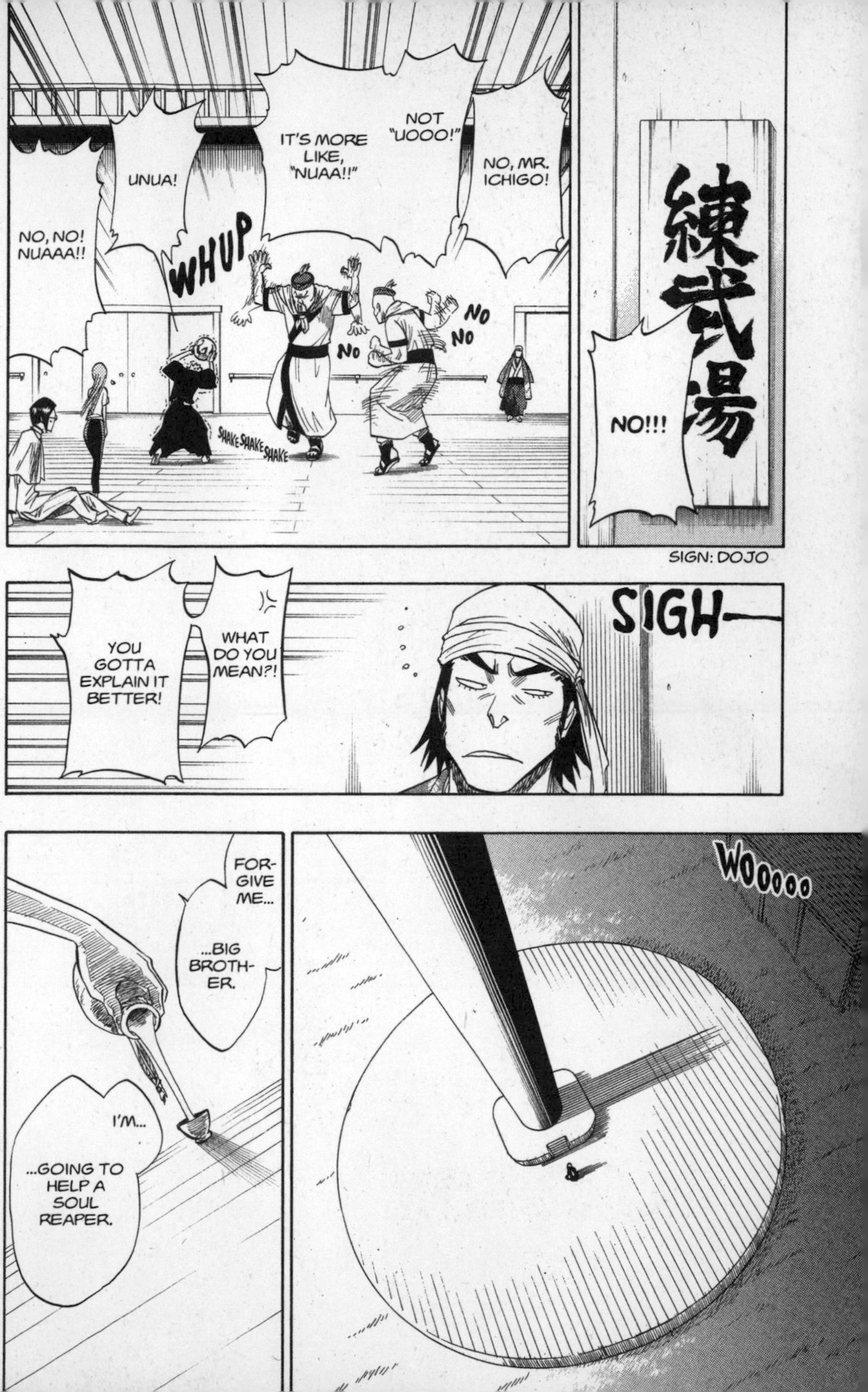
NO!!!
SIGN: DOJO
NO, MR. ICHIGO!
NOT "UOOO!"
IT'S MORE LIKE, "NUAA!!"
UNUA!
WHUP
NO NO
NO
NO, NO! NUAAA!!
SHAKE SHAKE SHAKE
SIGH—
WHAT DO YOU MEAN?!
YOU GOTTA EXPLAIN IT BETTER!
WOOOOO
FOR-GIVE ME...
...BIG BROTH-ER.
I'M...
...GOING TO HELP A SOUL REAPER.

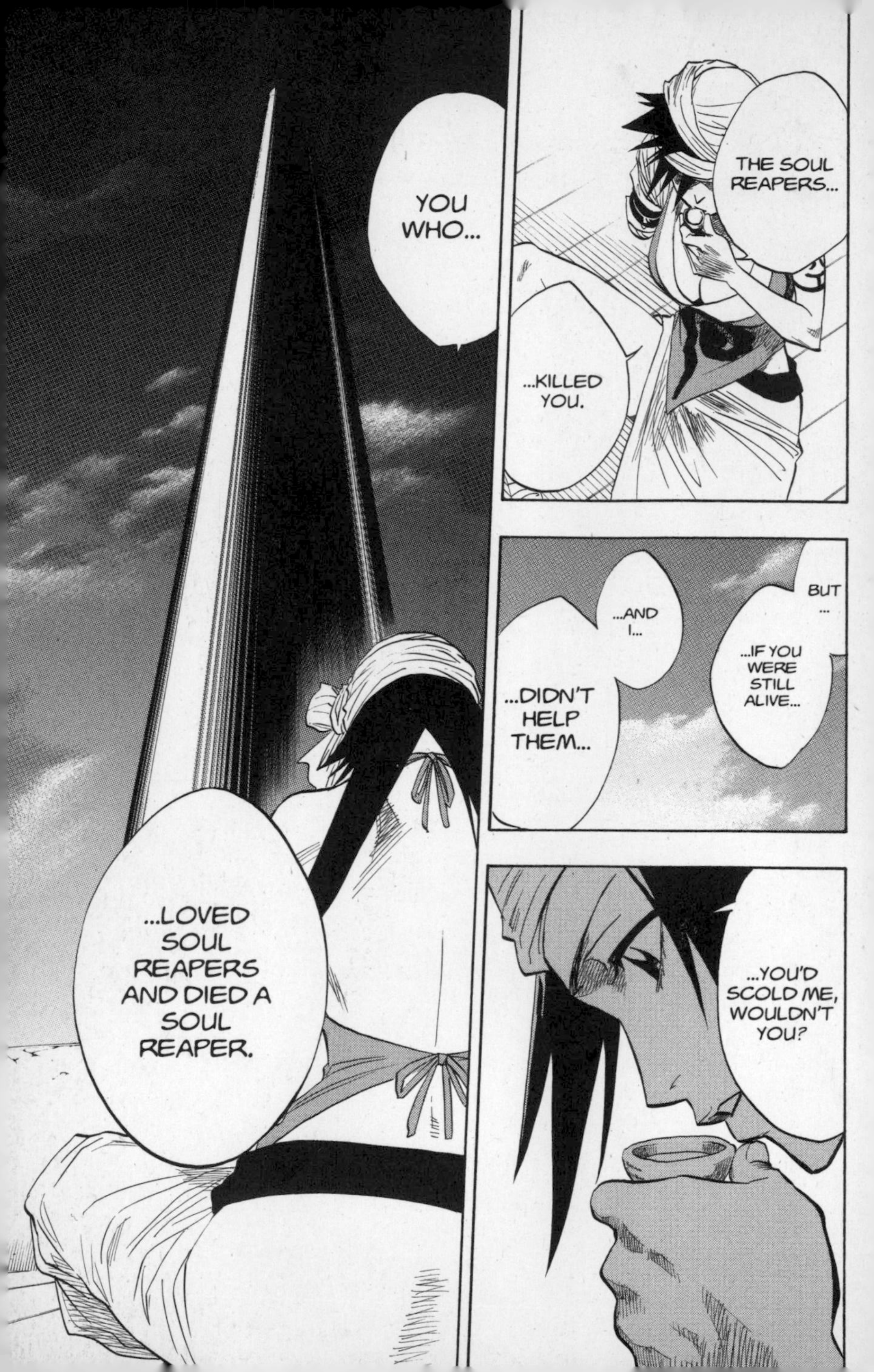
THE SOUL REAPERS...
...KILLED YOU.
...AND I...
...DIDN'T HELP THEM...
BUT...
...IF YOU WERE STILL ALIVE...
...YOU'D SCOLD ME, WOULDN'T YOU?
YOU WHO...
...LOVED SOUL REAPERS AND DIED A SOUL REAPER.

HOW TO DISTINGUISH KOGANEHIKO
FROM SHIROGANEHIKO.
LOTS OF PEOPLE CAN'T TELL
THE DIFFERENCE.
I THINK THEY'RE THE KIND OF TWINS
THAT DON'T LOOK ALIKE...

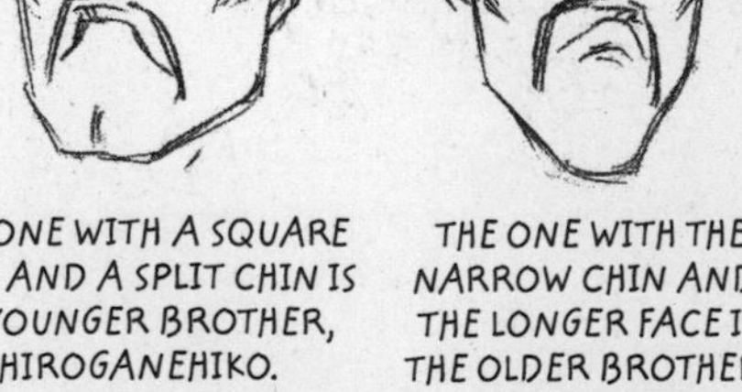

THE ONE WITH A SQUARE
FACE AND A SPLIT CHIN IS
THE YOUNGER BROTHER,
SHIROGANEHIKO.

THE ONE WITH THE
NARROW CHIN AND
THE LONGER FACE IS
THE OLDER BROTHER,
KOGANEHIKO.

81. Twelve-Tone Rendezvous

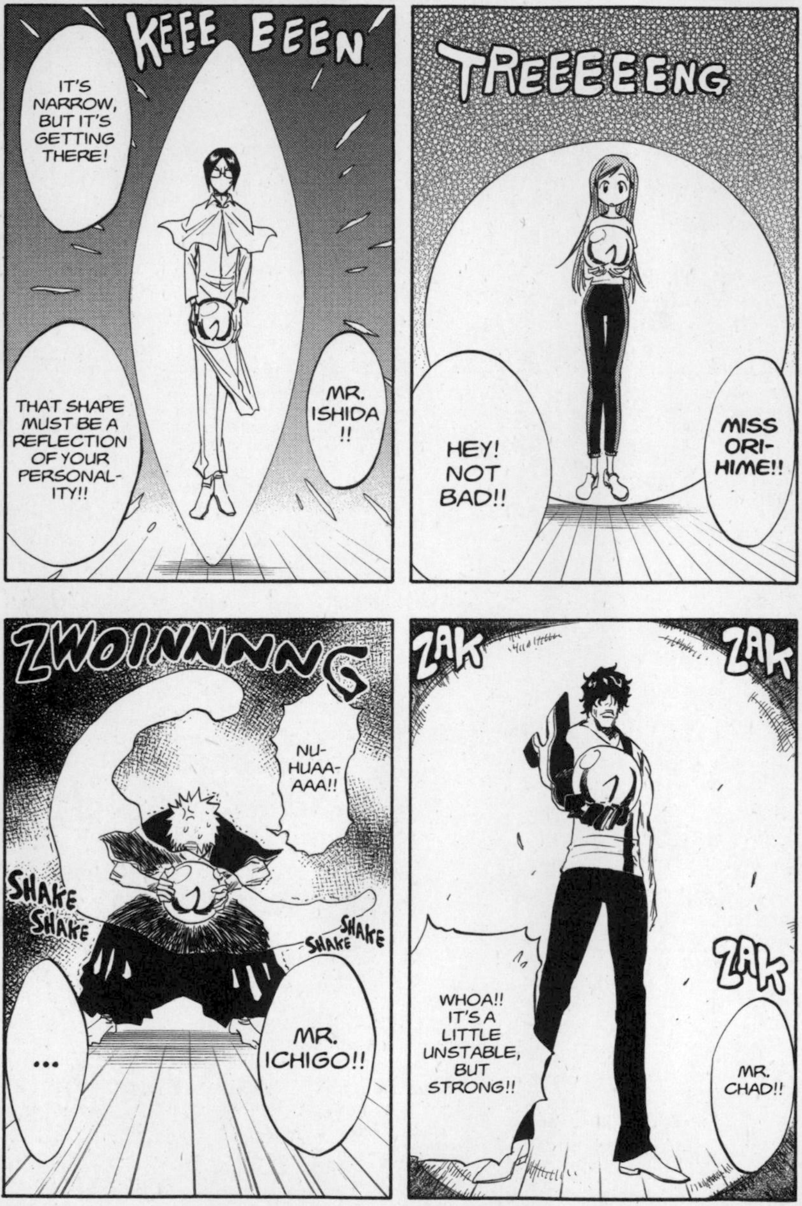
TREEEEEENG
MISS ORI-HIME!!
HEY! NOT BAD!!
KEEE EEEN
MR. ISHIDA!!
IT'S NARROW, BUT IT'S GETTING THERE!
THAT SHAPE MUST BE A REFLECTION OF YOUR PERSONAL-ITY!!
ZAK ZAK
ZAK
MR. CHAD!!
WHOA!! IT'S A LITTLE UNSTABLE, BUT STRONG!!
ZWOINNNNG
NU-HUAA-AAA!!
SHAKE SHAKE
SHAKE SHAKE
MR. ICHIGO!!
...

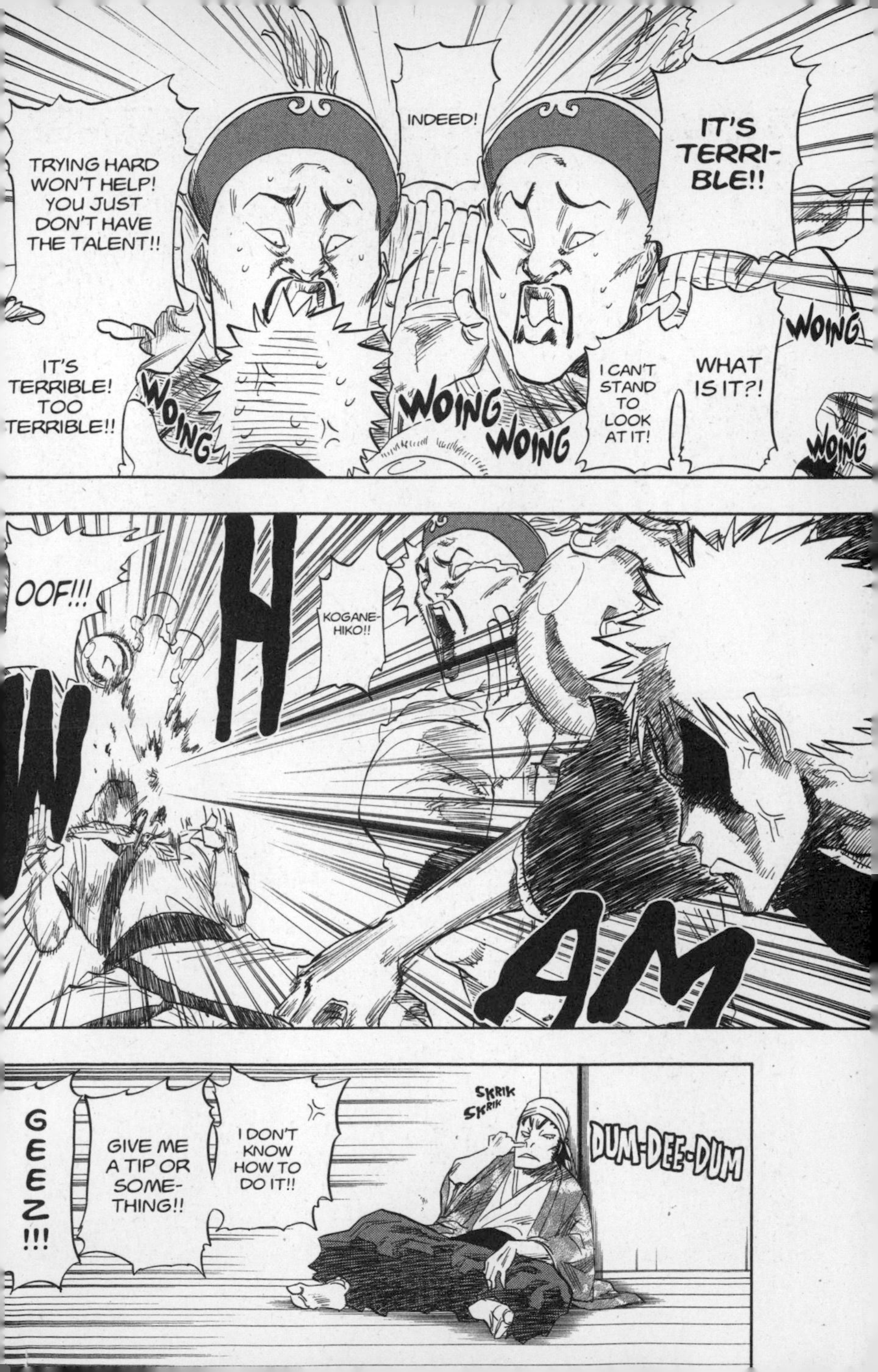
IT'S TERRIBLE!!
WOING
WHAT IS IT?!
WOING
I CAN'T STAND TO LOOK AT IT!
INDEED!
WOING WOING
TRYING HARD WON'T HELP! YOU JUST DON'T HAVE THE TALENT!!
IT'S TERRIBLE! TOO TERRIBLE!!
WOING
WHAM
KOGANE-HIKO!!
OOF!!!
DUM-DEE-DUM
SKRIK SKRIK
I DON'T KNOW HOW TO DO IT!!
GIVE ME A TIP OR SOMETHING!!
GEEZ!!!

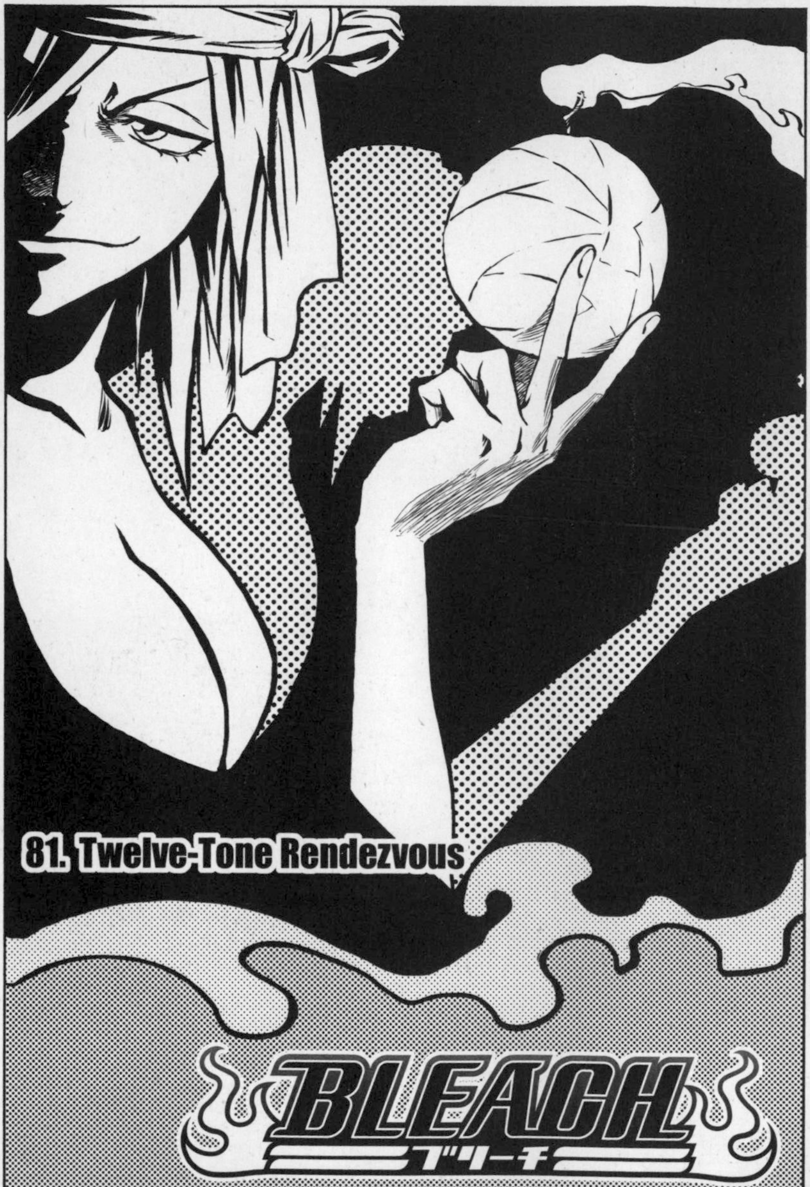
81. Twelve-Tone Rendezvous
BLEACH
ブリーチ

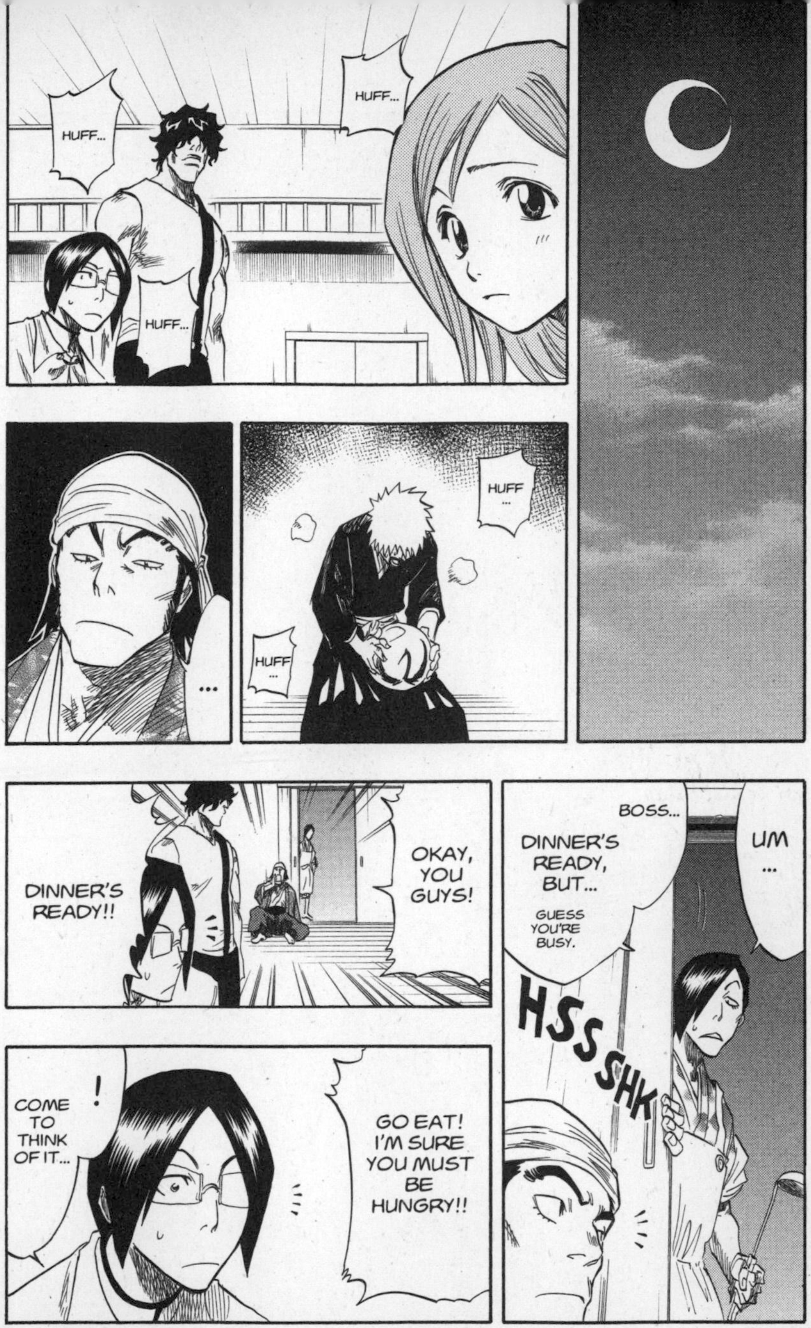
HUFF...
HUFF...
HUFF...
HUFF ...
HUFF ...
...
BOSS...
DINNER'S READY, BUT...
GUESS YOU'RE BUSY.
UM ...
HSS SHK
OKAY, YOU GUYS!
DINNER'S READY!!
GO EAT! I'M SURE YOU MUST BE HUNGRY!!
!
COME TO THINK OF IT...

READ THIS WAY

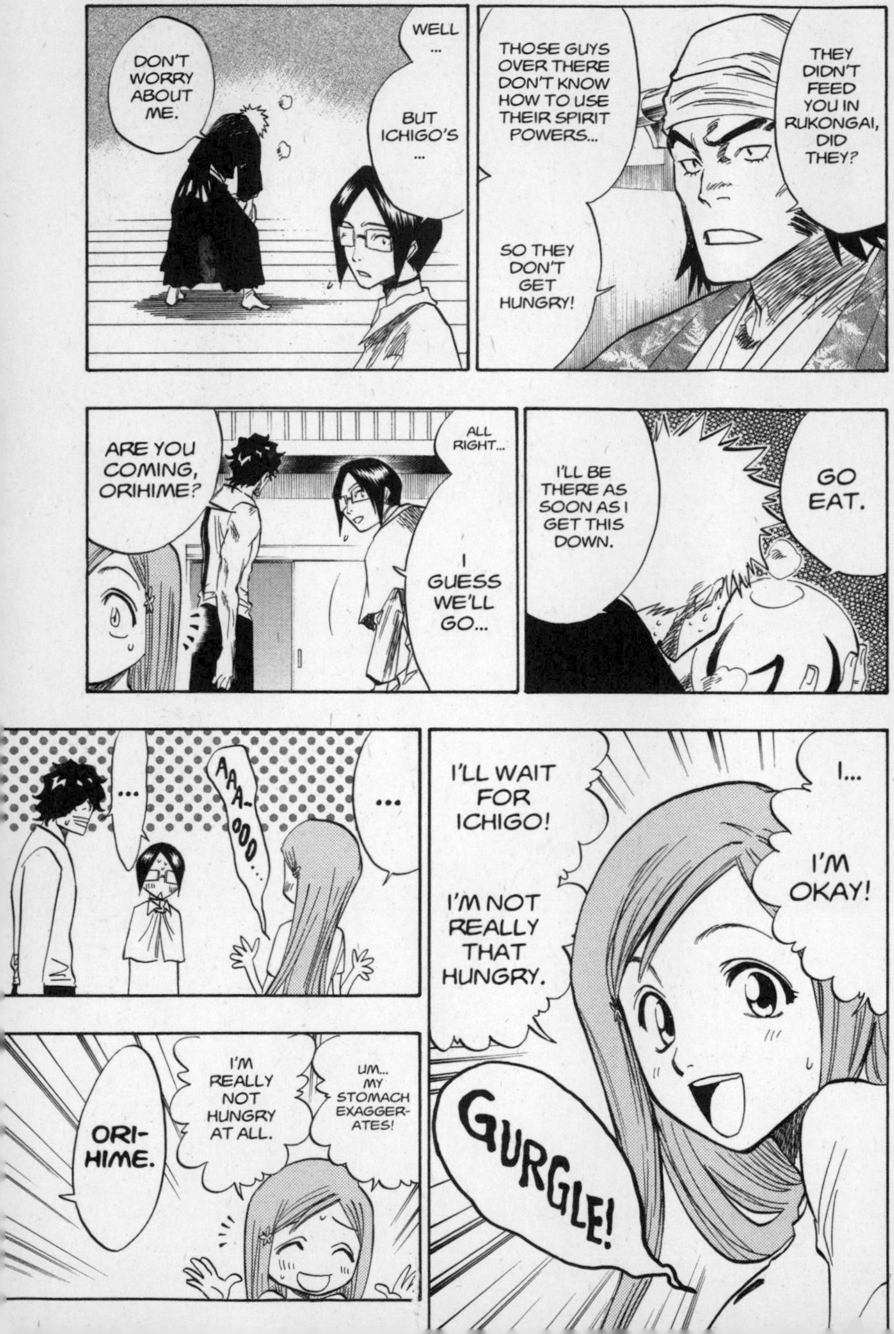
THEY DIDN'T FEED YOU IN RUKONGAI, DID THEY?
THOSE GUYS OVER THERE DON'T KNOW HOW TO USE THEIR SPIRIT POWERS...
SO THEY DON'T GET HUNGRY!
WELL ...
BUT ICHIGO'S ...
DON'T WORRY ABOUT ME.
GO EAT.
I'LL BE THERE AS SOON AS I GET THIS DOWN.
ALL RIGHT...
I GUESS WE'LL GO...
ARE YOU COMING, ORIHIME?
I...
I'M OKAY!
I'LL WAIT FOR ICHIGO!
I'M NOT REALLY THAT HUNGRY.
GURGLE!
...
AAA-OOO...
...
UM... MY STOMACH EXAGGER-ATES!
I'M REALLY NOT HUNGRY AT ALL.
ORI-HIME.

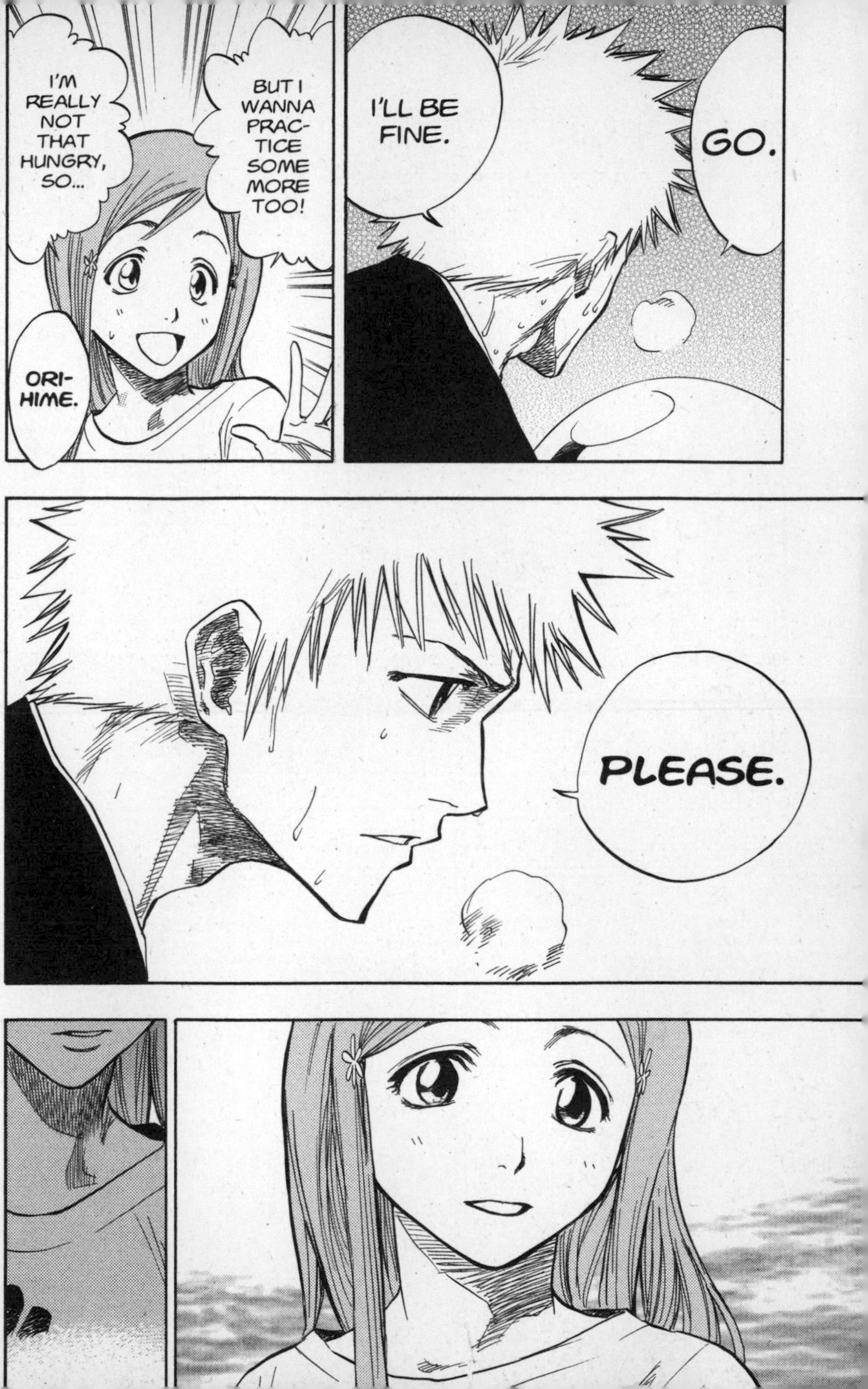
GO.
I'LL BE FINE.
BUT I WANNA PRAC-TICE SOME MORE TOO!
I'M REALLY NOT THAT HUNGRY, SO...
ORI-HIME.
PLEASE.

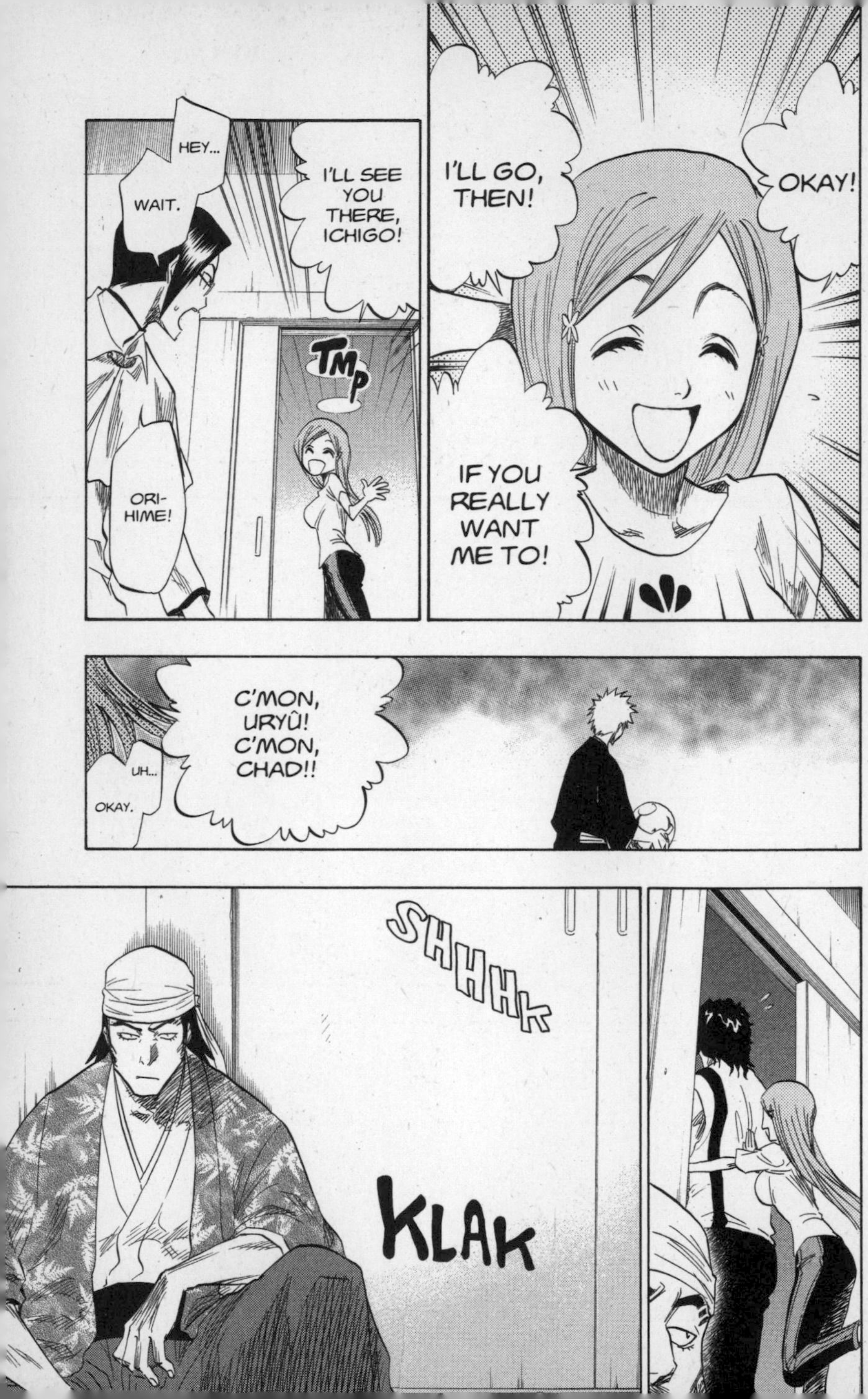
OKAY!
I'LL GO, THEN!
IF YOU REALLY WANT ME TO!
I'LL SEE YOU THERE, ICHIGO!
HEY... WAIT.
TMP
ORI-HIME!
C'MON, URYÛ! C'MON, CHAD!!
UH... OKAY.
SHHHK
KLAK

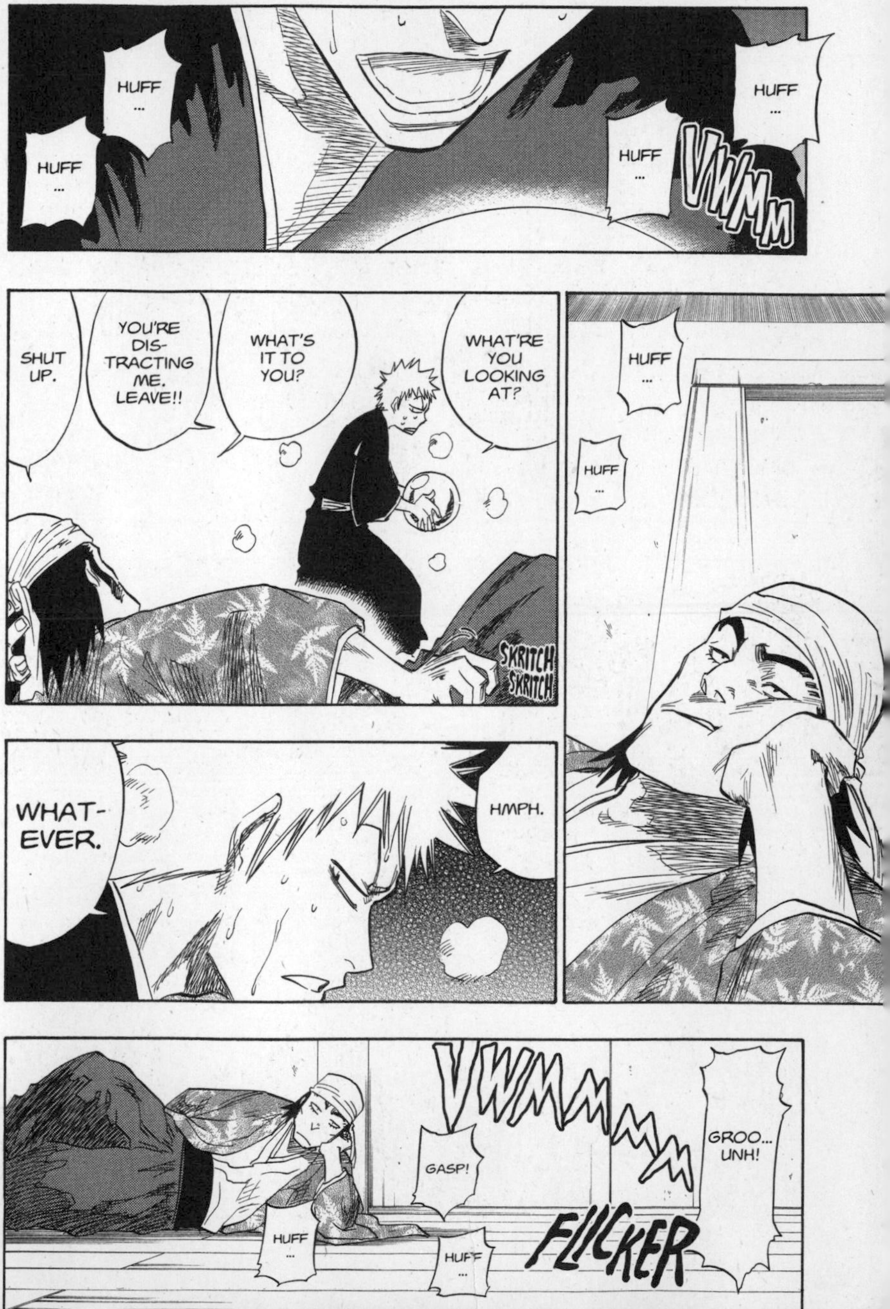
HUFF...
HUFF...
VWMM
HUFF...
HUFF...
HUFF...
HUFF...
WHAT'RE YOU LOOKING AT?
WHAT'S IT TO YOU?
YOU'RE DIS-TRACTING ME. LEAVE!!
SHUT UP.
SKRITCH SKRITCH
HMPH.
WHAT-EVER.
GROO... UNH!
VWMMMMM
GASP!
FLICKER
HUFF...
HUFF...

READ THIS WAY

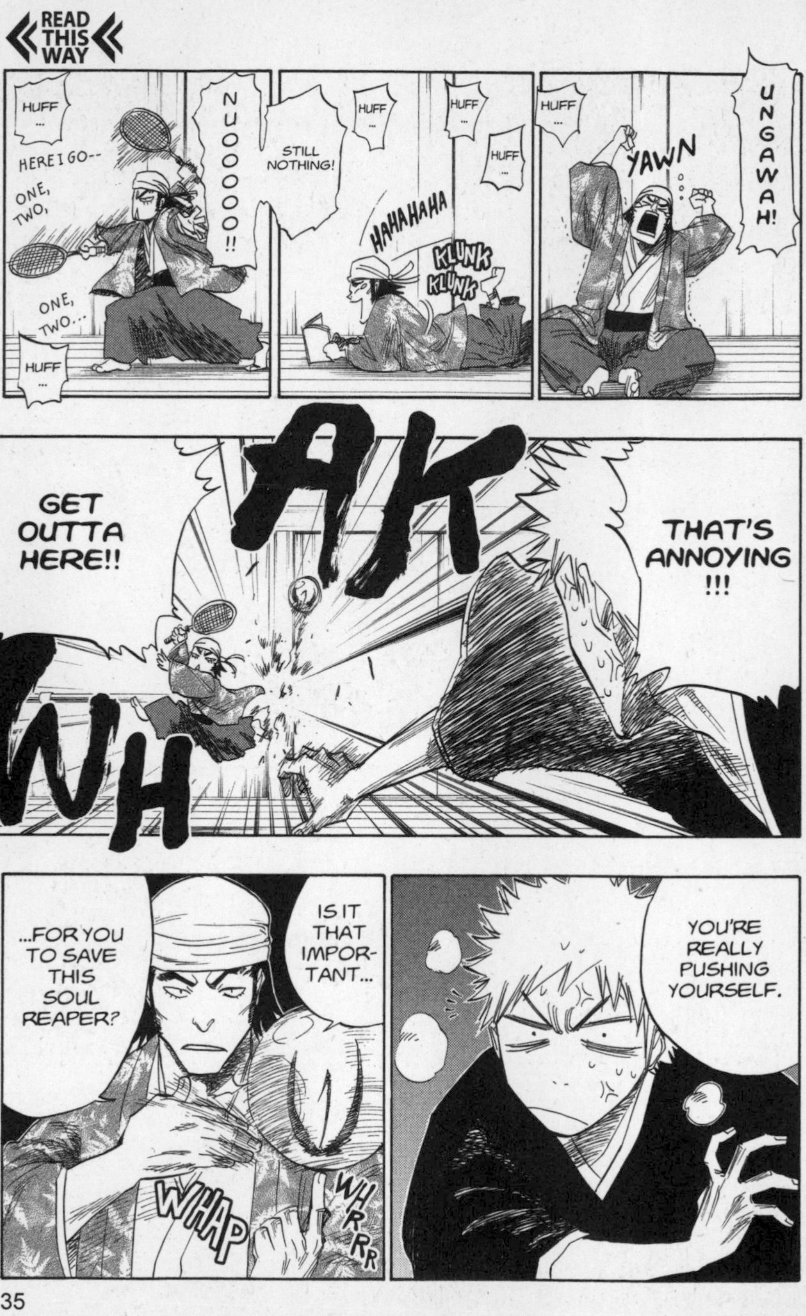
HUFF ...
YAWN
UNGAWAH!
HUFF ...
HUFF ...
HUFF ...
HAHAHAHA
KLUNK KLUNK
STILL NOTHING!
NUOOOOOO!!
HUFF ...
HERE I GO--
ONE, TWO,
ONE, TWO...
HUFF ...
THAT'S ANNOYING !!!
WHAK
GET OUTTA HERE!!
YOU'RE REALLY PUSHING YOURSELF.
IS IT THAT IMPOR-TANT...
...FOR YOU TO SAVE THIS SOUL REAPER?
WHRRR
WHAP

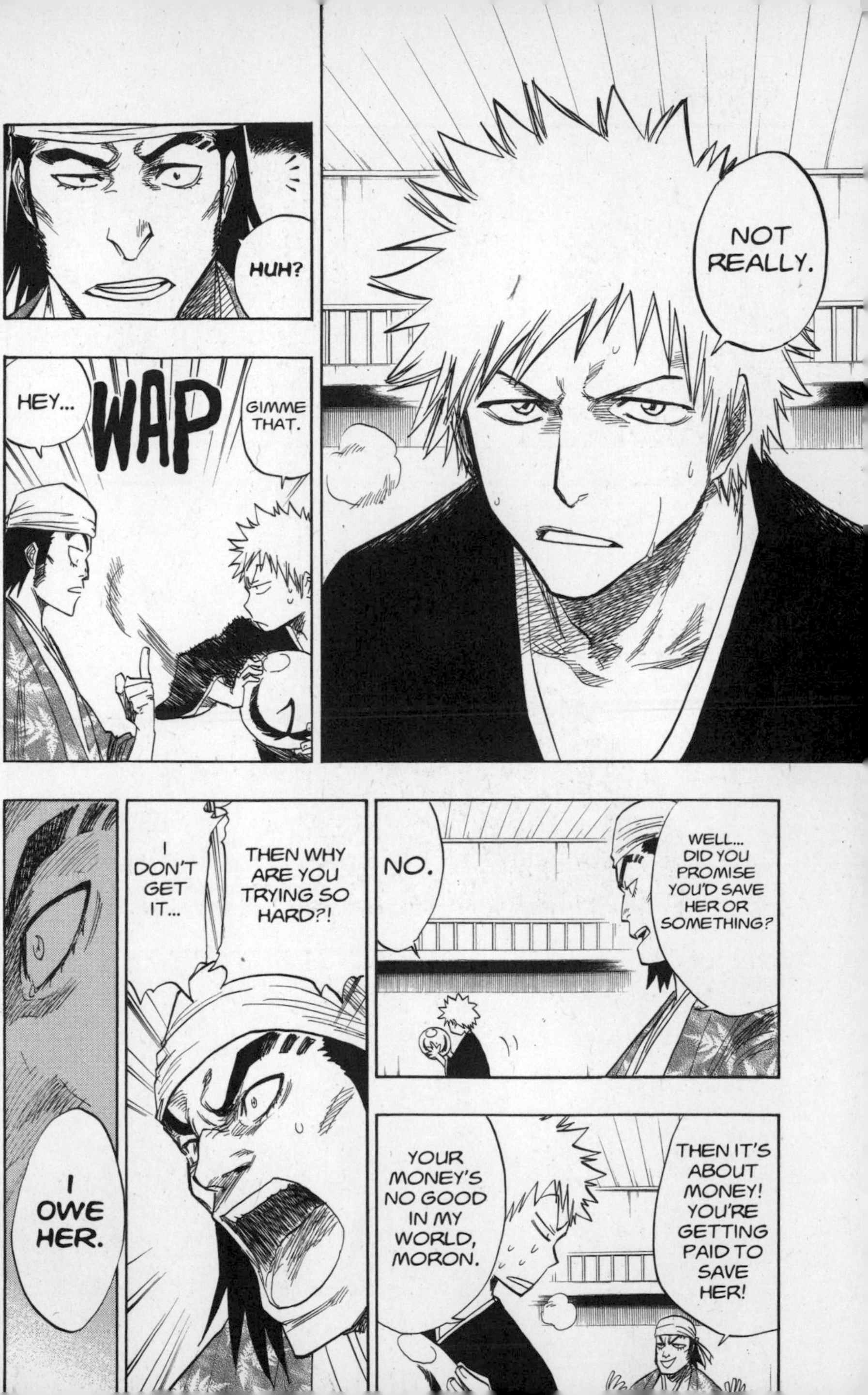
NOT REALLY.
HUH?
GIMME THAT.
WAP
HEY...
WELL... DID YOU PROMISE YOU'D SAVE HER OR SOMETHING?
NO.
THEN IT'S ABOUT MONEY! YOU'RE GETTING PAID TO SAVE HER!
YOUR MONEY'S NO GOOD IN MY WORLD, MORON.
THEN WHY ARE YOU TRYING SO HARD?!
I DON'T GET IT...
I OWE HER.

READ THIS WAY

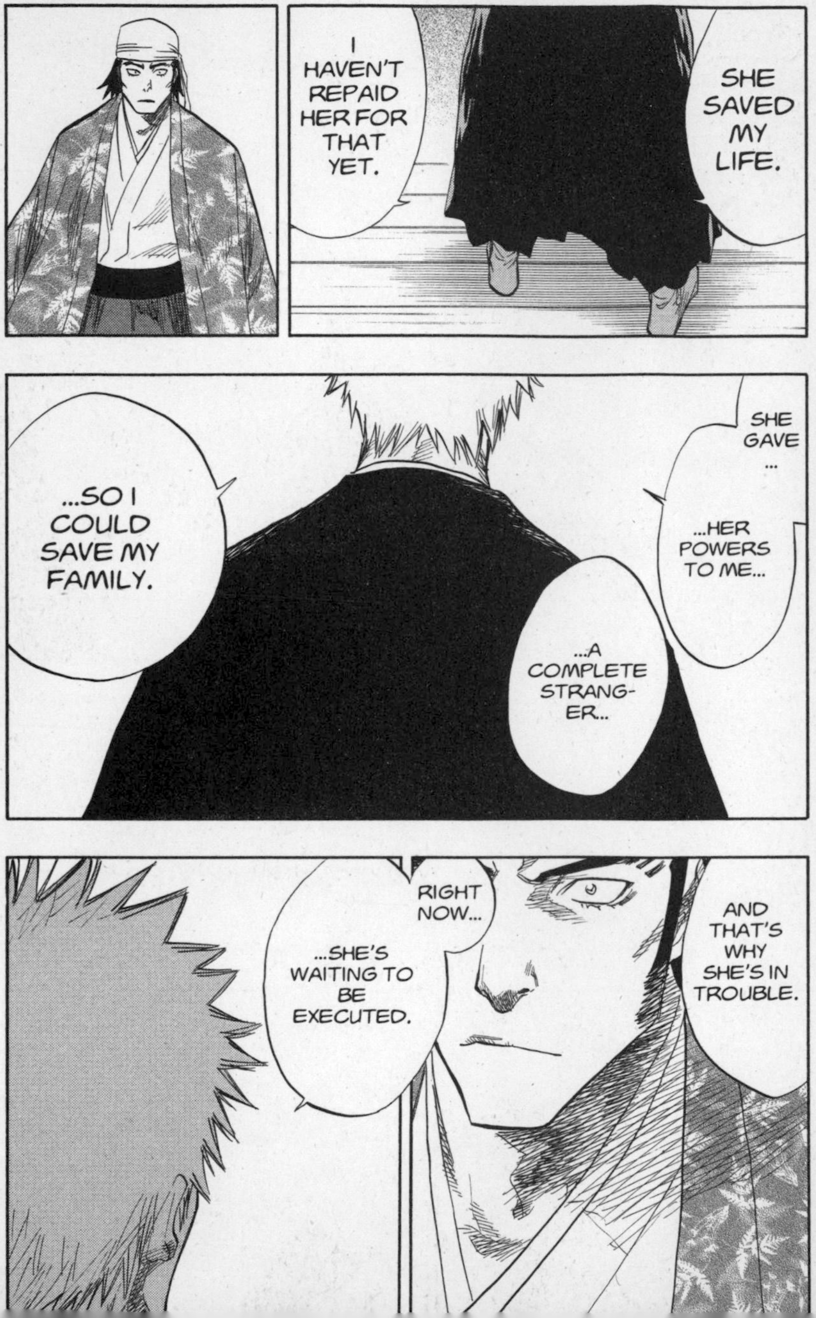
SHE SAVED MY LIFE.
I HAVEN'T REPAID HER FOR THAT YET.
SHE GAVE ...
...HER POWERS TO ME...
...A COMPLETE STRANGER..
...SO I COULD SAVE MY FAMILY.
AND THAT'S WHY SHE'S IN TROUBLE.
RIGHT NOW...
...SHE'S WAITING TO BE EXECUTED.

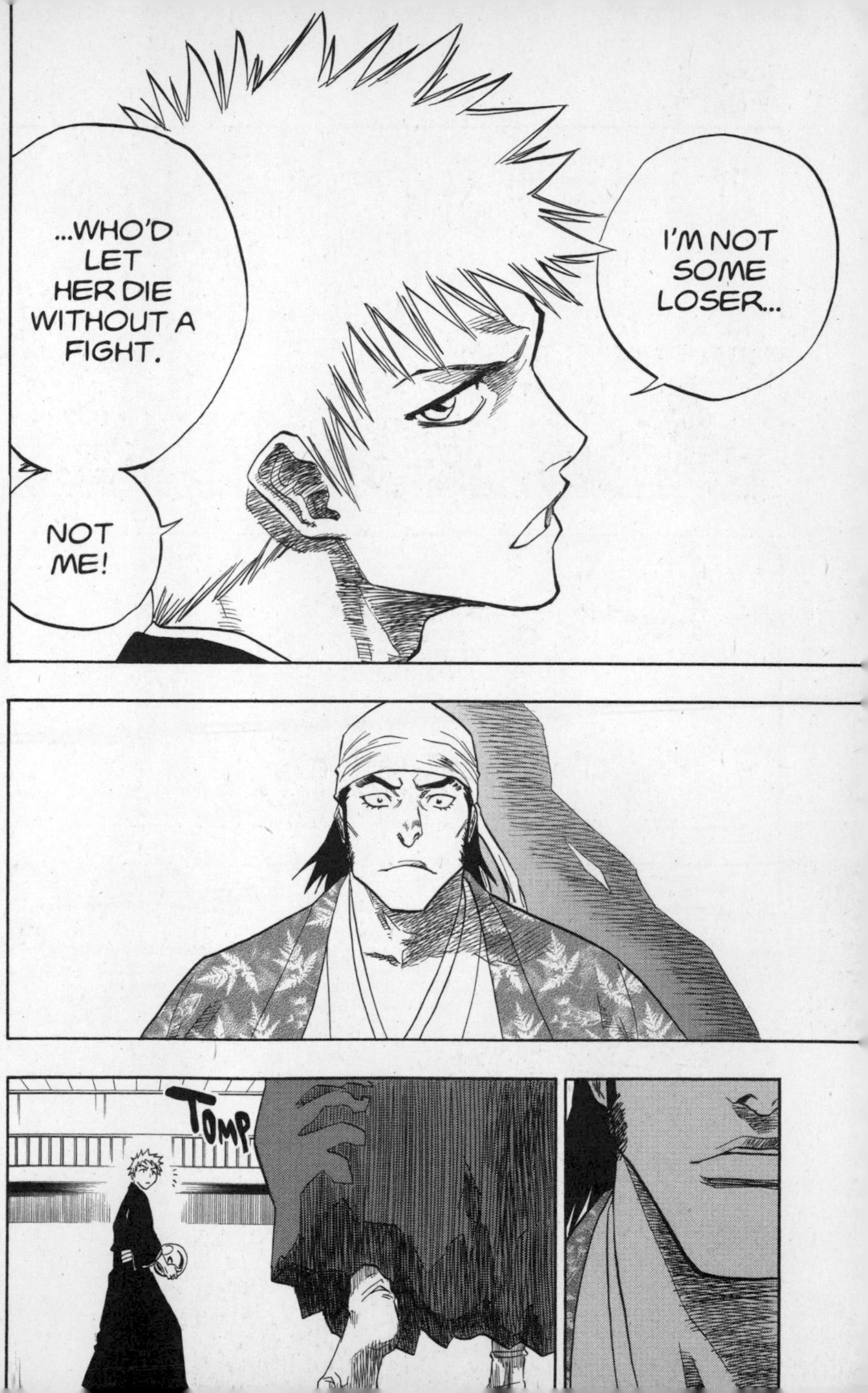
I'M NOT SOME LOSER...
...WHO'D LET HER DIE WITHOUT A FIGHT.
NOT ME!
TOMP

READ THIS WAY

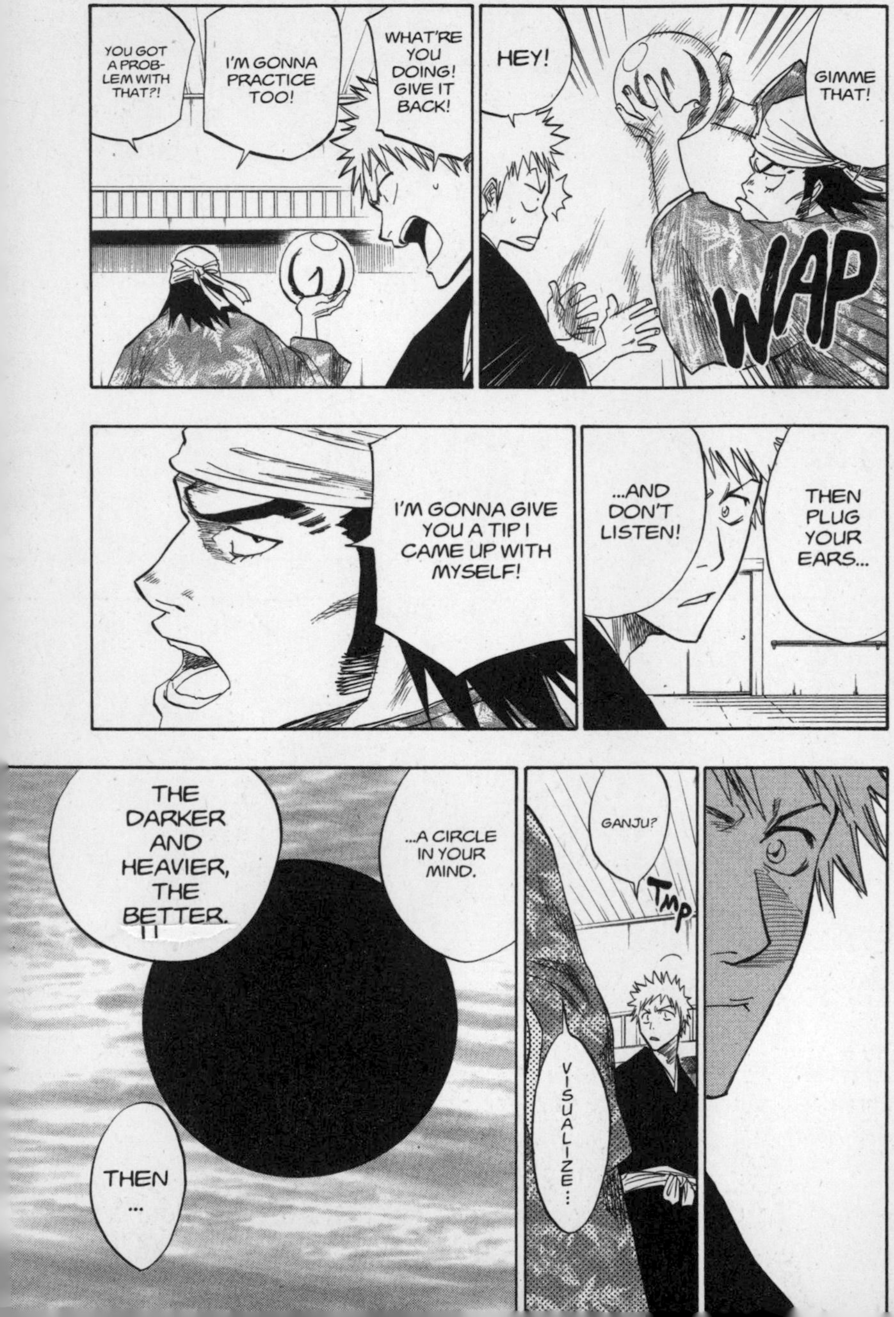

GIMME THAT!
HEY!
WAP
WHAT'RE YOU DOING! GIVE IT BACK!
I'M GONNA PRACTICE TOO!
YOU GOT A PROB-LEM WITH THAT?!
THEN PLUG YOUR EARS...
...AND DON'T LISTEN!
I'M GONNA GIVE YOU A TIP I CAME UP WITH MYSELF!
GANJU?
TMP
VISUALIZE...
...A CIRCLE IN YOUR MIND.
THE DARKER AND HEAVIER, THE BETTER.
THEN...

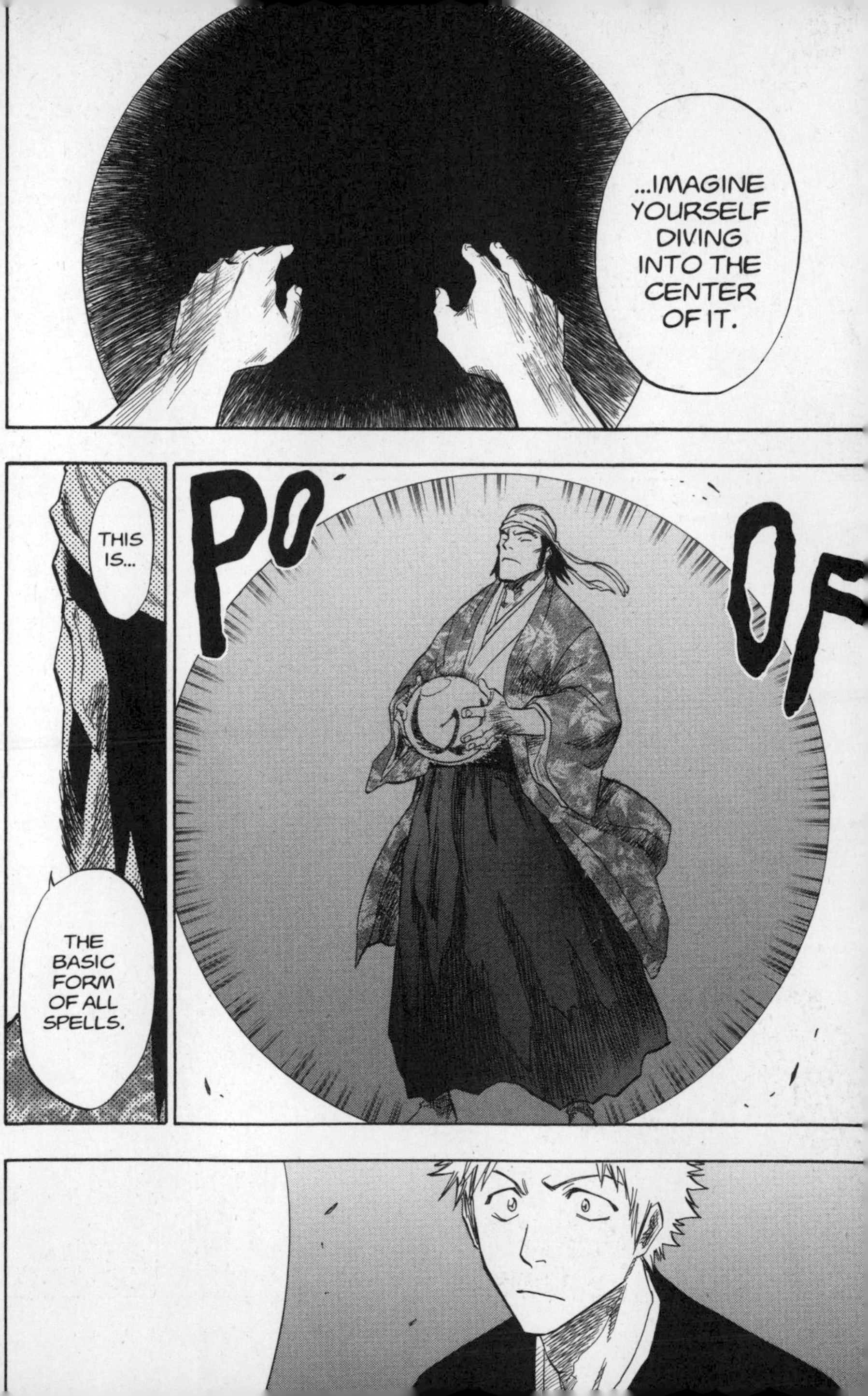
...IMAGINE YOURSELF DIVING INTO THE CENTER OF IT.
POOF
THIS IS...
THE BASIC FORM OF ALL SPELLS.

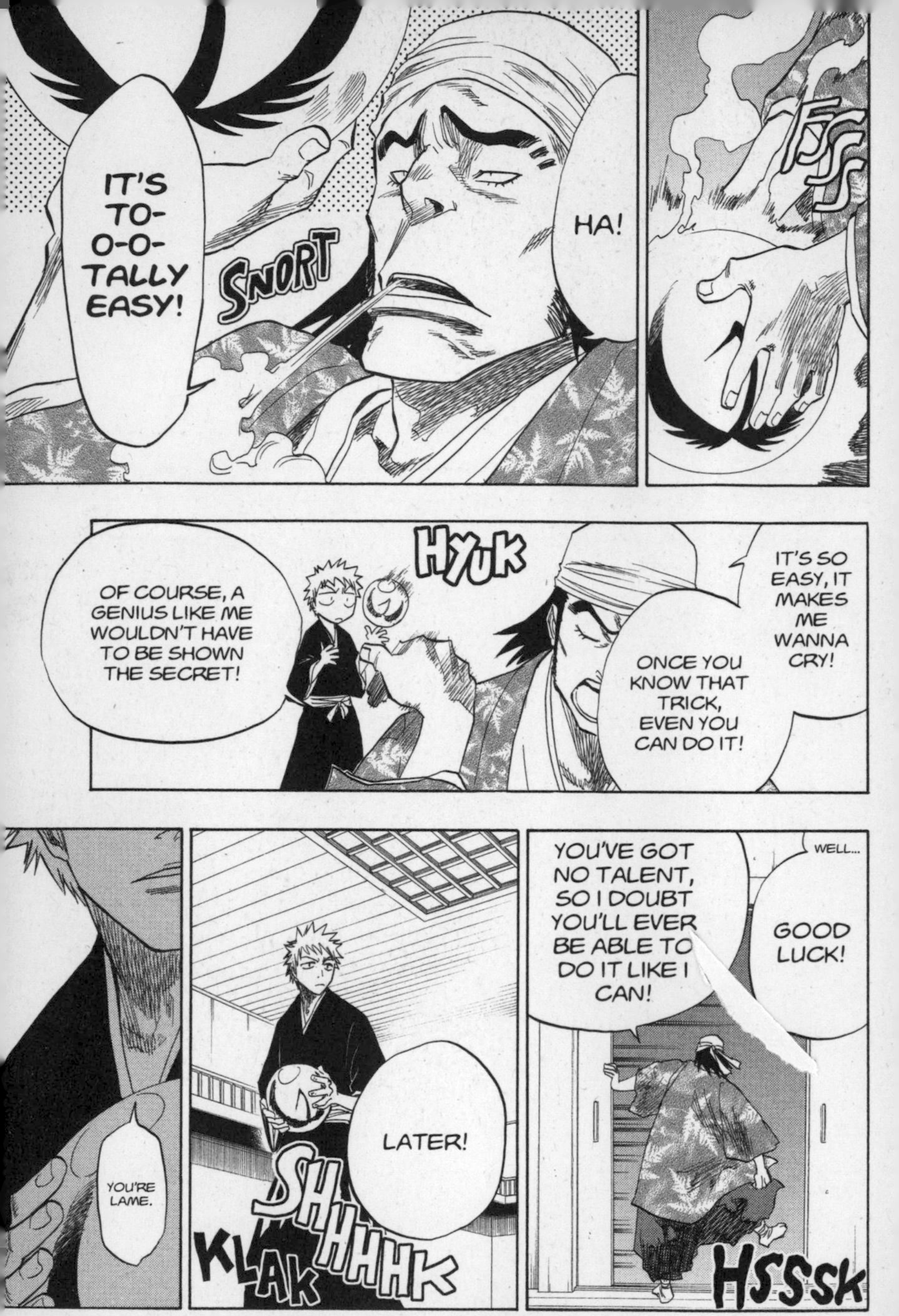
FSS
HA!
SNORT
IT'S TO-O-O-TALLY EASY!
IT'S SO EASY, IT MAKES ME WANNA CRY!
ONCE YOU KNOW THAT TRICK, EVEN YOU CAN DO IT!
HYUK
OF COURSE, A GENIUS LIKE ME WOULDN'T HAVE TO BE SHOWN THE SECRET!
WELL...
GOOD LUCK!
YOU'VE GOT NO TALENT, SO I DOUBT YOU'LL EVER BE ABLE TO DO IT LIKE I CAN!
HSSSK
LATER!
SHHHHHK
KLAK
YOU'RE LAME.

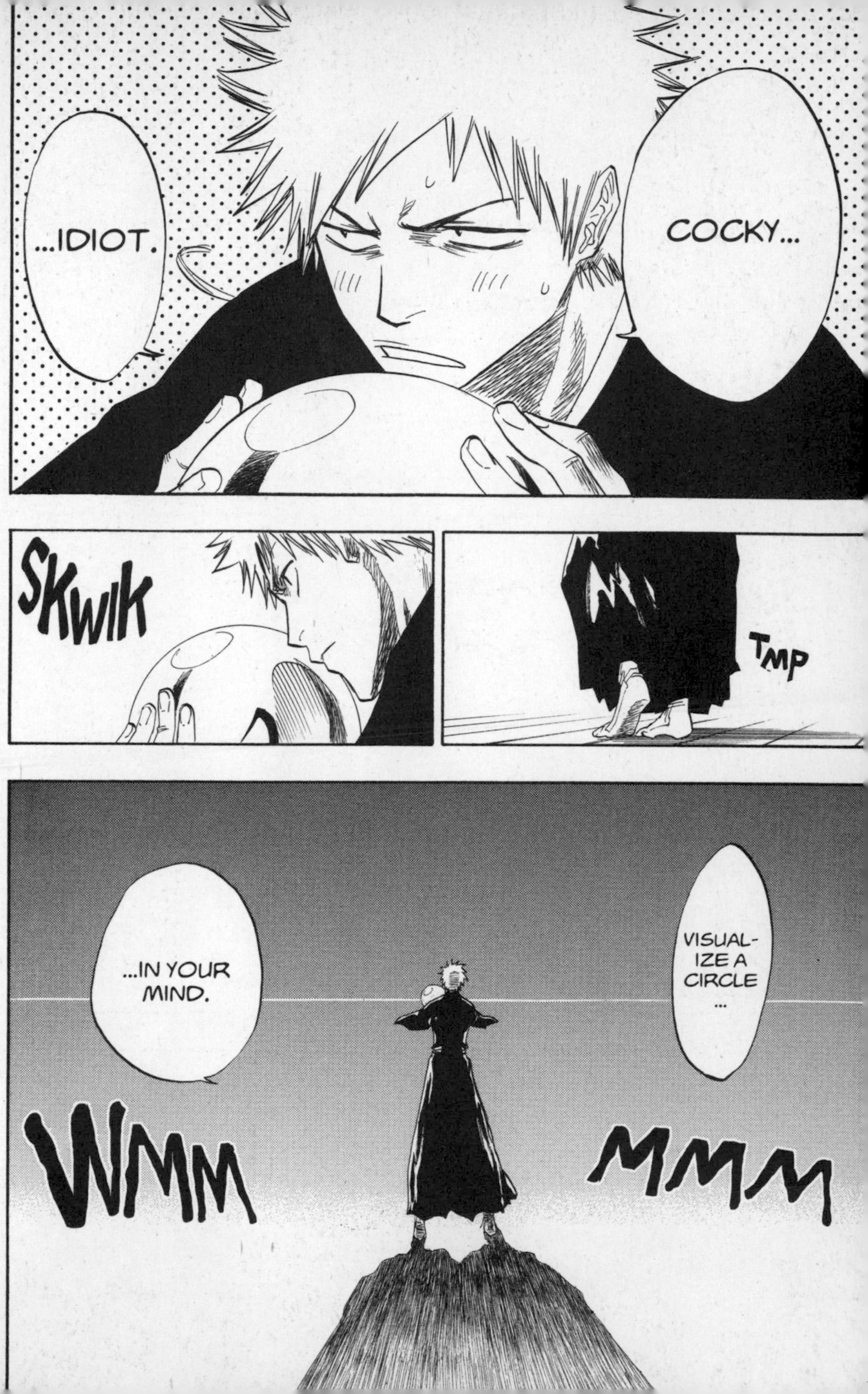
COCKY...
...IDIOT.
TMP
SKWIK
VISUALIZE A CIRCLE ...
...IN YOUR MIND.
WMM MMM

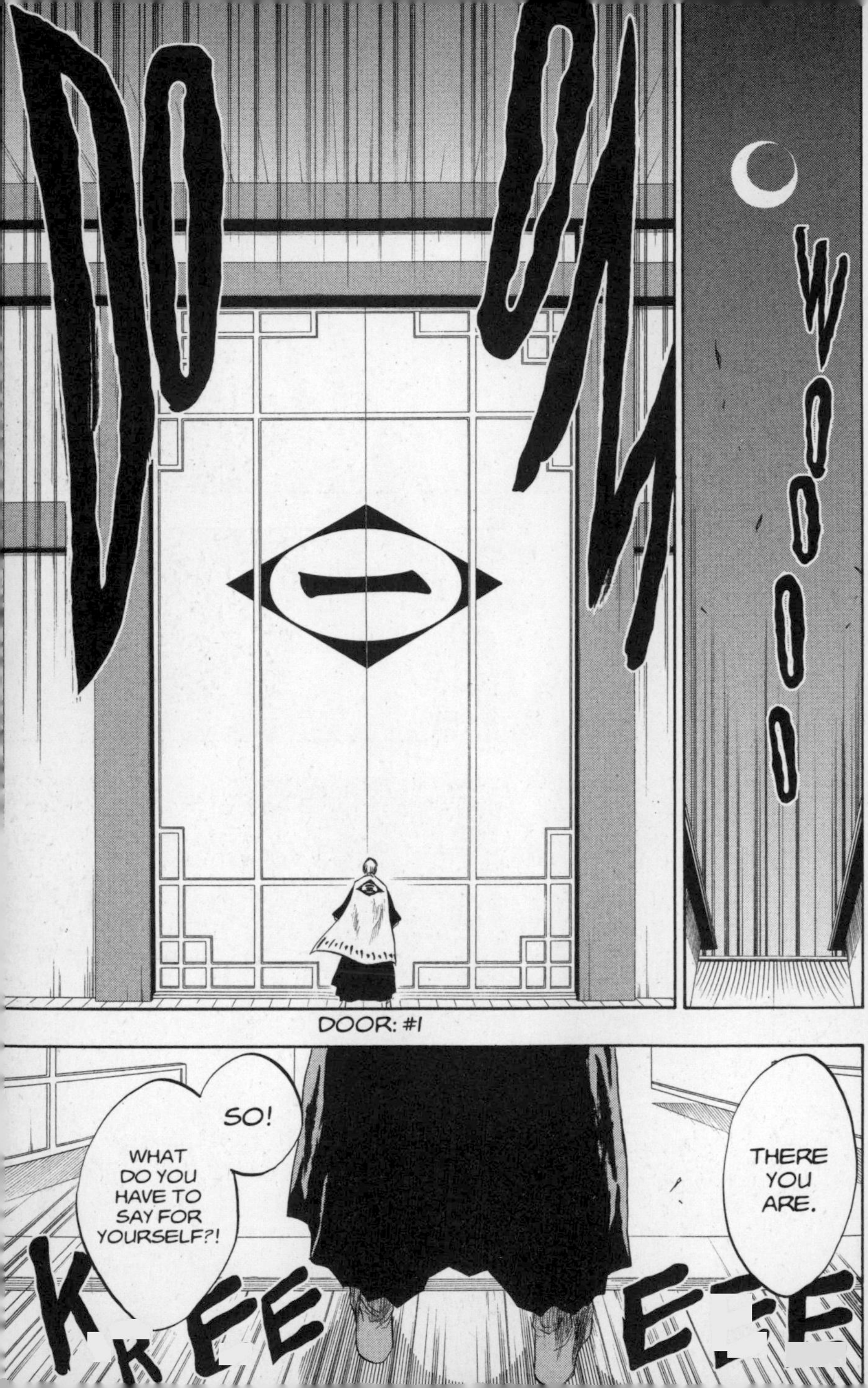
WOOOOO
DOOR: #1
THERE YOU ARE.
SO!
WHAT DO YOU HAVE TO SAY FOR YOURSELF?!

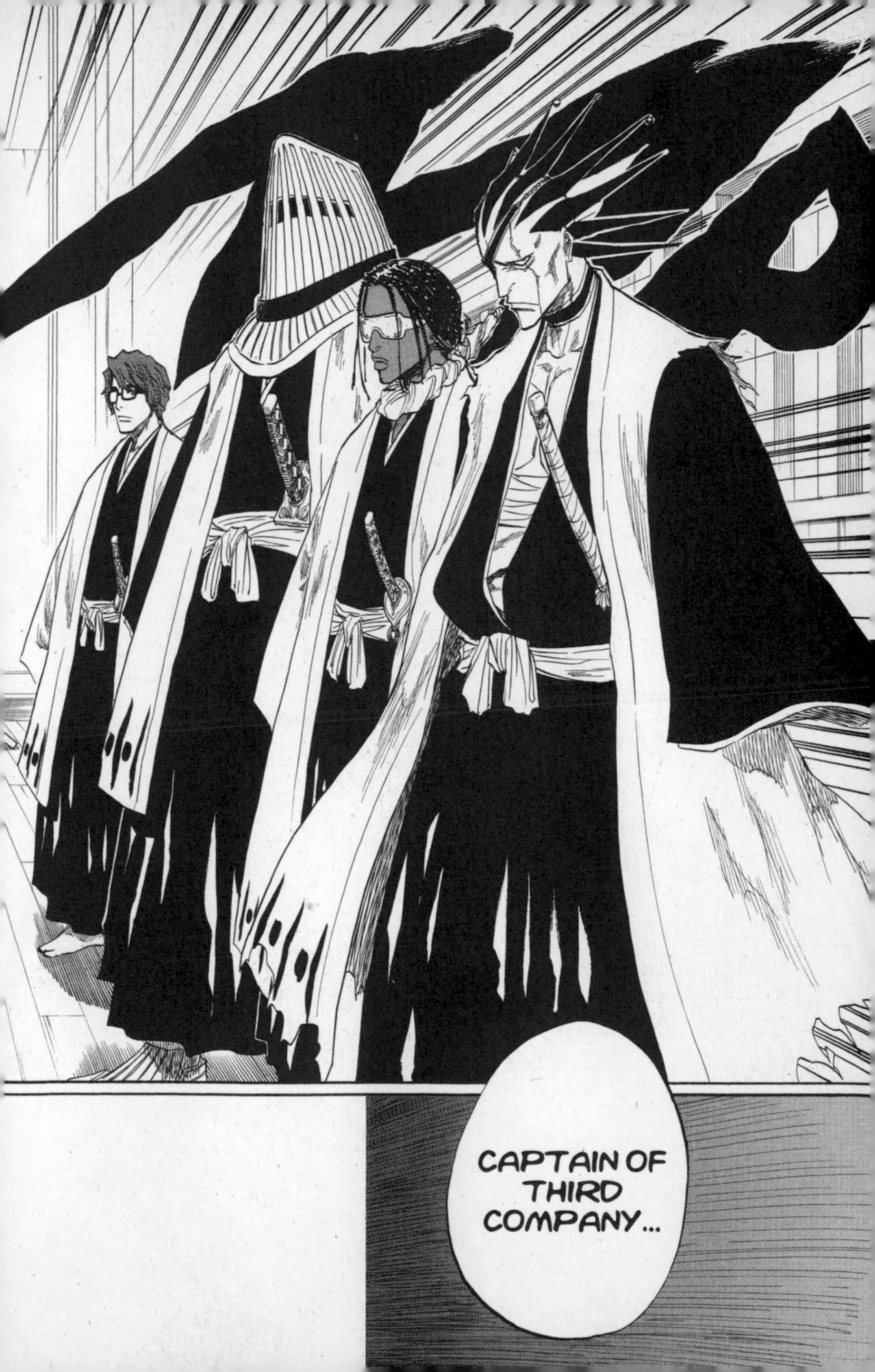
CAPTAIN OF THIRD COMPANY...

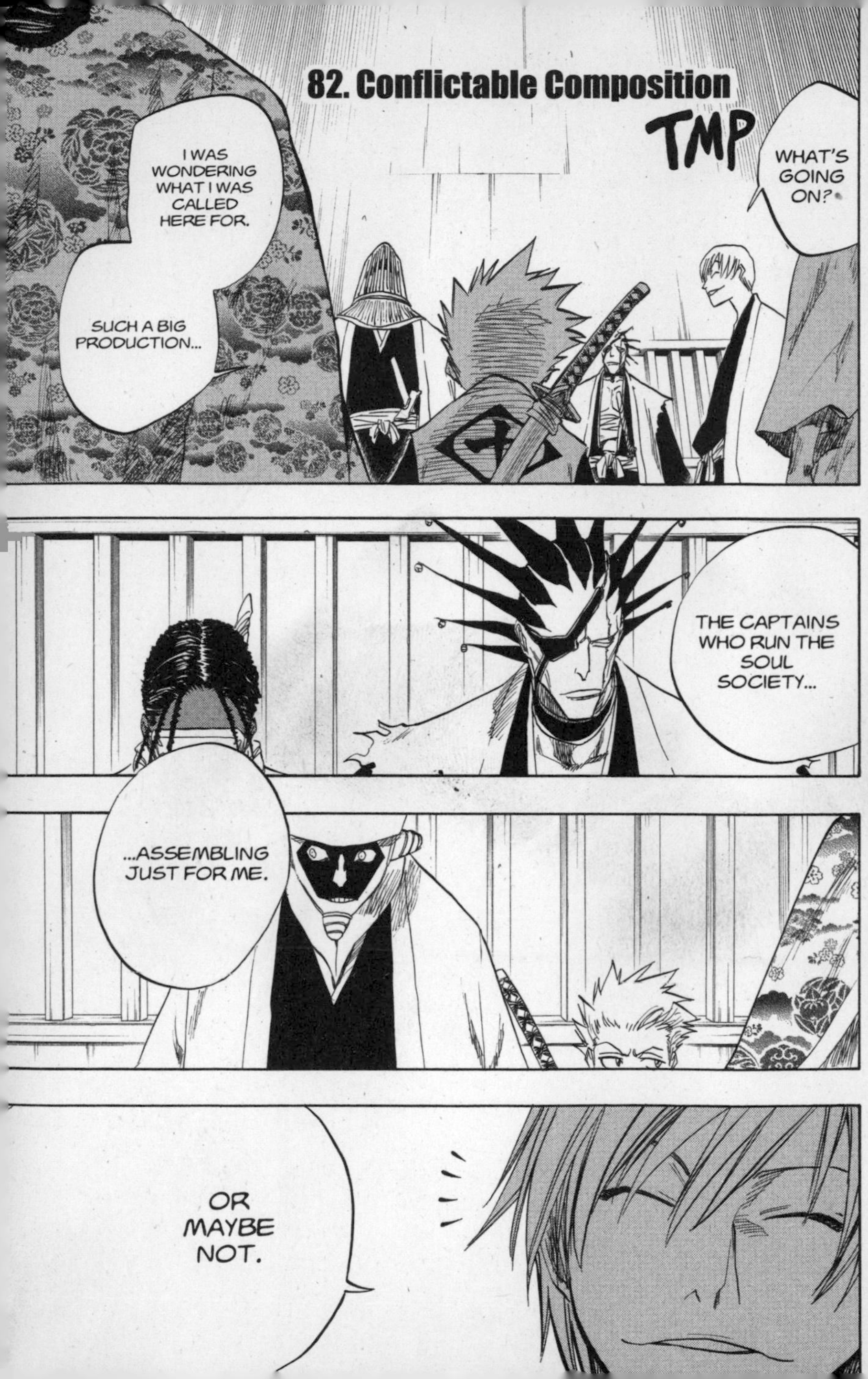
82. Conflictable Composition
TMP
WHAT'S GOING ON?
I WAS WONDERING WHAT I WAS CALLED HERE FOR.
SUCH A BIG PRODUCTION...
THE CAPTAINS WHO RUN THE SOUL SOCIETY...
...ASSEMBLING JUST FOR ME.
OR MAYBE NOT.

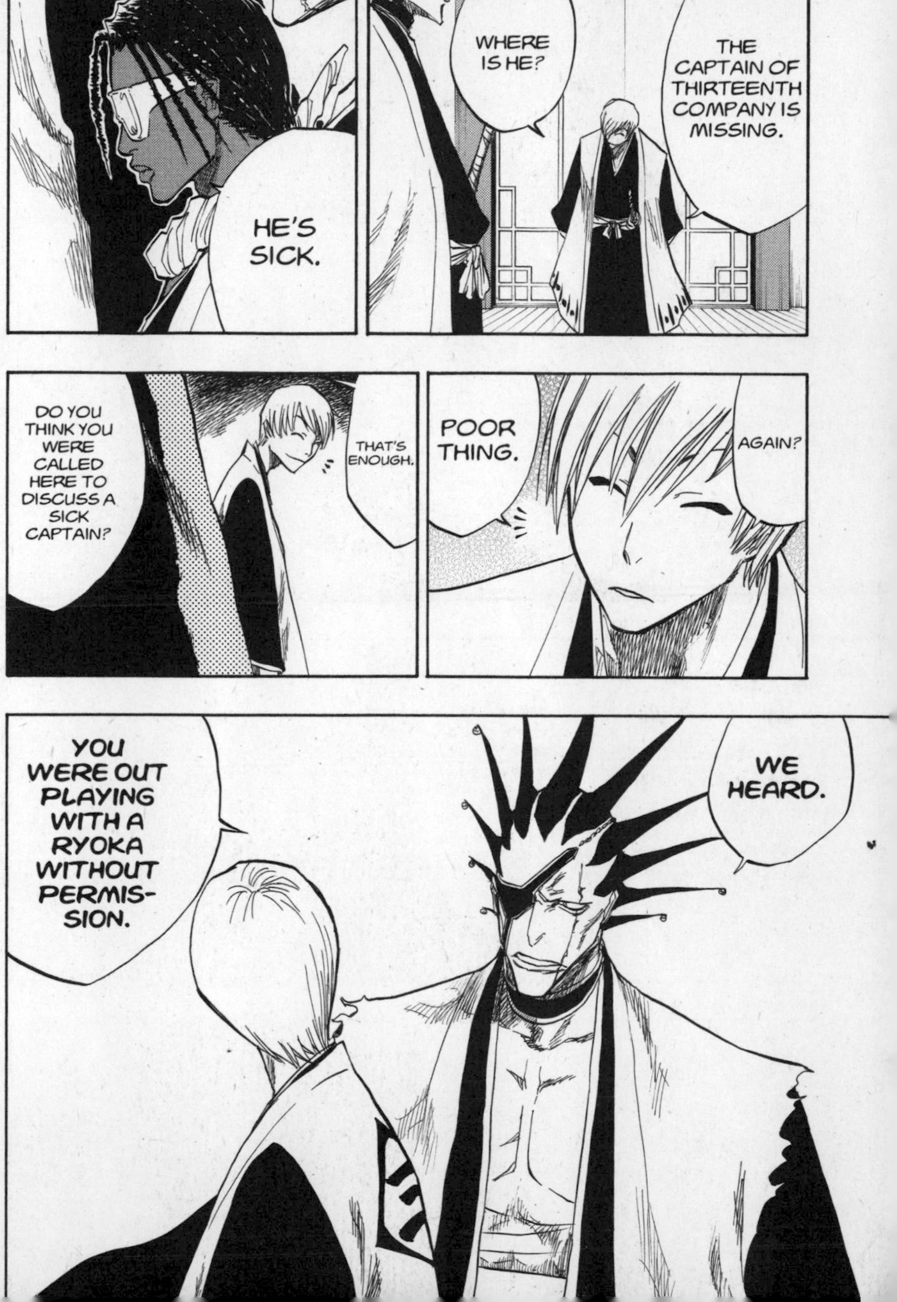
THE CAPTAIN OF THIRTEENTH COMPANY IS MISSING.
WHERE IS HE?
HE'S SICK.
AGAIN?
POOR THING.
THAT'S ENOUGH.
DO YOU THINK YOU WERE CALLED HERE TO DISCUSS A SICK CAPTAIN?
WE HEARD.
YOU WERE OUT PLAYING WITH A RYOKA WITHOUT PERMIS-SION.

READ THIS WAY

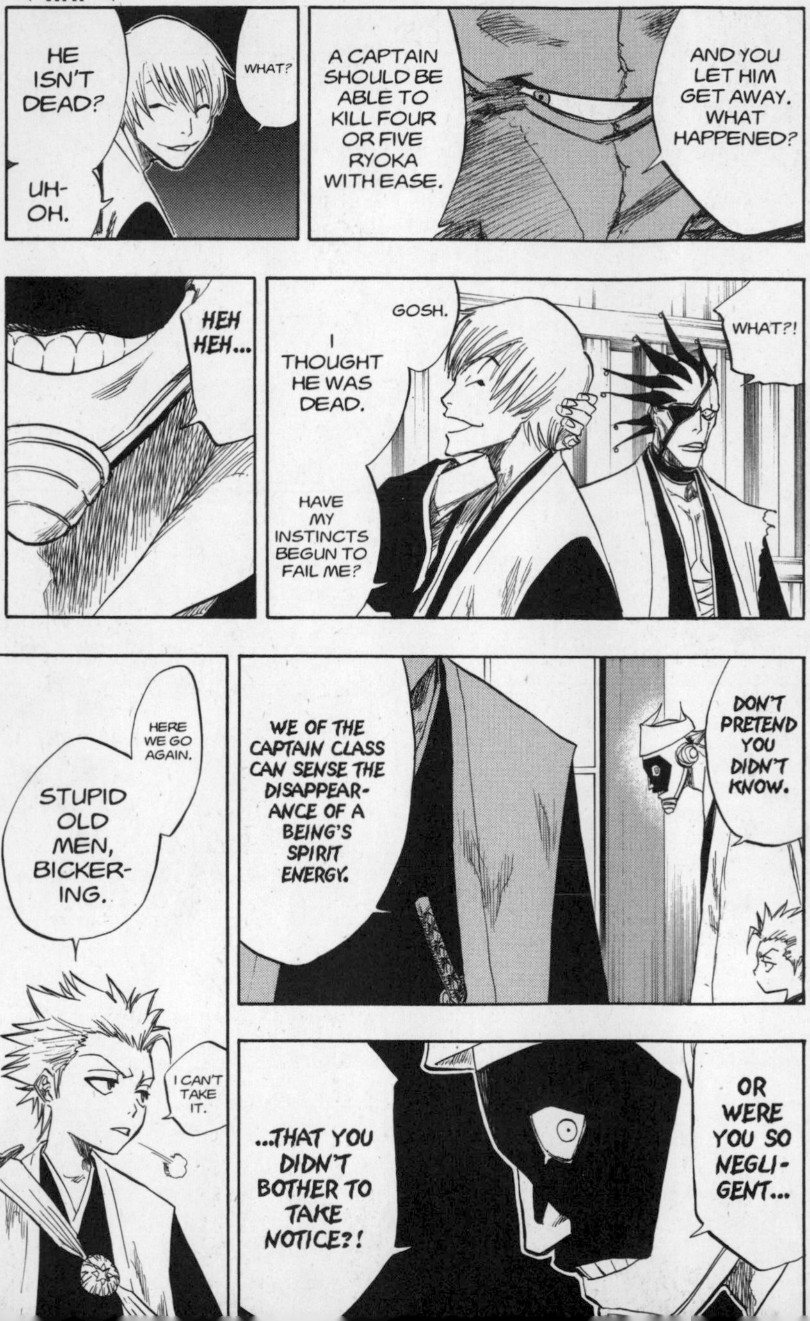
A CAPTAIN SHOULD BE ABLE TO KILL FOUR OR FIVE RYOKA WITH EASE.
AND YOU LET HIM GET AWAY. WHAT HAPPENED?
WHAT?
HE ISN'T DEAD?
UH-OH.
WHAT?!
GOSH.
I THOUGHT HE WAS DEAD.
HAVE MY INSTINCTS BEGUN TO FAIL ME?
HEH HEH...
DON'T PRETEND YOU DIDN'T KNOW.
WE OF THE CAPTAIN CLASS CAN SENSE THE DISAPPEARANCE OF A BEING'S SPIRIT ENERGY.
OR WERE YOU SO NEGLIGENT...
...THAT YOU DIDN'T BOTHER TO TAKE NOTICE?!
HERE WE GO AGAIN.
STUPID OLD MEN, BICKERING.
I CAN'T TAKE IT.

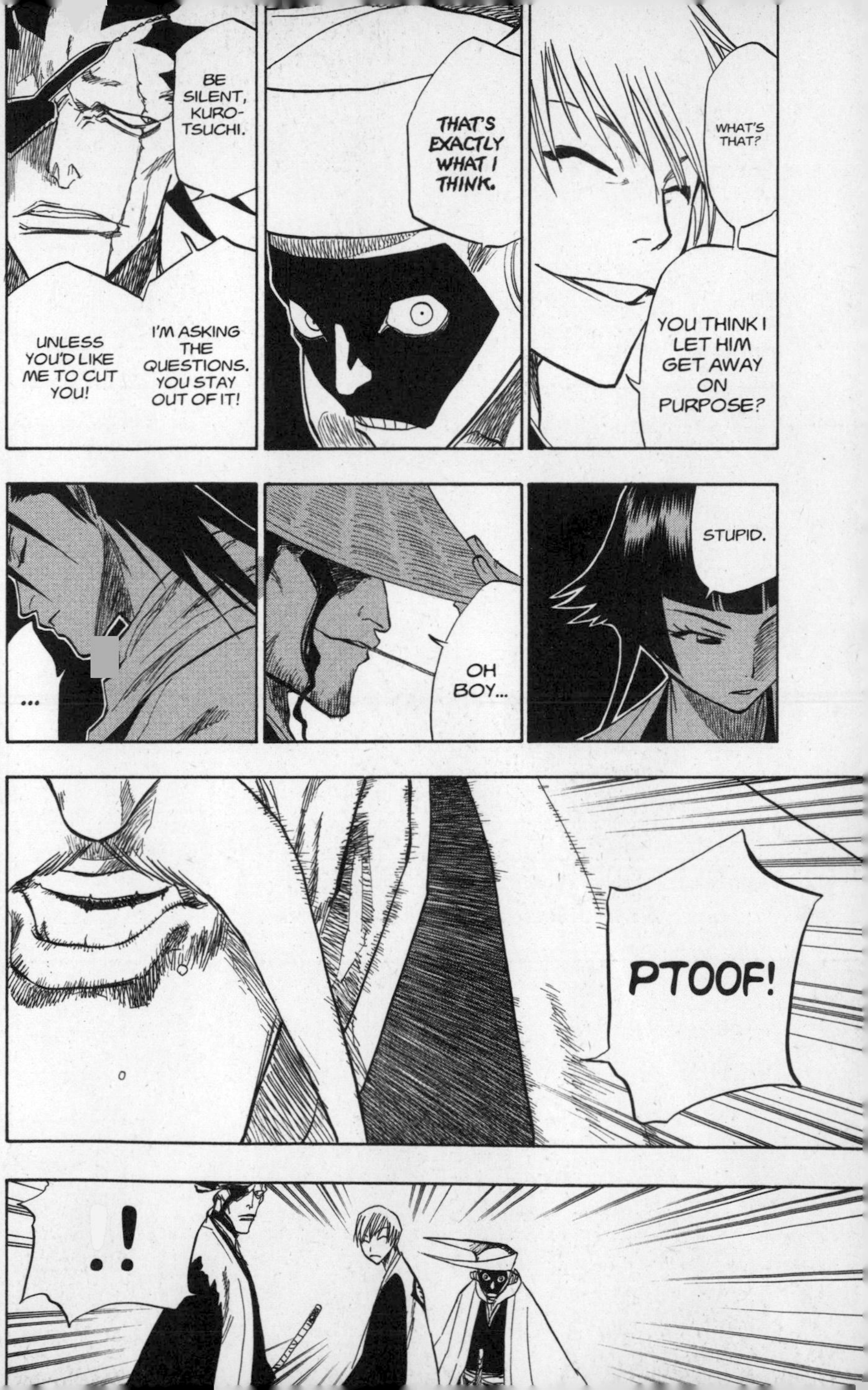
WHAT'S THAT?
YOU THINK I LET HIM GET AWAY ON PURPOSE?
THAT'S EXACTLY WHAT I THINK.
BE SILENT, KURO-TSUCHI.
I'M ASKING THE QUESTIONS. YOU STAY OUT OF IT!
UNLESS YOU'D LIKE ME TO CUT YOU!
STUPID.
OH BOY...
...
PTOOF!
!!

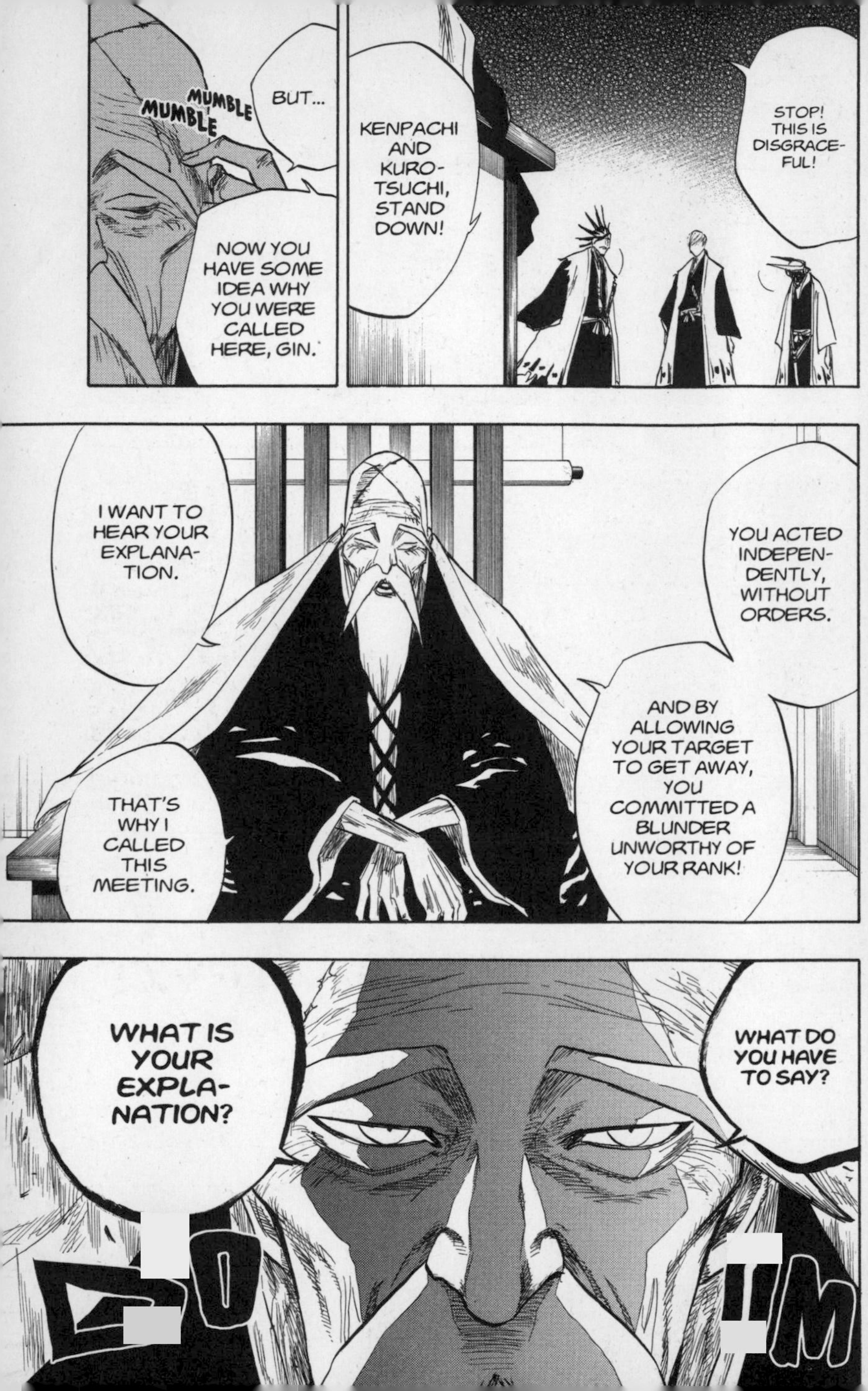
STOP! THIS IS DISGRACE-FUL!
KENPACHI AND KURO-TSUCHI, STAND DOWN!
BUT...
MUMBLE MUMBLE
NOW YOU HAVE SOME IDEA WHY YOU WERE CALLED HERE, GIN.
YOU ACTED INDEPEN-DENTLY, WITHOUT ORDERS.
AND BY ALLOWING YOUR TARGET TO GET AWAY, YOU COMMITTED A BLUNDER UNWORTHY OF YOUR RANK!
I WANT TO HEAR YOUR EXPLANA-TION.
THAT'S WHY I CALLED THIS MEETING.
WHAT DO YOU HAVE TO SAY?
WHAT IS YOUR EXPLA-NATION?

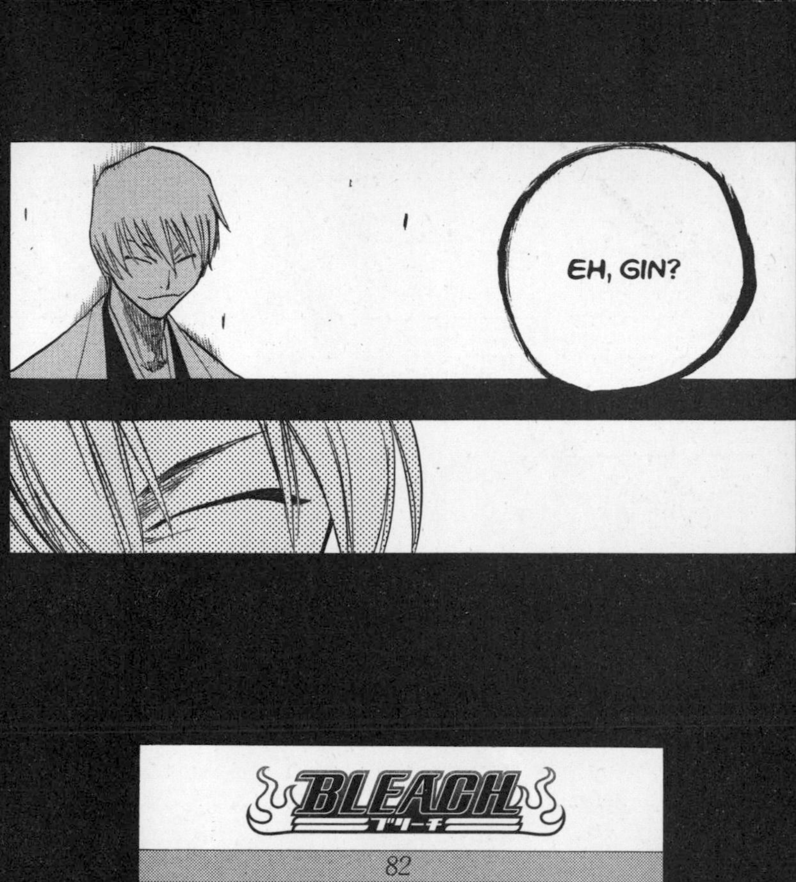
EH, GIN?

82
Conflictable Composition

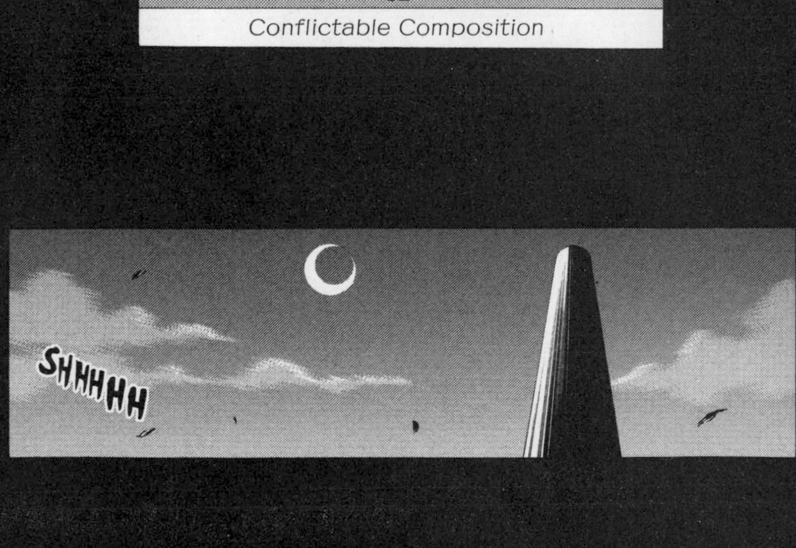
SHHHHH

READ THIS WAY

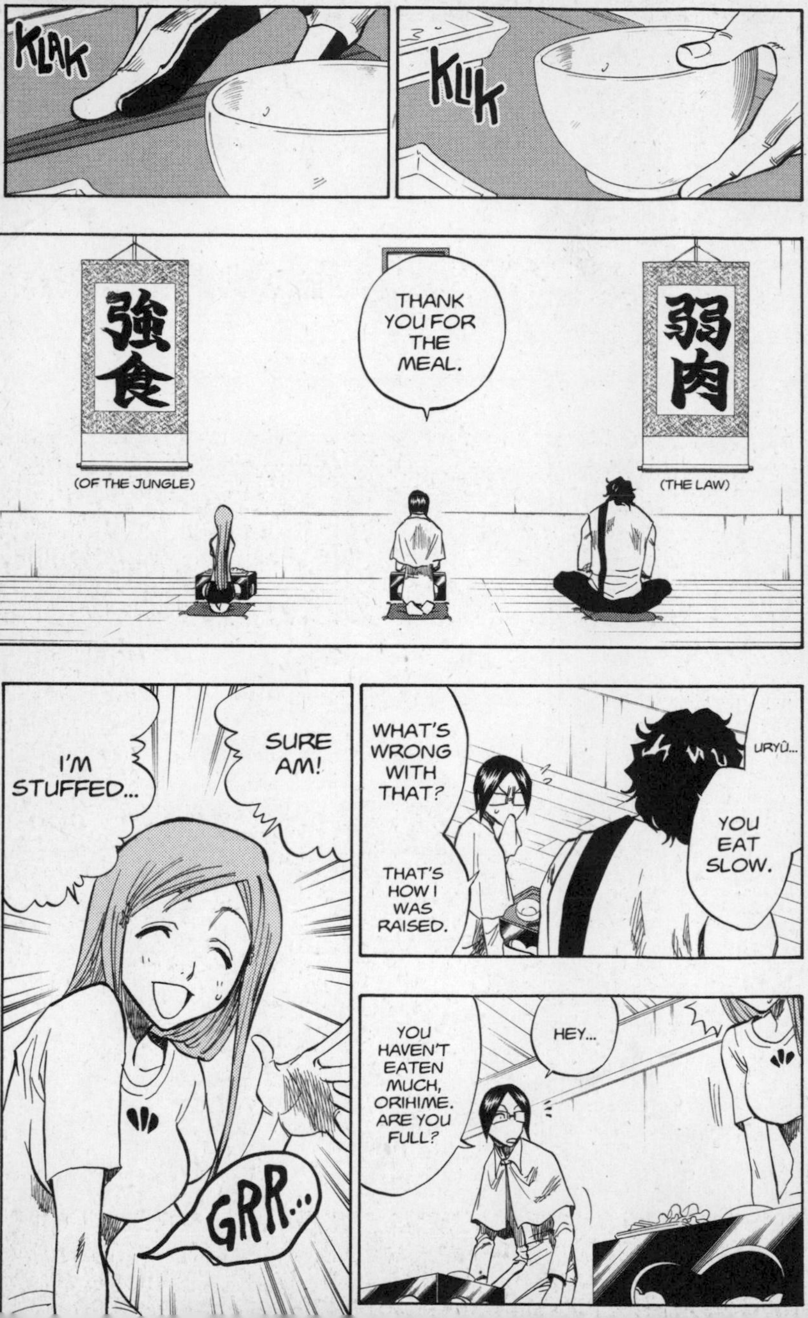
KLIK
KLAK
弱肉
(THE LAW)
THANK YOU FOR THE MEAL.
強食
(OF THE JUNGLE)
URYŪ...
YOU EAT SLOW.
WHAT'S WRONG WITH THAT?
THAT'S HOW I WAS RAISED.
HEY...
YOU HAVEN'T EATEN MUCH, ORIHIME. ARE YOU FULL?
SURE AM!
I'M STUFFED...
GRR...

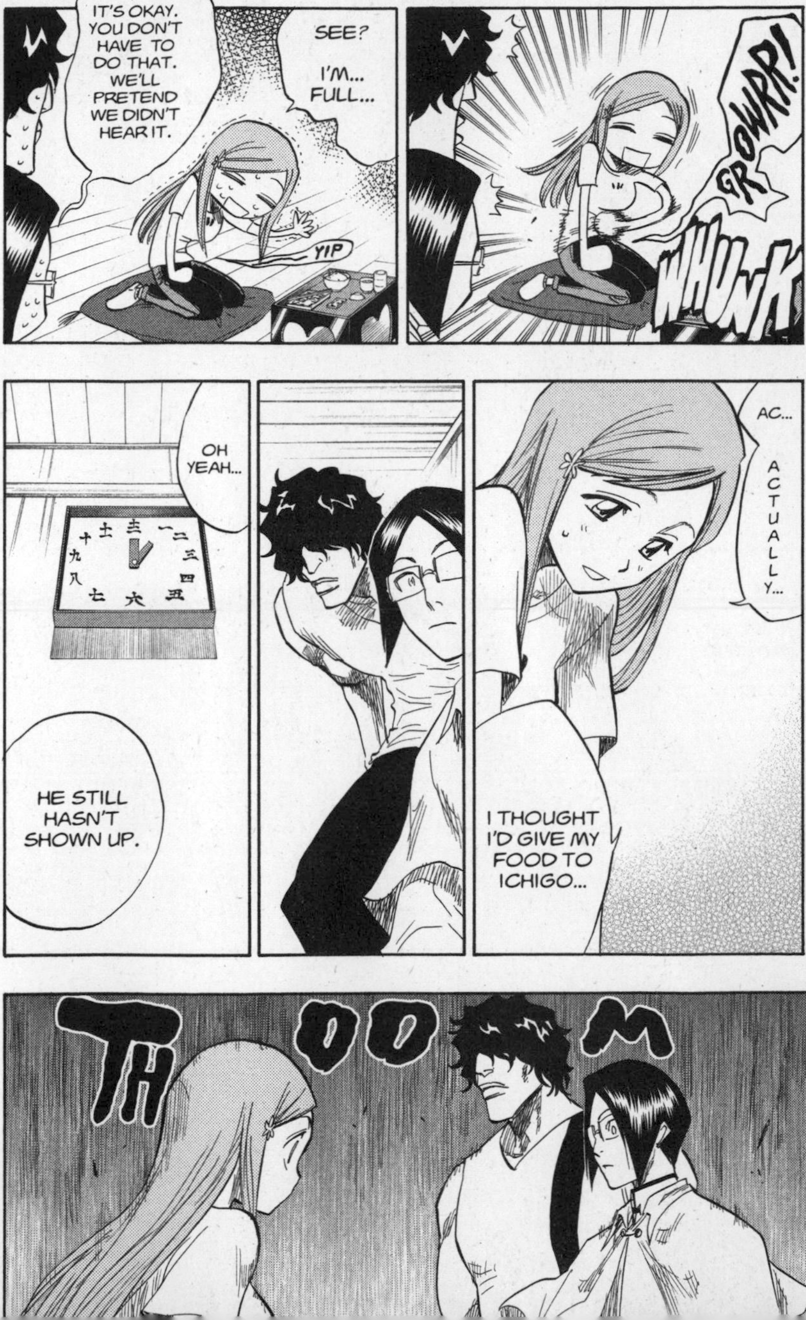
GROWRR!
WHUNK!
SEE?
I'M... FULL...
IT'S OKAY. YOU DON'T HAVE TO DO THAT. WE'LL PRETEND WE DIDN'T HEAR IT.
YIP
AC...
ACTUALLY...
I THOUGHT I'D GIVE MY FOOD TO ICHIGO...
OH YEAH...
HE STILL HASN'T SHOWN UP.
THOOOM

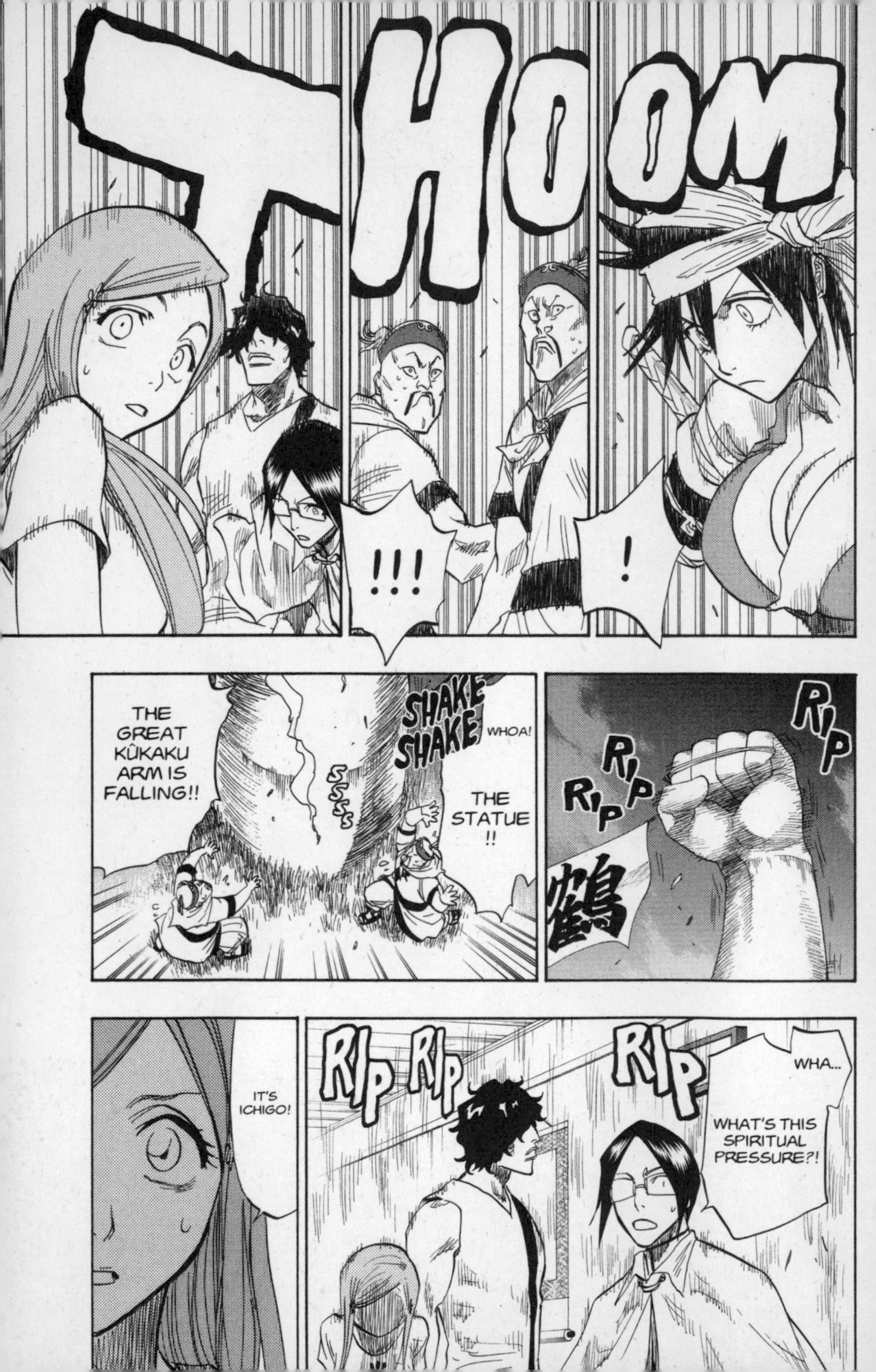
THOOM
!
!!!
RIP RIP RIP
鶴
SHAKE SHAKE
WHOA!
THE STATUE !!
SSSS
THE GREAT KÛKAKU ARM IS FALLING!!
RIP RIP RIP
WHA...
WHAT'S THIS SPIRITUAL PRESSURE?!
IT'S ICHIGO!

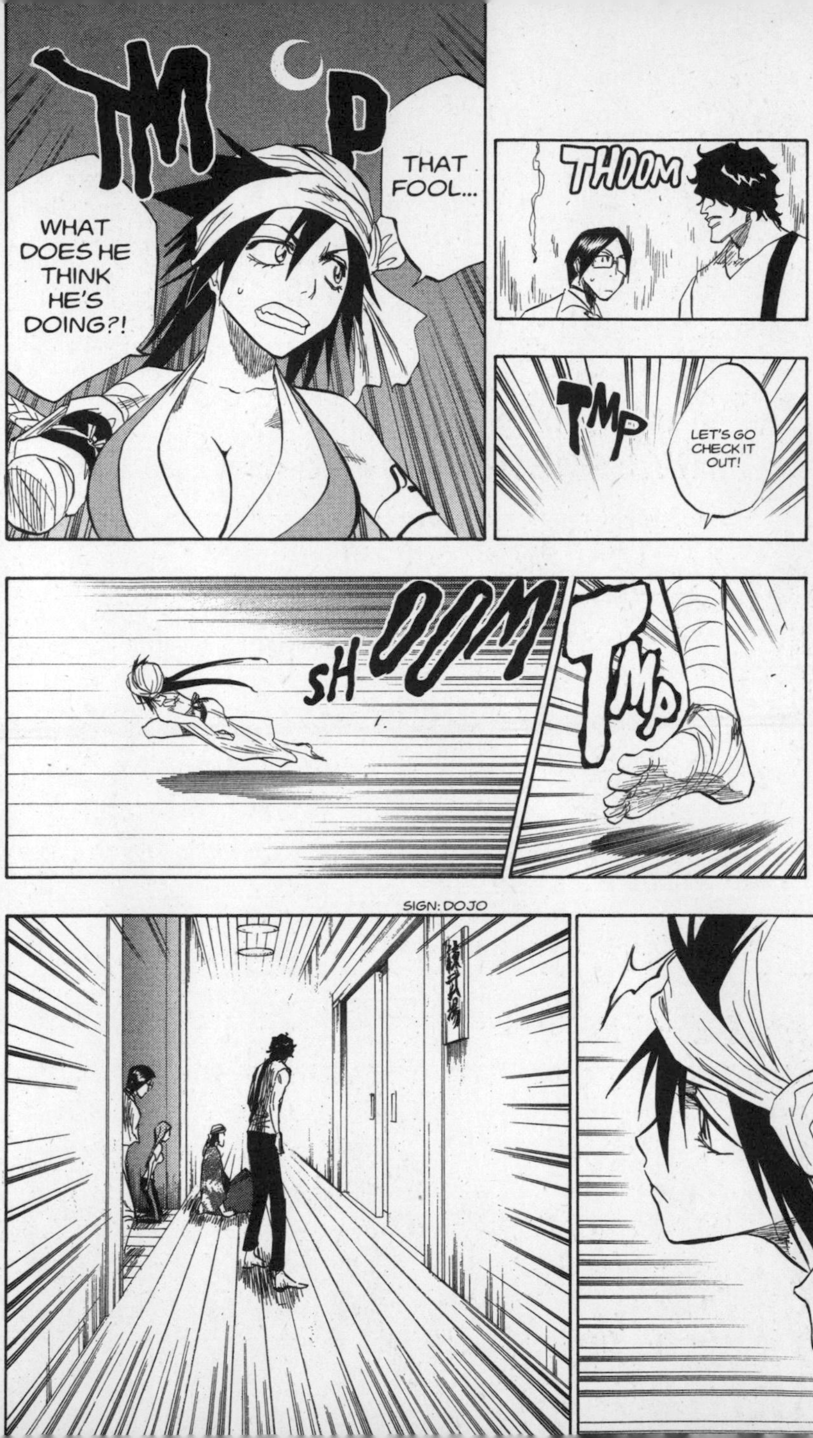
THOOM
LET'S GO CHECK IT OUT!
TMP
TMP
THAT FOOL...
WHAT DOES HE THINK HE'S DOING?!
TMP
SHOOM
SIGN: DOJO

READ THIS WAY

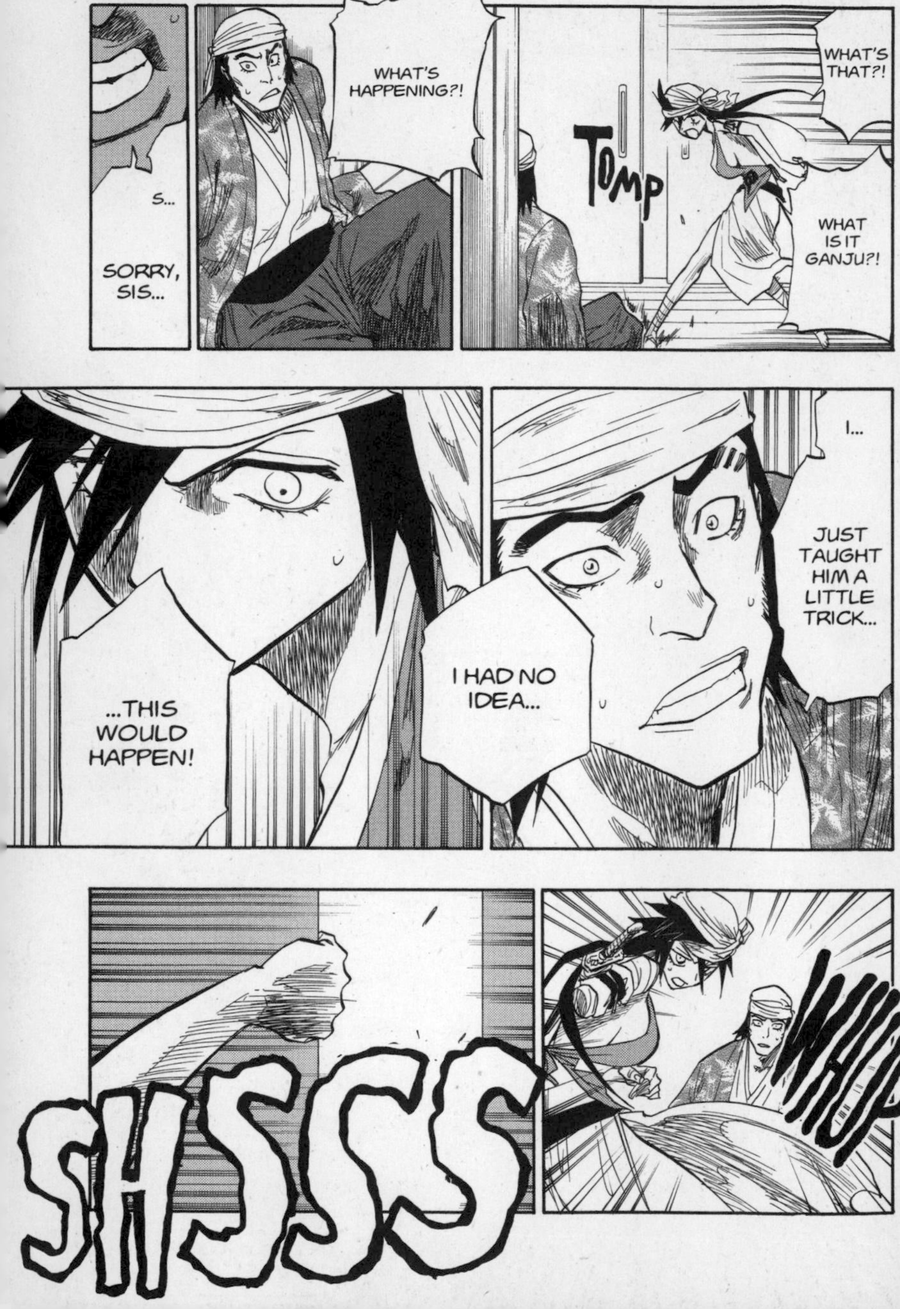
WHAT'S THAT?!
TOMP
WHAT IS IT GANJU?!
WHAT'S HAPPENING?!
S...
SORRY, SIS...
I...
JUST TAUGHT HIM A LITTLE TRICK...
I HAD NO IDEA...
...THIS WOULD HAPPEN!
WHIP
SHSSS

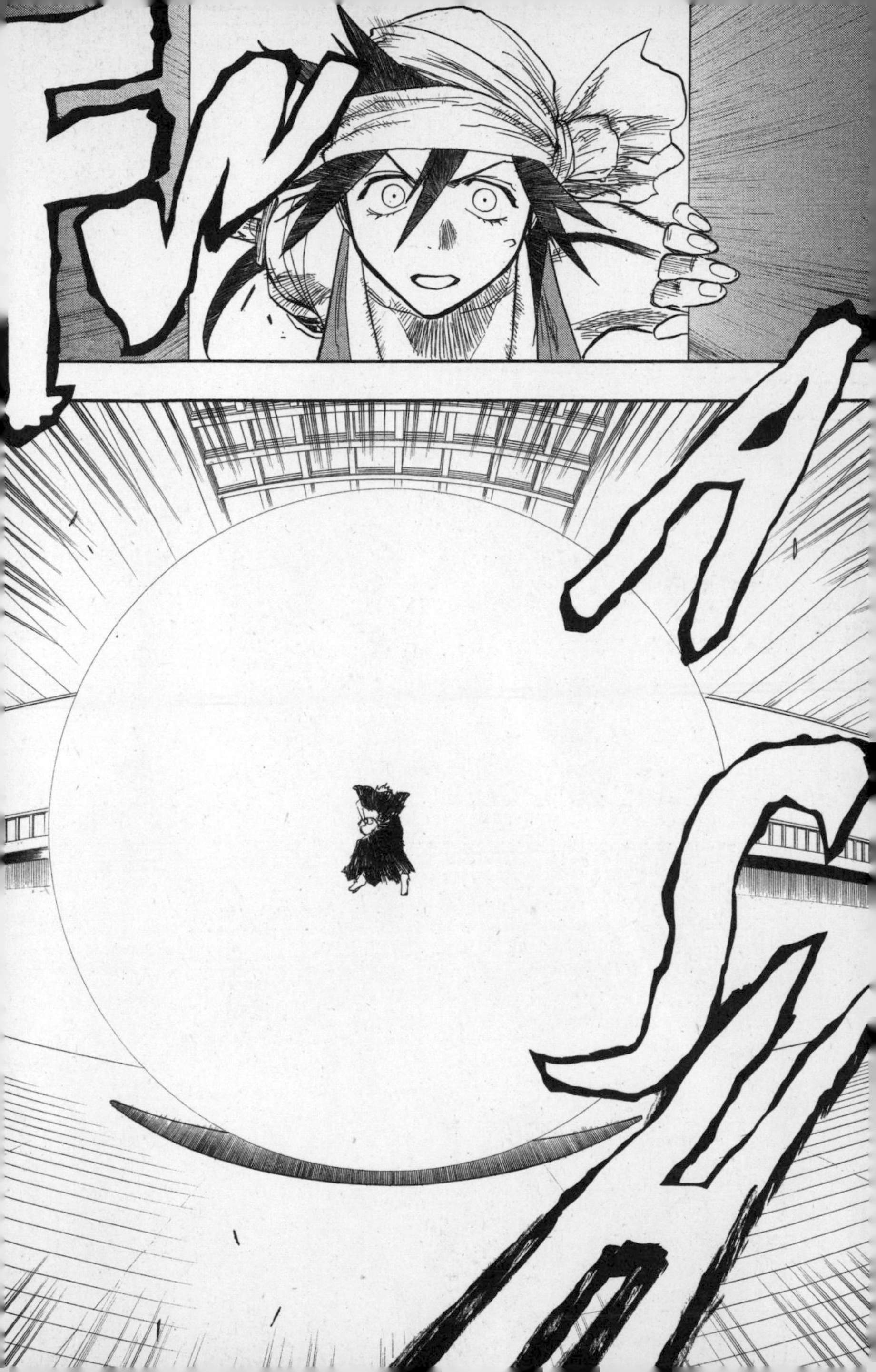

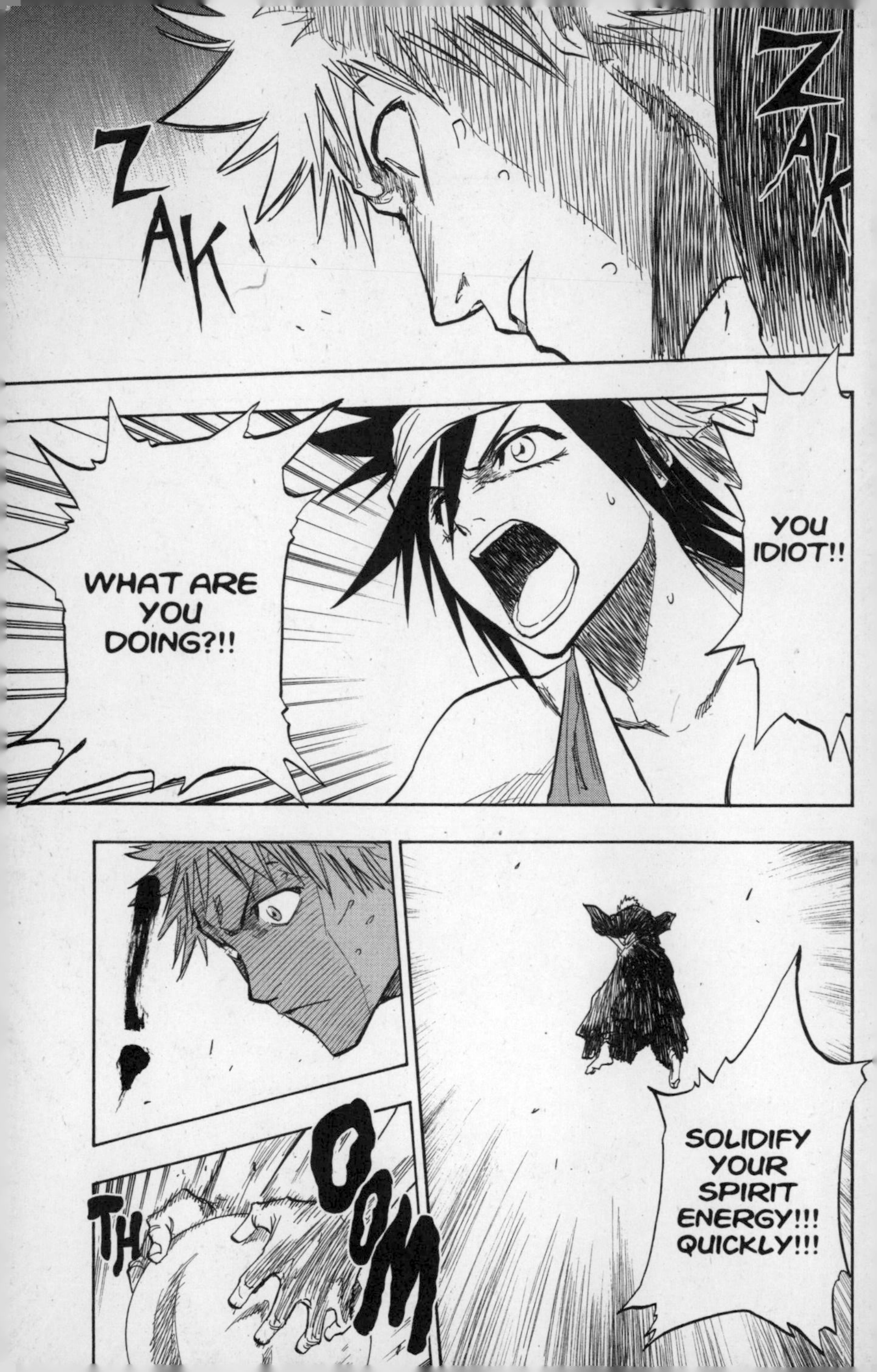
ZAK
ZAK
YOU IDIOT!!
WHAT ARE YOU DOING?!!
SOLIDIFY YOUR SPIRIT ENERGY!!! QUICKLY!!!
!
THOOM

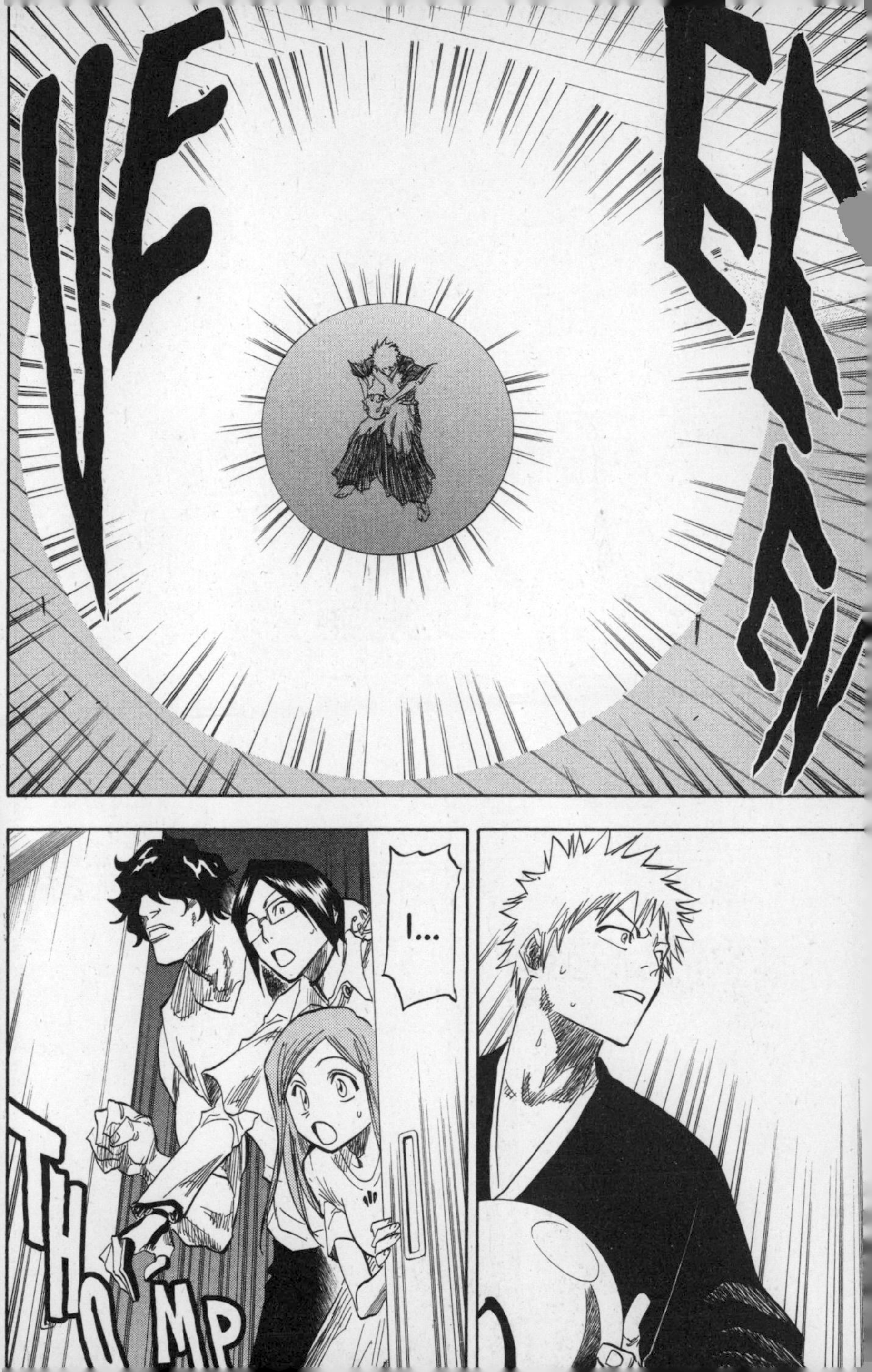
I...
THOOMP

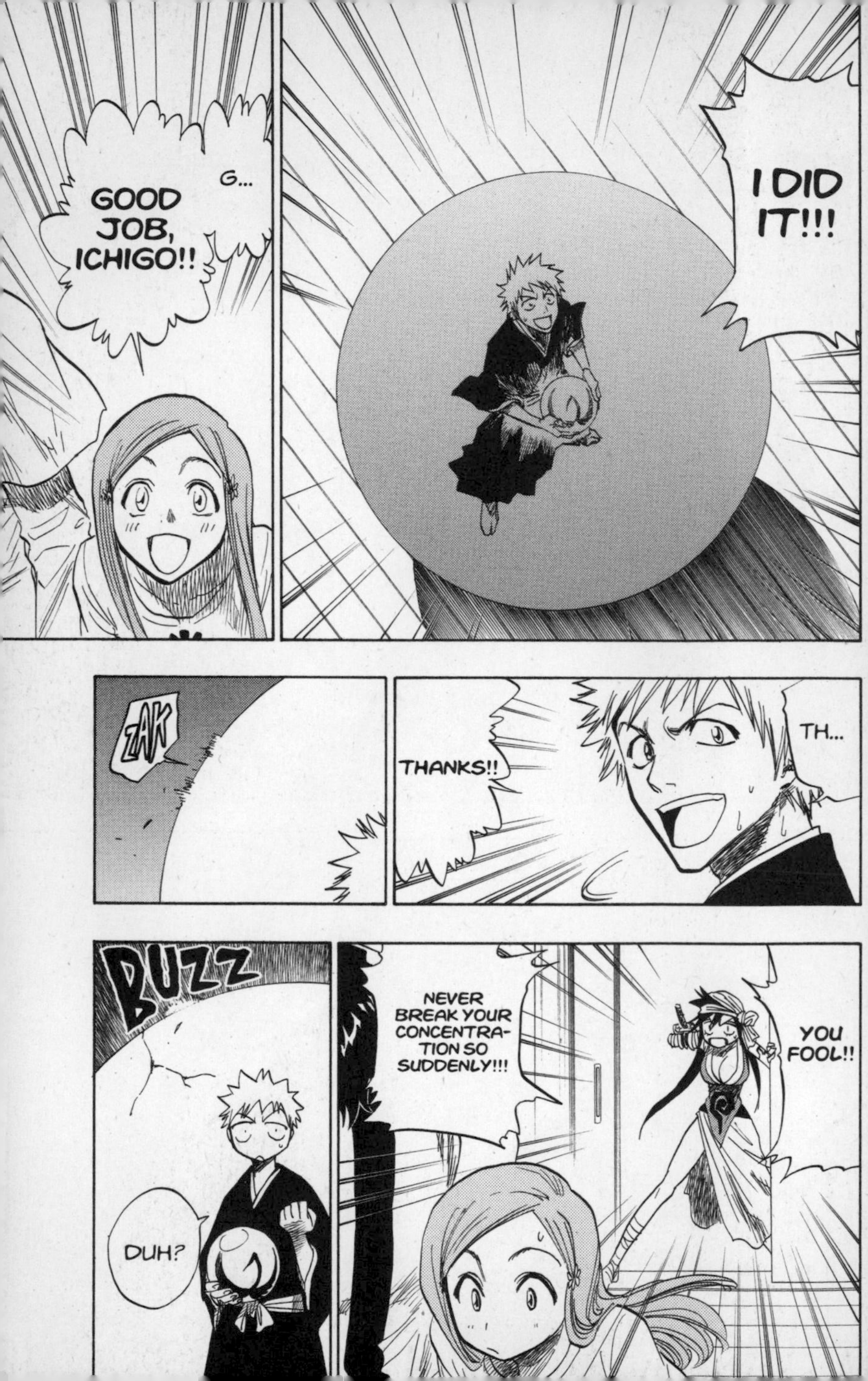
I DID IT!!!
G...
GOOD JOB, ICHIGO!!
TH...
THANKS!!
ZAK
YOU FOOL!!
NEVER BREAK YOUR CONCENTRATION SO SUDDENLY!!!
BUZZ
DUH?

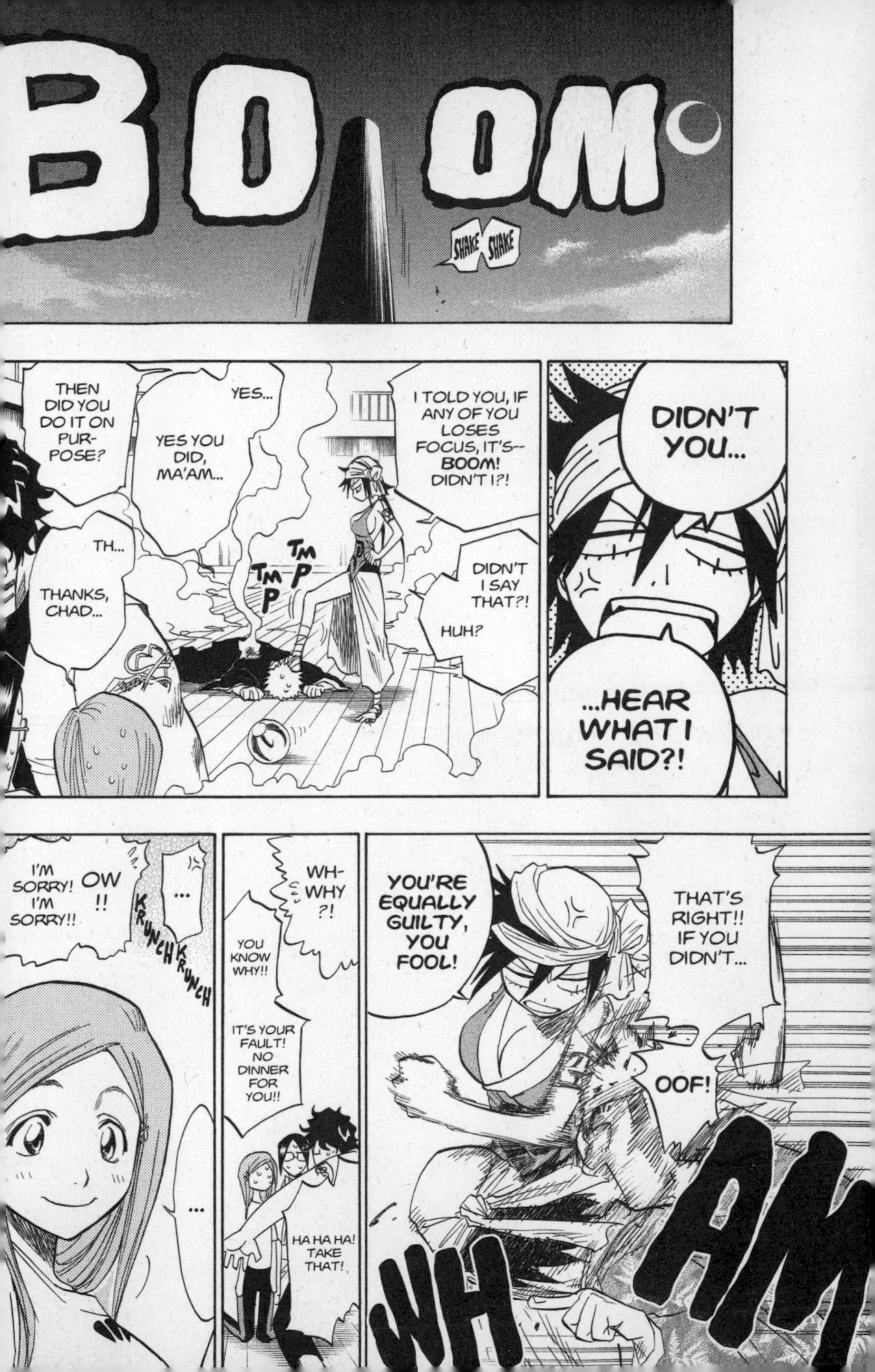
BOOM
SHAKE SHAKE
DIDN'T YOU...
...HEAR WHAT I SAID?!
I TOLD YOU, IF ANY OF YOU LOSES FOCUS, IT'S-- BOOM! DIDN'T I?!
DIDN'T I SAY THAT?!
HUH?
YES...
YES YOU DID, MA'AM...
TMP TMP
THEN DID YOU DO IT ON PUR-POSE?
TH...
THANKS, CHAD...
THAT'S RIGHT!! IF YOU DIDN'T...
YOU'RE EQUALLY GUILTY, YOU FOOL!
OOF!
WHAM
WH- WHY ?!
YOU KNOW WHY!!
IT'S YOUR FAULT! NO DINNER FOR YOU!!
HA HA HA! TAKE THAT!
...
KRUNCH KRUNCH
OW !!
I'M SORRY! I'M SORRY!!
...

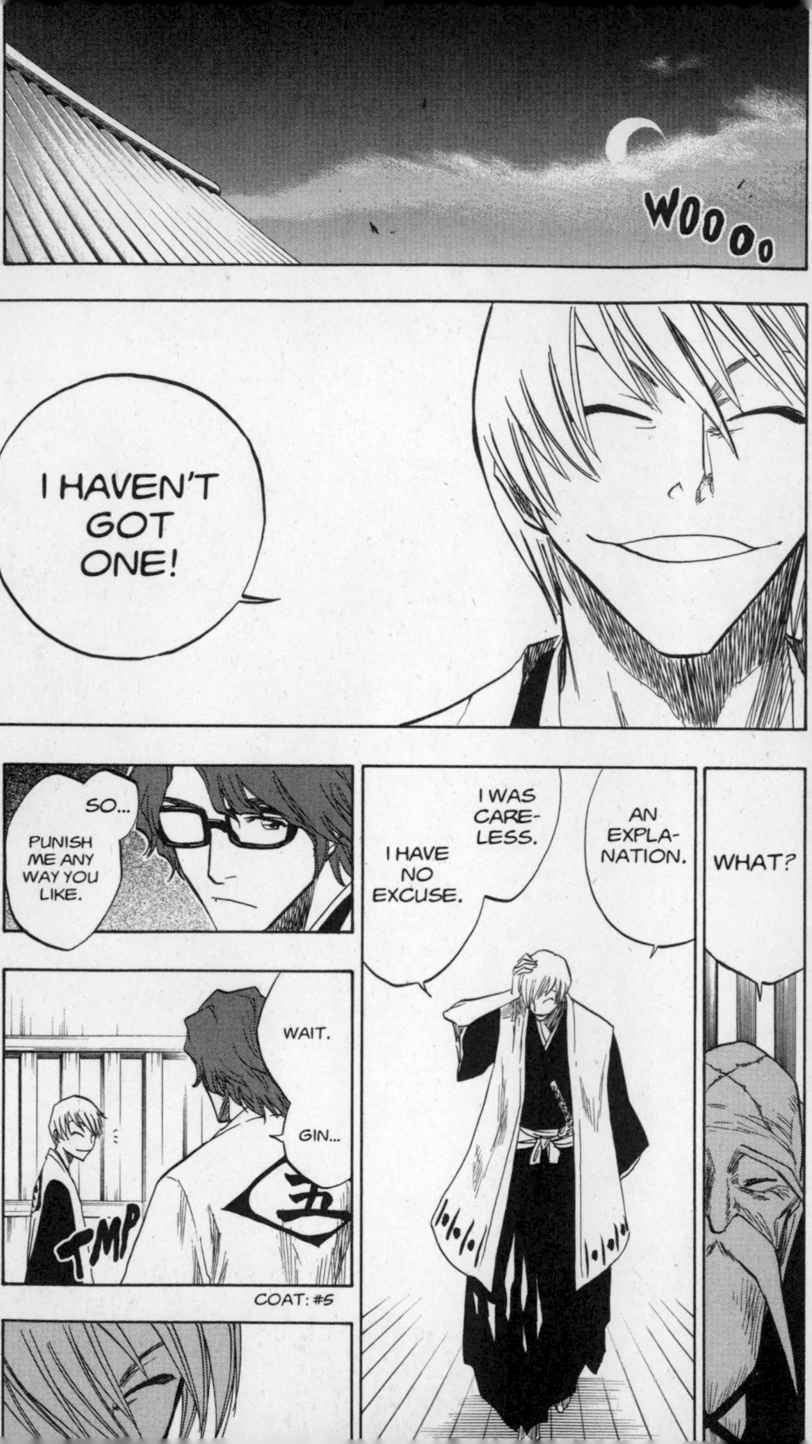
WOOOO
I HAVEN'T GOT ONE!
WHAT?
AN EXPLANATION.
I WAS CARELESS.
I HAVE NO EXCUSE.
SO...
PUNISH ME ANY WAY YOU LIKE.
WAIT.
GIN...
TMP
COAT: #5

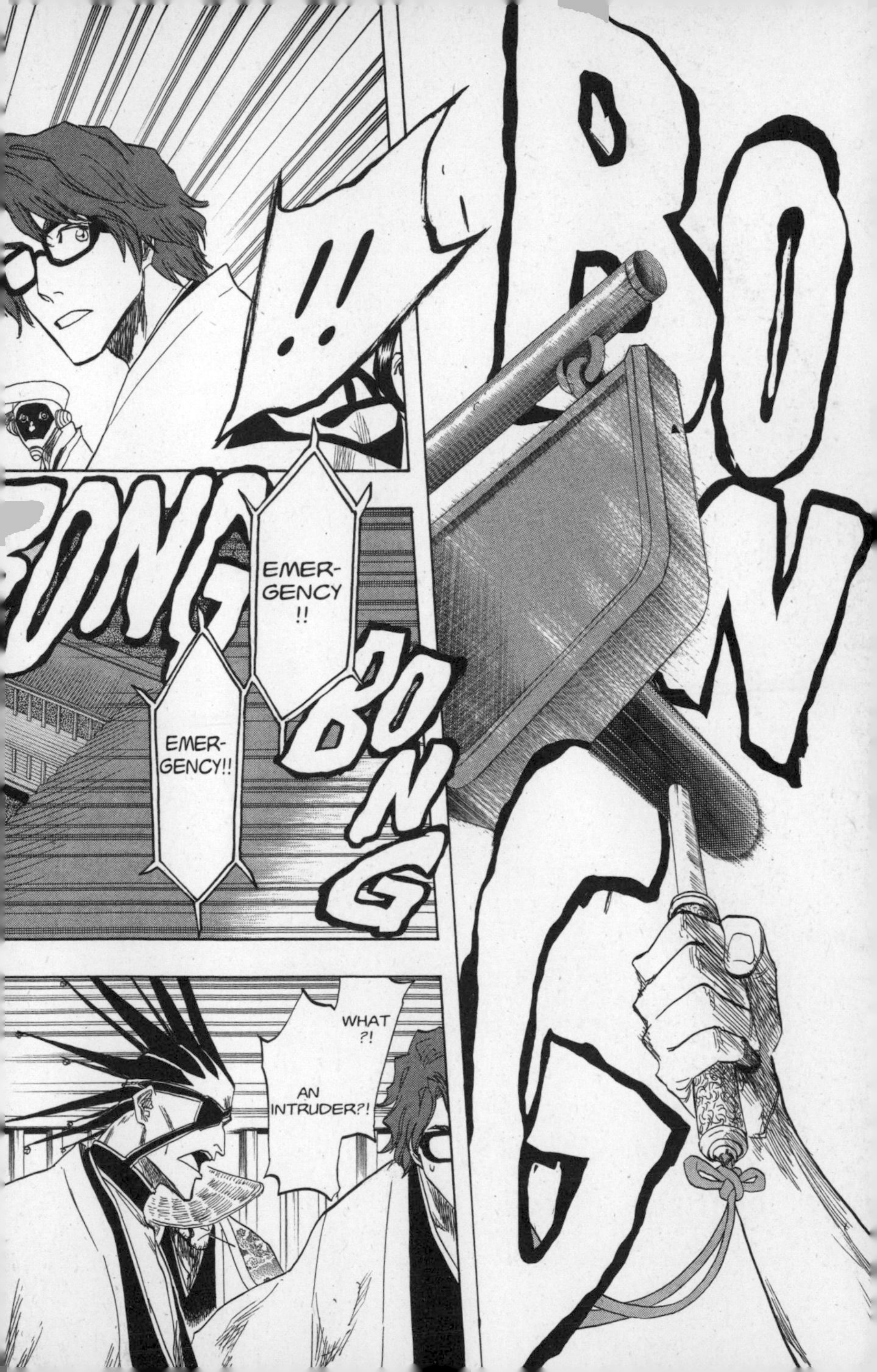
BONG
!!
EMERGENCY!!
EMERGENCY!!
ONG
BONG
WHAT?!
AN INTRUDER?!

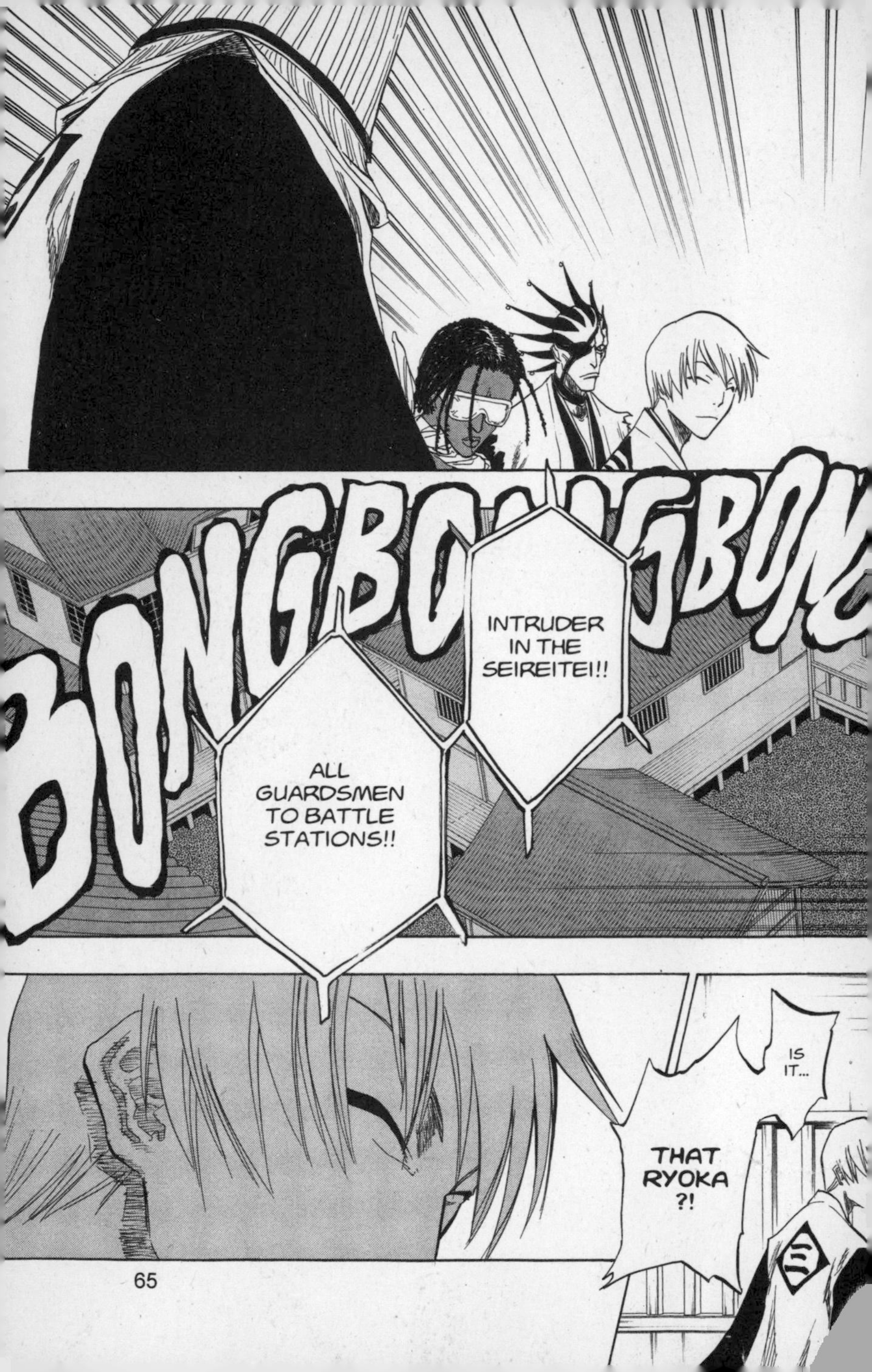

BONGBONGBON
INTRUDER IN THE SEIREITEI!!
ALL GUARDSMEN TO BATTLE STATIONS!!
IS IT...
THAT RYOKA ?!

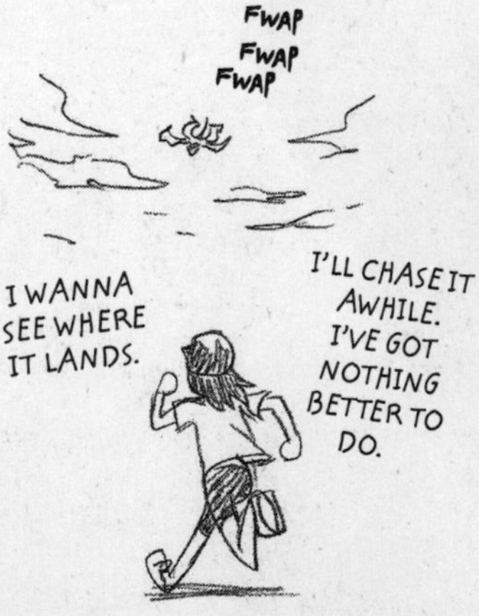
FWAP
FWAP
FWAP
I'LL CHASE IT AWHILE. I'VE GOT NOTHING BETTER TO DO.
I WANNA SEE WHERE IT LANDS.

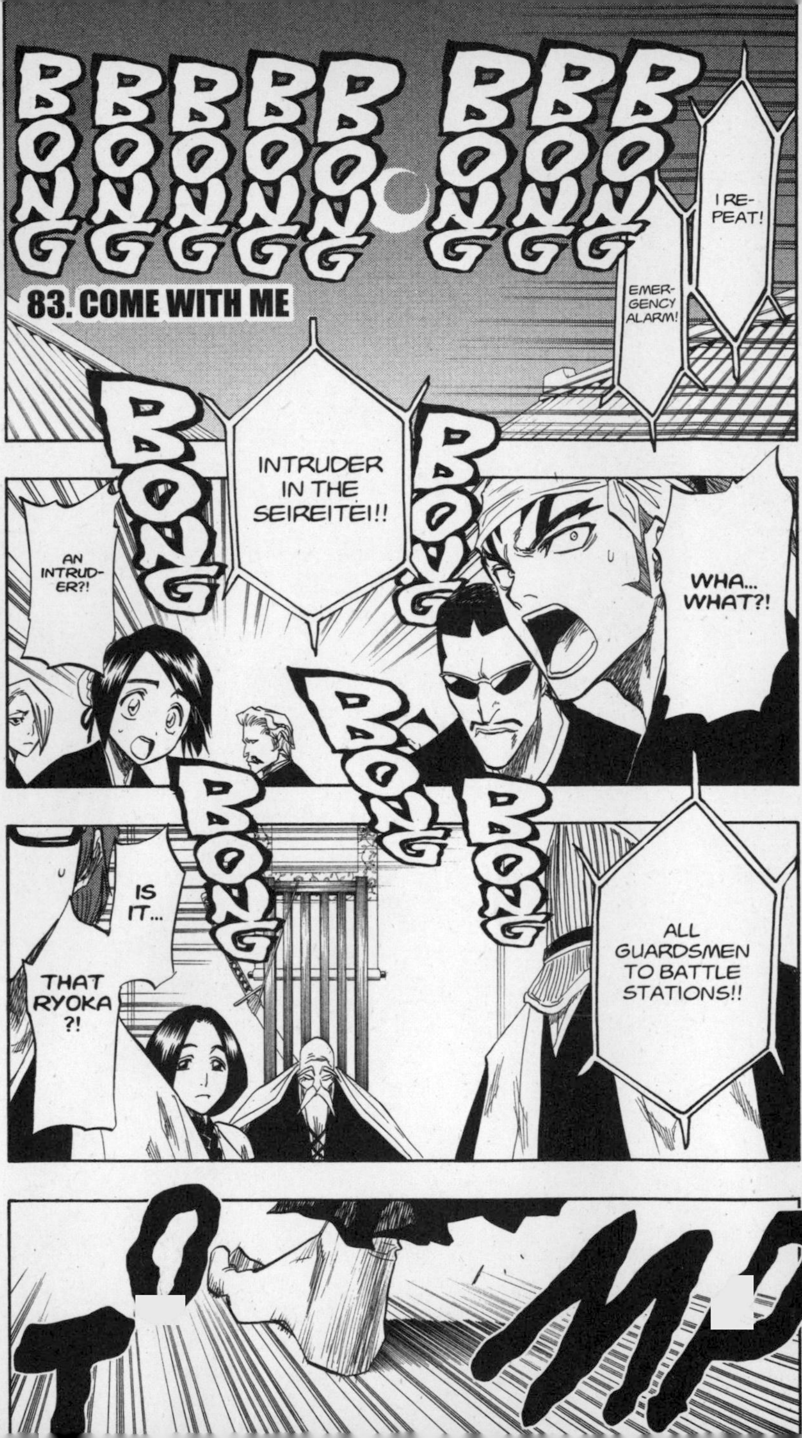
BONG BONG BONG BONG BONG BONG BONG BONG
83. COME WITH ME
I RE-PEAT!
EMERGENCY ALARM!
INTRUDER IN THE SEIREITEI!!
BONG
BONG
WHA... WHAT?!
AN INTRUDER?!
BONG
BONG
BONG
ALL GUARDSMEN TO BATTLE STATIONS!!
IS IT...
THAT RYOKA?!

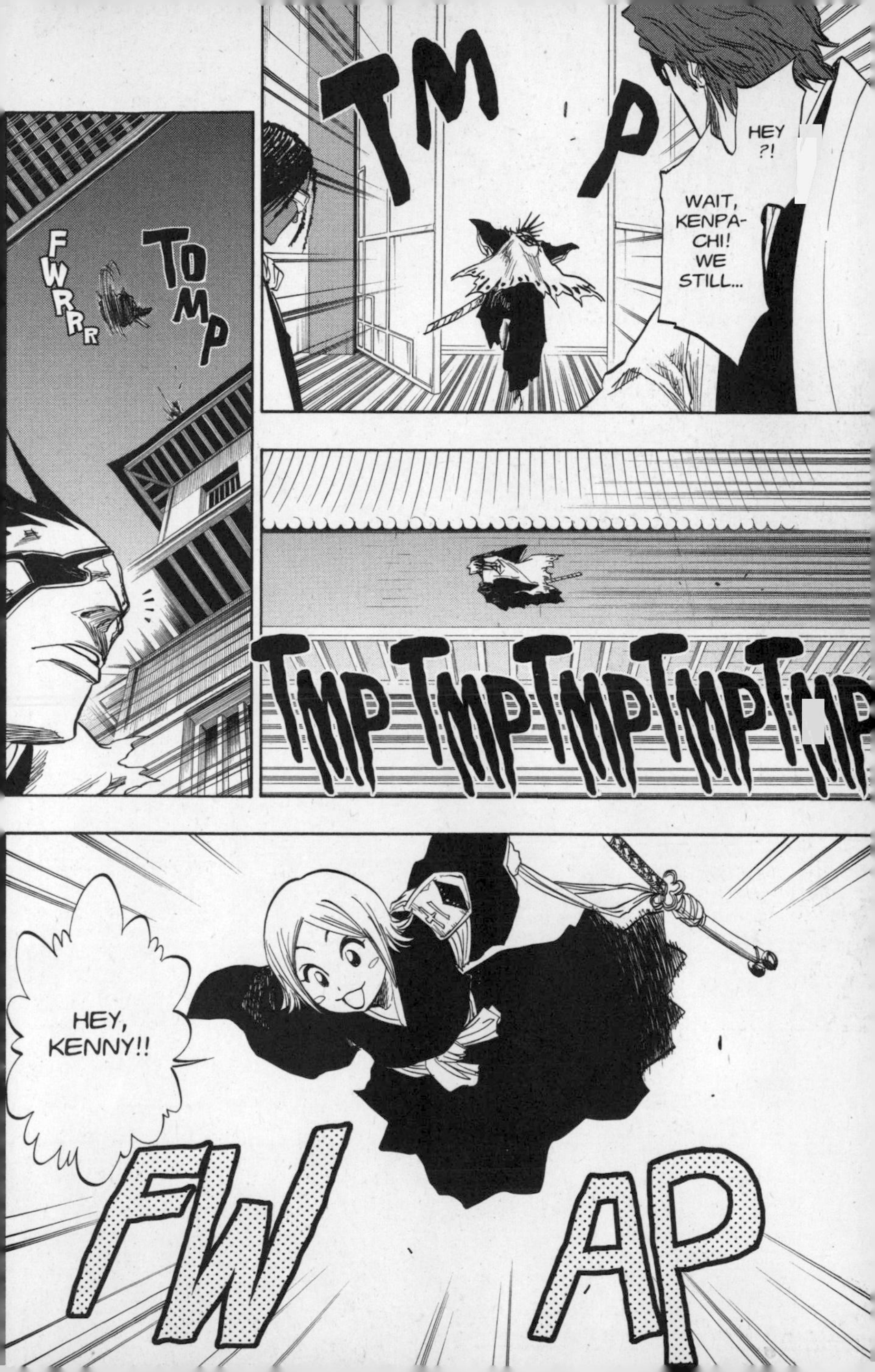
TM P
HEY ?!
WAIT, KENPACHI! WE STILL...
TMPTMPTMPTMPTMP
FWRRR
TOMP
HEY, KENNY!!
FW AP

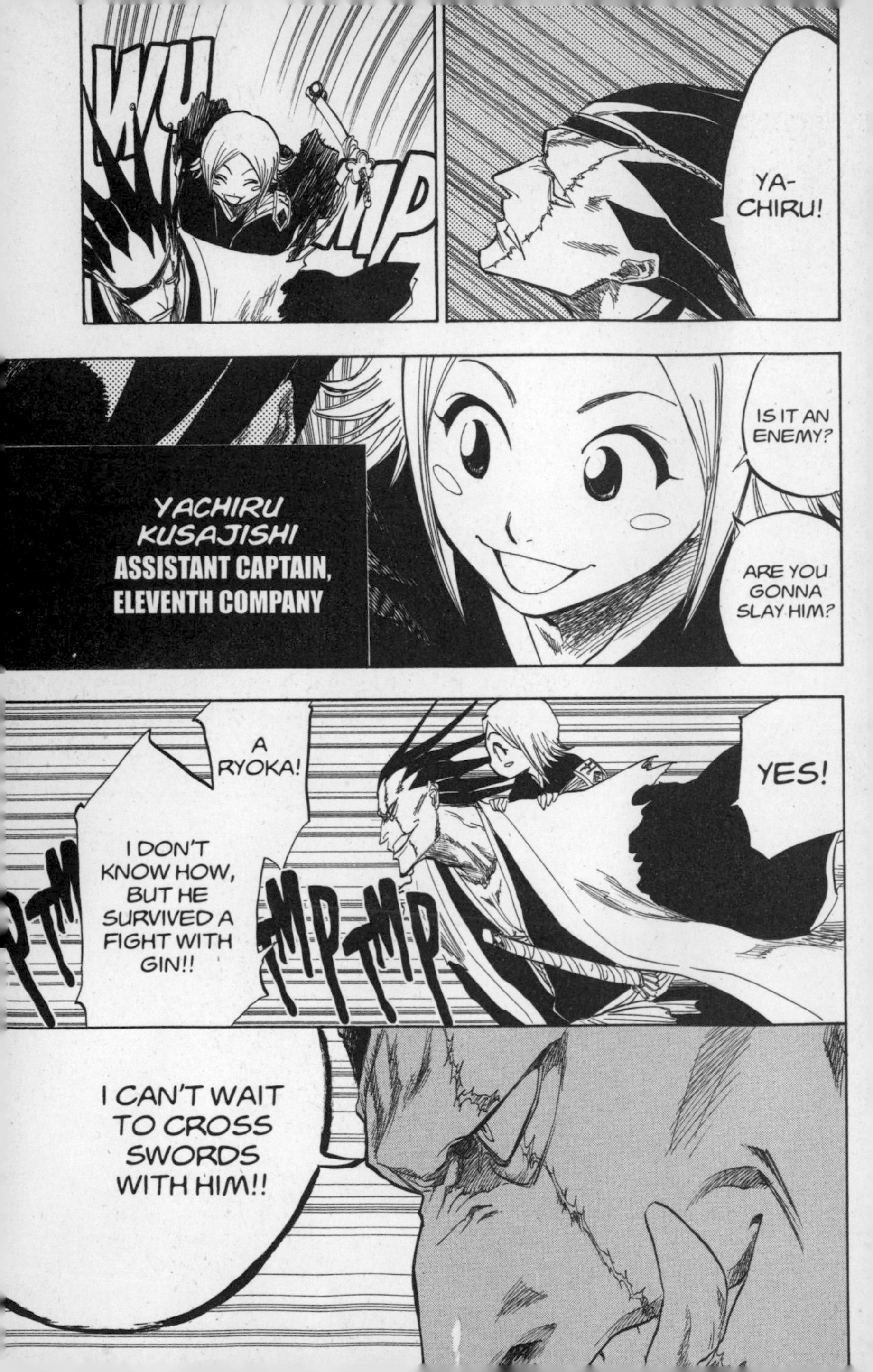
YA-CHIRU!
IS IT AN ENEMY?
ARE YOU GONNA SLAY HIM?
YACHIRU KUSAJISHI
ASSISTANT CAPTAIN, ELEVENTH COMPANY
YES!
A RYOKA!
I DON'T KNOW HOW, BUT HE SURVIVED A FIGHT WITH GIN!!
I CAN'T WAIT TO CROSS SWORDS WITH HIM!!

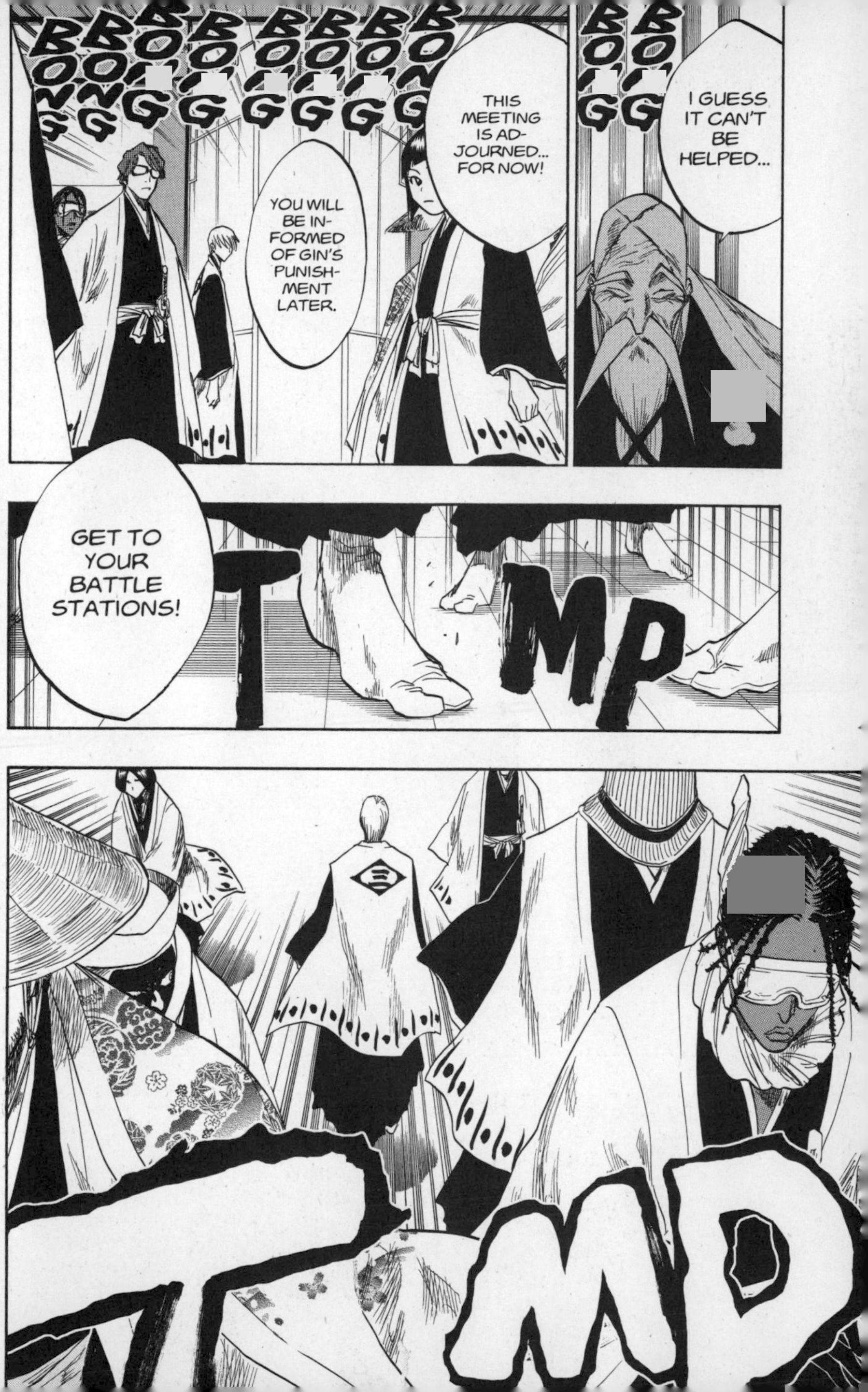
BOONG BOONG
I GUESS IT CAN'T BE HELPED...
BOOONG BOOONG BOOONG BOOONG BOOONG BOOONG
THIS MEETING IS AD-JOURNED... FOR NOW!
YOU WILL BE IN-FORMED OF GIN'S PUNISH-MENT LATER.
GET TO YOUR BATTLE STATIONS!
TMP
TMP

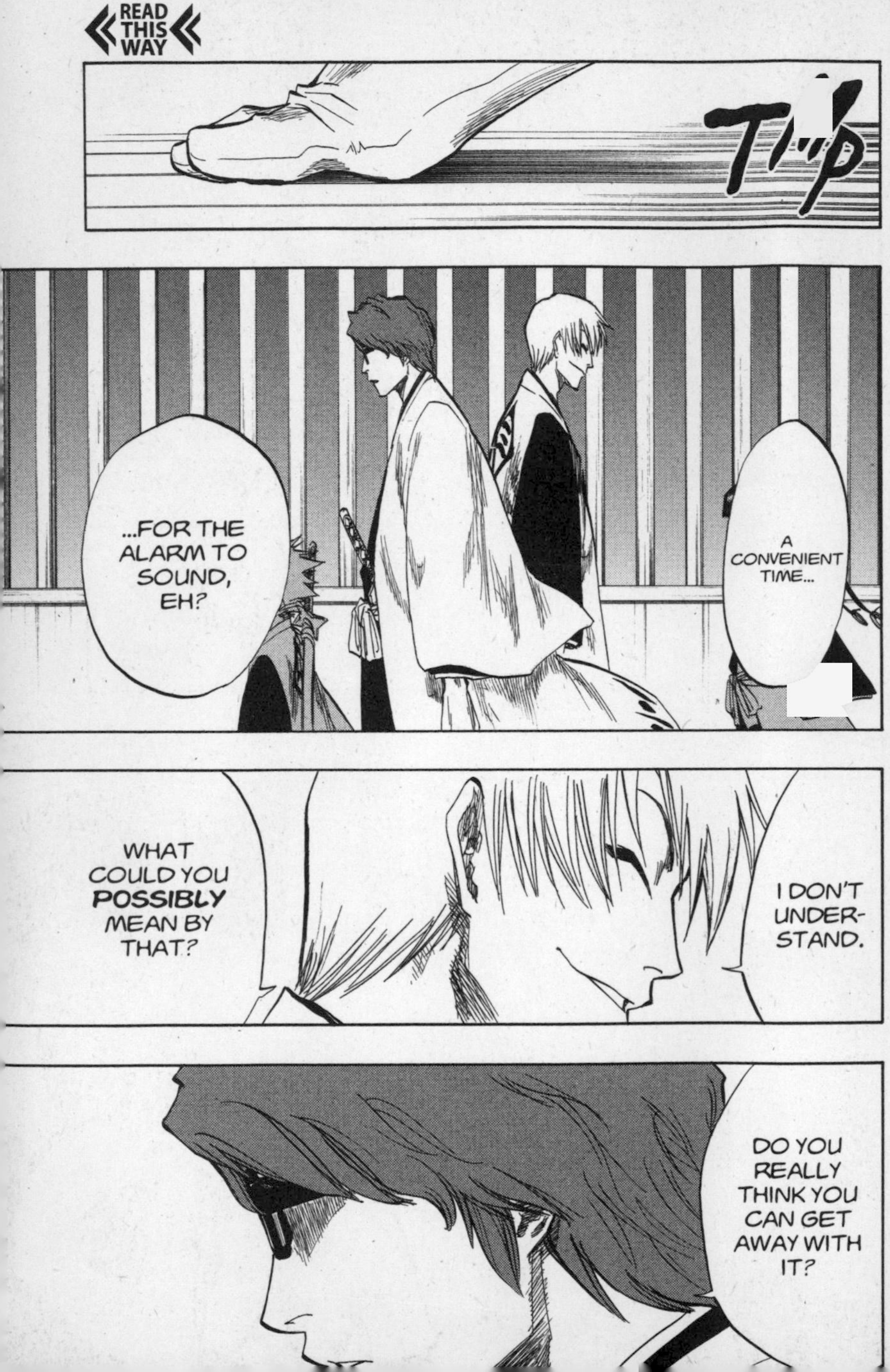
READ THIS WAY
A CONVENIENT TIME...
...FOR THE ALARM TO SOUND, EH?
I DON'T UNDER-STAND.
WHAT COULD YOU **POSSIBLY** MEAN BY THAT?
DO YOU REALLY THINK YOU CAN GET AWAY WITH IT?

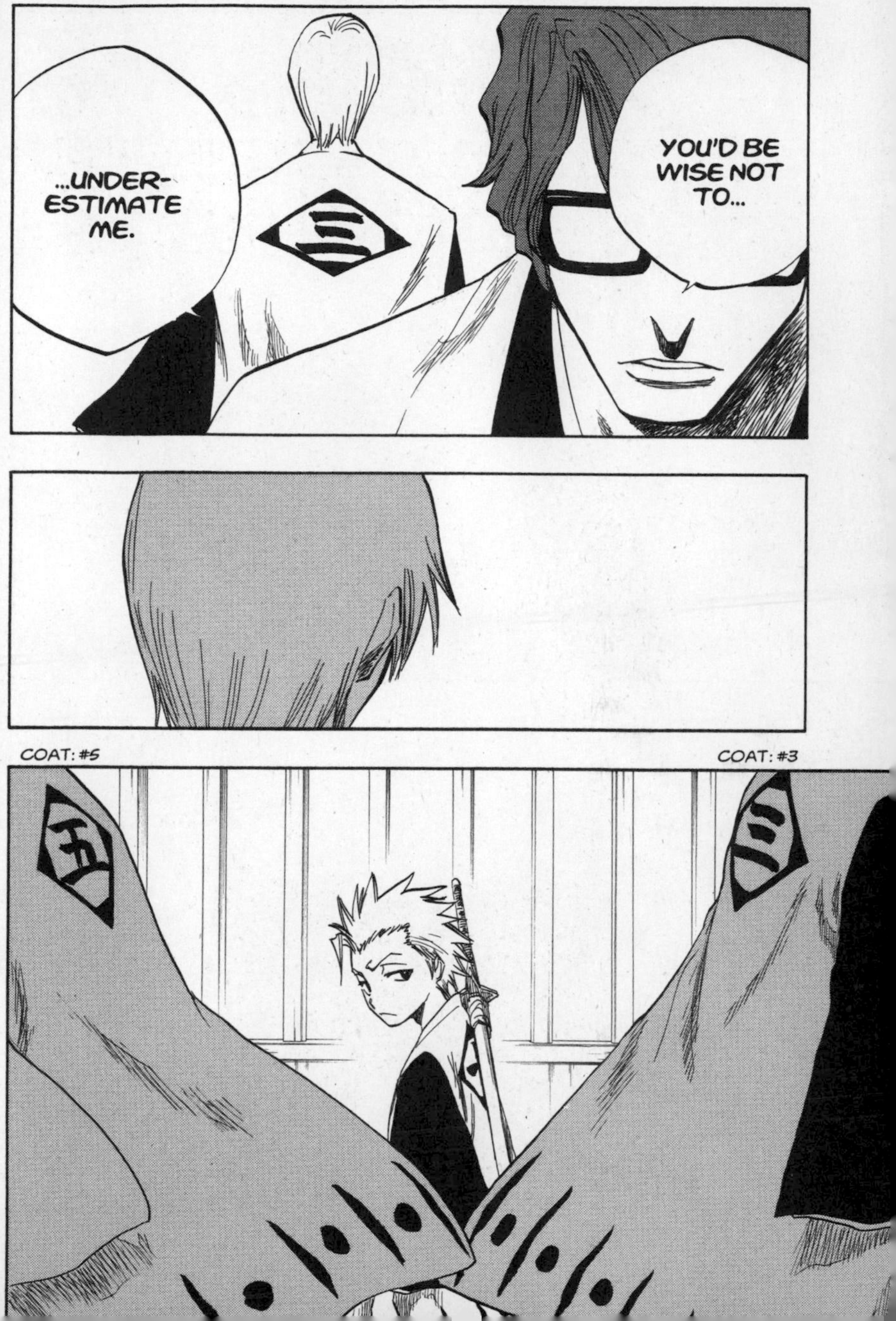
YOU'D BE WISE NOT TO...
...UNDER-ESTIMATE ME.
COAT: #3
COAT: #5

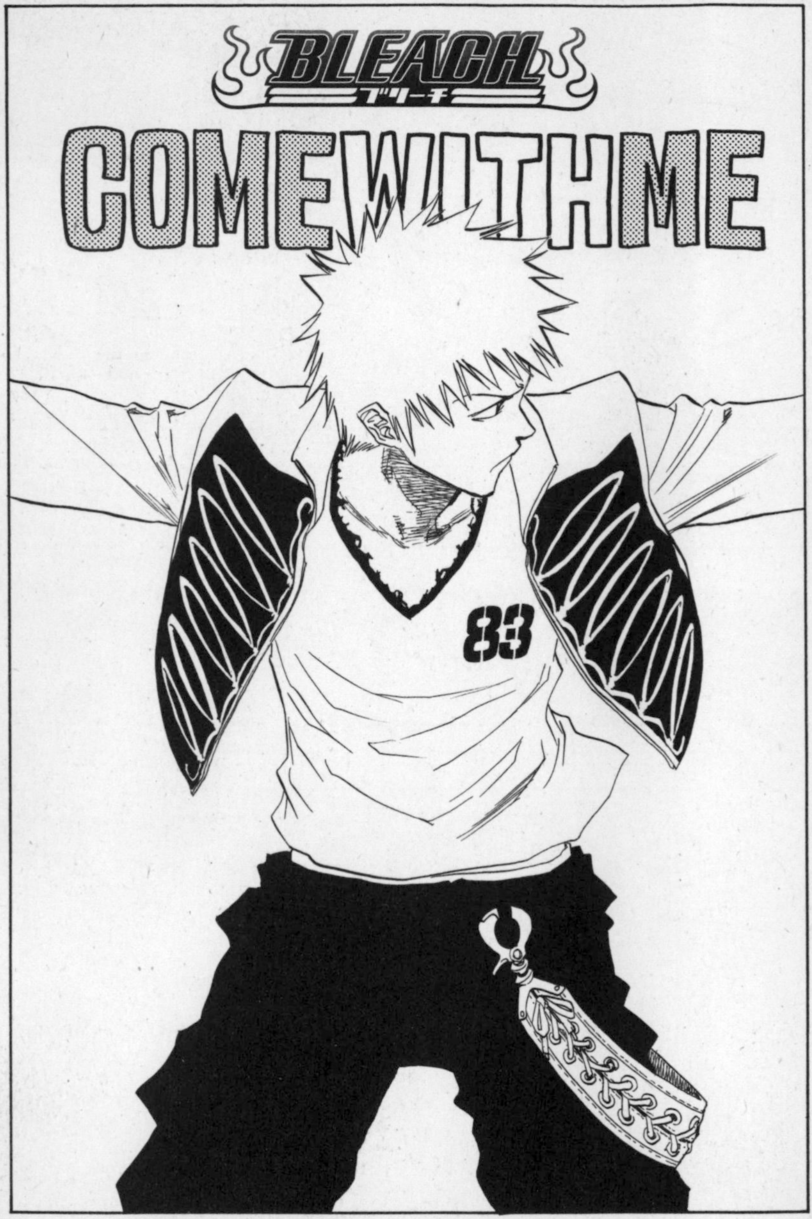
BLEACH
ブリーチ
COME WITH ME
83

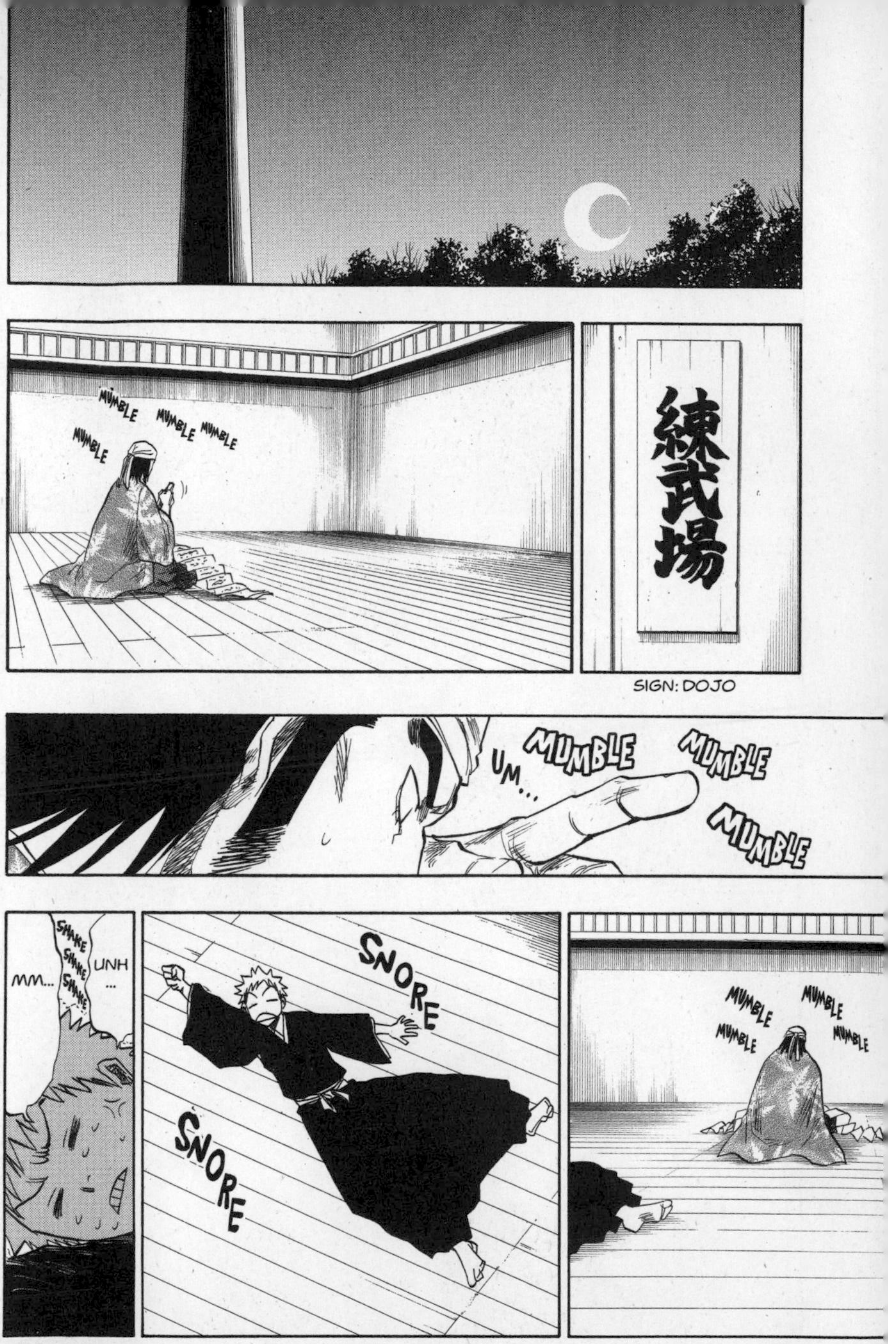
練武場
SIGN: DOJO
MUMBLE
MUMBLE
MUMBLE
MUMBLE
UM...
MUMBLE
MUMBLE
MUMBLE
MUMBLE
MUMBLE
MUMBLE
MUMBLE
SNORE
SNORE
UNH...
SHAKE
SHAKE
SHAKE
MM...

READ THIS WAY

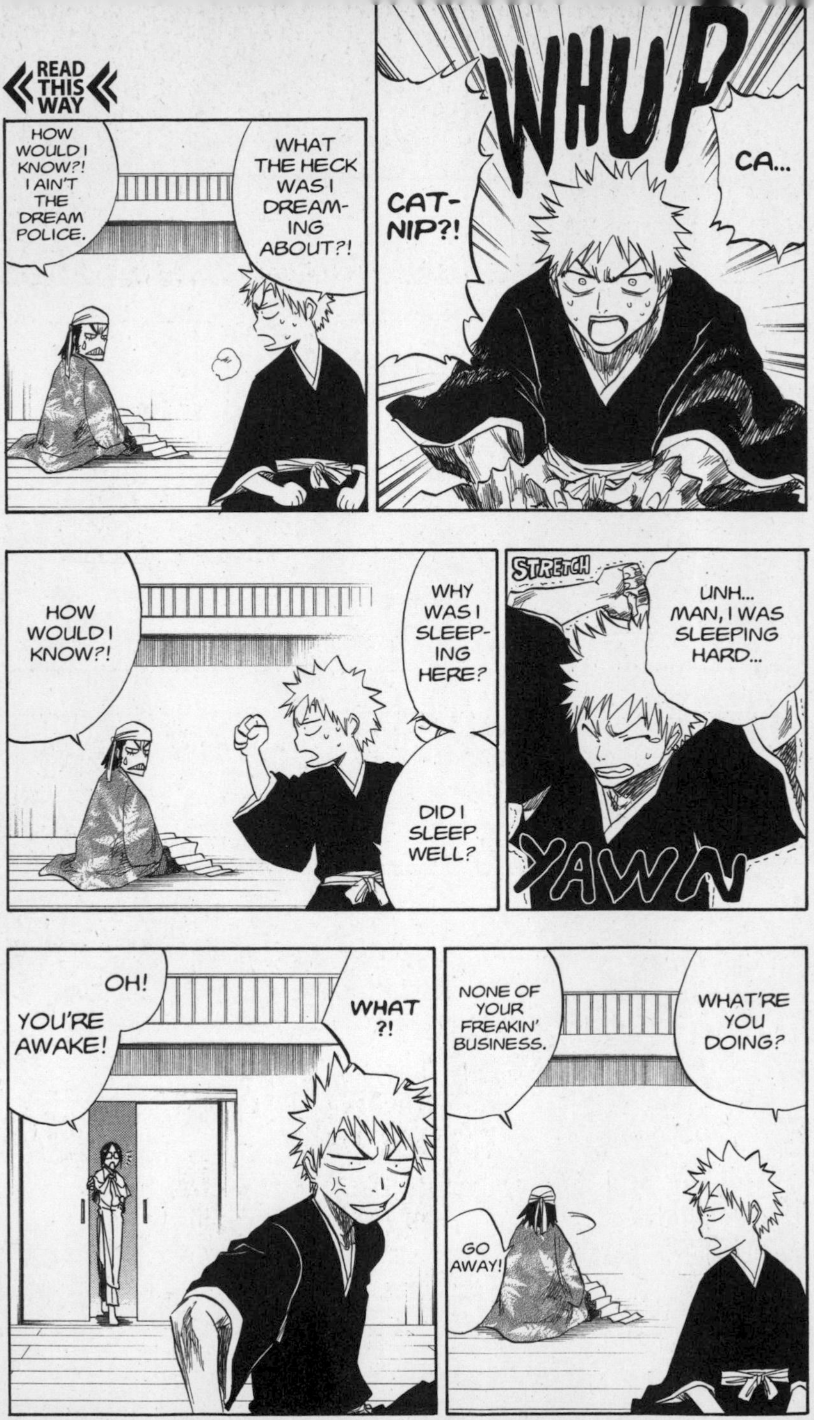
WHUP
CA...
CAT-NIP?!
WHAT THE HECK WAS I DREAMING ABOUT?!
HOW WOULD I KNOW?! I AIN'T THE DREAM POLICE.
STRETCH
UNH... MAN, I WAS SLEEPING HARD...
YAWN
WHY WAS I SLEEPING HERE?
DID I SLEEP WELL?
HOW WOULD I KNOW?!
WHAT'RE YOU DOING?
NONE OF YOUR FREAKIN' BUSINESS.
GO AWAY!
WHAT ?!
OH!
YOU'RE AWAKE!

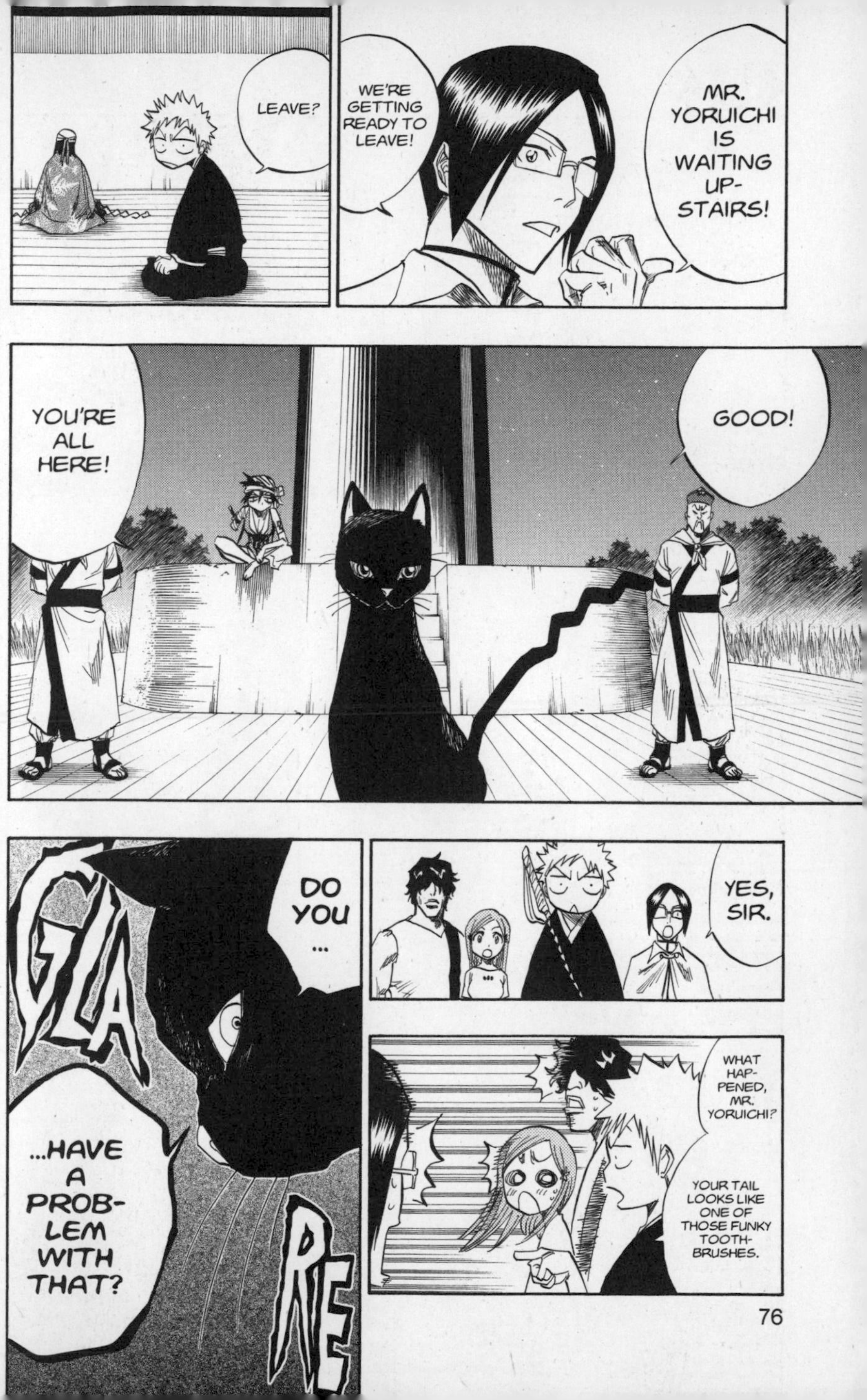
MR. YORUICHI IS WAITING UP-STAIRS!
WE'RE GETTING READY TO LEAVE!
LEAVE?
GOOD!
YOU'RE ALL HERE!
YES, SIR.
WHAT HAP-PENED, MR. YORUICHI?
YOUR TAIL LOOKS LIKE ONE OF THOSE FUNKY TOOTH-BRUSHES.
DO YOU ...
GLARE
...HAVE A PROB-LEM WITH THAT?

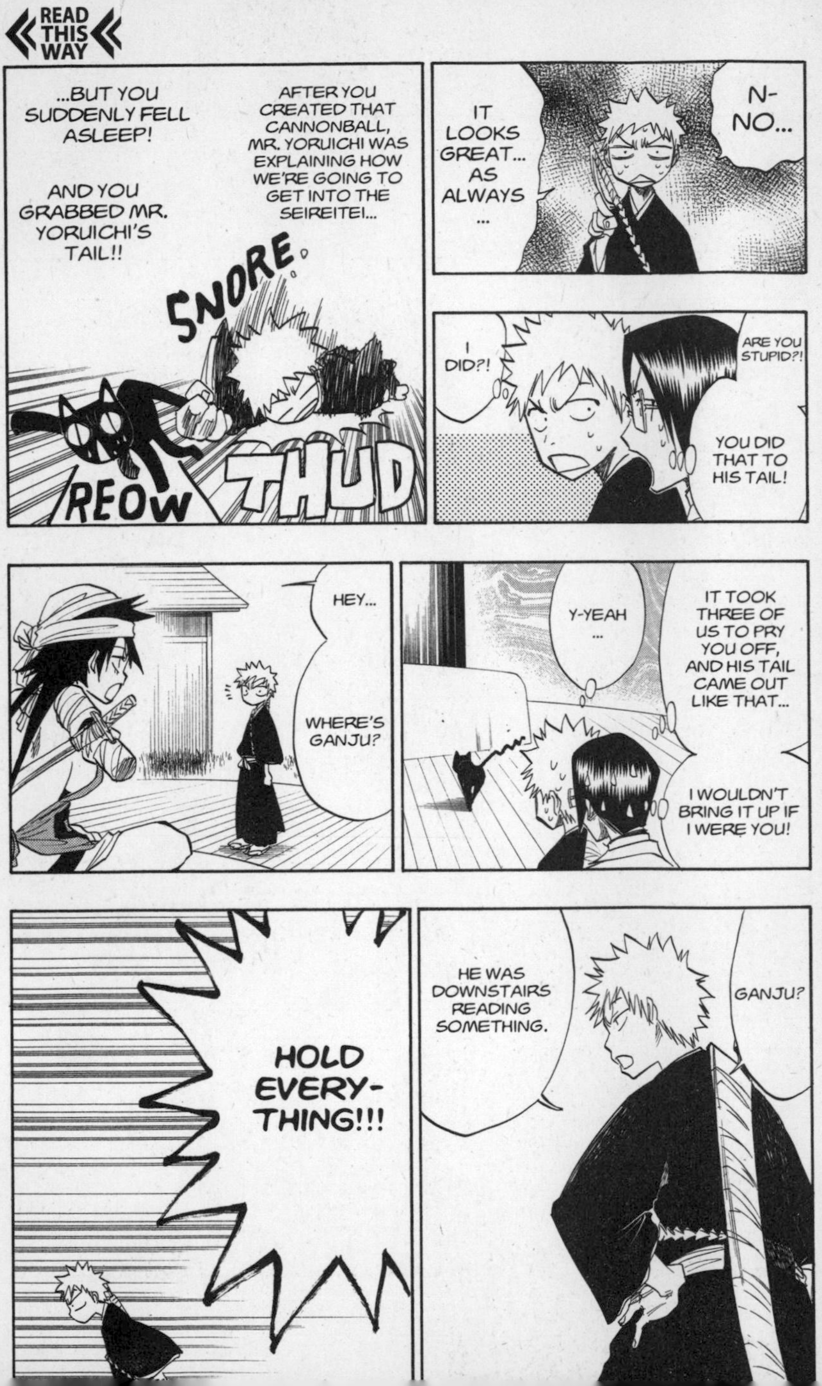
READ THIS WAY
N-NO...
IT LOOKS GREAT... AS ALWAYS ...
ARE YOU STUPID?!
I DID?!
YOU DID THAT TO HIS TAIL!
AFTER YOU CREATED THAT CANNONBALL, MR. YORUICHI WAS EXPLAINING HOW WE'RE GOING TO GET INTO THE SEIREITEI...
...BUT YOU SUDDENLY FELL ASLEEP!
AND YOU GRABBED MR. YORUICHI'S TAIL!!
SNORE
THUD
REOW
IT TOOK THREE OF US TO PRY YOU OFF, AND HIS TAIL CAME OUT LIKE THAT...
Y-YEAH ...
I WOULDN'T BRING IT UP IF I WERE YOU!
HEY...
WHERE'S GANJU?
GANJU?
HE WAS DOWNSTAIRS READING SOMETHING.
HOLD EVERY-THING!!!

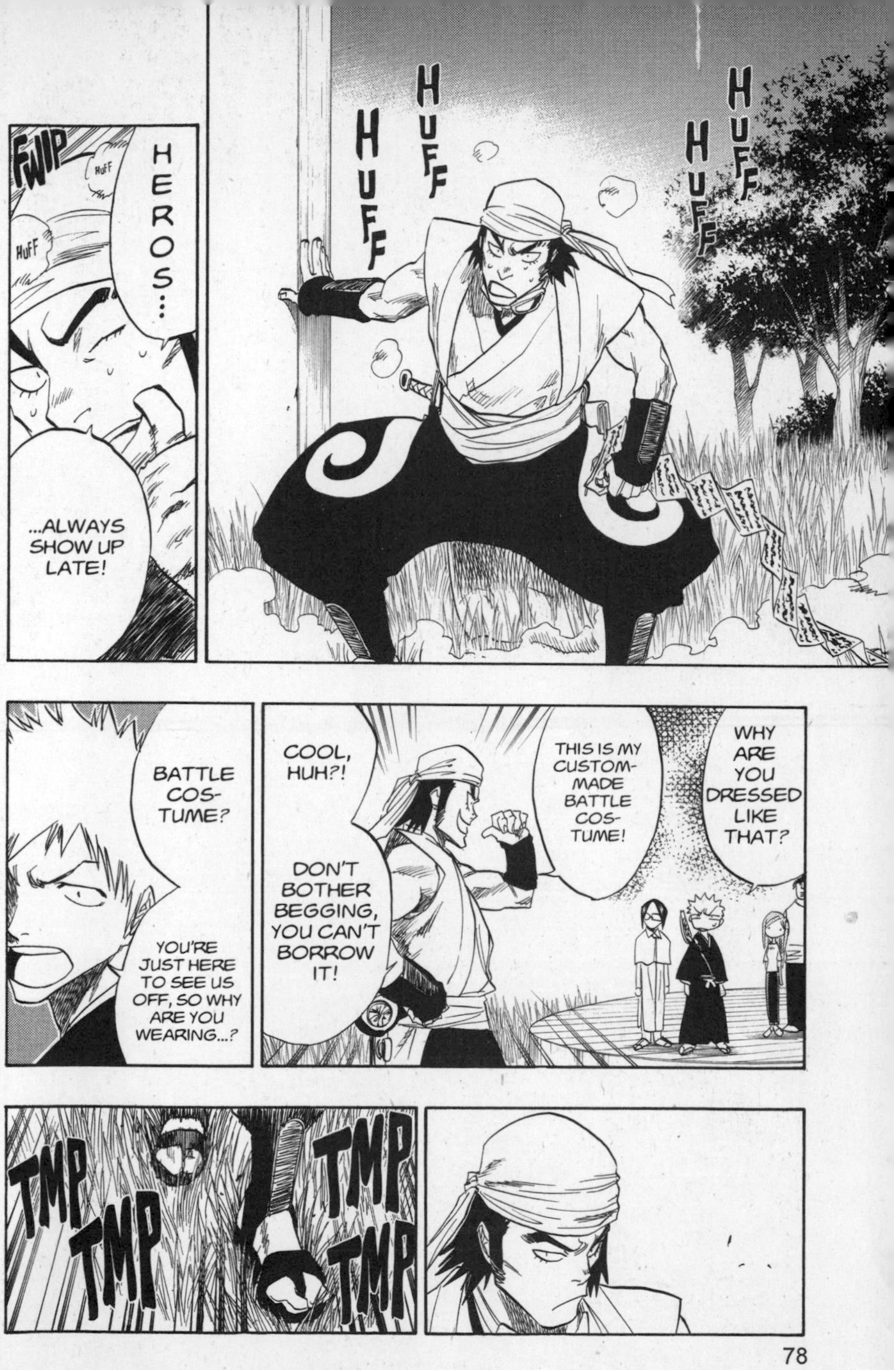
HUFF
HUFF
HUFF
HUFF
FWIP
HUFF
HUFF
HEROS...
...ALWAYS SHOW UP LATE!
WHY ARE YOU DRESSED LIKE THAT?
THIS IS MY CUSTOM-MADE BATTLE COS-TUME!
COOL, HUH?!
DON'T BOTHER BEGGING, YOU CAN'T BORROW IT!
BATTLE COS-TUME?
YOU'RE JUST HERE TO SEE US OFF, SO WHY ARE YOU WEARING...?
TMP TMP
TMP TMP

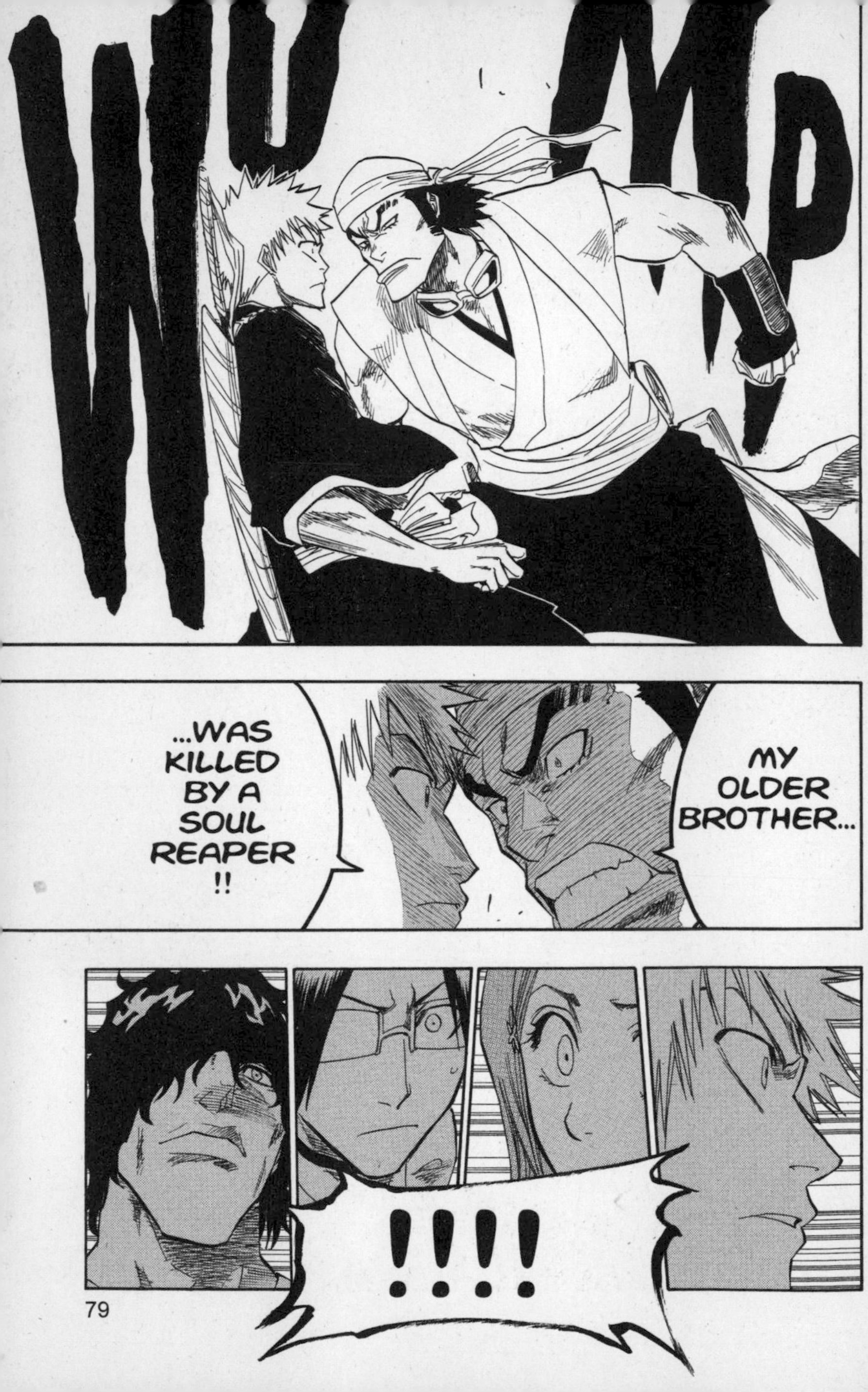
WHUMP
MY OLDER BROTHER...
...WAS KILLED BY A SOUL REAPER!!
!!!!

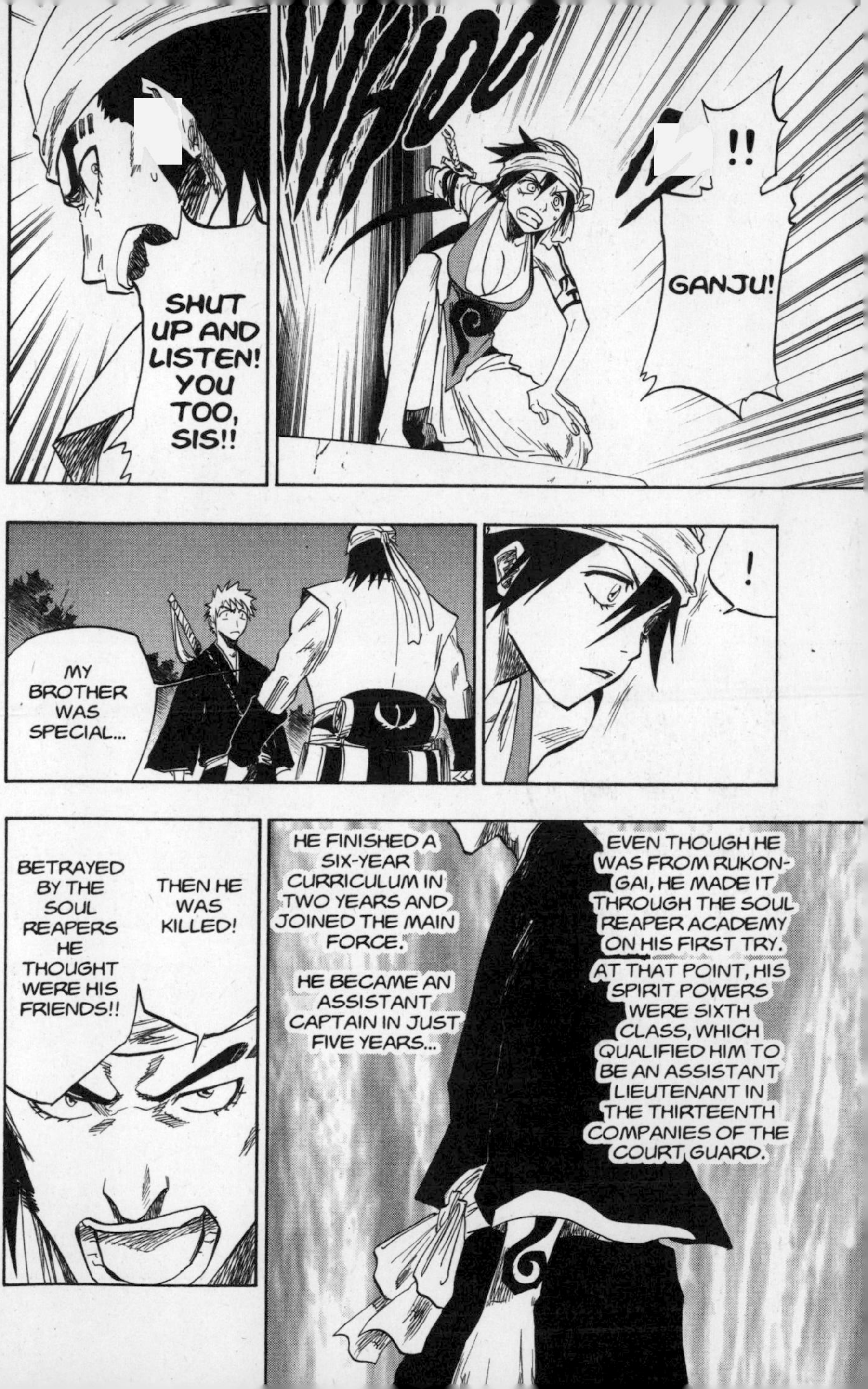

WHOO
!!
GANJU!
SHUT UP AND LISTEN! YOU TOO, SIS!!
!
MY BROTHER WAS SPECIAL...
EVEN THOUGH HE WAS FROM RUKON-GAI, HE MADE IT THROUGH THE SOUL REAPER ACADEMY ON HIS FIRST TRY.
AT THAT POINT, HIS SPIRIT POWERS WERE SIXTH CLASS, WHICH QUALIFIED HIM TO BE AN ASSISTANT LIEUTENANT IN THE THIRTEENTH COMPANIES OF THE COURT GUARD.
HE FINISHED A SIX-YEAR CURRICULUM IN TWO YEARS AND JOINED THE MAIN FORCE.
HE BECAME AN ASSISTANT CAPTAIN IN JUST FIVE YEARS...
THEN HE WAS KILLED!
BETRAYED BY THE SOUL REAPERS HE THOUGHT WERE HIS FRIENDS!!

READ THIS WAY

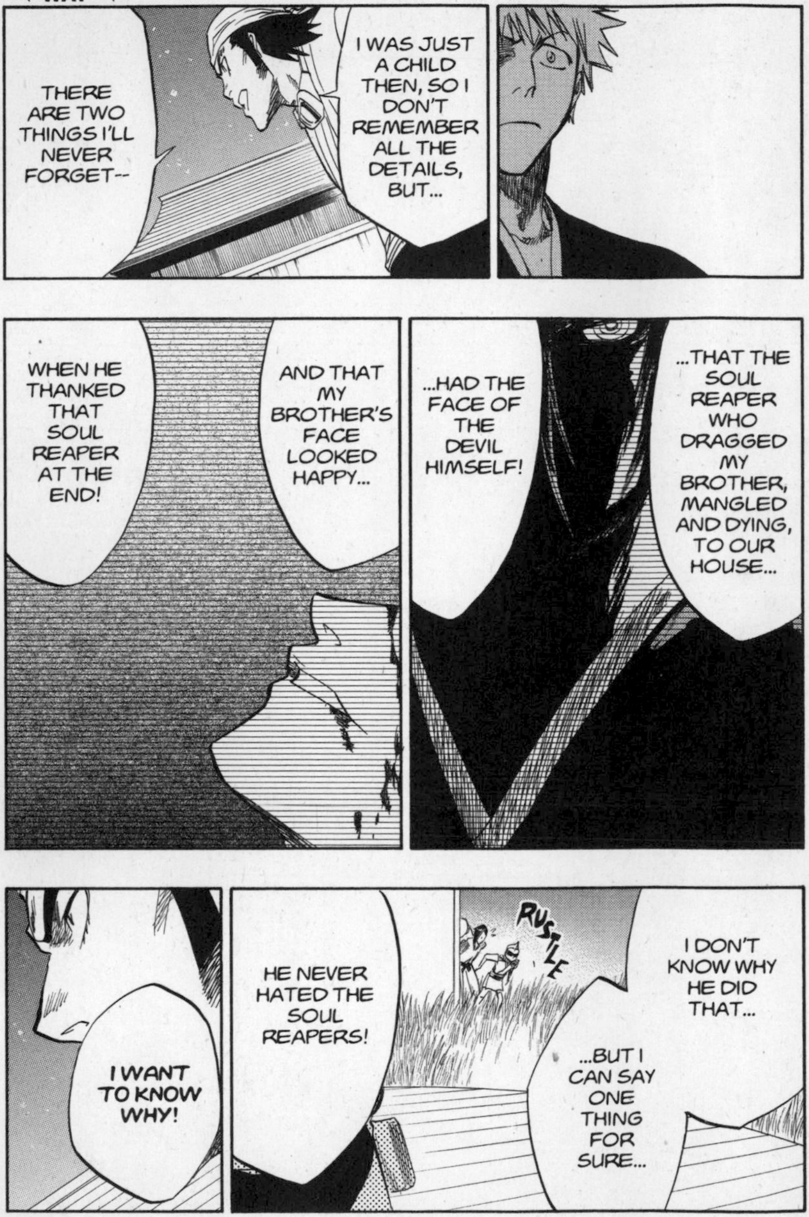
I WAS JUST A CHILD THEN, SO I DON'T REMEMBER ALL THE DETAILS, BUT...
THERE ARE TWO THINGS I'LL NEVER FORGET--
...THAT THE SOUL REAPER WHO DRAGGED MY BROTHER, MANGLED AND DYING, TO OUR HOUSE...
...HAD THE FACE OF THE DEVIL HIMSELF!
AND THAT MY BROTHER'S FACE LOOKED HAPPY...
WHEN HE THANKED THAT SOUL REAPER AT THE END!
I DON'T KNOW WHY HE DID THAT...
RUSTLE
...BUT I CAN SAY ONE THING FOR SURE...
HE NEVER HATED THE SOUL REAPERS!
I WANT TO KNOW WHY!

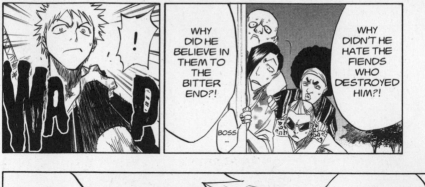

WHY DIDN'T HE HATE THE FIENDS WHO DESTROYED HIM?!
WHY DID HE BELIEVE IN THEM TO THE BITTER END?!
BOSS ...
!
WAP
YOU'RE NOT LIKE THE OTHER SOUL REAPERS!
THAT'S THE FEELING I GET!
IF I GO WITH YOU, MAYBE I'LL FIND SOME-THING OUT.
THAT'S THE FEEL-ING I GET!
THAT'S WHY...
...I'M GOING TO HELP YOU GUYS!

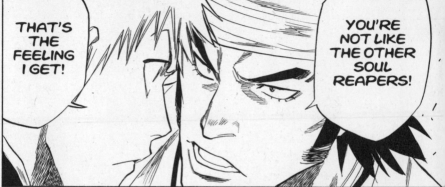

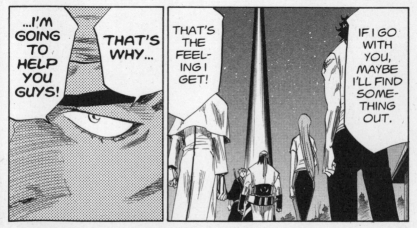

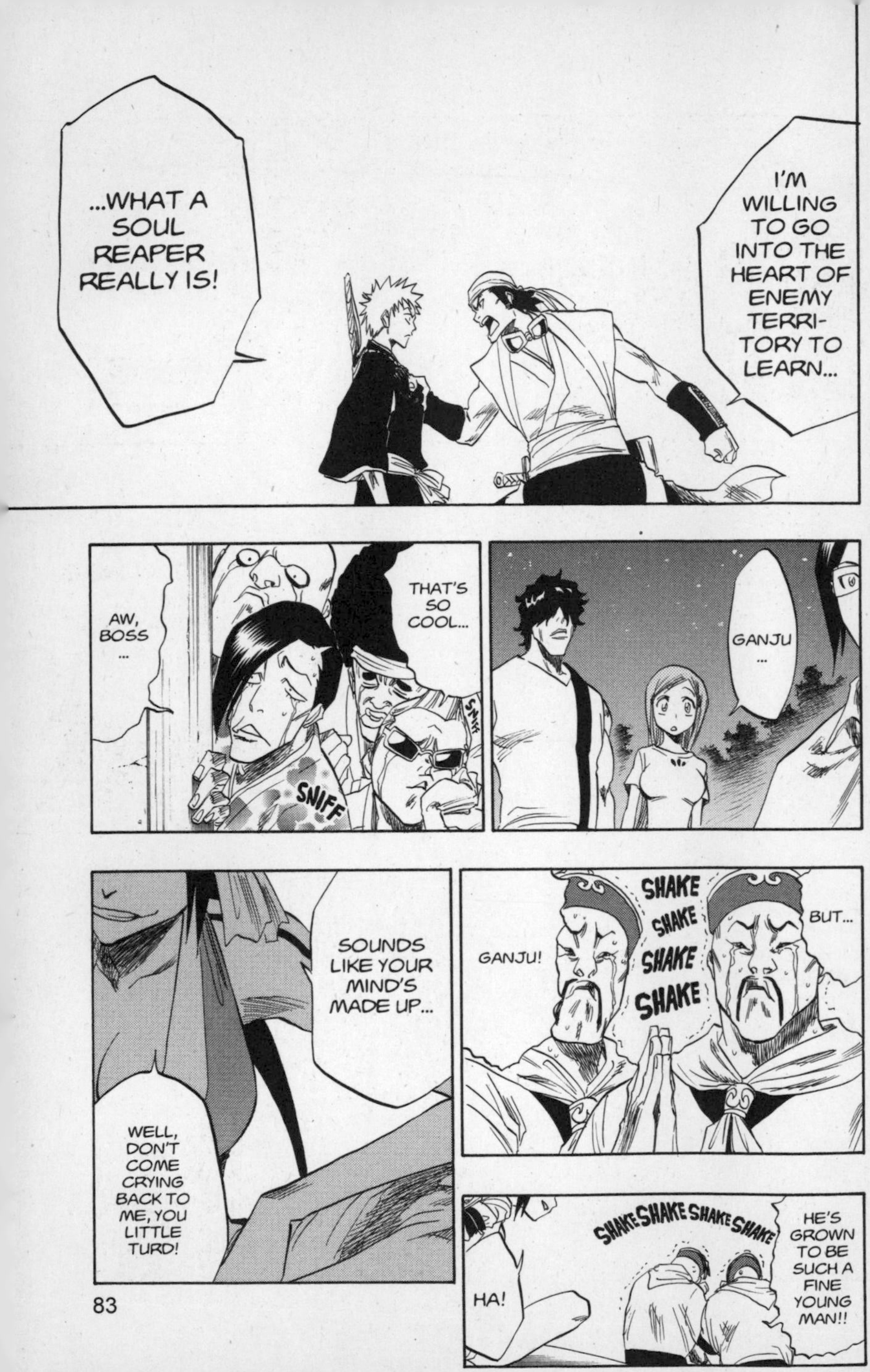
I'M WILLING TO GO INTO THE HEART OF ENEMY TERRI-TORY TO LEARN...
...WHAT A SOUL REAPER REALLY IS!
GANJU...
THAT'S SO COOL...
SNIFF
AW, BOSS...
SNIFF
BUT...
SHAKE SHAKE SHAKE SHAKE
GANJU!
HE'S GROWN TO BE SUCH A FINE YOUNG MAN!!
SHAKE SHAKE SHAKE SHAKE
HA!
SOUNDS LIKE YOUR MIND'S MADE UP...
WELL, DON'T COME CRYING BACK TO ME, YOU LITTLE TURD!

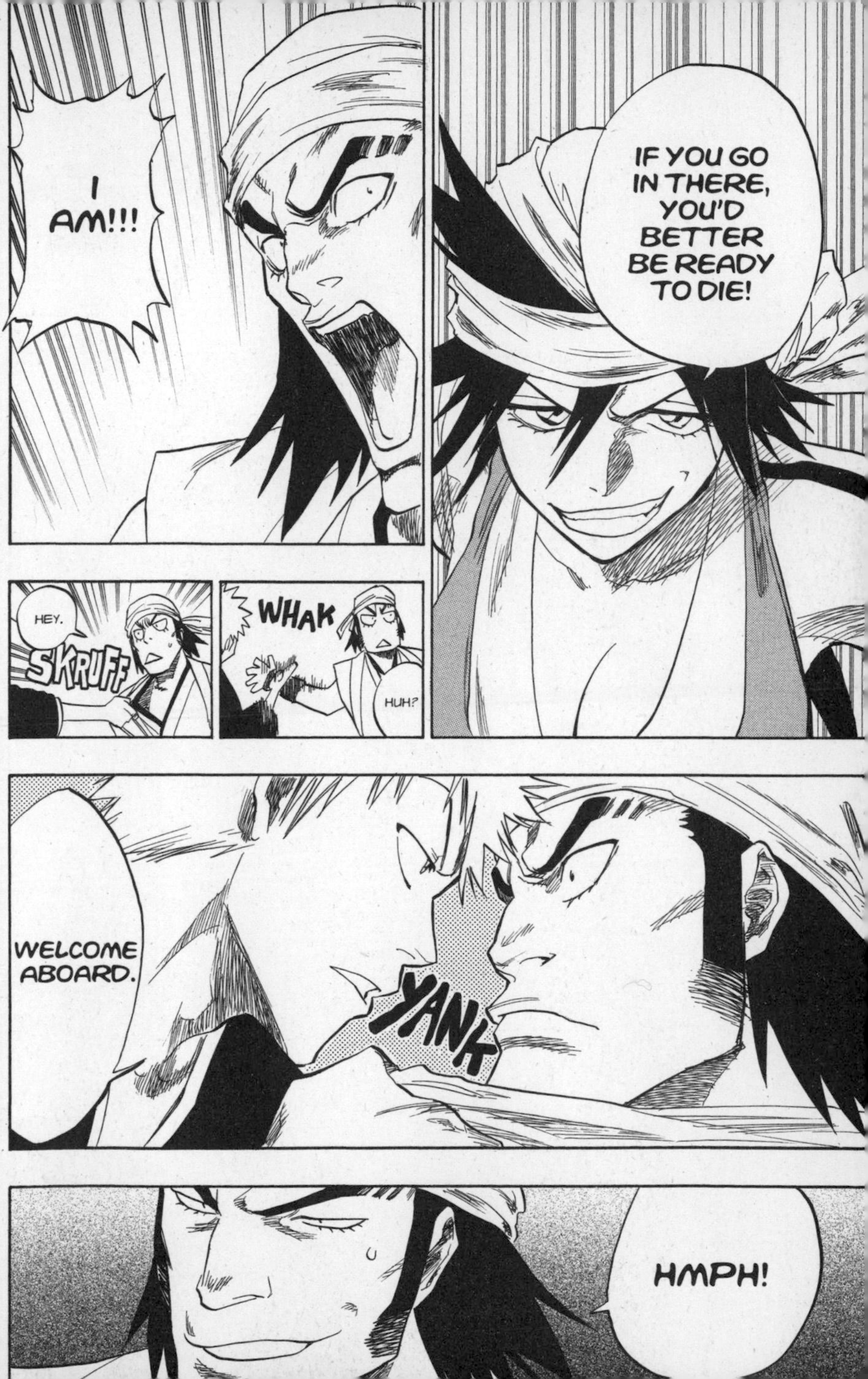
IF YOU GO IN THERE, YOU'D BETTER BE READY TO DIE!
I AM!!!
WHAK
HUH?
HEY.
SKRUFF
YANK
WELCOME ABOARD.
HMPH!

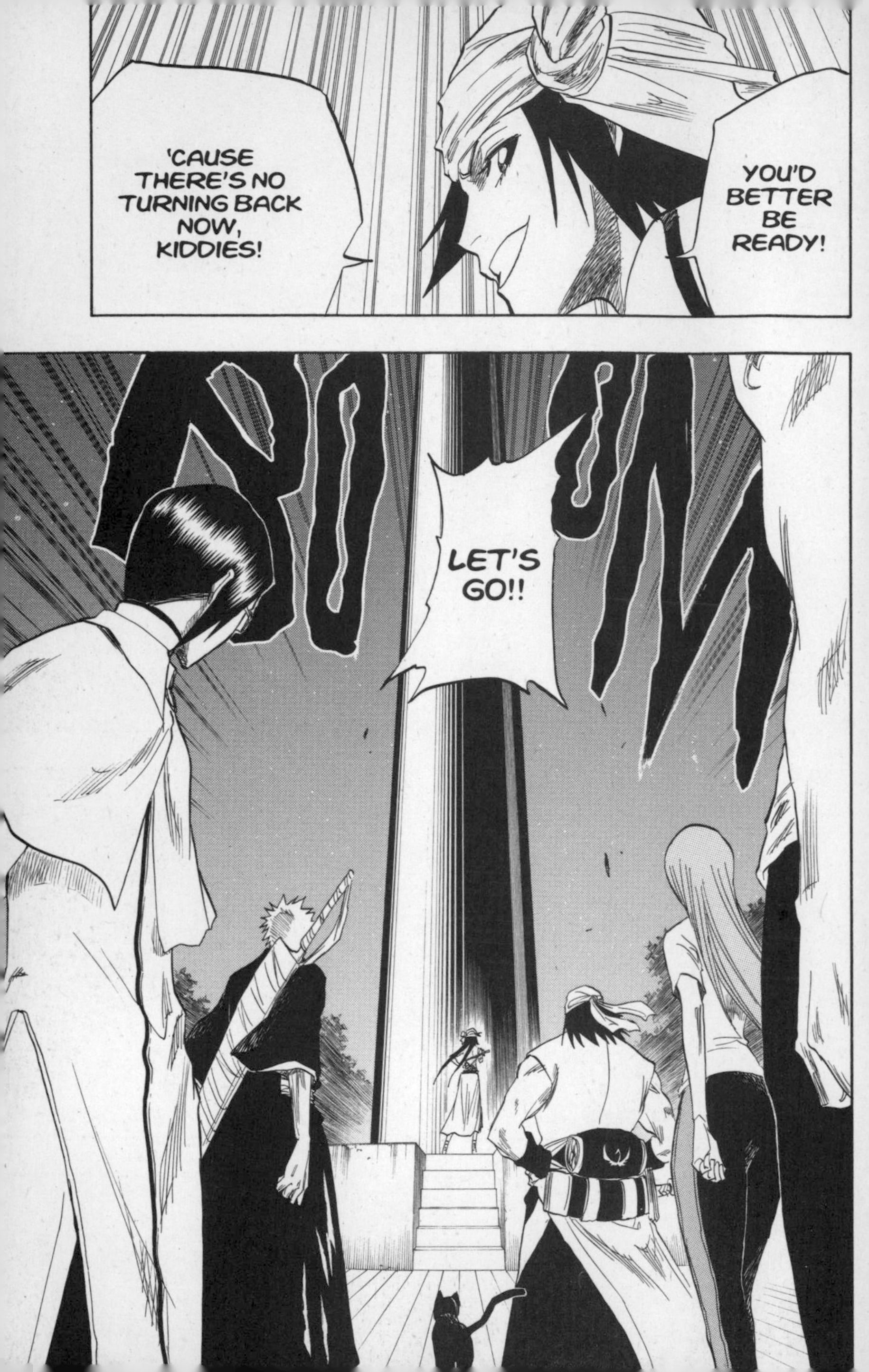
YOU'D BETTER BE READY!
'CAUSE THERE'S NO TURNING BACK NOW, KIDDIES!
LET'S GO!!

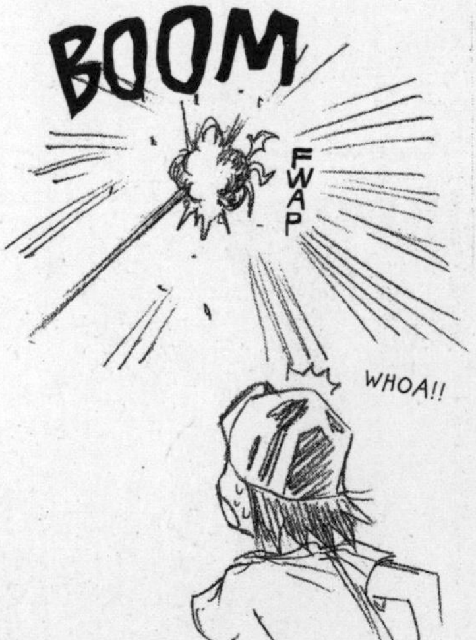
BOOM
FWAP
WHOA!!

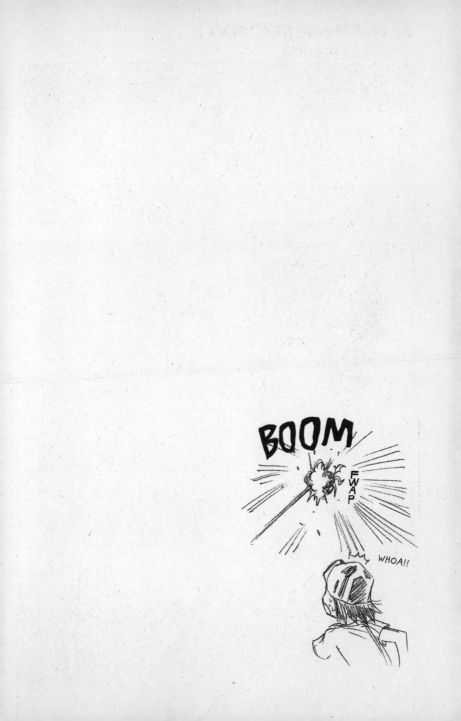

84. The Shooting Star Project 2
(Tattoo on the Sky)

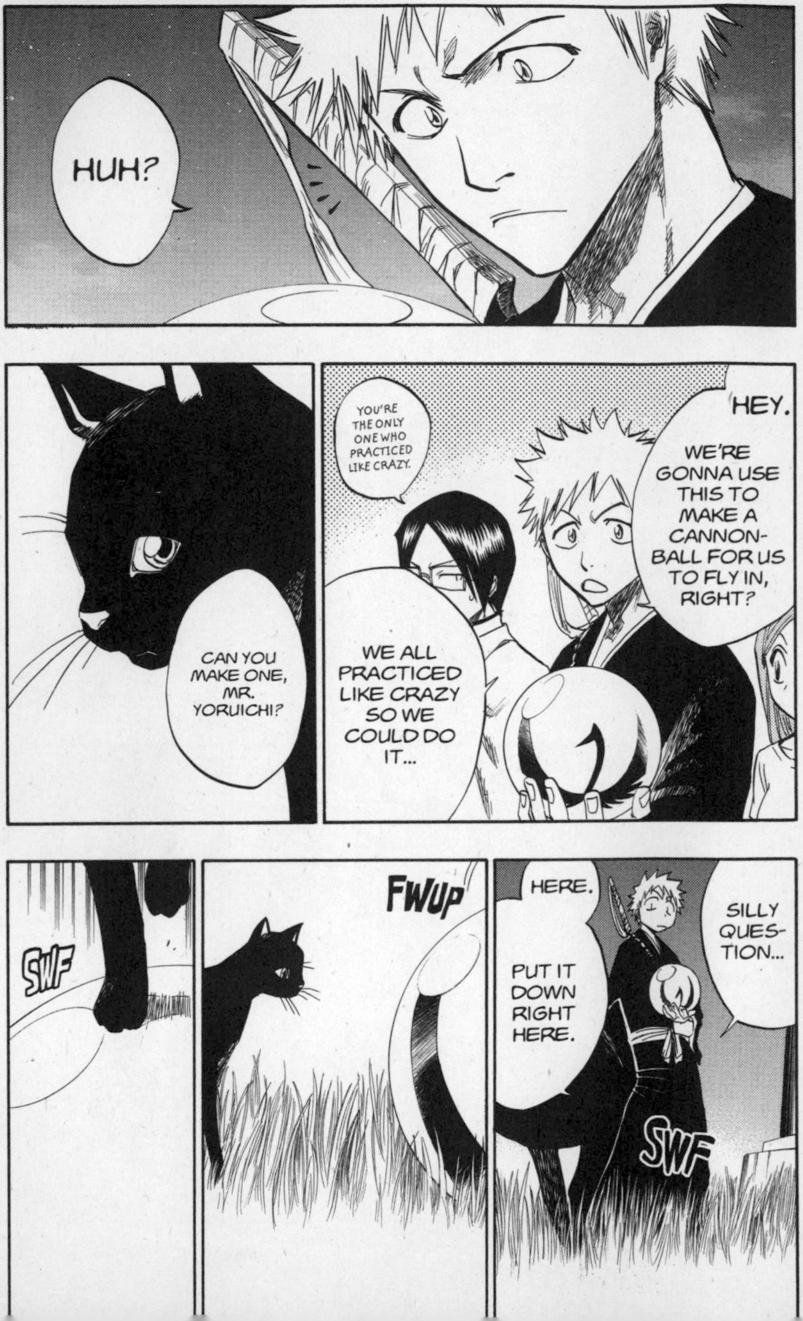
HUH?
HEY.
WE'RE GONNA USE THIS TO MAKE A CANNON-BALL FOR US TO FLY IN, RIGHT?
WE ALL PRACTICED LIKE CRAZY SO WE COULD DO IT...
YOU'RE THE ONLY ONE WHO PRACTICED LIKE CRAZY.
CAN YOU MAKE ONE, MR. YORUICHI?
SILLY QUES-TION...
HERE.
PUT IT DOWN RIGHT HERE.
SWF
FWUP
SWF

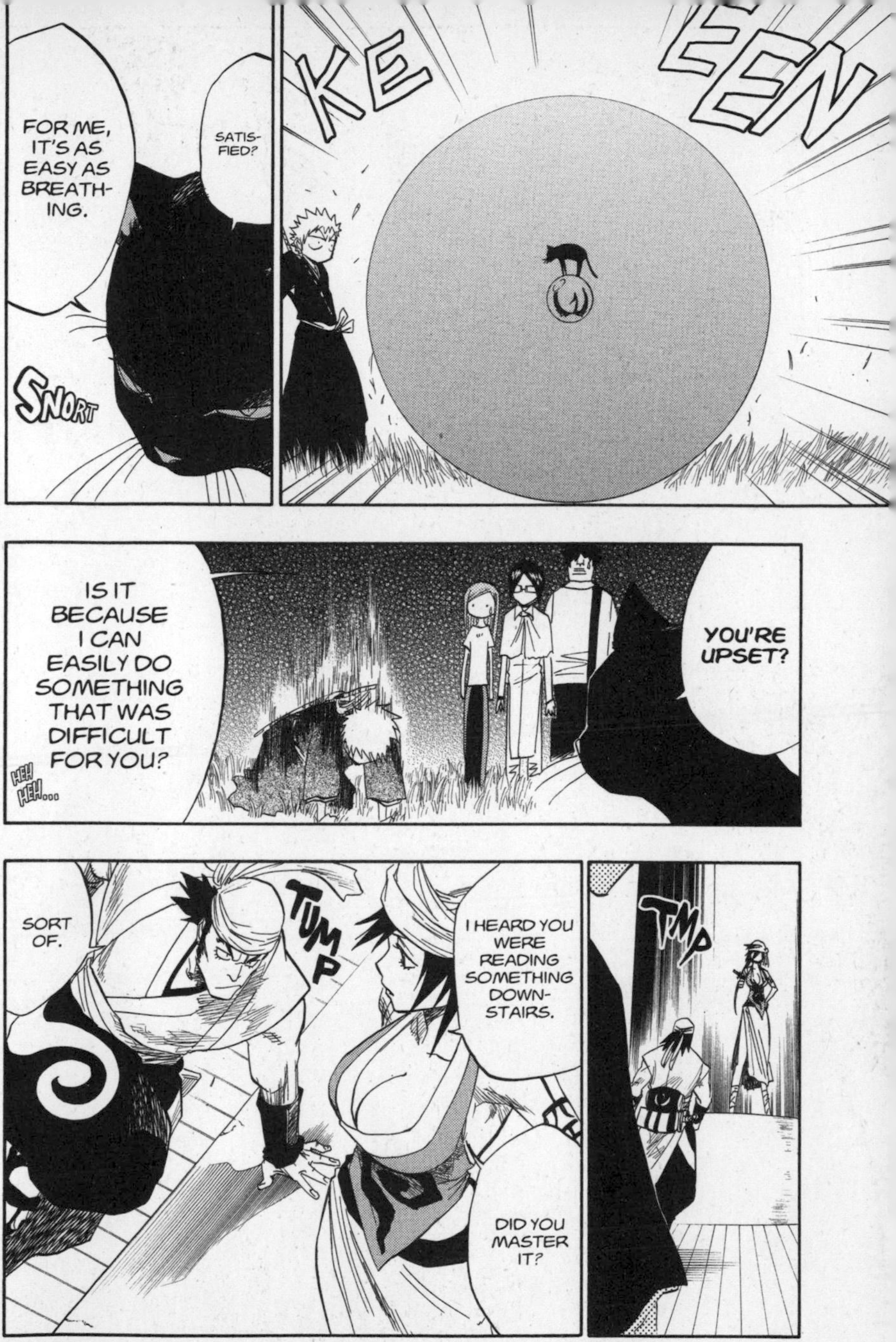
KE EEN
SATIS-FIED?
FOR ME, IT'S AS EASY AS BREATH-ING.
SNORT
YOU'RE UPSET?
IS IT BECAUSE I CAN EASILY DO SOMETHING THAT WAS DIFFICULT FOR YOU?
HEH HEH...
TMP
I HEARD YOU WERE READING SOMETHING DOWN-STAIRS.
TUMP
DID YOU MASTER IT?
SORT OF.

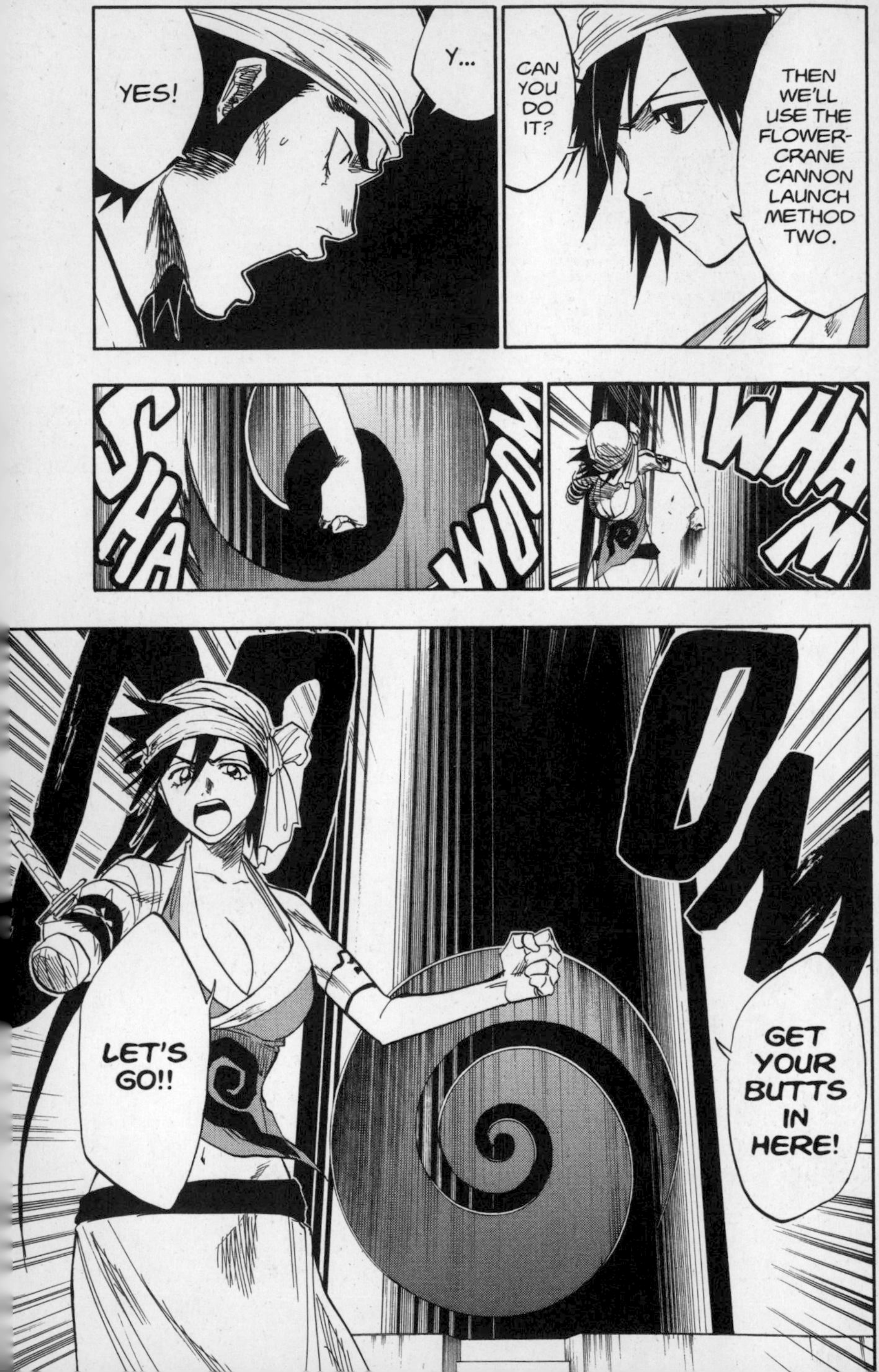
THEN WE'LL USE THE FLOWER-CRANE CANNON LAUNCH METHOD TWO.
CAN YOU DO IT?
Y...
YES!
WHAM
WOOM
SHA
GET YOUR BUTTS IN HERE!
LET'S GO!!

BLEACH ブリーチ

TMP
TMP
TMP
TMP
TMP
THE SUN WILL BE UP SOON.
THAT'S OUR CUE TO BEGIN THE LAUNCH CEREMONY.
SKR

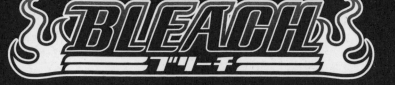

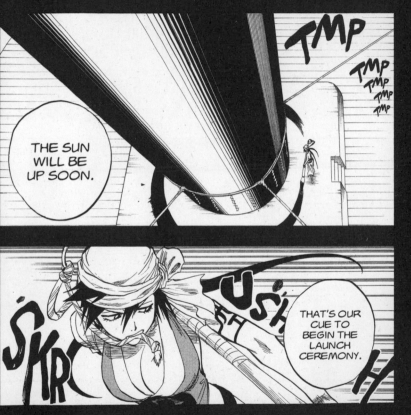

84. The Shooting Star Project 2 (Tattoo on the Sky)

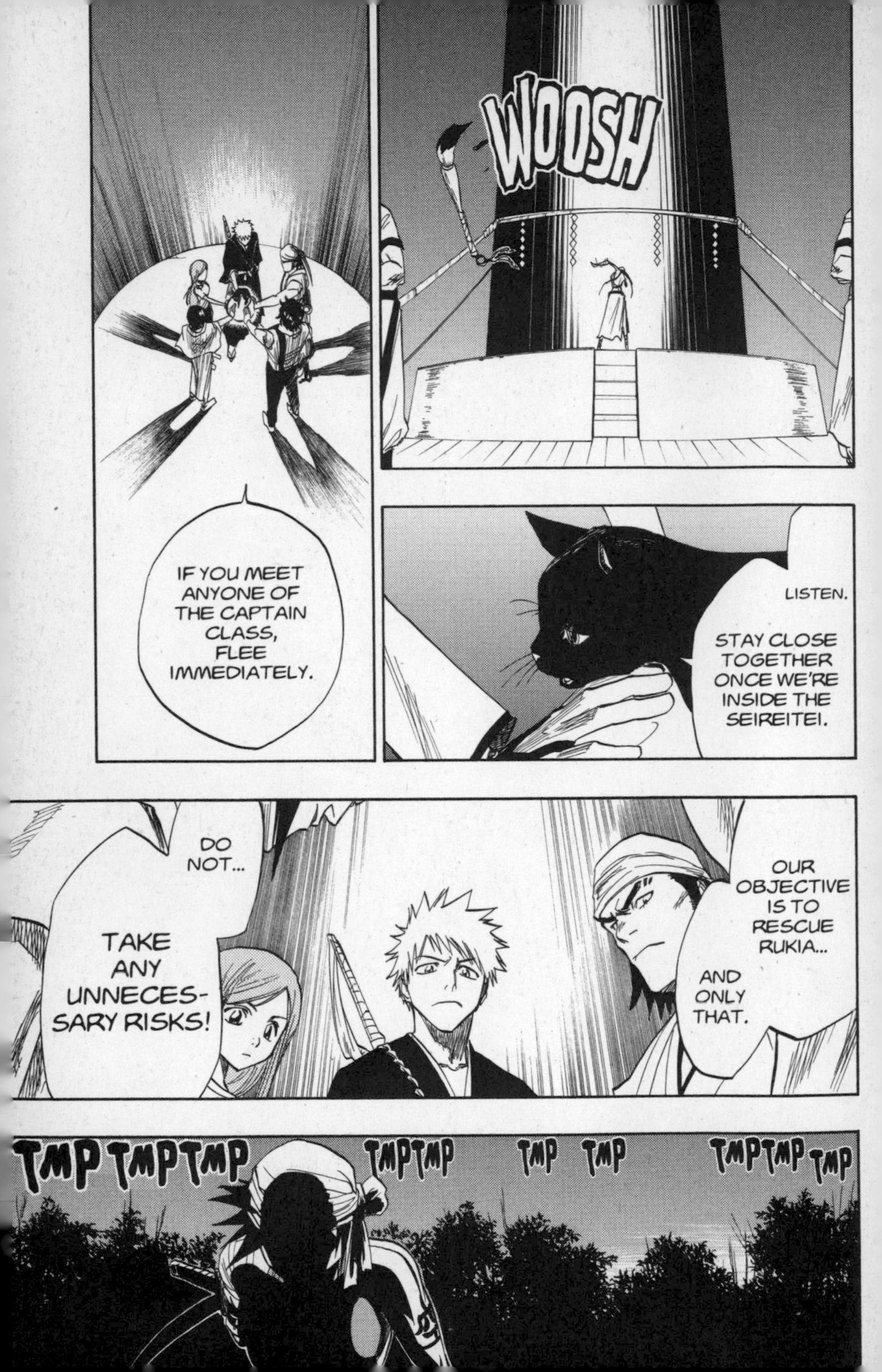
WOOSH
LISTEN.
STAY CLOSE TOGETHER ONCE WE'RE INSIDE THE SEIREITEI.
IF YOU MEET ANYONE OF THE CAPTAIN CLASS, FLEE IMMEDIATELY.
OUR OBJECTIVE IS TO RESCUE RUKIA...
AND ONLY THAT.
DO NOT...
TAKE ANY UNNECES-SARY RISKS!
TMPTMP TMP
TMP
TMP
TMPTMP
TMP TMPTMP

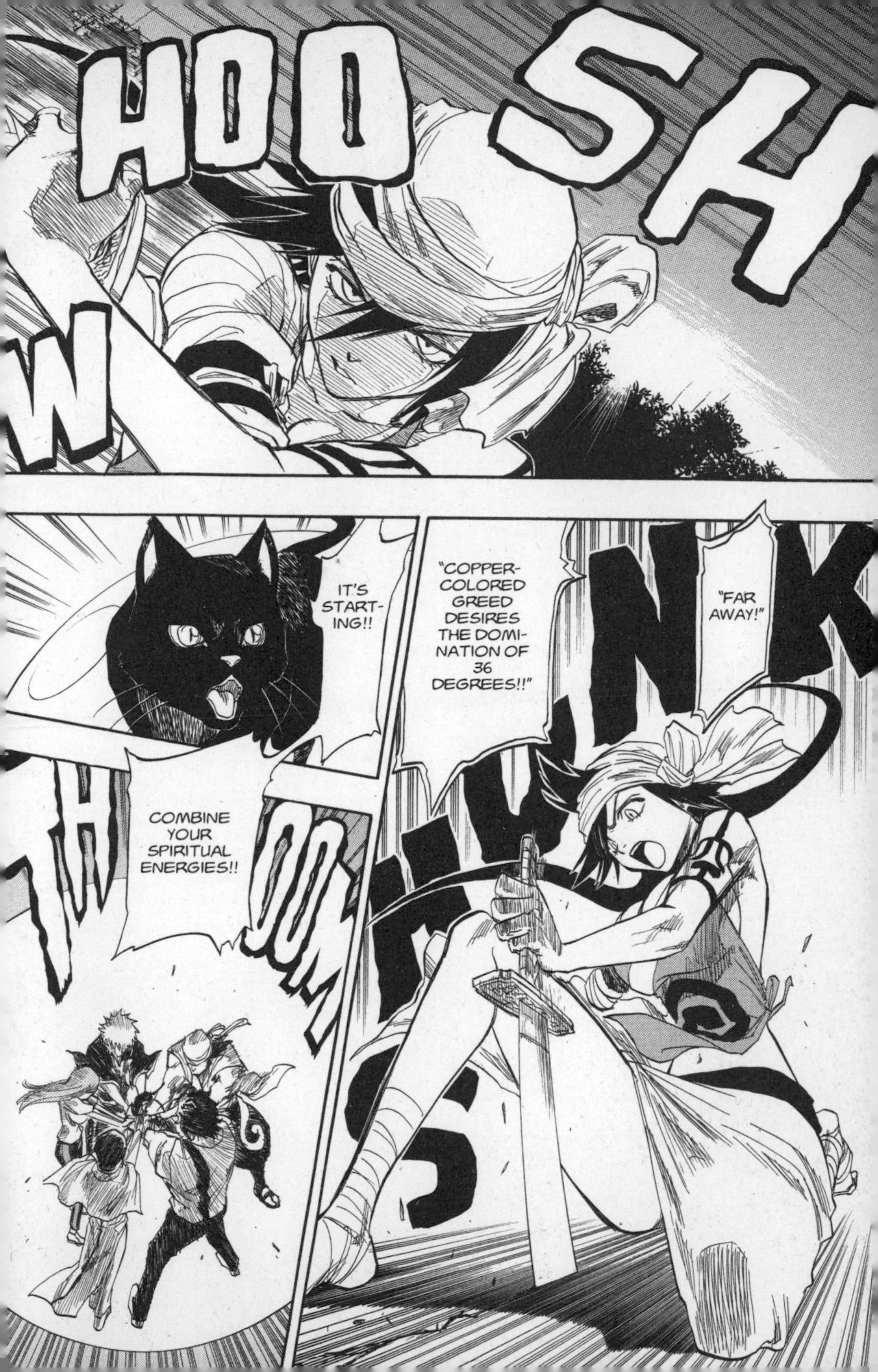
WHOOSH
"FAR AWAY!"
"COPPER-COLORED GREED DESIRES THE DOMINATION OF 36 DEGREES!!"
IT'S STARTING!!
COMBINE YOUR SPIRITUAL ENERGIES!!

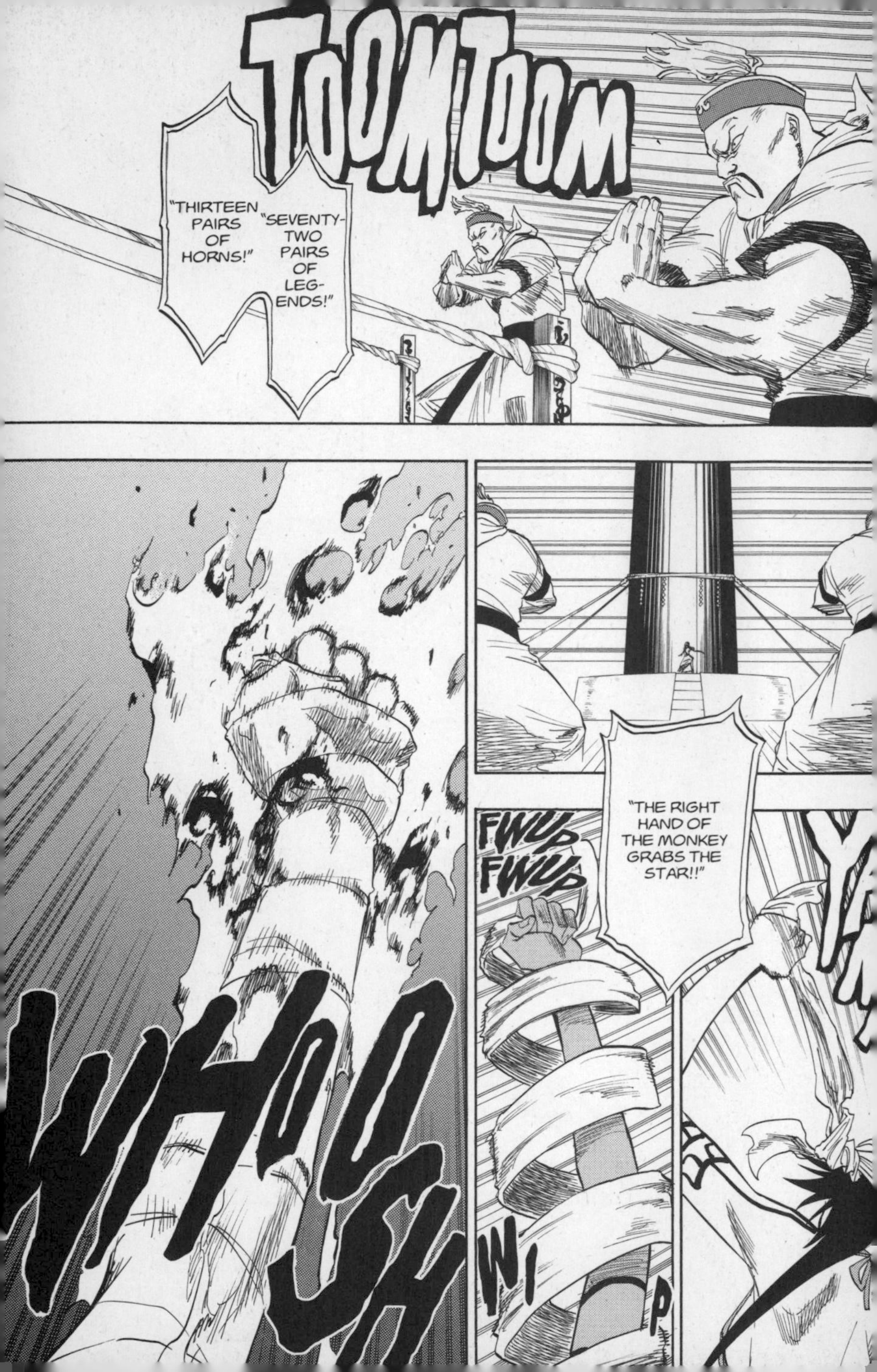
TOOM TOOM
"THIRTEEN PAIRS OF HORNS!"
"SEVENTY-TWO PAIRS OF LEG-ENDS!"
"THE RIGHT HAND OF THE MONKEY GRABS THE STAR!!"
FWUP FWUP
WIP
WHOOSH

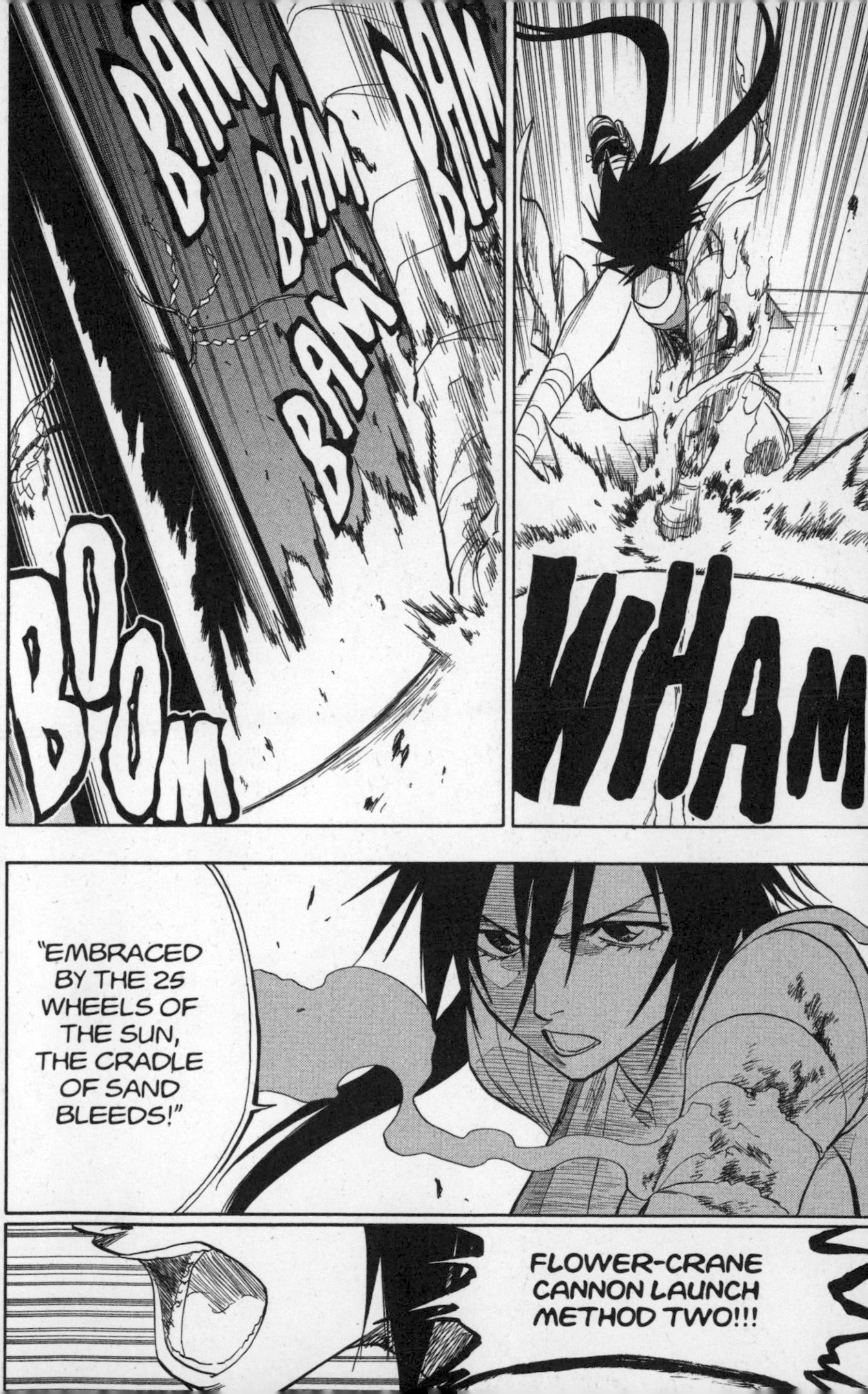
WHAM
BAM
BAM
BAM
BAM
BOOM
"EMBRACED BY THE 25 WHEELS OF THE SUN, THE CRADLE OF SAND BLEEDS!"
FLOWER-CRANE CANNON LAUNCH METHOD TWO!!!

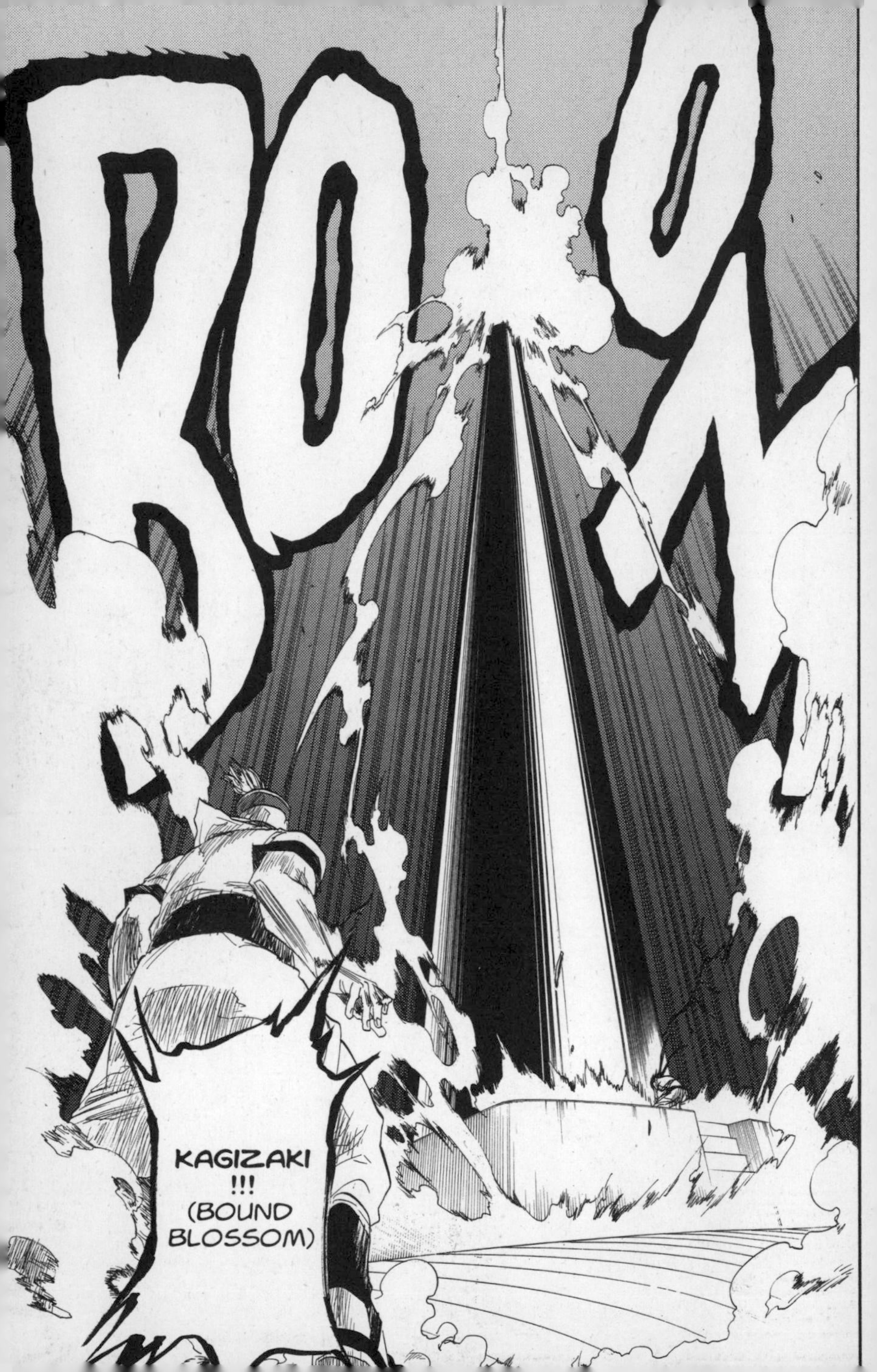
DOOM
KAGIZAKI !!! (BOUND BLOSSOM)

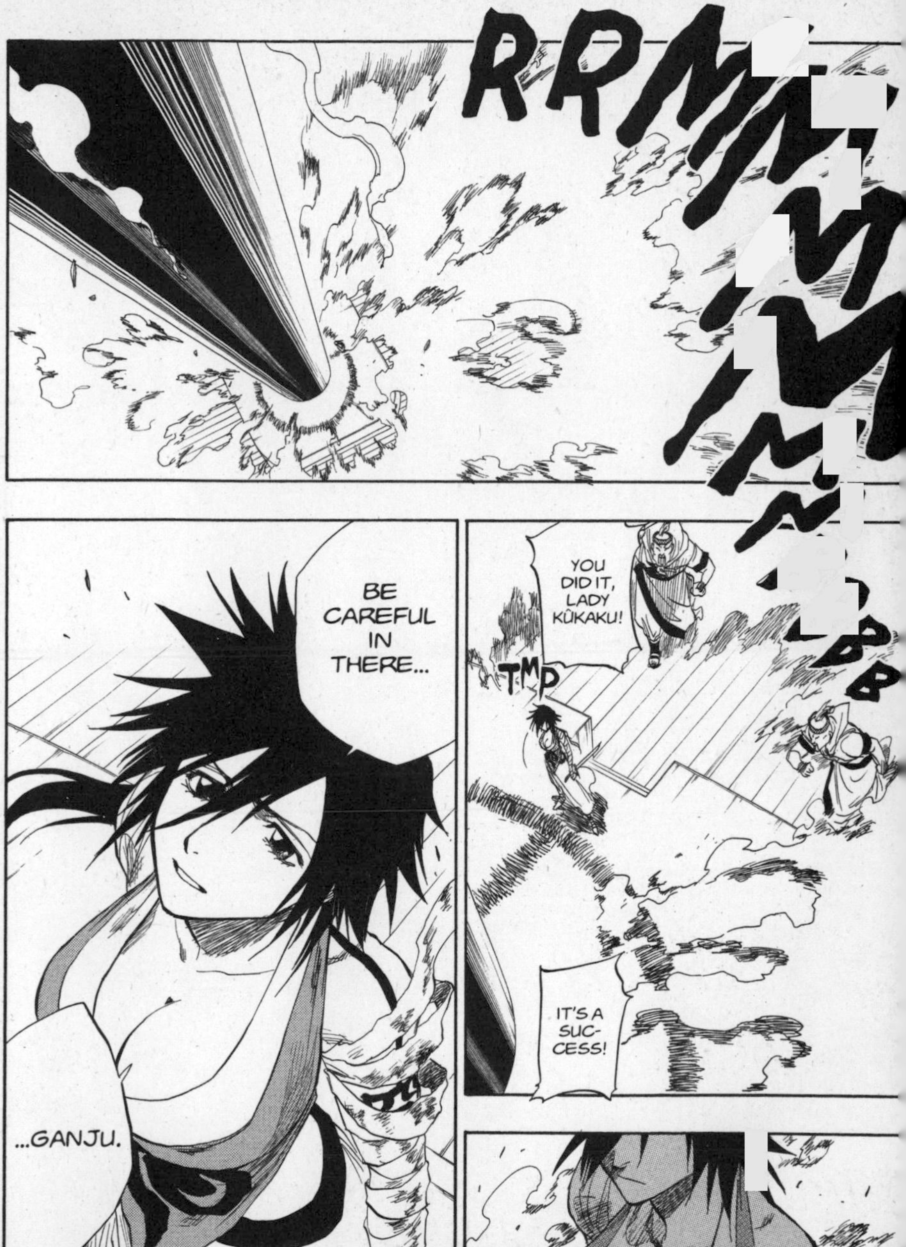
RRM
YOU DID IT, LADY KÛKAKU!
TMP
IT'S A SUC-CESS!
BE CAREFUL IN THERE...
...GANJU.

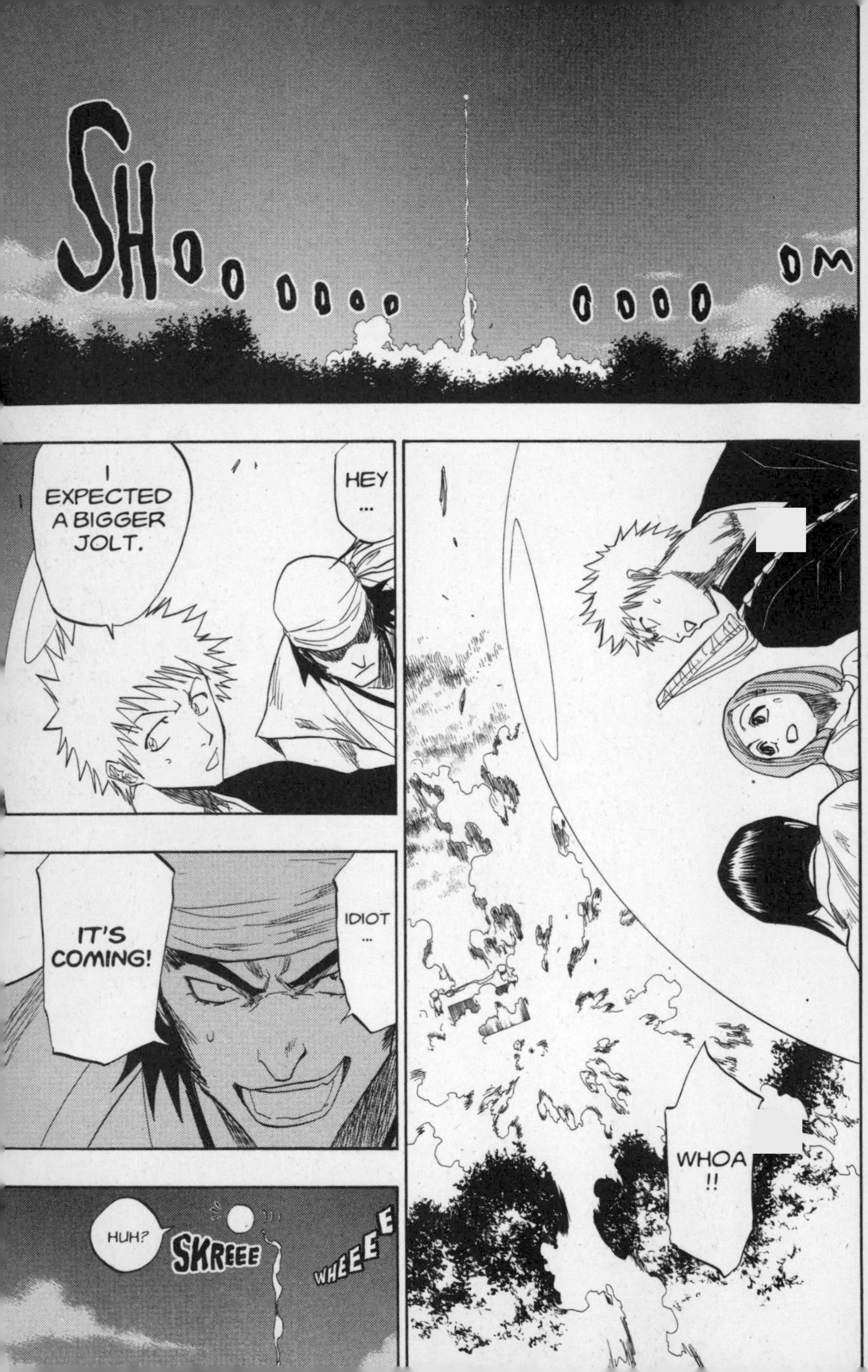
SHOOOOOOOOOOOOM
WHOA !!
HEY ...
I EXPECTED A BIGGER JOLT.
IDIOT ...
IT'S COMING!
WHEEEE
SKREEE
HUH?

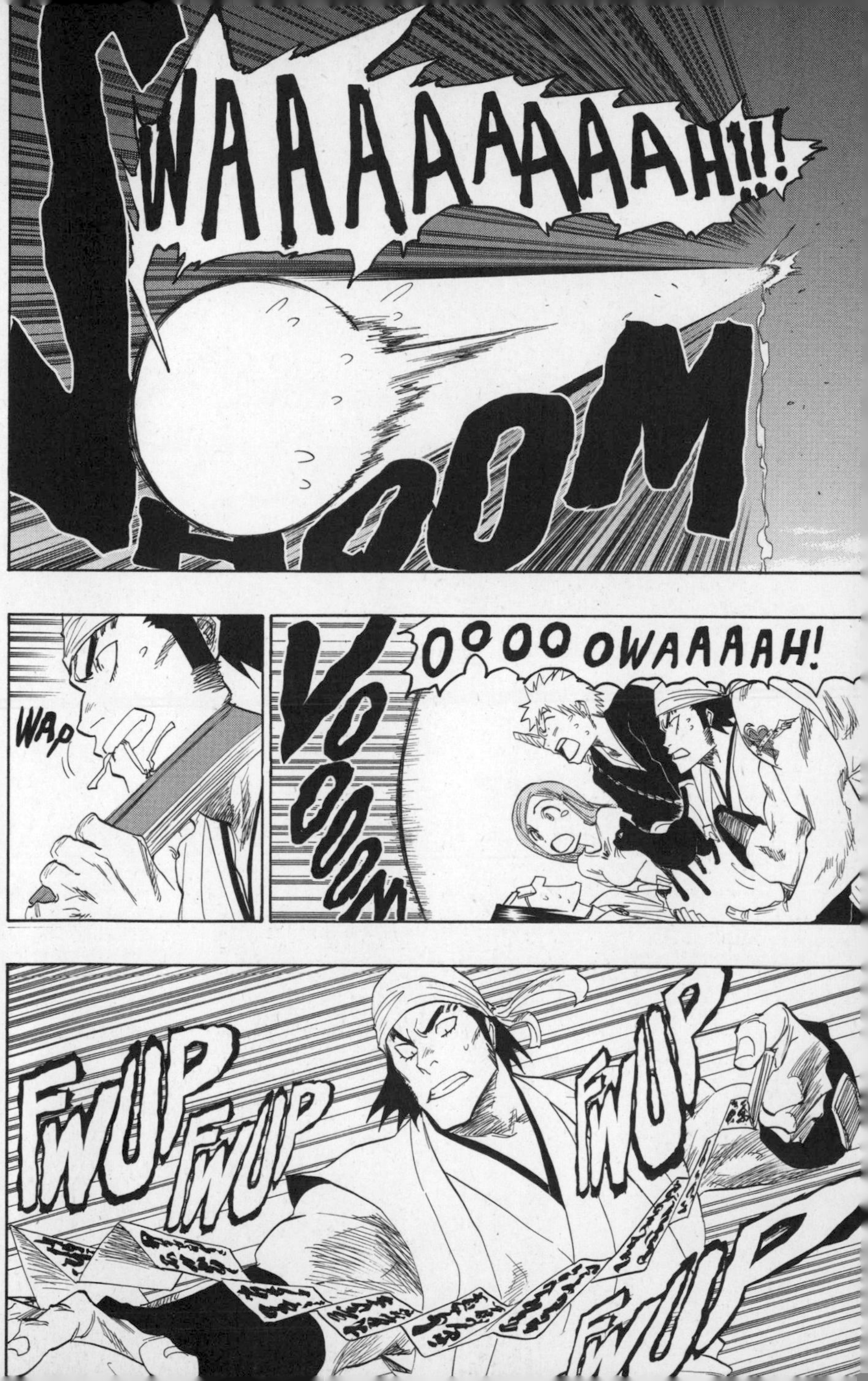
WAAAAAAAH!!!
HOOM
OOOO OWAAAAAH!
VOOOOOM
WAP
FWUP
FWUP
FWUP
FWUP

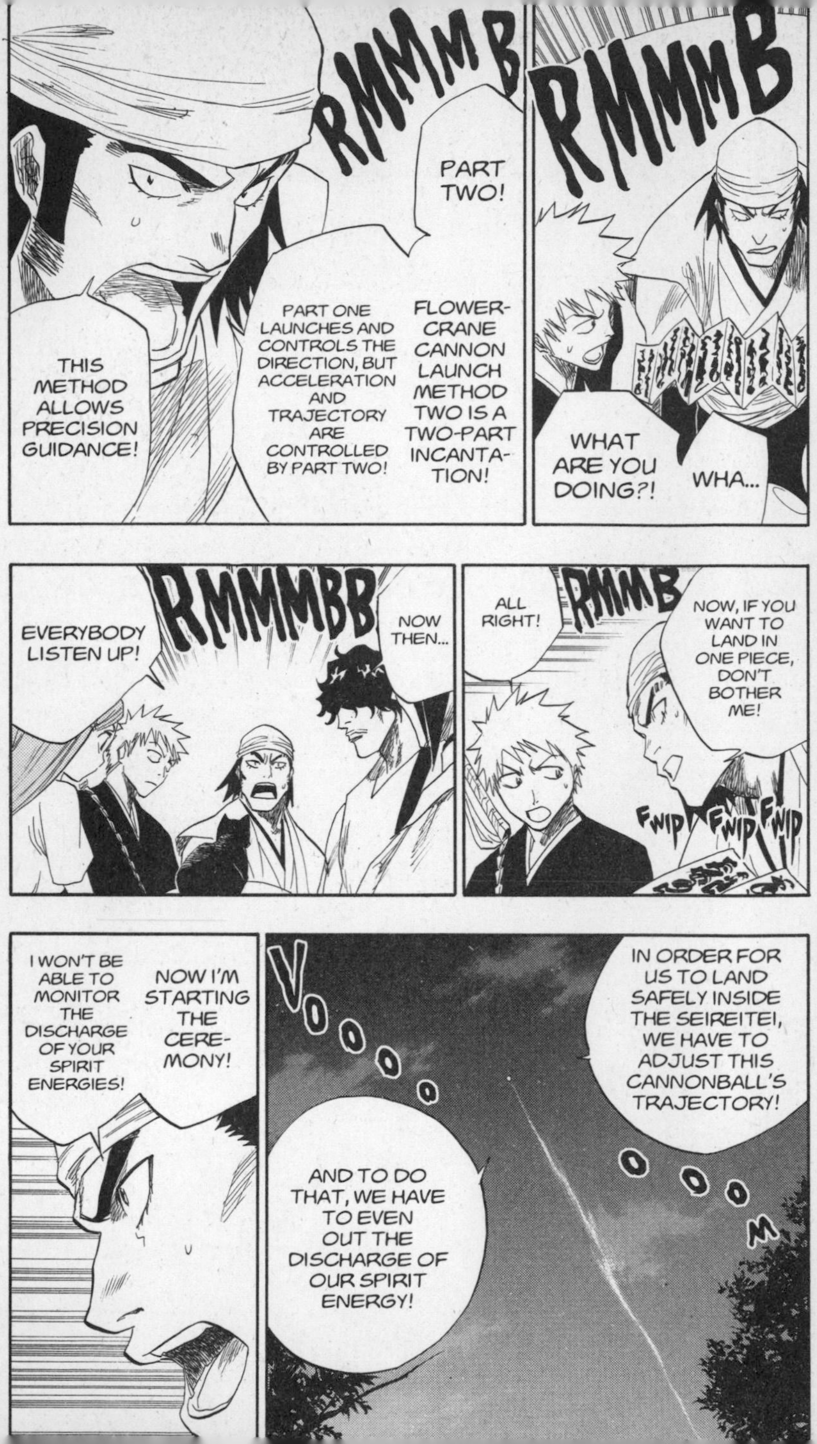
RMMMB
WHA...
WHAT ARE YOU DOING?!
RMMMB
PART TWO!
FLOWER-CRANE CANNON LAUNCH METHOD TWO IS A TWO-PART INCANTATION!
PART ONE LAUNCHES AND CONTROLS THE DIRECTION, BUT ACCELERATION AND TRAJECTORY ARE CONTROLLED BY PART TWO!
THIS METHOD ALLOWS PRECISION GUIDANCE!
RMMB
NOW, IF YOU WANT TO LAND IN ONE PIECE, DON'T BOTHER ME!
ALL RIGHT!
FWIP FWIP FWIP
NOW THEN...
RMMMBB
EVERYBODY LISTEN UP!
IN ORDER FOR US TO LAND SAFELY INSIDE THE SEIREITEI, WE HAVE TO ADJUST THIS CANNONBALL'S TRAJECTORY!
VOOOOOOOOM
AND TO DO THAT, WE HAVE TO EVEN OUT THE DISCHARGE OF OUR SPIRIT ENERGY!
NOW I'M STARTING THE CEREMONY!
I WON'T BE ABLE TO MONITOR THE DISCHARGE OF YOUR SPIRIT ENERGIES!

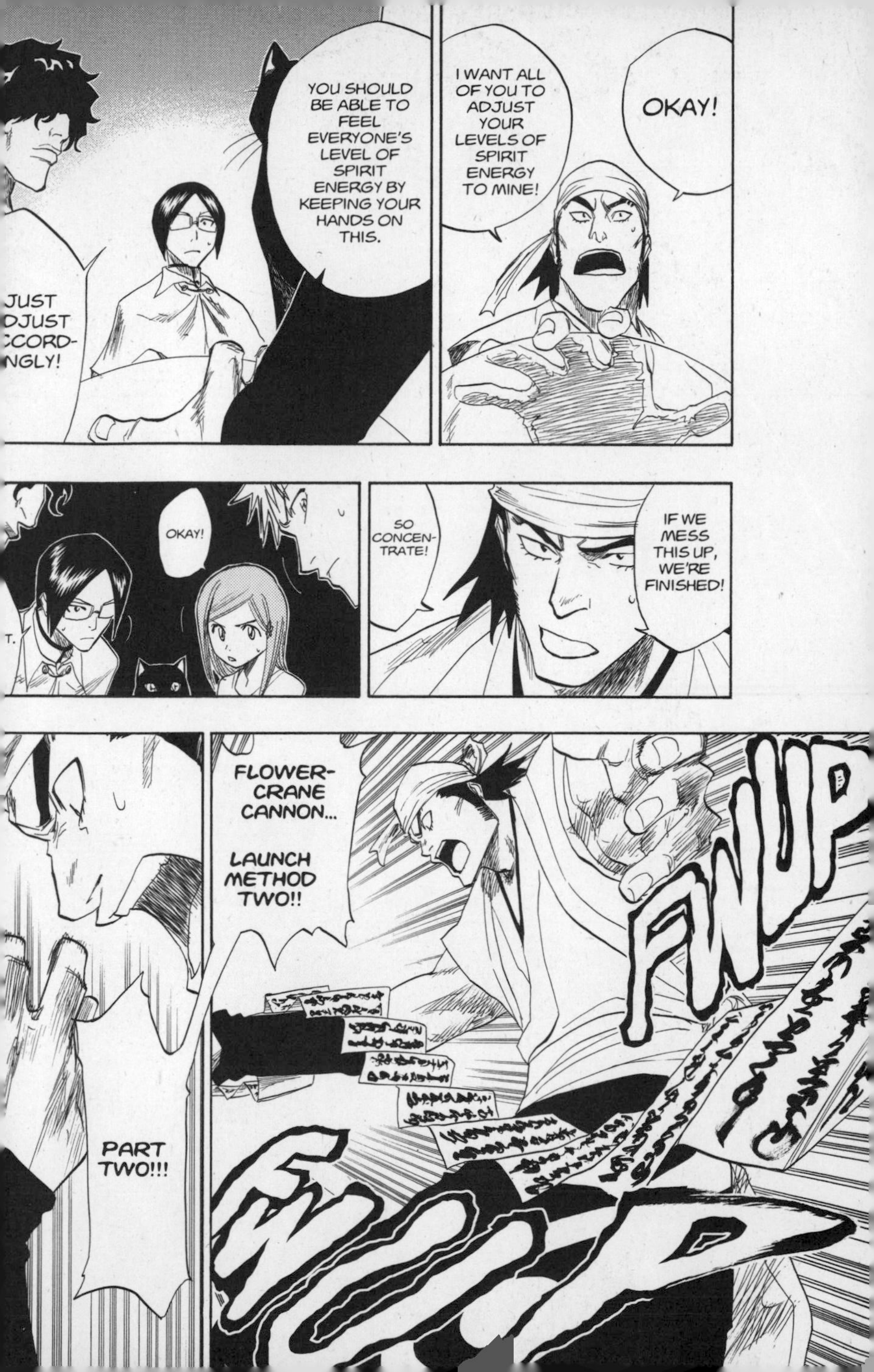
I WANT ALL OF YOU TO ADJUST YOUR LEVELS OF SPIRIT ENERGY TO MINE!
OKAY!
YOU SHOULD BE ABLE TO FEEL EVERYONE'S LEVEL OF SPIRIT ENERGY BY KEEPING YOUR HANDS ON THIS.
JUST DJUST CCORD- NGLY!
IF WE MESS THIS UP, WE'RE FINISHED!
SO CONCEN- TRATE!
OKAY!
T.
FLOWER- CRANE CANNON...
LAUNCH METHOD TWO!!
FWUP
PART TWO!!!

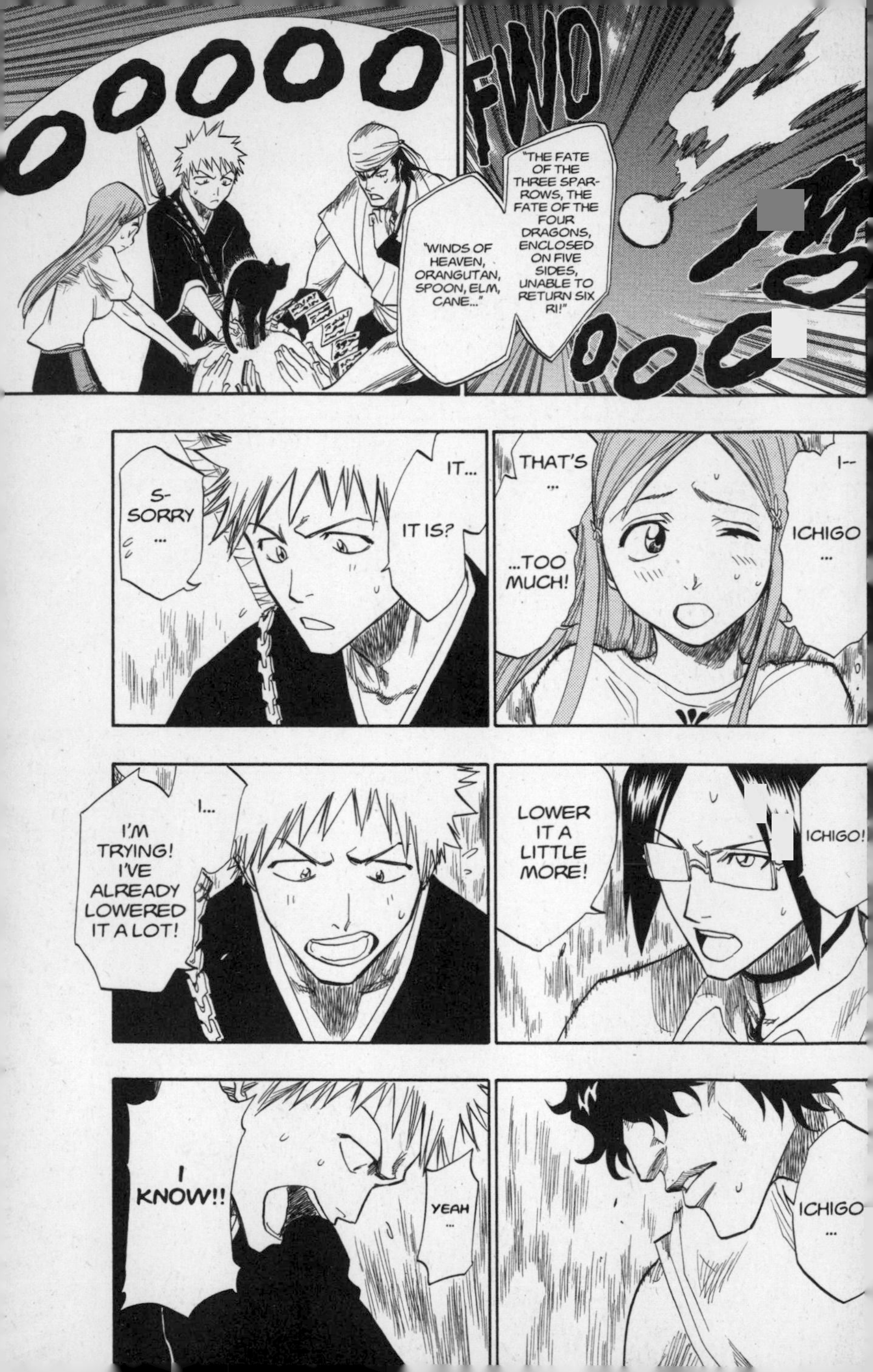
FWO
"THE FATE OF THE THREE SPARROWS, THE FATE OF THE FOUR DRAGONS, ENCLOSED ON FIVE SIDES, UNABLE TO RETURN SIX RI!"
"WINDS OF HEAVEN, ORANGUTAN, SPOON, ELM, CANE..."
OOOOO
I-- ICHIGO...
THAT'S... ...TOO MUCH!
IT... IT IS?
S-SORRY...
ICHIGO!
LOWER IT A LITTLE MORE!
I... I'M TRYING! I'VE ALREADY LOWERED IT A LOT!
ICHIGO...
YEAH...
I KNOW!!

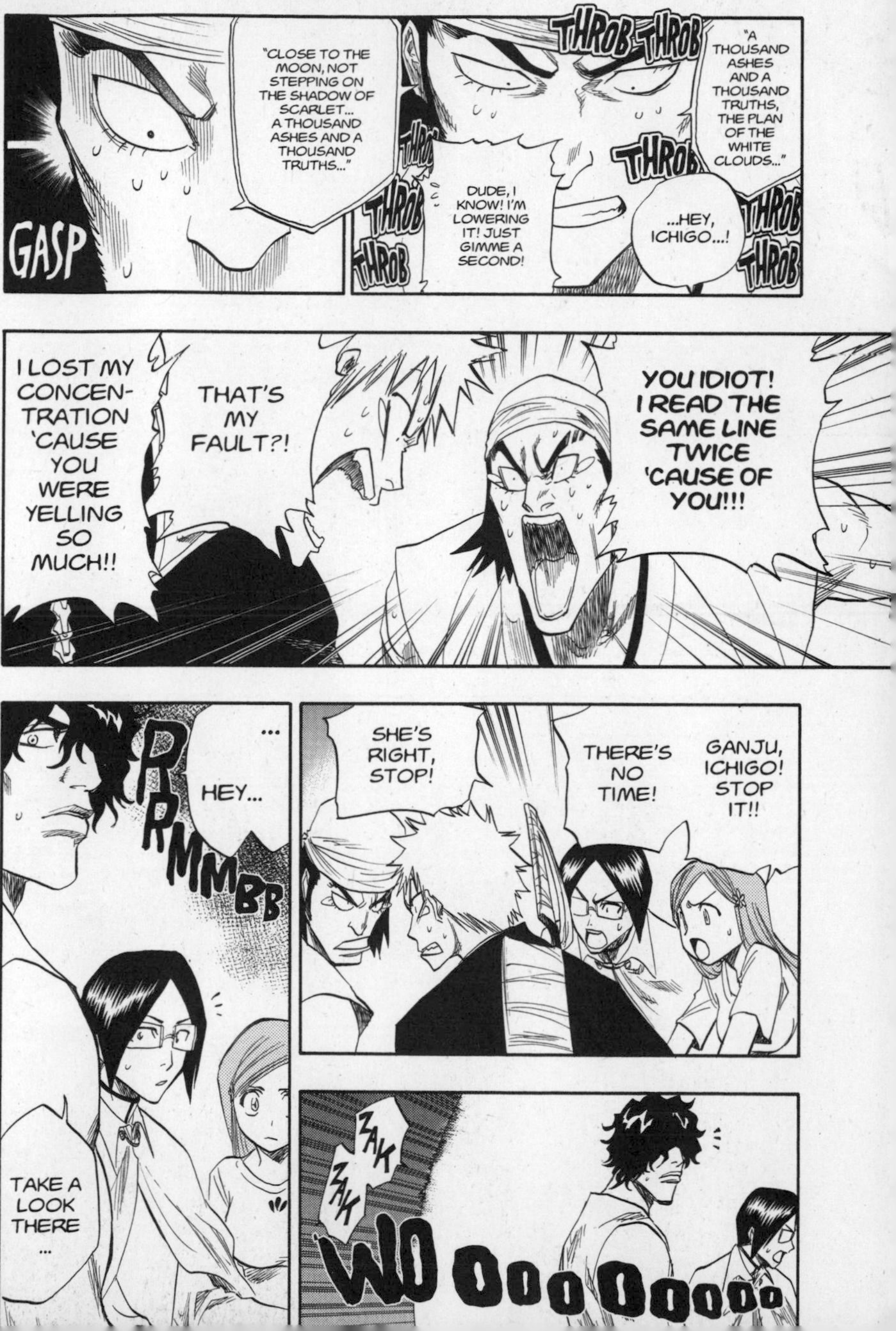
THROB THROB
"A THOUSAND ASHES AND A THOUSAND TRUTHS, THE PLAN OF THE WHITE CLOUDS..."
THROB
...HEY, ICHIGO...!
DUDE, I KNOW! I'M LOWERING IT! JUST GIMME A SECOND!
THROB
THROB
THROB
THROB
THROB
"CLOSE TO THE MOON, NOT STEPPING ON THE SHADOW OF SCARLET... A THOUSAND ASHES AND A THOUSAND TRUTHS..."
GASP
YOU IDIOT! I READ THE SAME LINE TWICE 'CAUSE OF YOU!!!
THAT'S MY FAULT?!
I LOST MY CONCEN-TRATION 'CAUSE YOU WERE YELLING SO MUCH!!
GANJU, ICHIGO! STOP IT!!
THERE'S NO TIME!
SHE'S RIGHT, STOP!
ZAK ZAK
WOOOOOOOOOO
...
HEY...
RRMMBB
TAKE A LOOK THERE ...

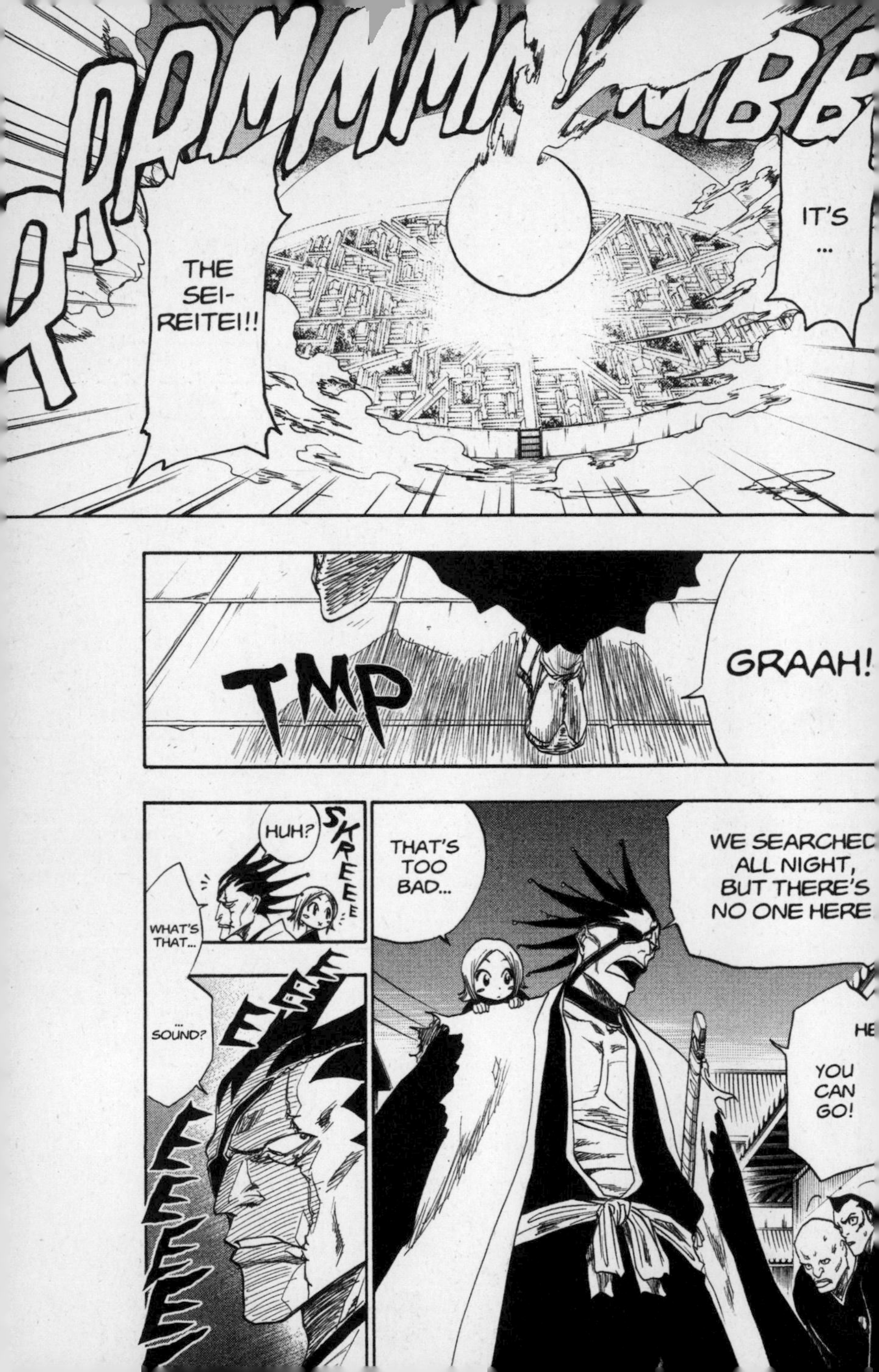
IT'S ...
THE SEI-REITEI!!!
GRAAH!
TMP
WE SEARCHED ALL NIGHT, BUT THERE'S NO ONE HERE
HE
YOU CAN GO!
THAT'S TOO BAD...
HUH?
SKREEEE
WHAT'S THAT...
... SOUND?
EEEEEEEE

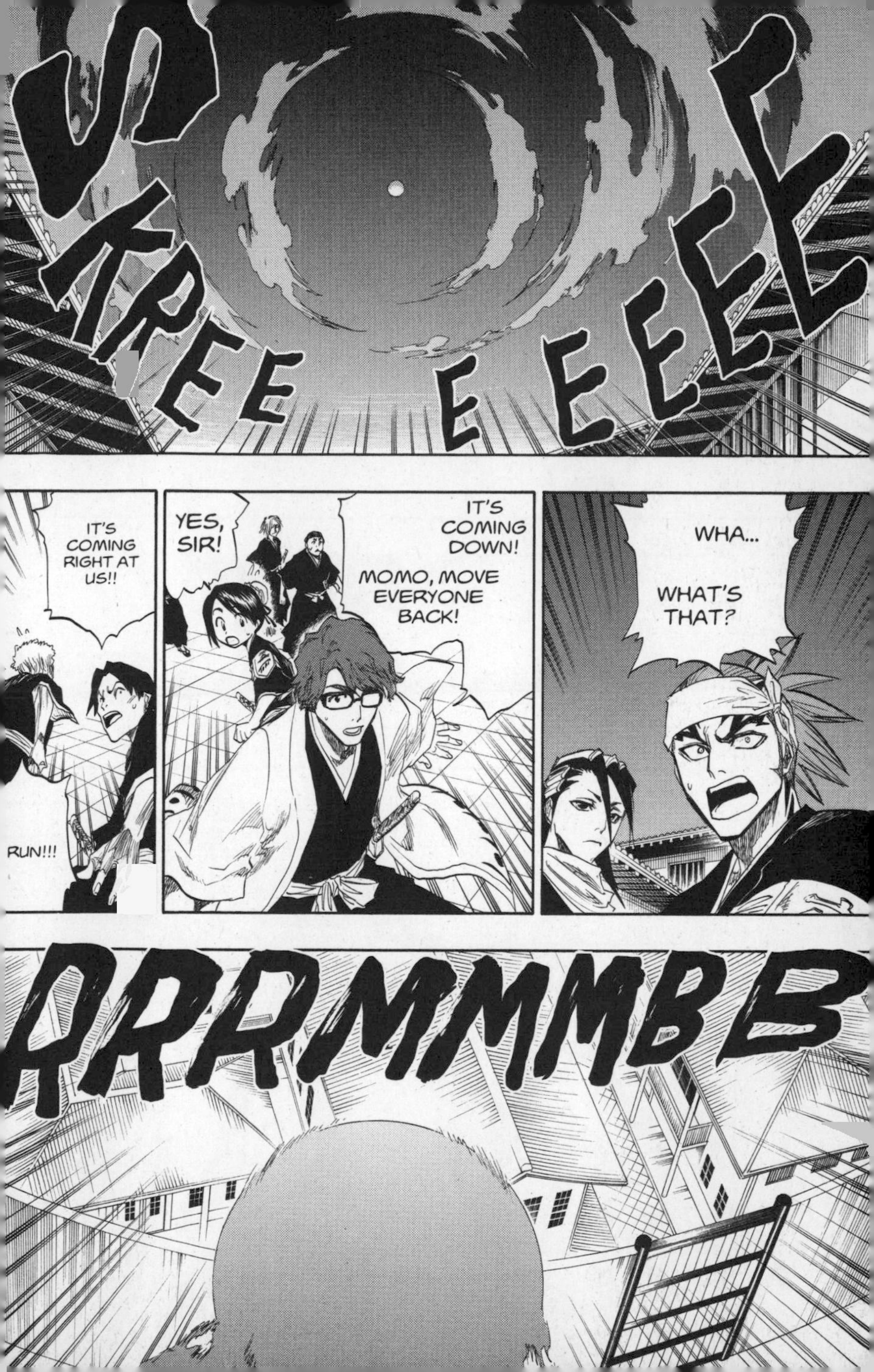
SKREEEEEEK
WHA...
WHAT'S THAT?
IT'S COMING DOWN!
MOMO, MOVE EVERYONE BACK!
YES, SIR!
IT'S COMING RIGHT AT US!!
RUN!!!
RRRMMMBB

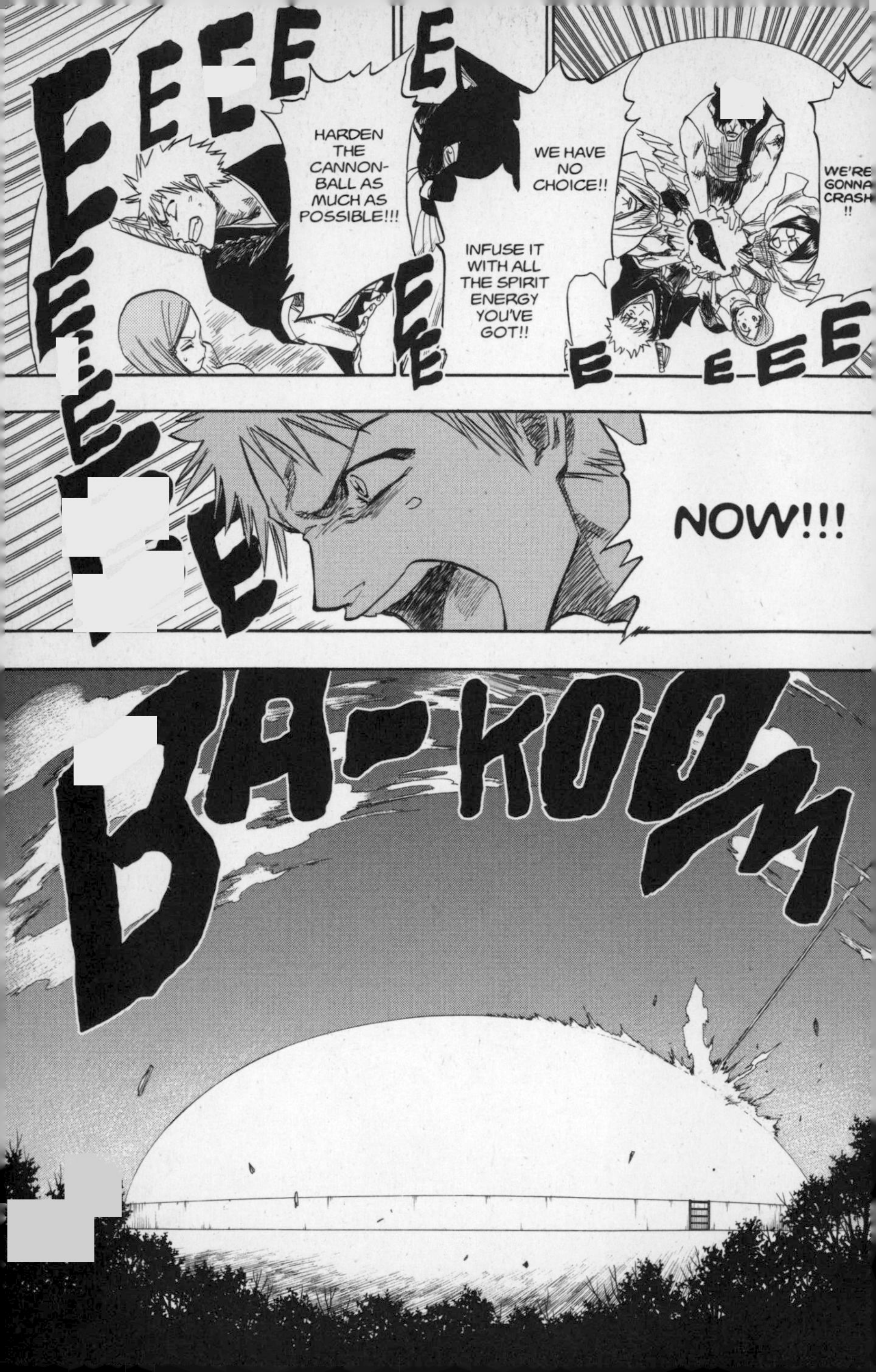
WE'RE GONNA CRASH!!
EEEE
WE HAVE NO CHOICE!!
INFUSE IT WITH ALL THE SPIRIT ENERGY YOU'VE GOT!!
EE
E
HARDEN THE CANNON-BALL AS MUCH AS POSSIBLE!!!
EEEE
NOW!!!
BA-KOOM

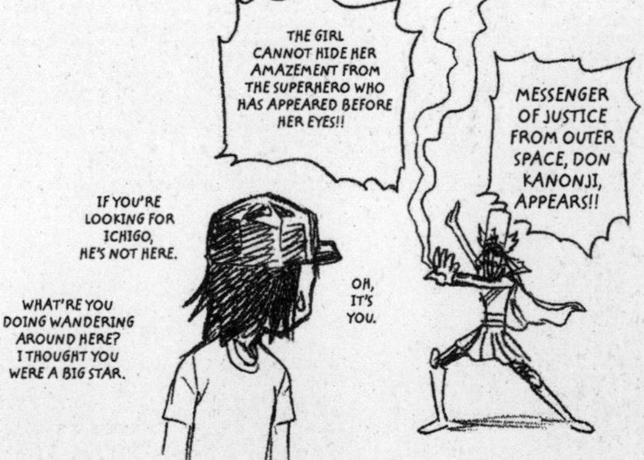
MESSENGER OF JUSTICE FROM OUTER SPACE, DON KANONJI, APPEARS!!
THE GIRL CANNOT HIDE HER AMAZEMENT FROM THE SUPERHERO WHO HAS APPEARED BEFORE HER EYES!!
OH, IT'S YOU.
IF YOU'RE LOOKING FOR ICHIGO, HE'S NOT HERE.
WHAT'RE YOU DOING WANDERING AROUND HERE? I THOUGHT YOU WERE A BIG STAR.

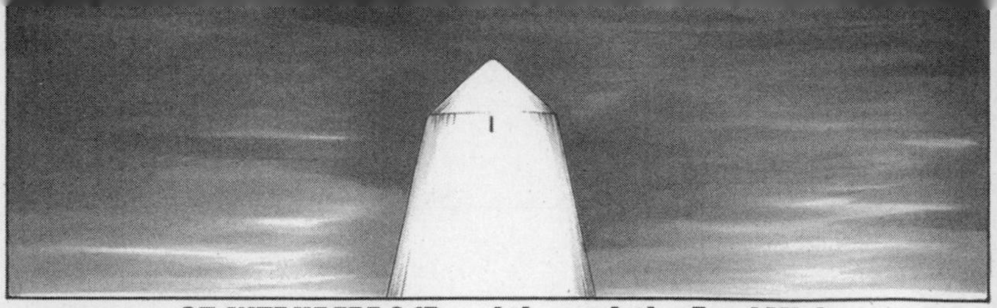

85.INTRUDERZ 2 (Breakthrough the Roof Mix)

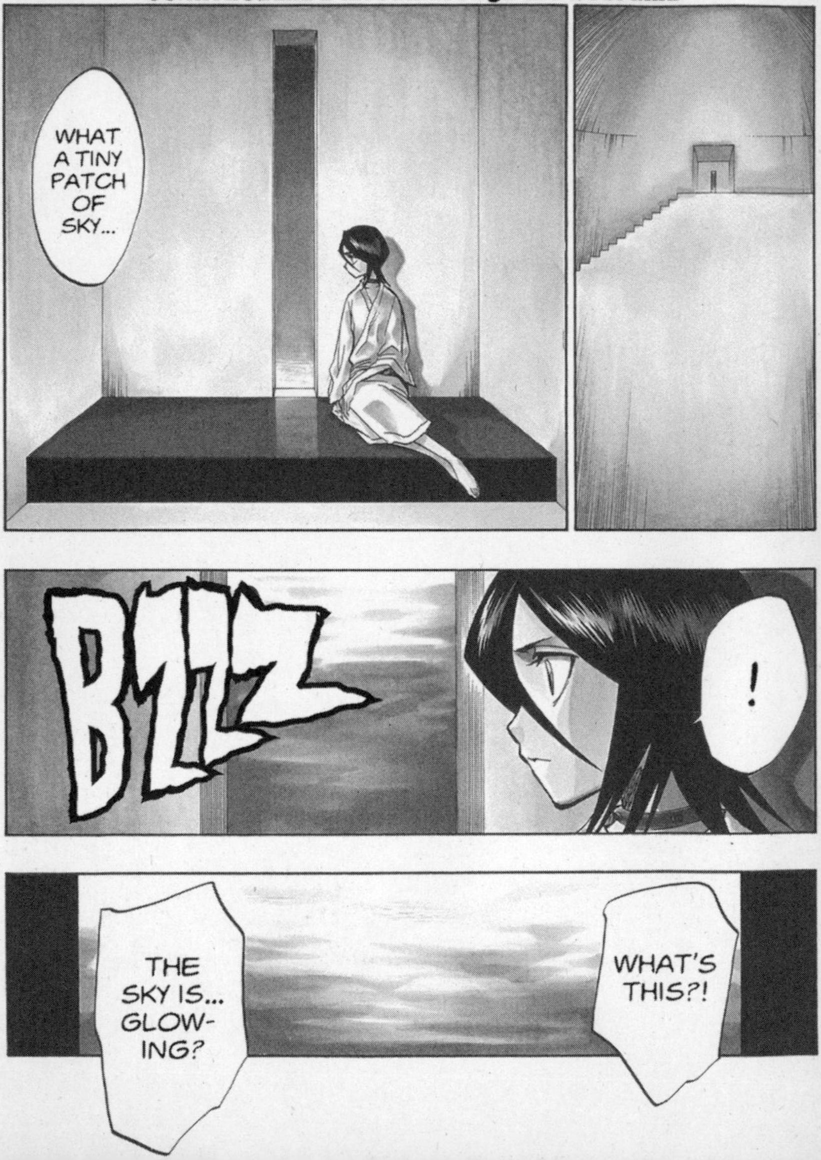
WHAT A TINY PATCH OF SKY...
!
BZZZ
WHAT'S THIS?!
THE SKY IS... GLOWING?

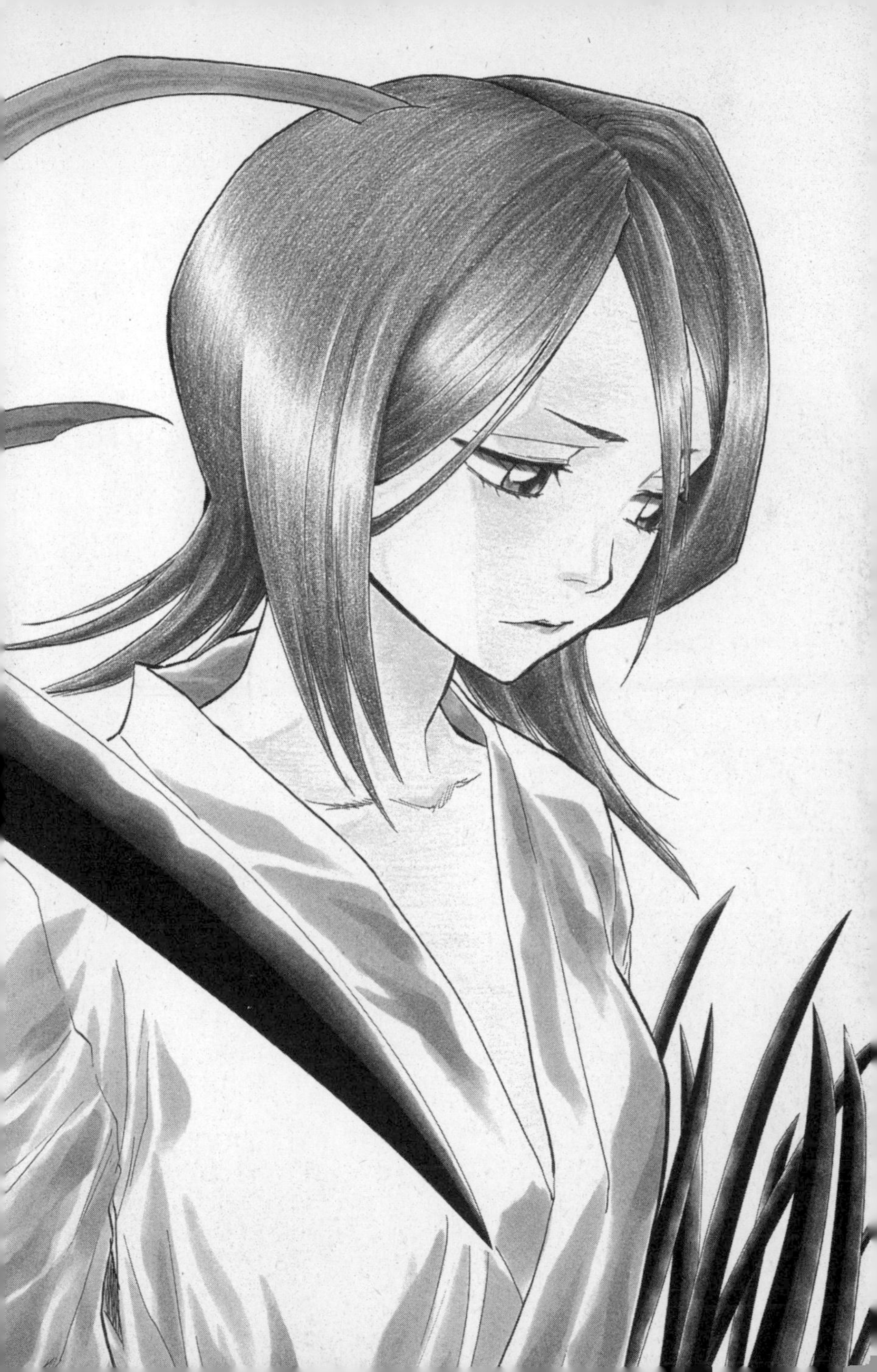

85. INTRUDERZ 2 (Breakthrough the Roof Mix)

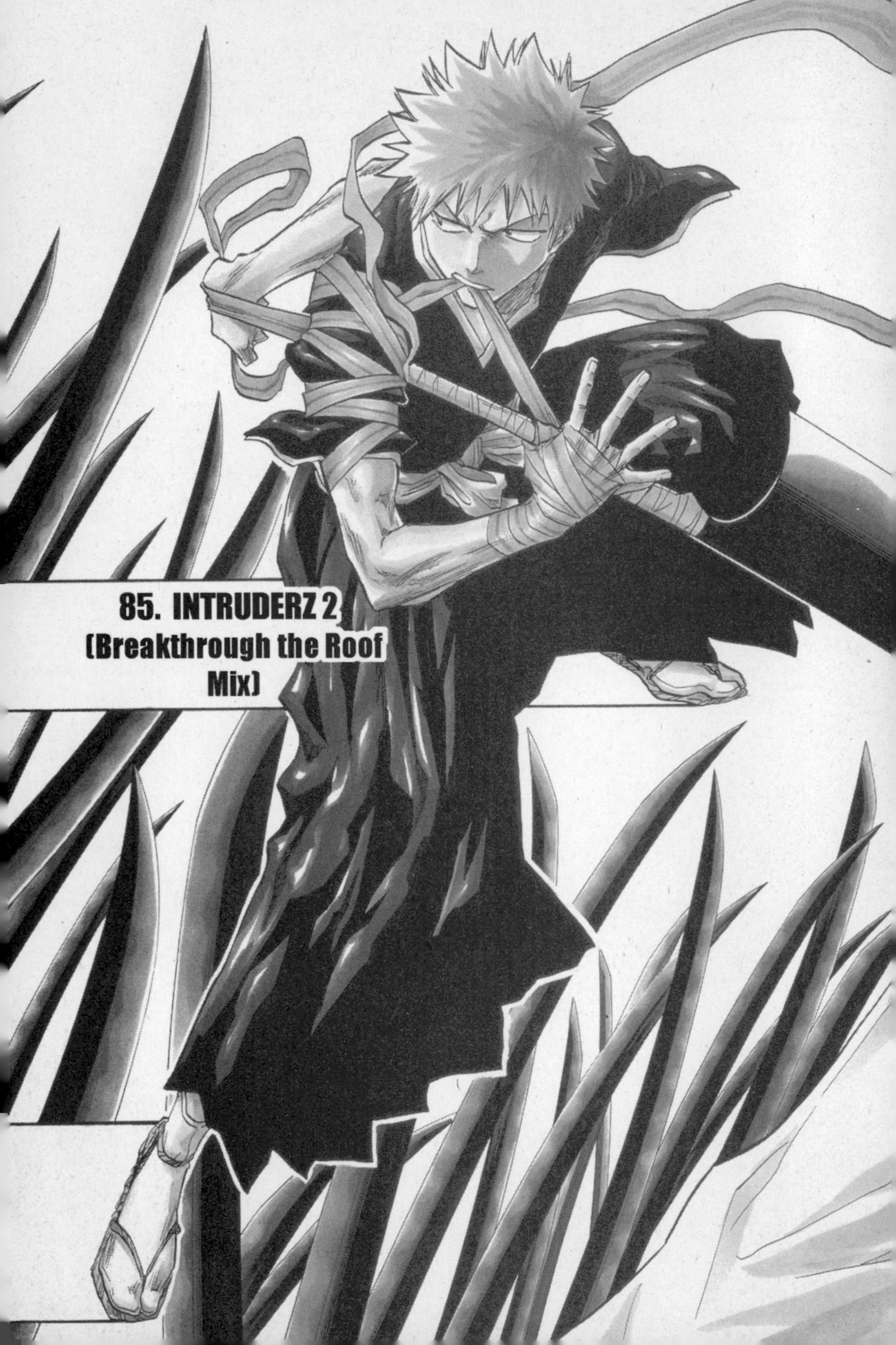

BLEACH
ブリーチ

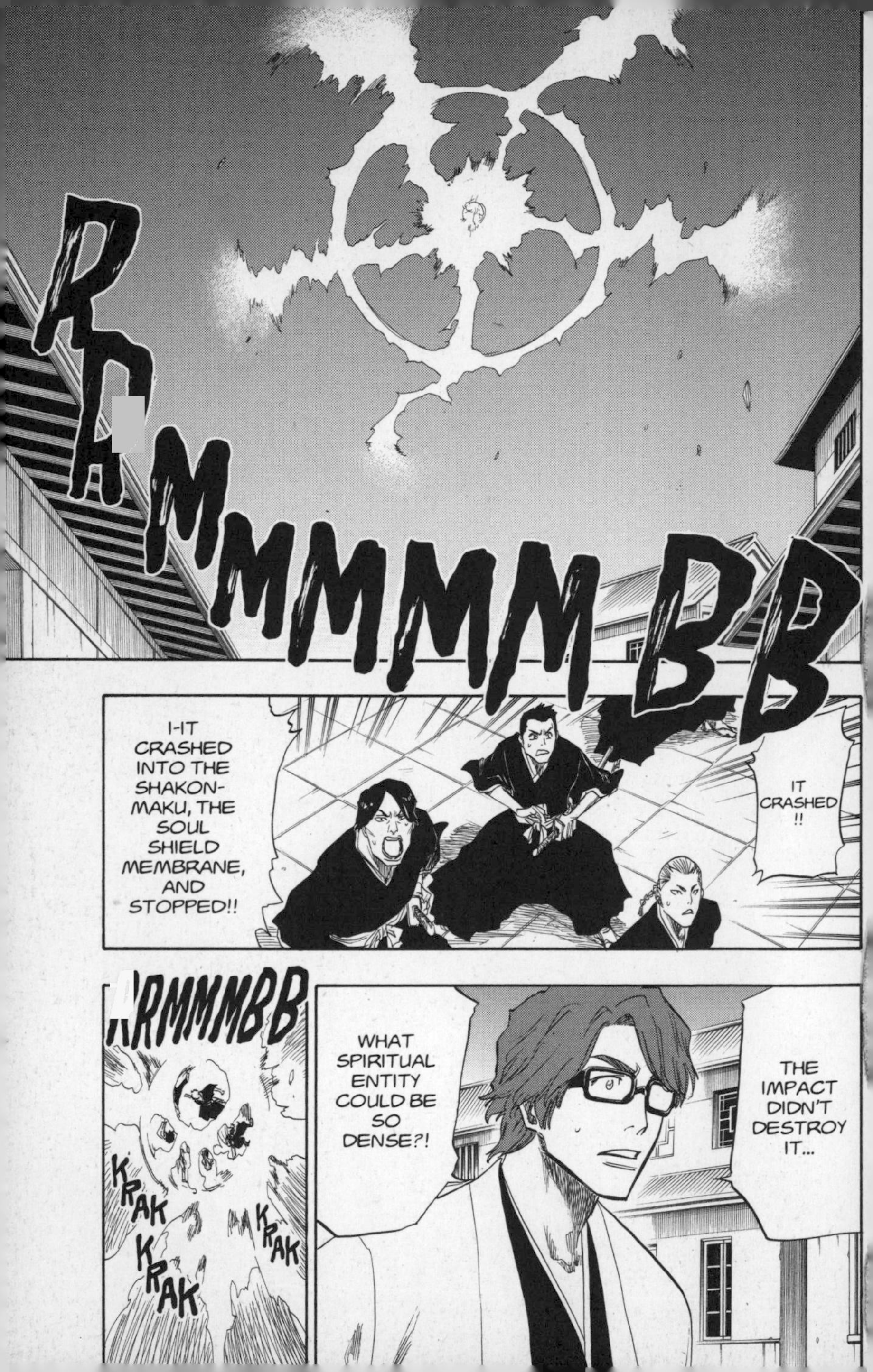
RRAMMMMMBB
IT CRASHED!!
I-IT CRASHED INTO THE SHAKON-MAKU, THE SOUL SHIELD MEMBRANE, AND STOPPED!!
THE IMPACT DIDN'T DESTROY IT...
WHAT SPIRITUAL ENTITY COULD BE SO DENSE?!
RMMMBB
KRAK
KRAK
KRAK

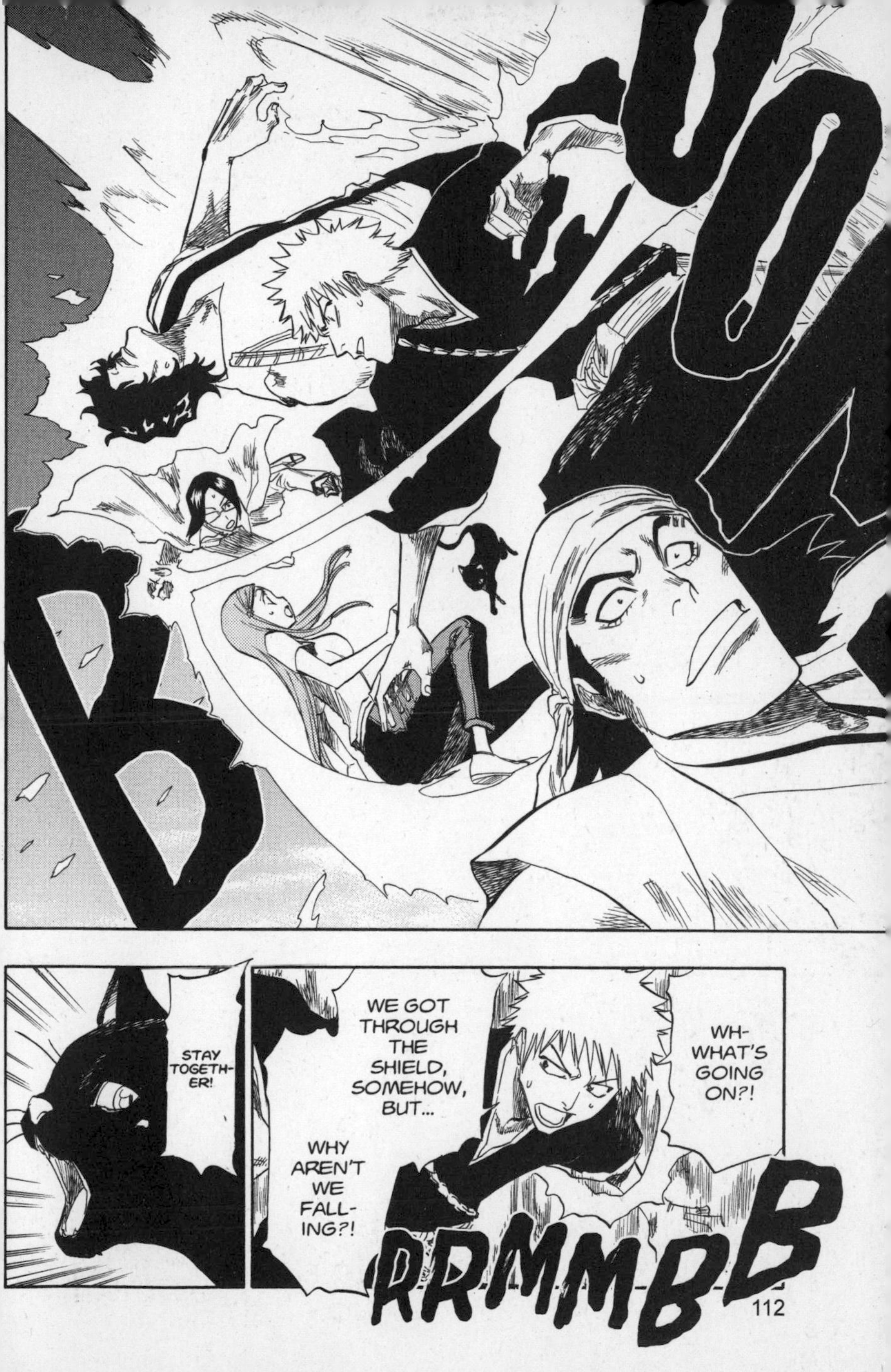
WH- WHAT'S GOING ON?!
WE GOT THROUGH THE SHIELD, SOMEHOW, BUT...
WHY AREN'T WE FALL- ING?!
RRMMBB
STAY TOGETH- ER!

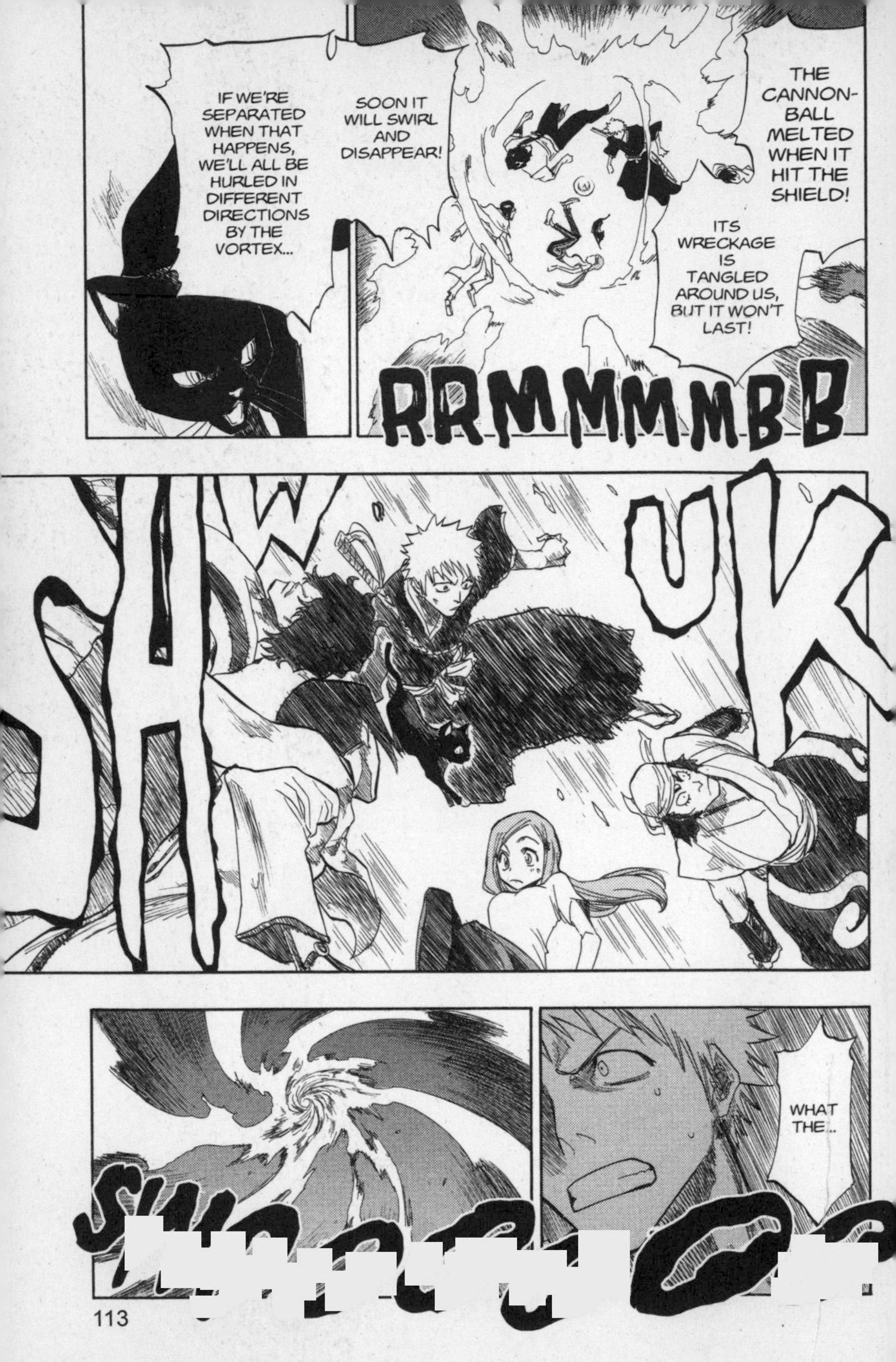
THE CANNON-BALL MELTED WHEN IT HIT THE SHIELD!
ITS WRECKAGE IS TANGLED AROUND US, BUT IT WON'T LAST!
SOON IT WILL SWIRL AND DISAPPEAR!
RRMMMMBB
IF WE'RE SEPARATED WHEN THAT HAPPENS, WE'LL ALL BE HURLED IN DIFFERENT DIRECTIONS BY THE VORTEX...
SHWUK
WHAT THE...

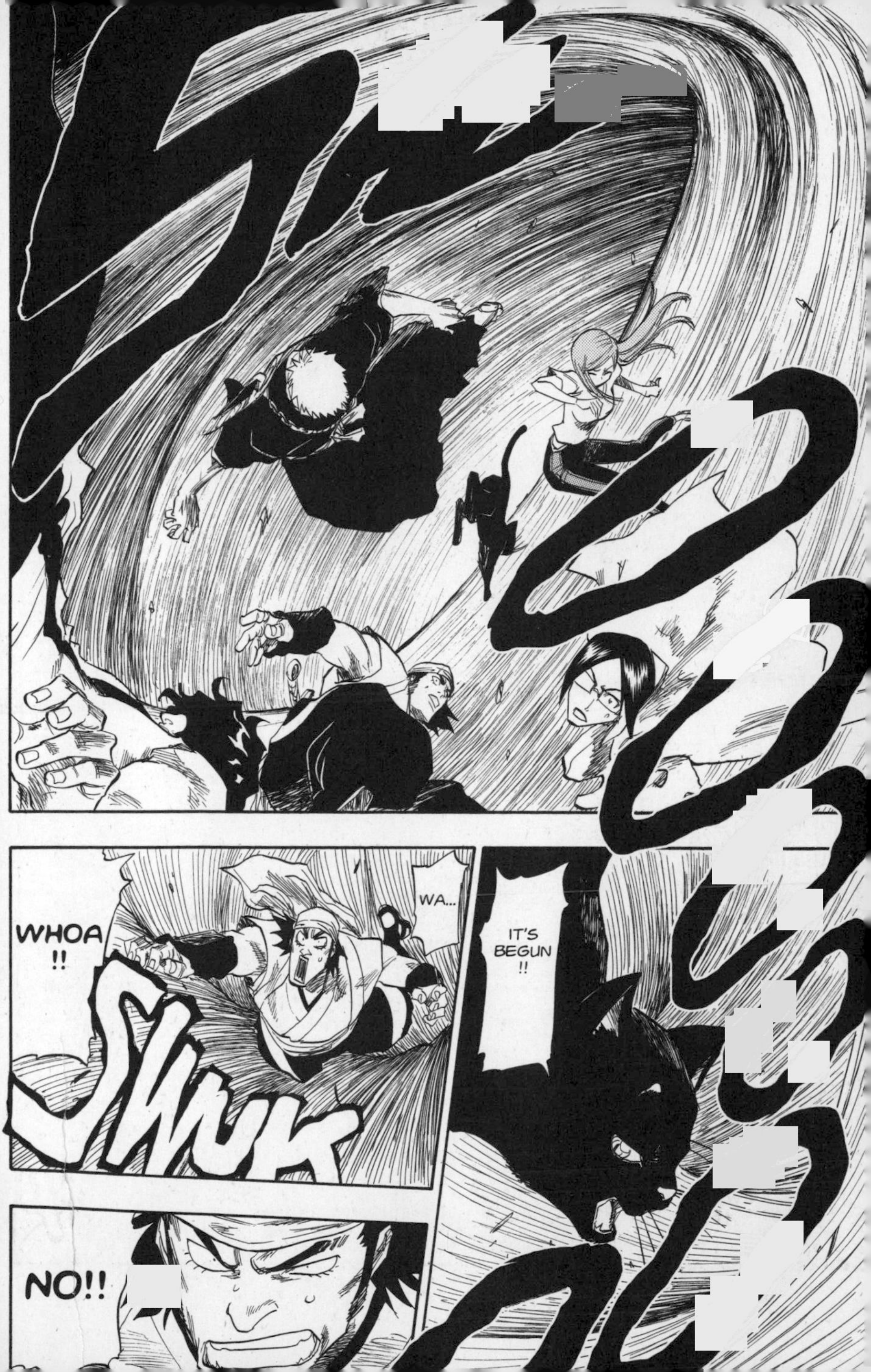
IT'S BEGUN !!
WA...
WHOA !!
NO!!

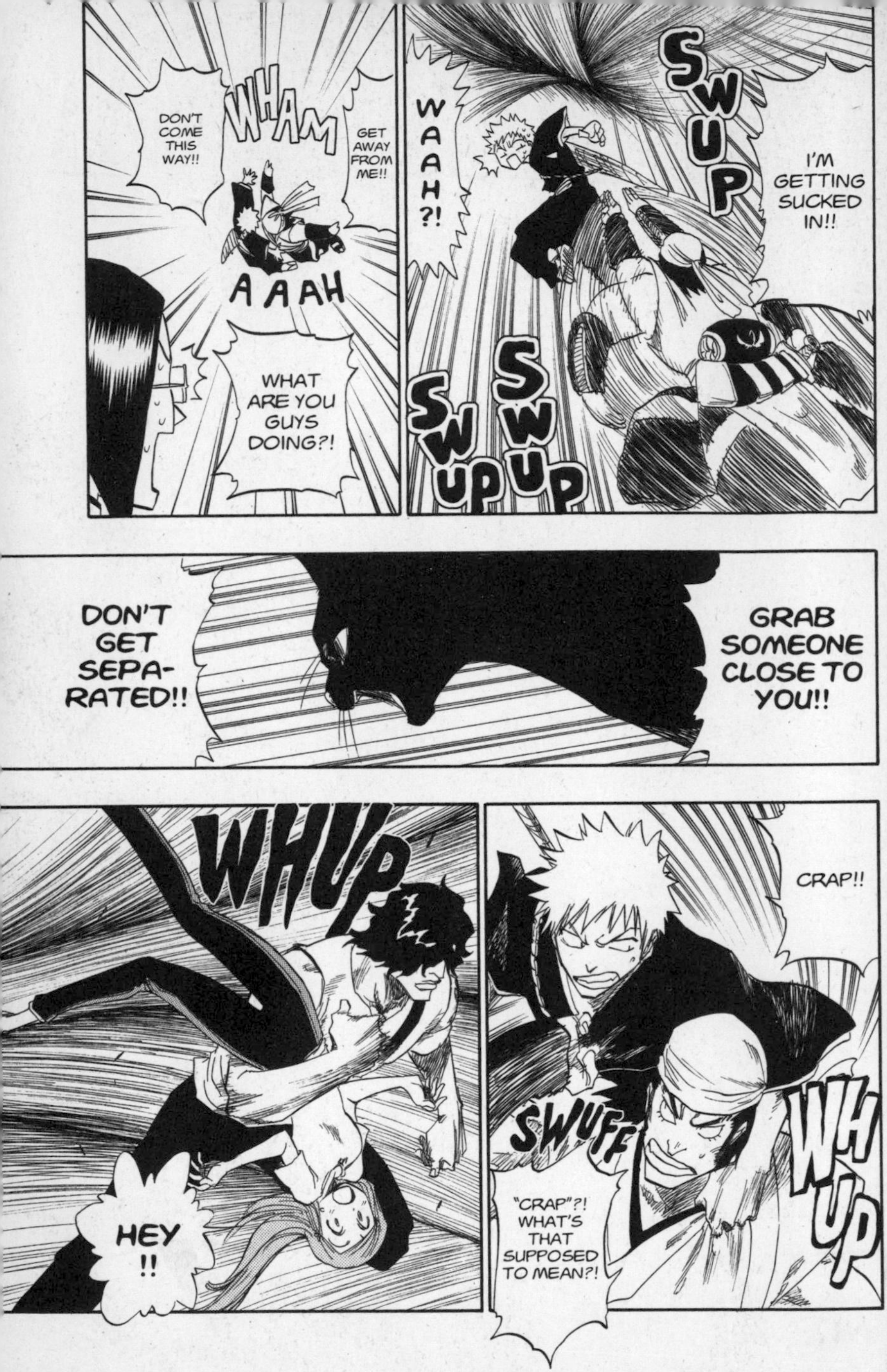
SWUP
I'M GETTING SUCKED IN!!
WAAAH?!
SWUP
SWUP
GET AWAY FROM ME!!
WHAM
DON'T COME THIS WAY!!
AAAH
WHAT ARE YOU GUYS DOING?!
GRAB SOMEONE CLOSE TO YOU!!
DON'T GET SEPA-RATED!!
CRAP!!
WHUP
SWUFF
"CRAP"?! WHAT'S THAT SUPPOSED TO MEAN?!
WHUP
HEY !!

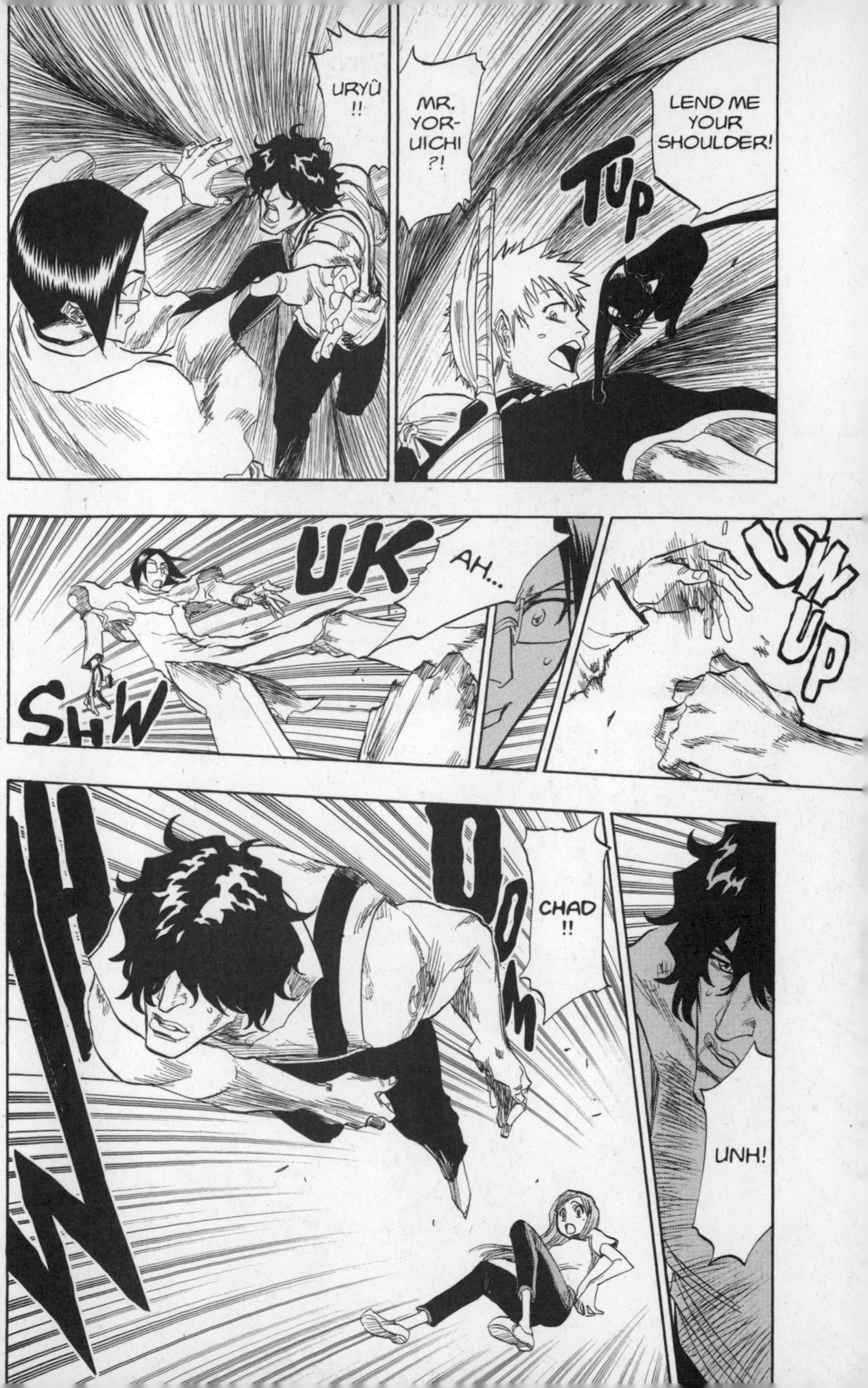
LEND ME YOUR SHOULDER!
TUP
MR. YOR-UICHI ?!
URYÛ !!
SW UP
AH...
UK
SHW
UNH!
DOOM
CHAD !!

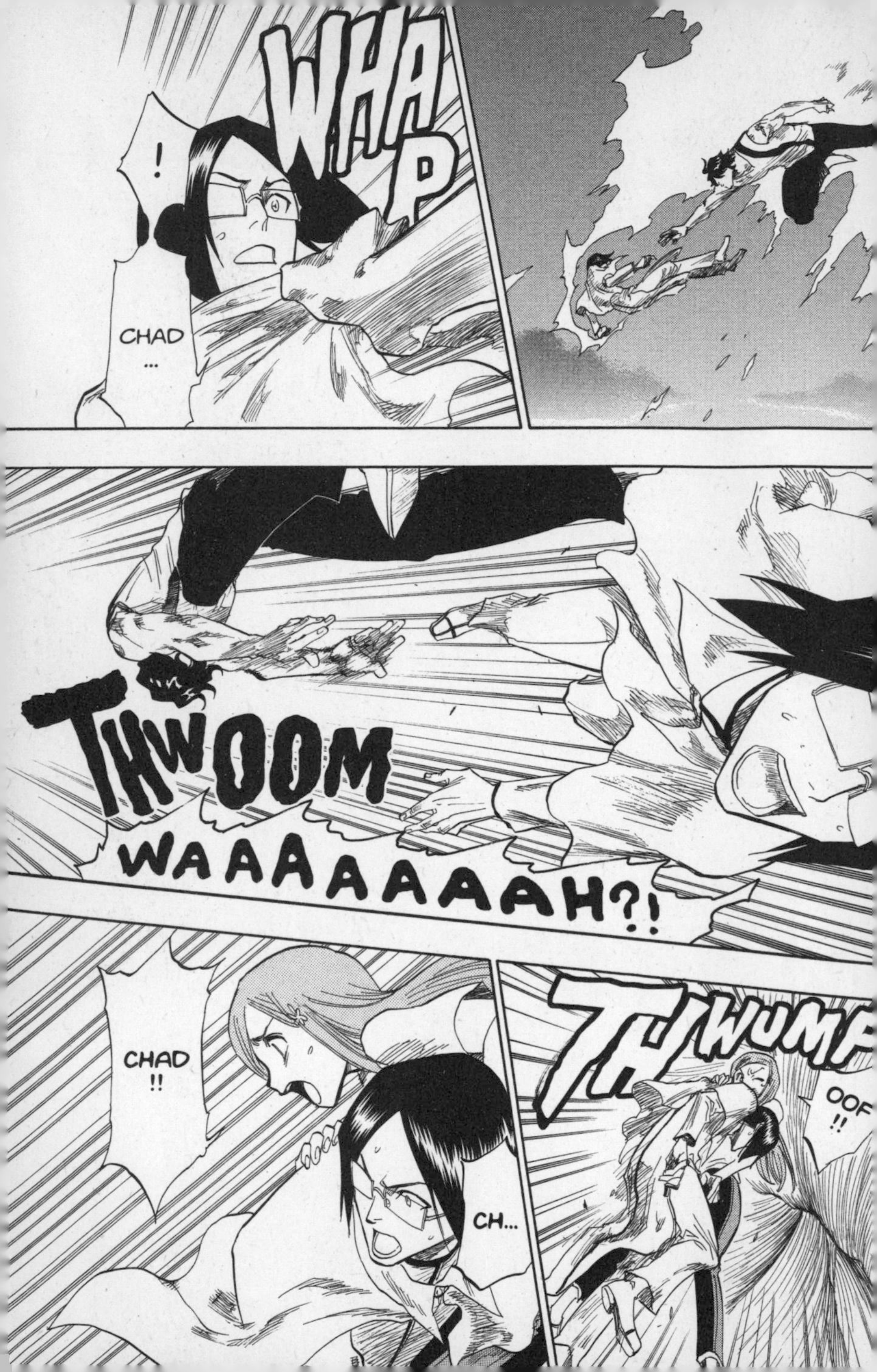
WHAP
!
CHAD
...
THWOOM
WAAAAAAAAH?!
THWUMP
OOF
!!
CHAD
!!
CH...

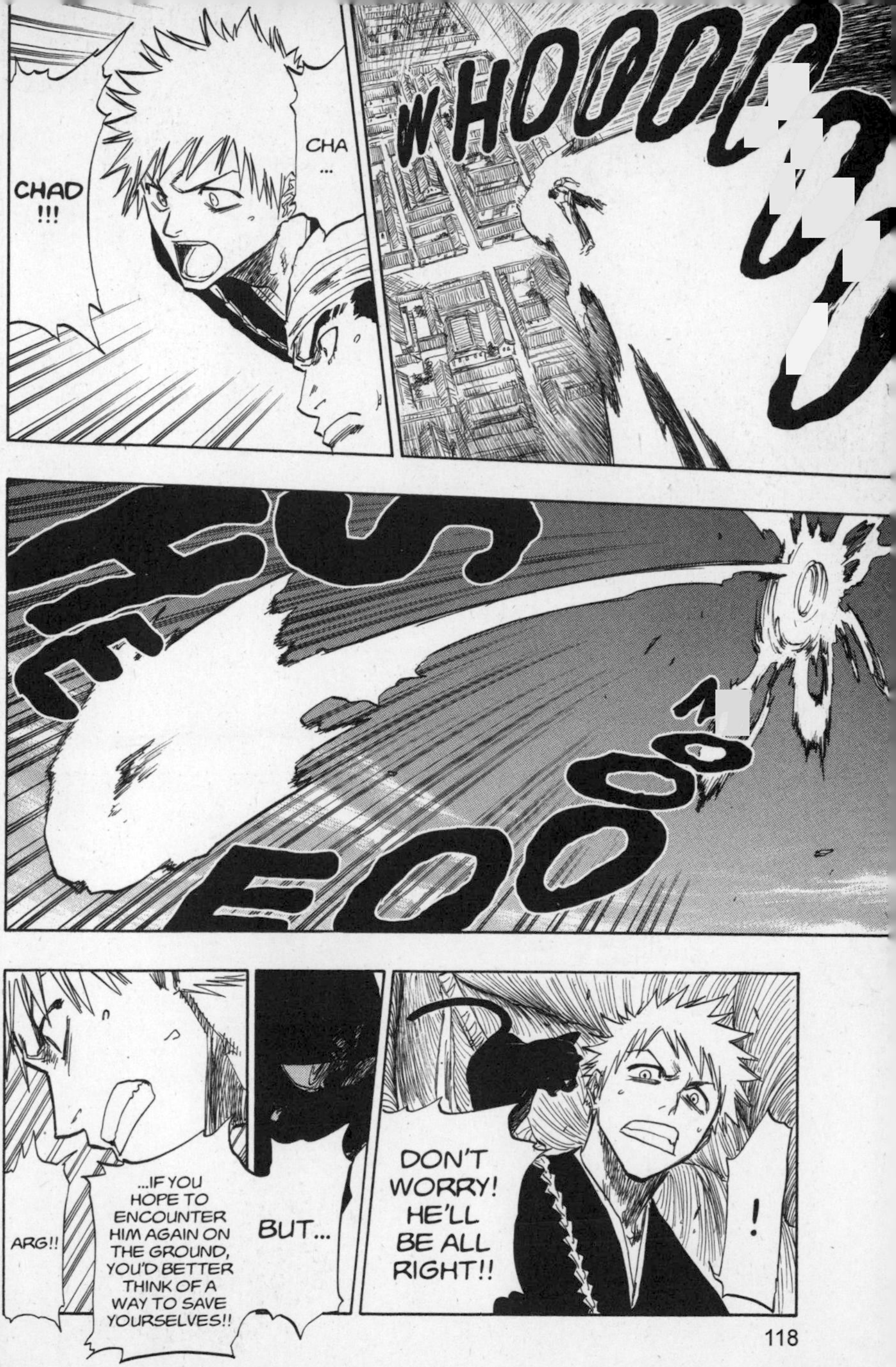
WHOOOO
CHA ...
CHAD !!!
!
DON'T WORRY! HE'LL BE ALL RIGHT!!
BUT...
...IF YOU HOPE TO ENCOUNTER HIM AGAIN ON THE GROUND, YOU'D BETTER THINK OF A WAY TO SAVE YOURSELVES!!
ARG!!

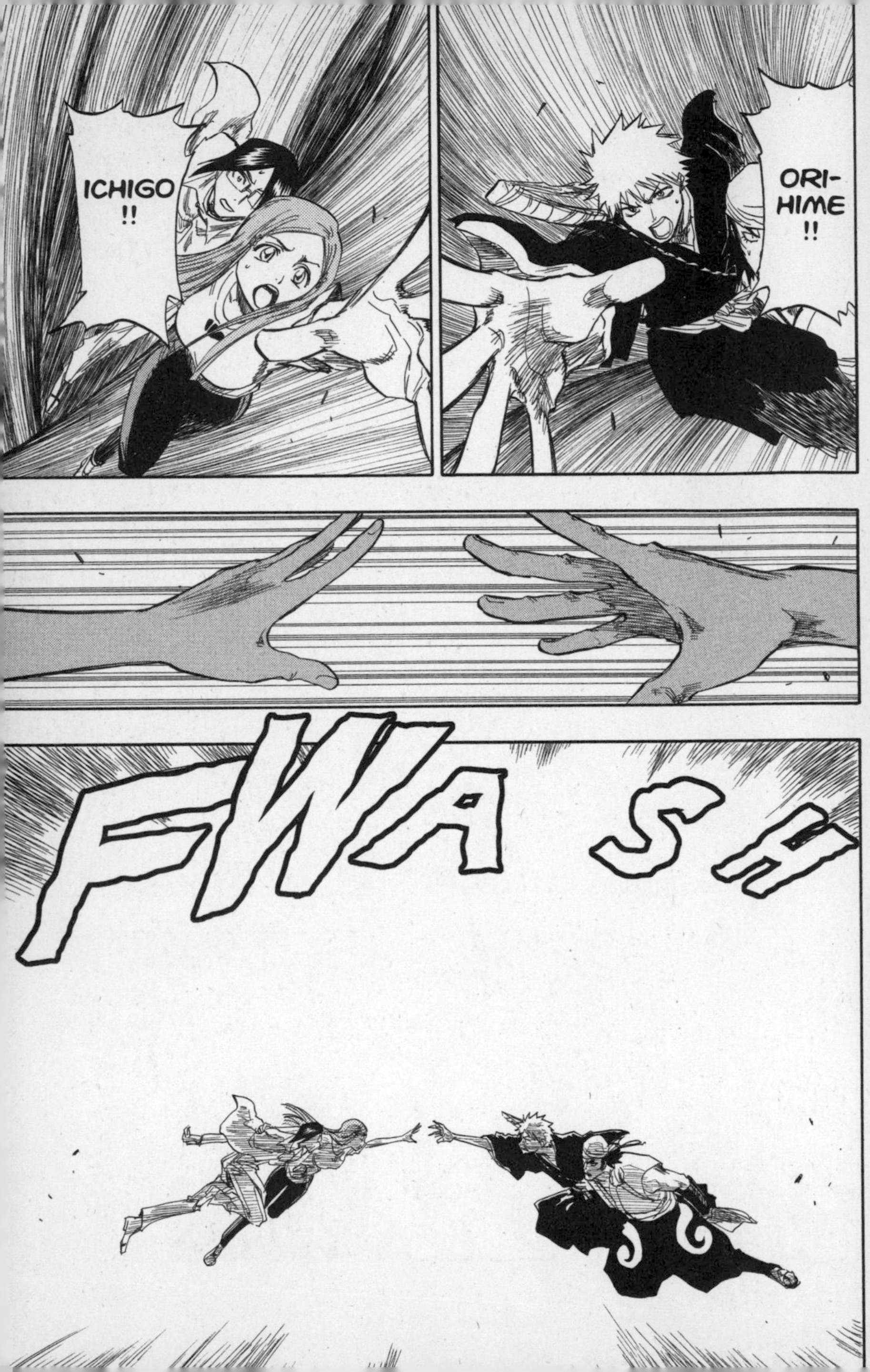
ORI-HIME !!
ICHIGO !!
FWASH

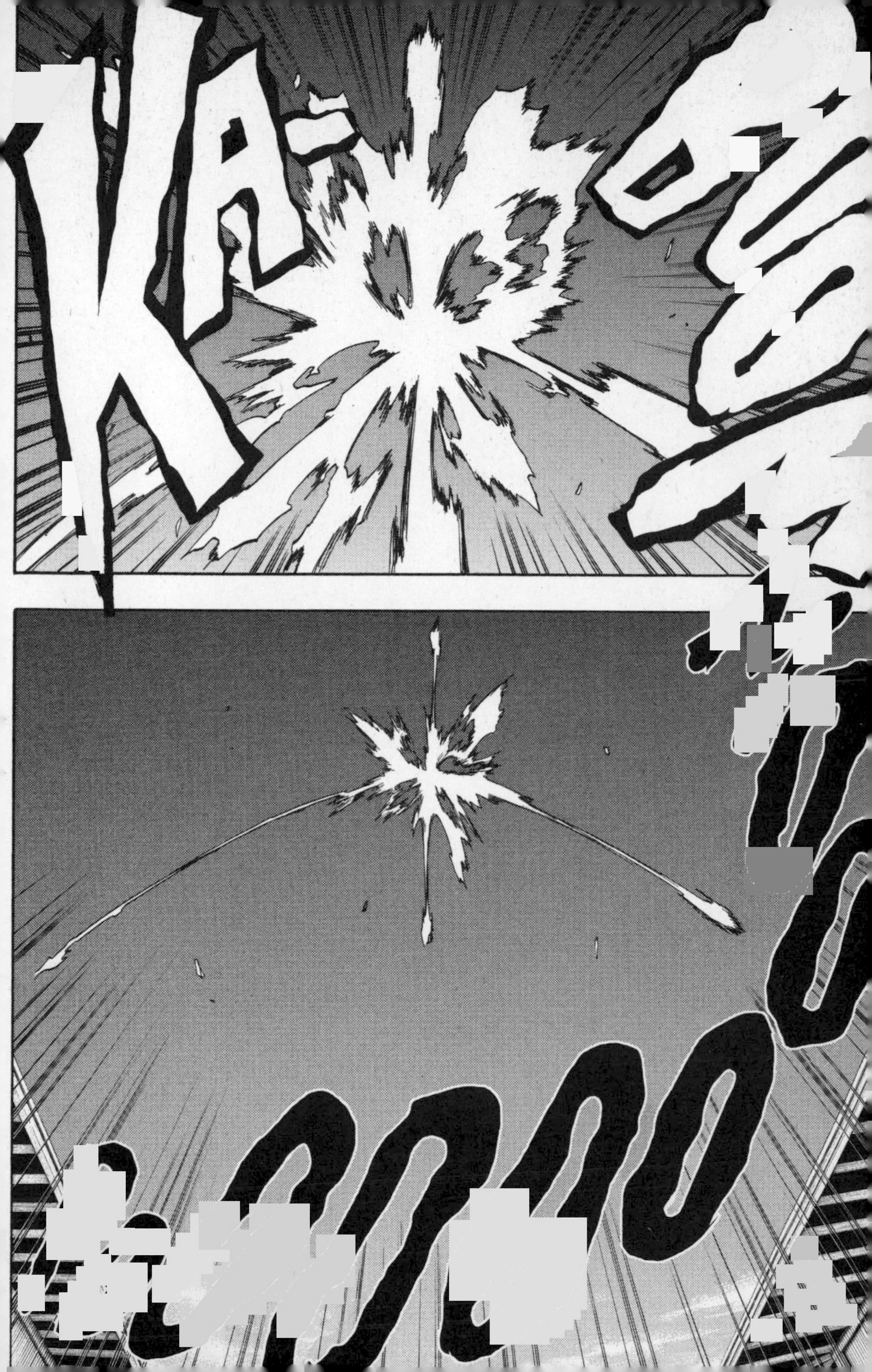

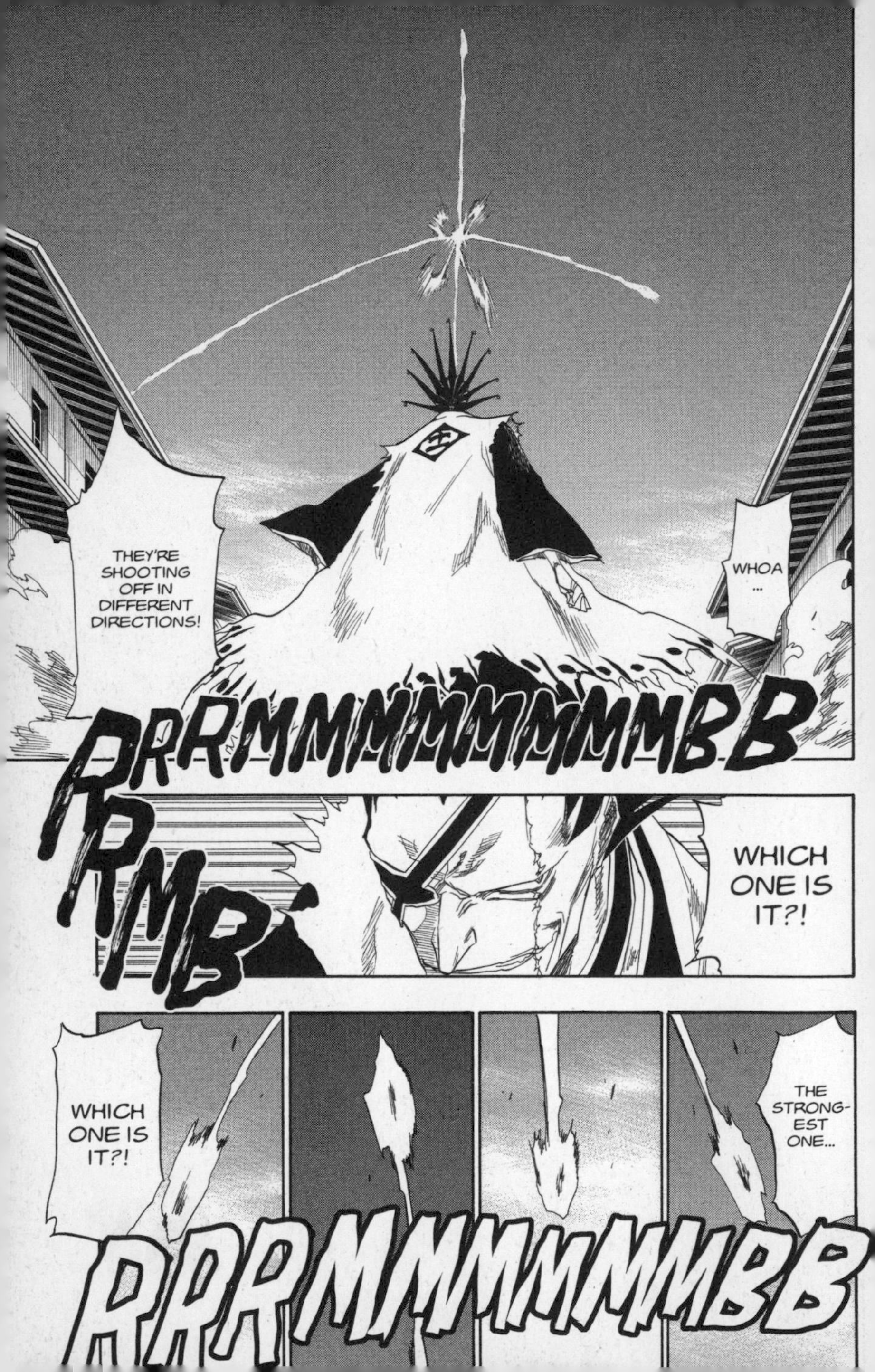
WHOA...
THEY'RE SHOOTING OFF IN DIFFERENT DIRECTIONS!
RRRMMMMMMMMMMBB
RRMB
WHICH ONE IS IT?!
THE STRONGEST ONE...
WHICH ONE IS IT?!
RRRMMMMMMMBB

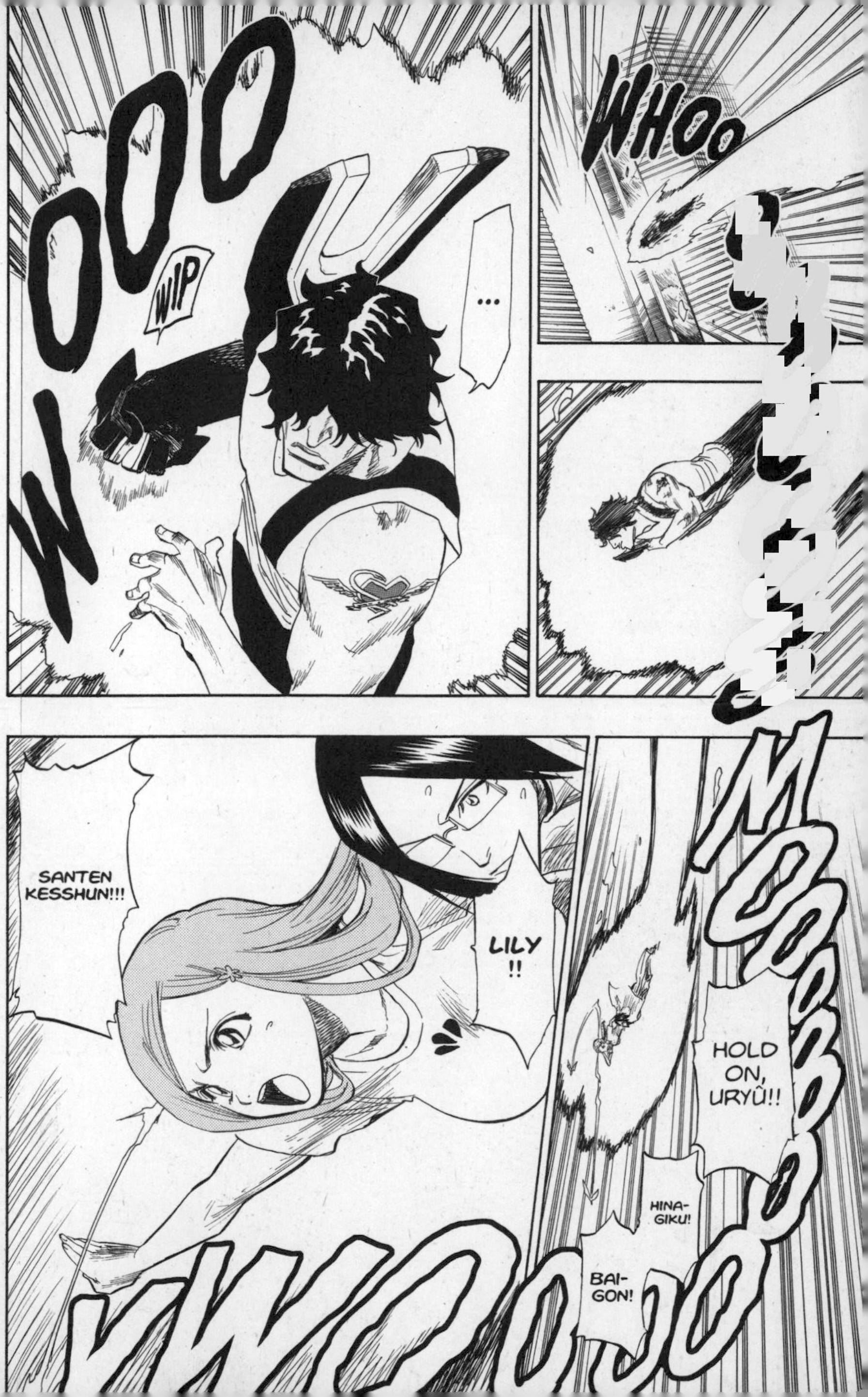
WHOO
WOOOO
WIP
...
HOLD ON, URYÛ!!
HINA-GIKU!
BAI-GON!
LILY !!
SANTEN KESSHUN!!!

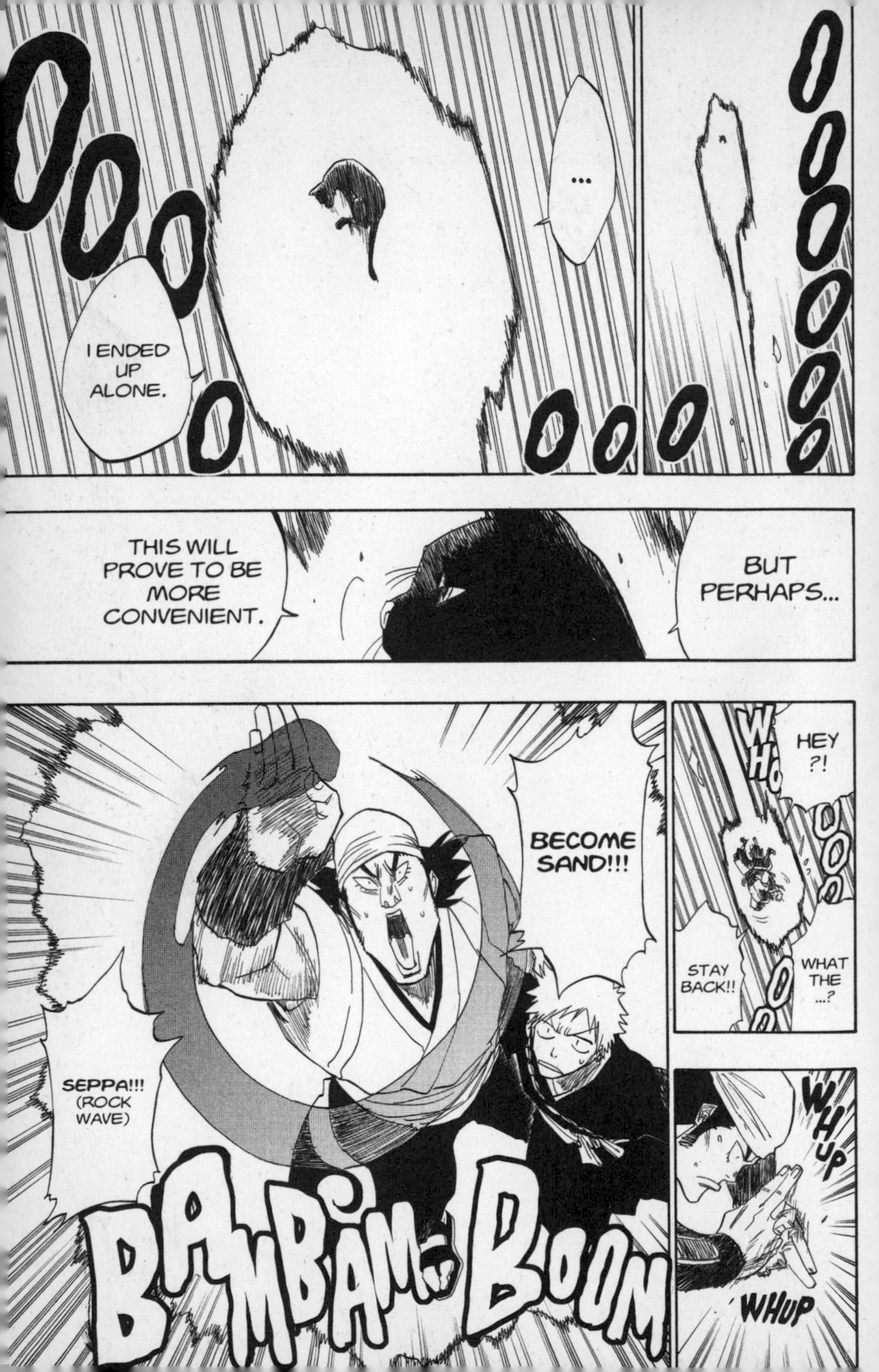

...
I ENDED UP ALONE.
BUT PERHAPS...
THIS WILL PROVE TO BE MORE CONVENIENT.
WHO
HEY ?!
WHAT THE ...?
STAY BACK!!
WHUP
WHUP
BECOME SAND!!!
SEPPA!!! (ROCK WAVE)
BAMBAM-BOOM

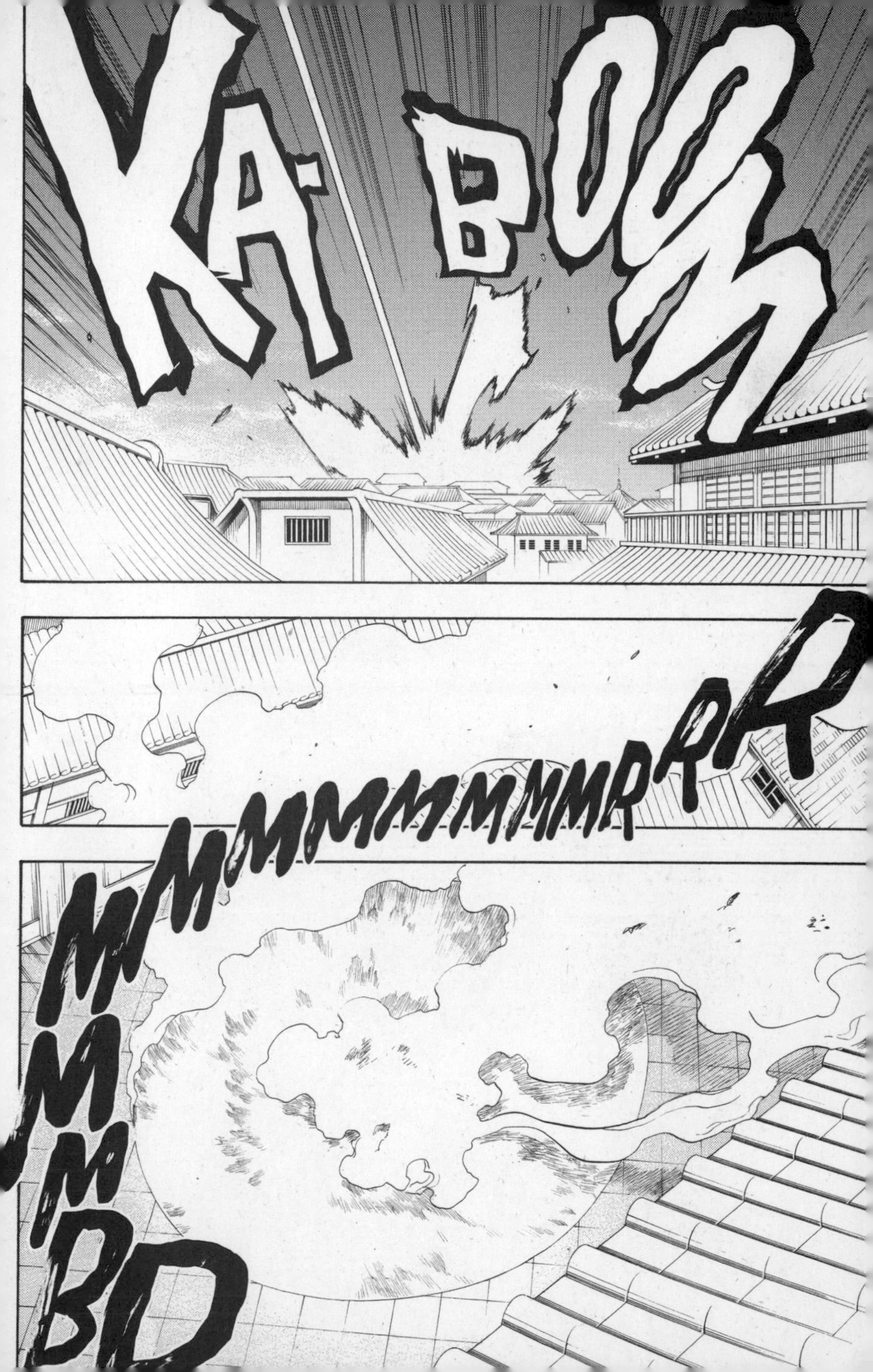
KA-BOOM
BDMMMMMMMMMMMMMMMMRRRRR

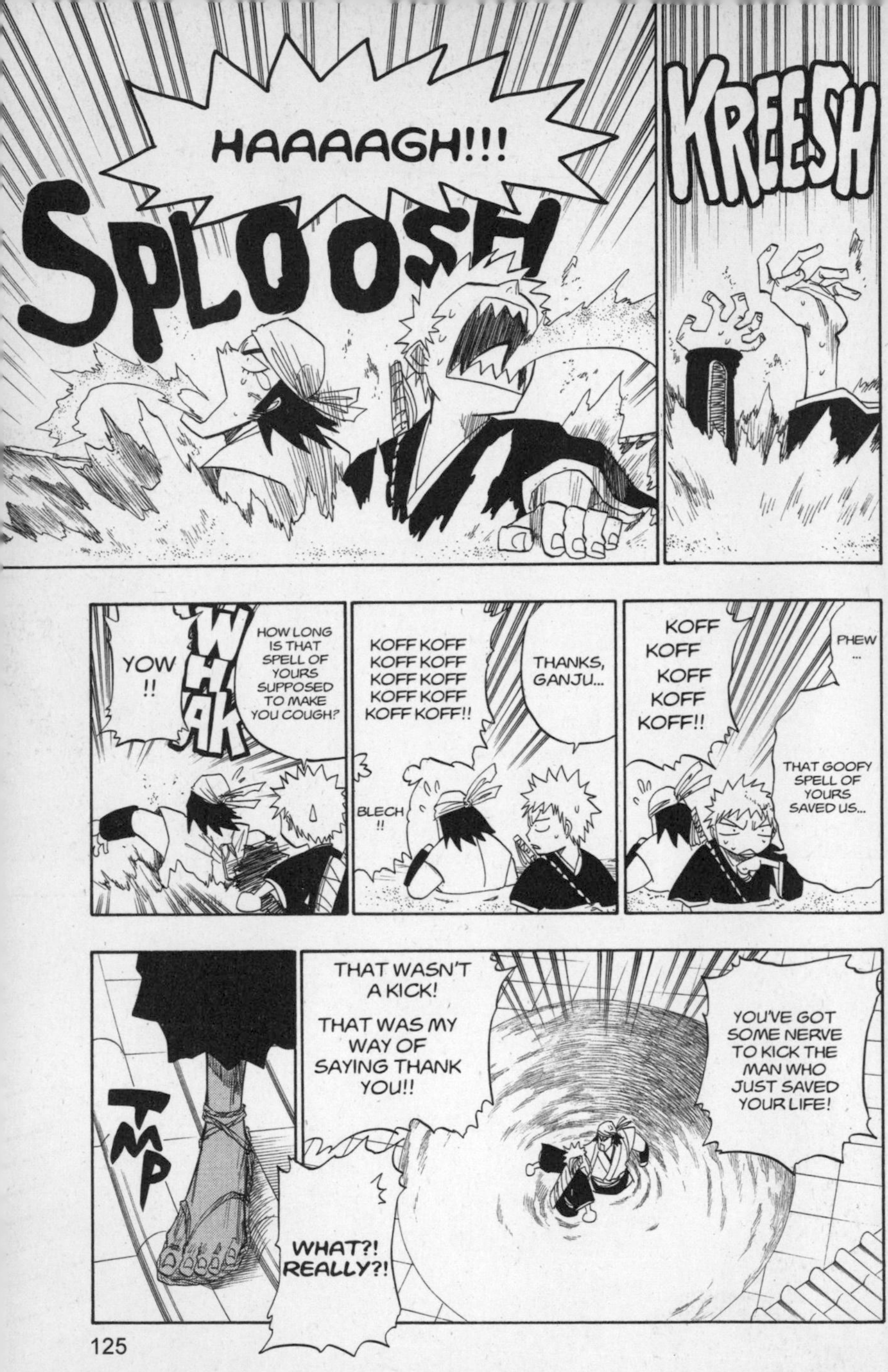
KREESH
HAAAAGH!!!
SPLOOSH
KOFF KOFF KOFF KOFF KOFF!!
PHEW ...
THAT GOOFY SPELL OF YOURS SAVED US...
KOFF KOFF KOFF KOFF KOFF KOFF KOFF KOFF KOFF KOFF!!
THANKS, GANJU...
BLECH !!
HOW LONG IS THAT SPELL OF YOURS SUPPOSED TO MAKE YOU COUGH?
WHAK
YOW !!
YOU'VE GOT SOME NERVE TO KICK THE MAN WHO JUST SAVED YOUR LIFE!
THAT WASN'T A KICK!
THAT WAS MY WAY OF SAYING THANK YOU!!
WHAT?! REALLY?!
TMP

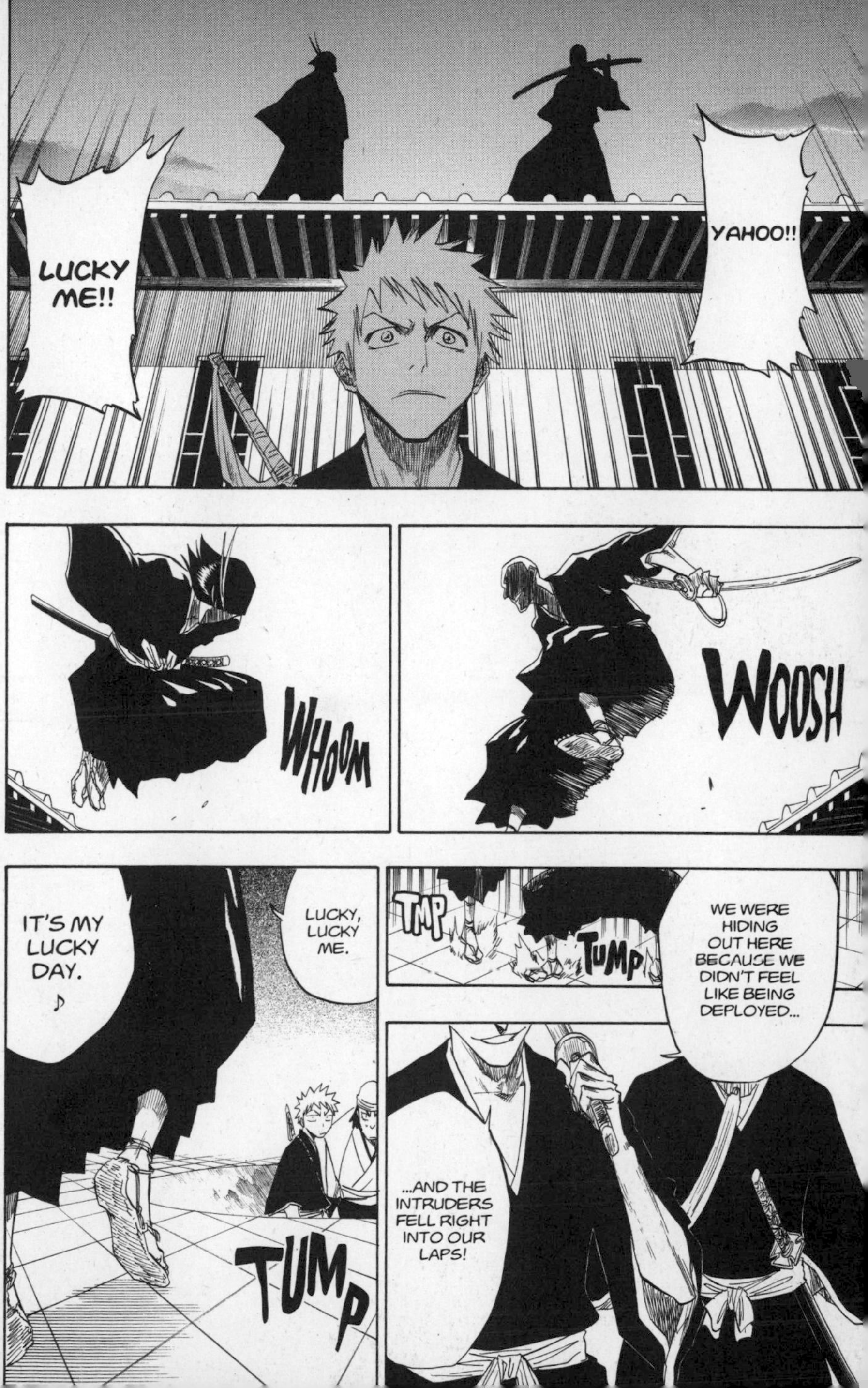
YAHOO!!
LUCKY ME!!
WOOSH
WHOOM
TMP
TUMP
WE WERE HIDING OUT HERE BECAUSE WE DIDN'T FEEL LIKE BEING DEPLOYED...
...AND THE INTRUDERS FELL RIGHT INTO OUR LAPS!
LUCKY, LUCKY ME.
IT'S MY LUCKY DAY. ♪
TUMP

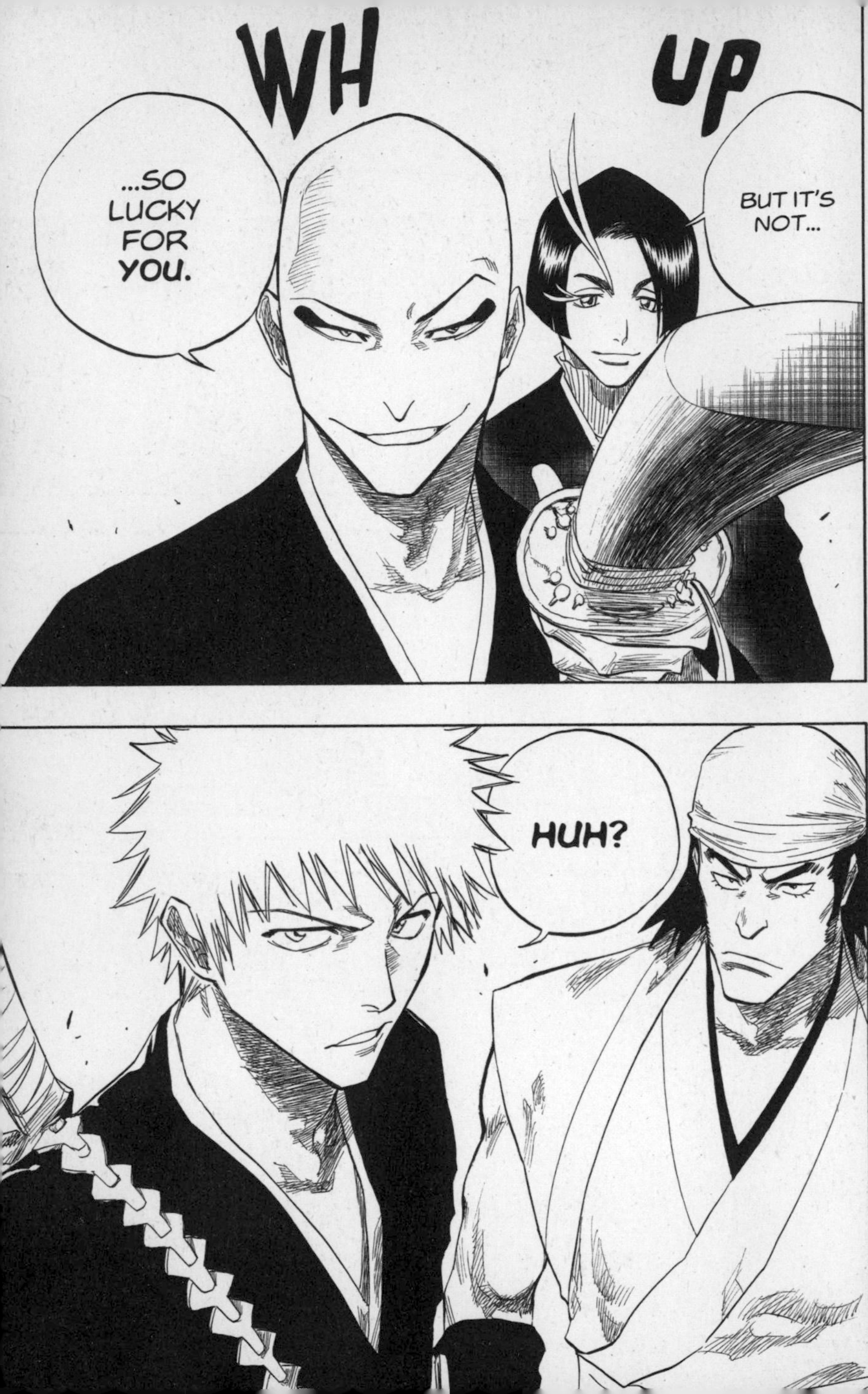
WH UP
BUT IT'S NOT...
...SO LUCKY FOR YOU.
HUH?

HEH HEH... I'D ALREADY DETECTED THE BOY'S SOUL WAVE, SO I KNEW HE WASN'T HOME! BUT RIGHT NOW I'M RECRUITING MEMBERS FOR THE KARAKURA SUPERHEROES, A SPECIAL UNIT THAT WILL PROTECT KARAKURA CITY FROM EVIL SPIRITS WHILE THE BOY IS AWAY!! SINCE YOU COULD SEE THAT THING, THAT MEANS YOU HAVE THE GIFT, SISTER OF THE BOY! SO, WHADDAYA SAY? WILL YOU DEFEND KARAKURA CITY WITH ME?! BY THE WAY, THE THING YOU SAW WAS AN EVIL SPIRIT, CALLED A HOLLOW...

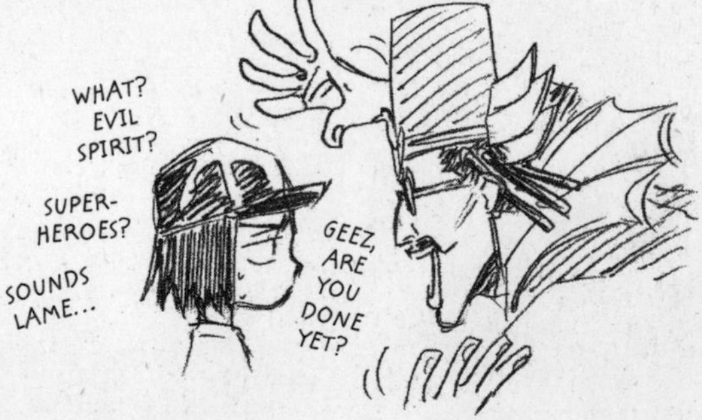
GEEZ, ARE YOU DONE YET?
WHAT? EVIL SPIRIT?
SUPER-HEROES?
SOUNDS LAME...

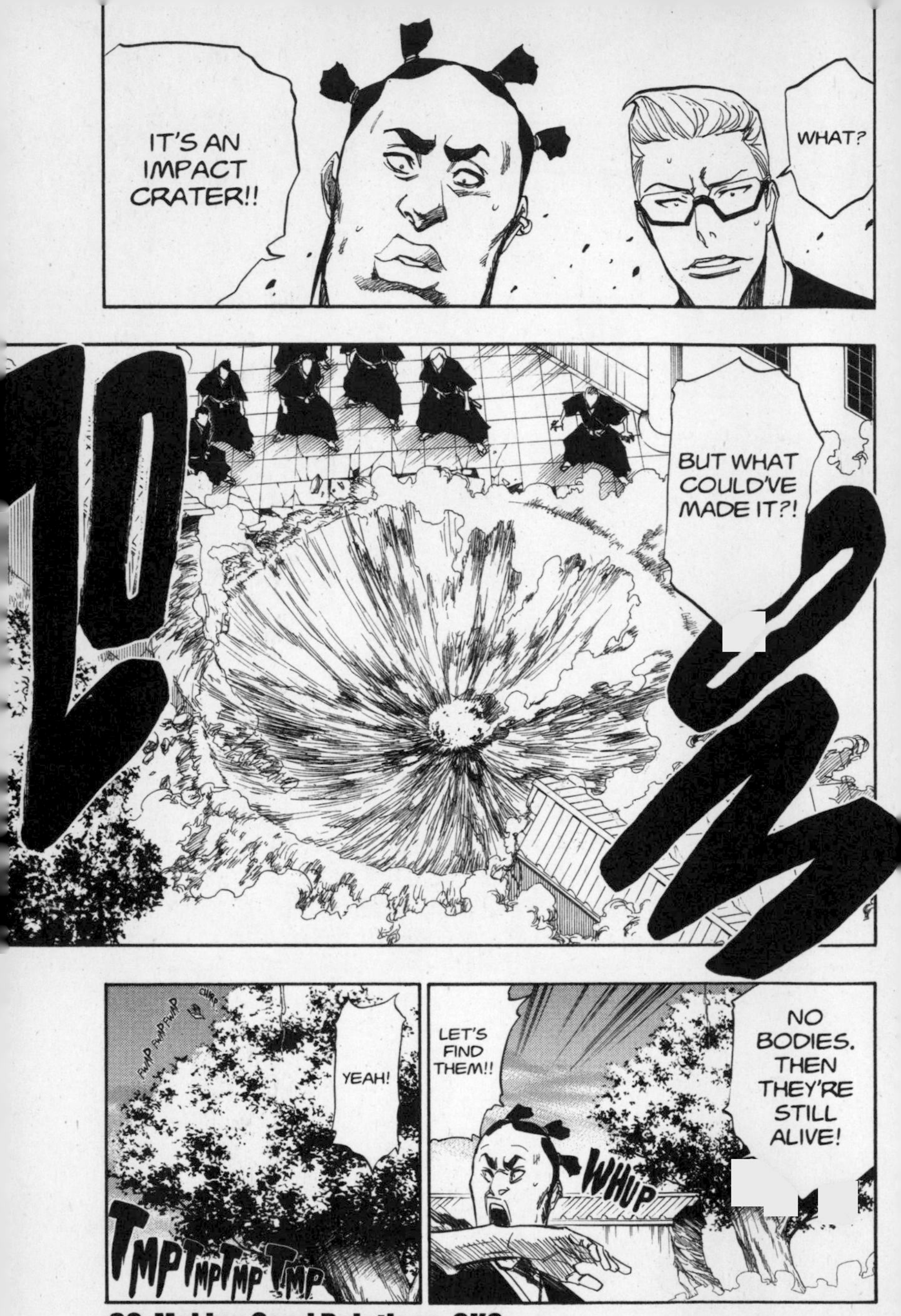
WHAT?
IT'S AN IMPACT CRATER!!
BUT WHAT COULD'VE MADE IT?!
NO BODIES. THEN THEY'RE STILL ALIVE!
WHUP
LET'S FIND THEM!!
YEAH!
TMP TMP TMP TMP

86. Making Good Relations, OK?

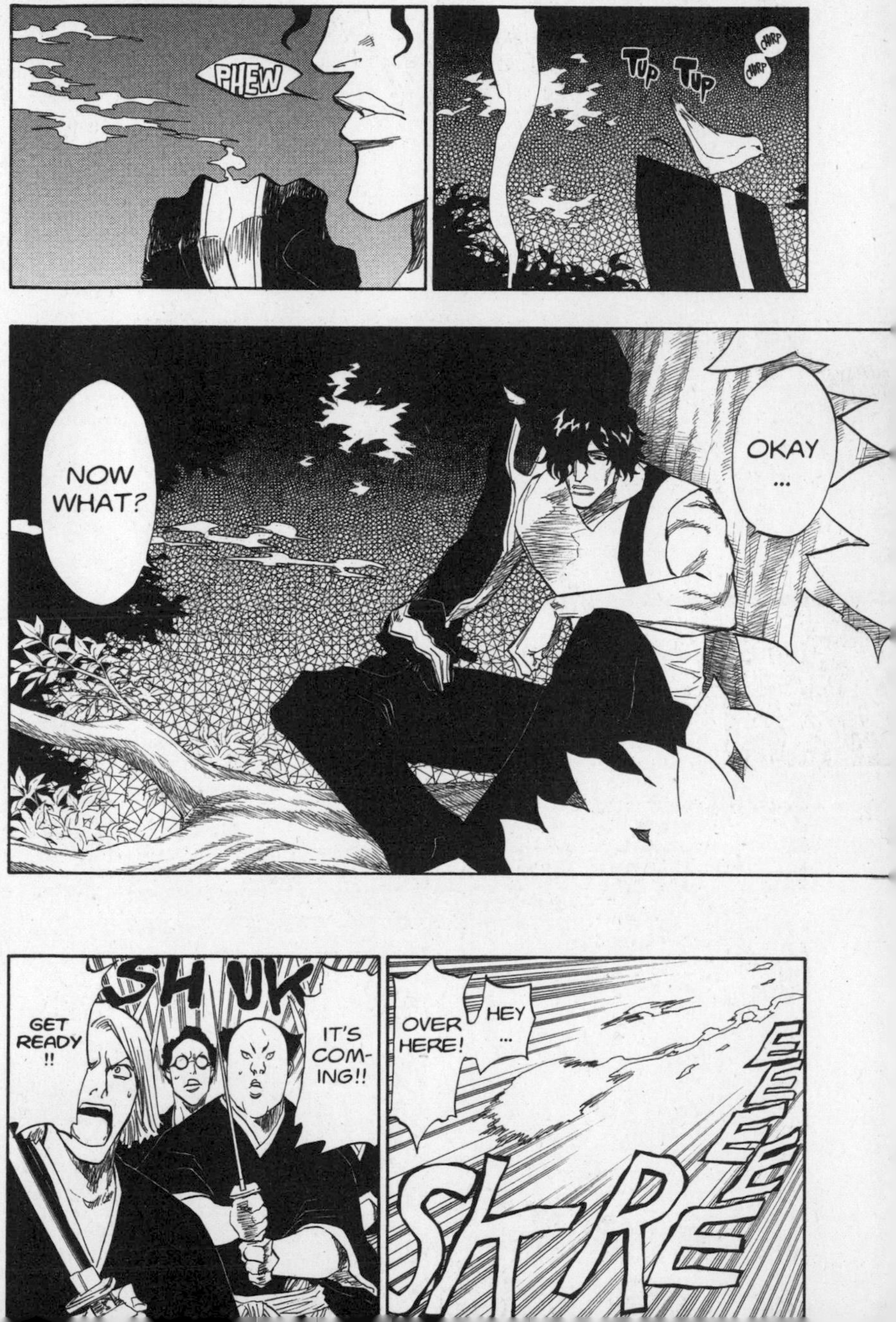
TUP TUP
CHIRP
CHIRP
PHEW
OKAY ...
NOW WHAT?
HEY ...
OVER HERE!
SHTREEEEEE
SHUK
IT'S COMING!!
GET READY!!

READ THIS WAY

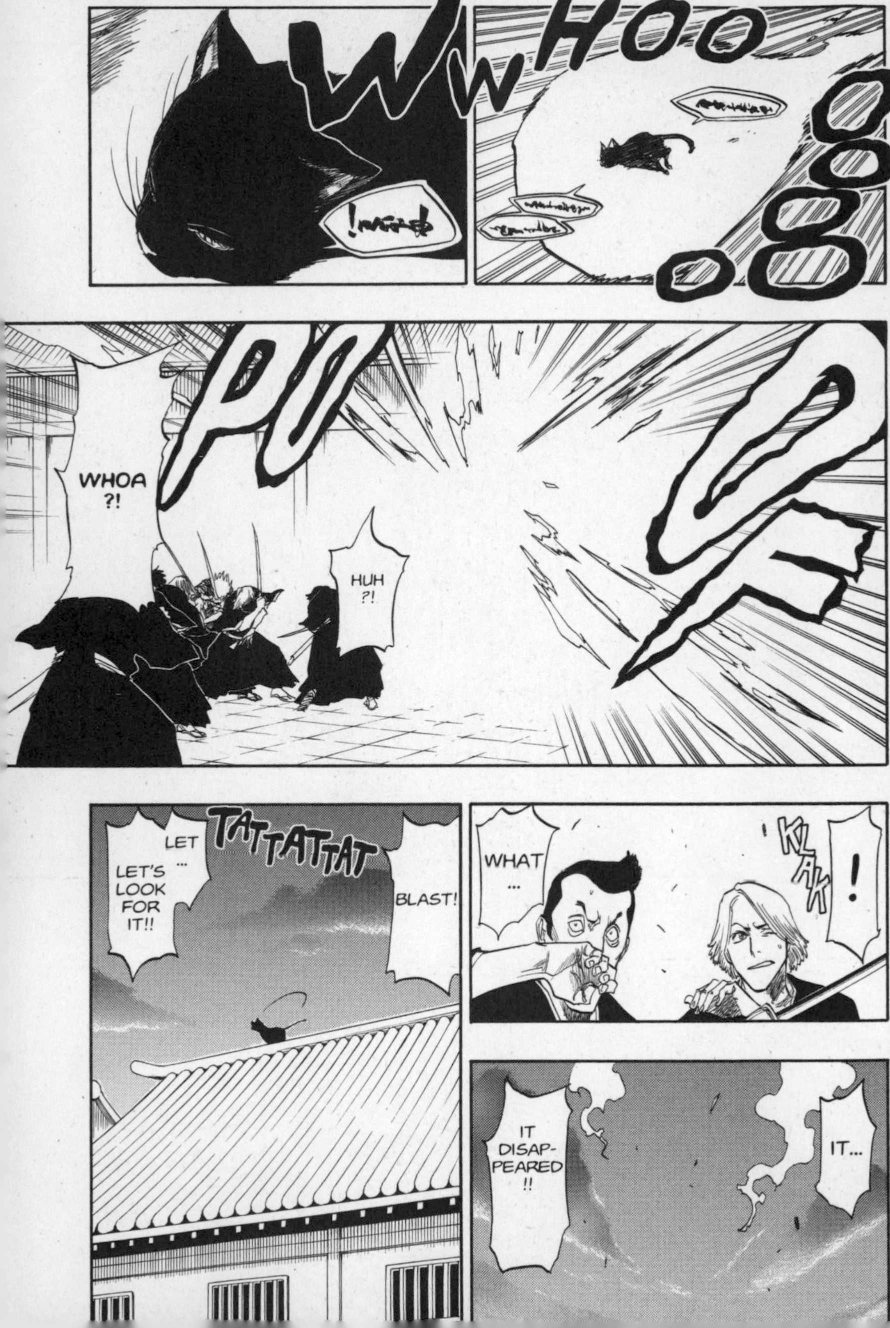
WWHOOOOOOOO
POOF
HUH ?!
WHOA ?!
KLAK
!
WHAT ...
IT...
IT DISAPPEARED!!
BLAST!
TATTATTAT
LET ... LET'S LOOK FOR IT!!

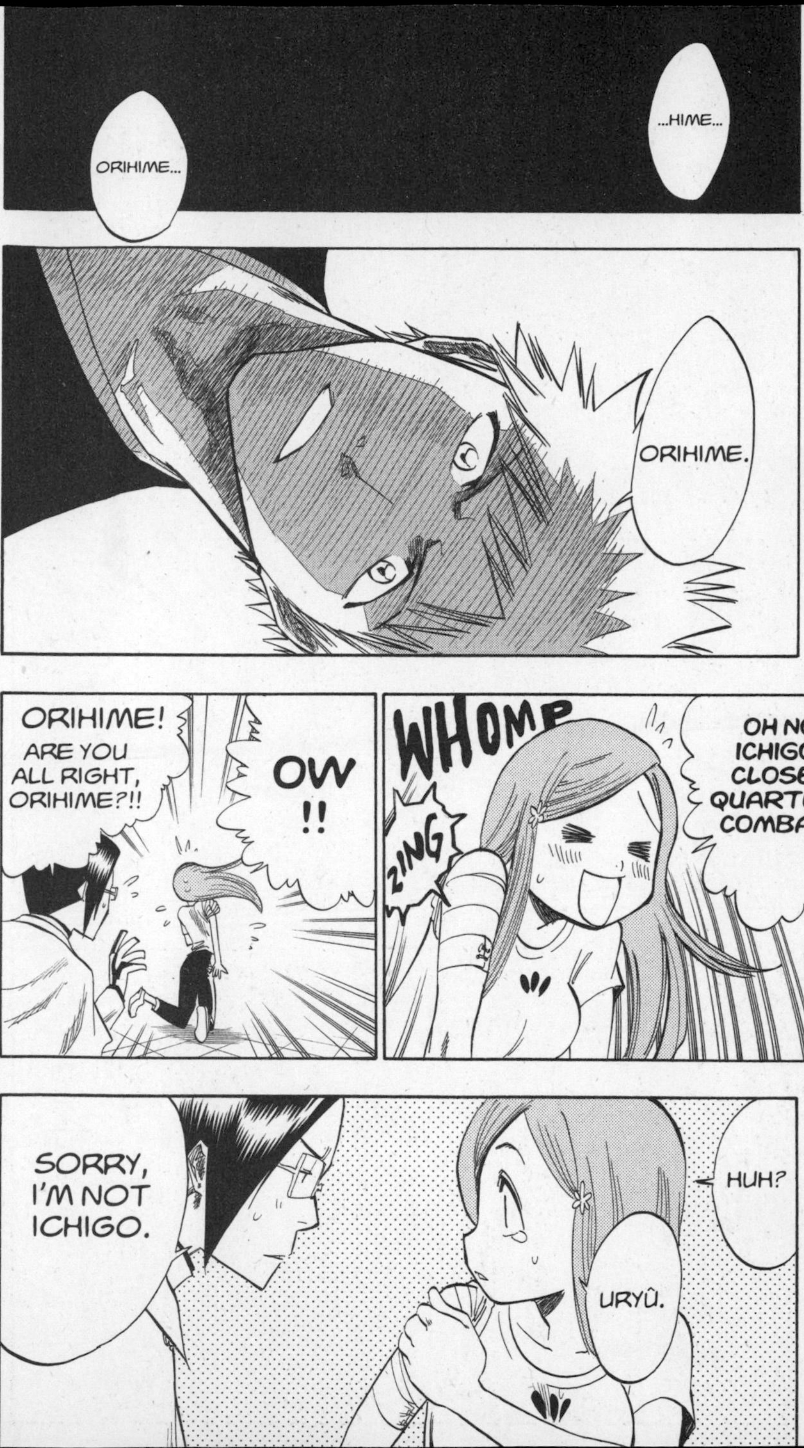
...HIME...
ORIHIME...
ORIHIME.
WHOMP
ZING
OH NO, ICHIGO!! CLOSE-QUARTERS COMBAT!!
OW !!
ORIHIME! ARE YOU ALL RIGHT, ORIHIME?!!
HUH?
URYÛ.
SORRY, I'M NOT ICHIGO.

READ THIS WAY

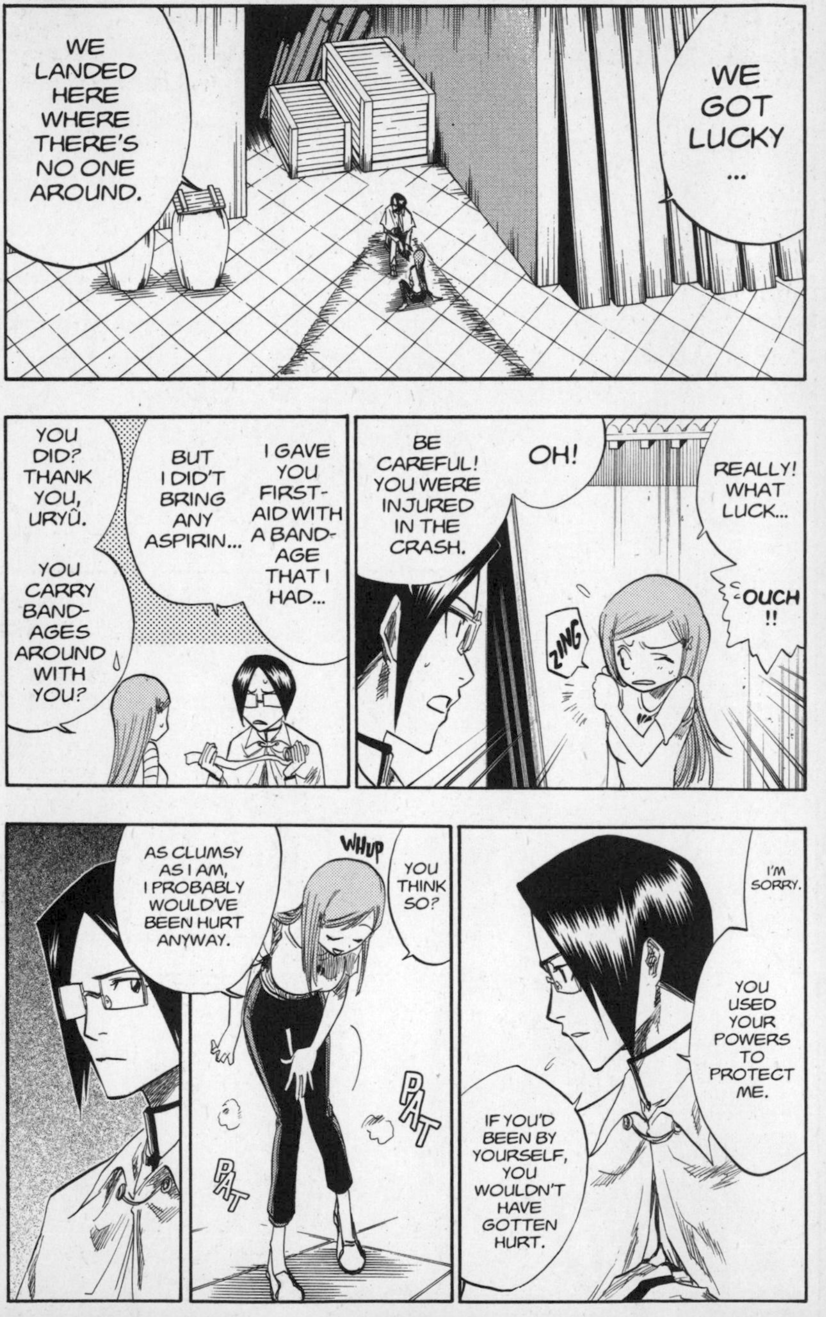
WE GOT LUCKY ...
WE LANDED HERE WHERE THERE'S NO ONE AROUND.
REALLY! WHAT LUCK...
OUCH!!
ZING
OH!
BE CAREFUL! YOU WERE INJURED IN THE CRASH.
I GAVE YOU FIRST-AID WITH A BANDAGE THAT I HAD...
BUT I DIDN'T BRING ANY ASPIRIN...
YOU DID? THANK YOU, URYŪ.
YOU CARRY BANDAGES AROUND WITH YOU?
I'M SORRY.
YOU USED YOUR POWERS TO PROTECT ME.
IF YOU'D BEEN BY YOURSELF, YOU WOULDN'T HAVE GOTTEN HURT.
WHUP
YOU THINK SO?
AS CLUMSY AS I AM, I PROBABLY WOULD'VE BEEN HURT ANYWAY.
PAT
PAT

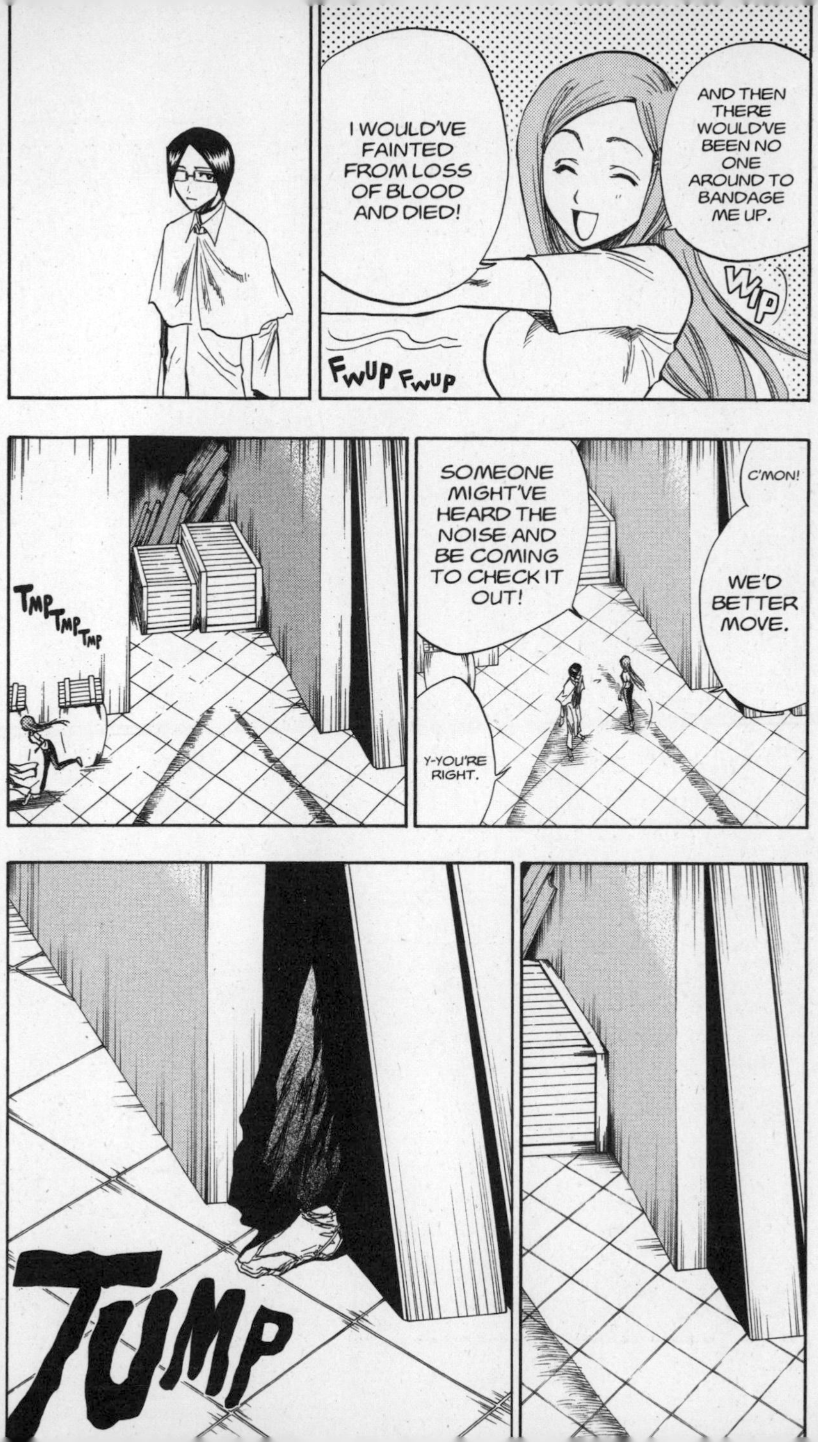
AND THEN THERE WOULD'VE BEEN NO ONE AROUND TO BANDAGE ME UP.
I WOULD'VE FAINTED FROM LOSS OF BLOOD AND DIED!
WIP
FWUP FWUP
C'MON!
WE'D BETTER MOVE.
SOMEONE MIGHT'VE HEARD THE NOISE AND BE COMING TO CHECK IT OUT!
Y-YOU'RE RIGHT.
TMP TMP TMP
TUMP

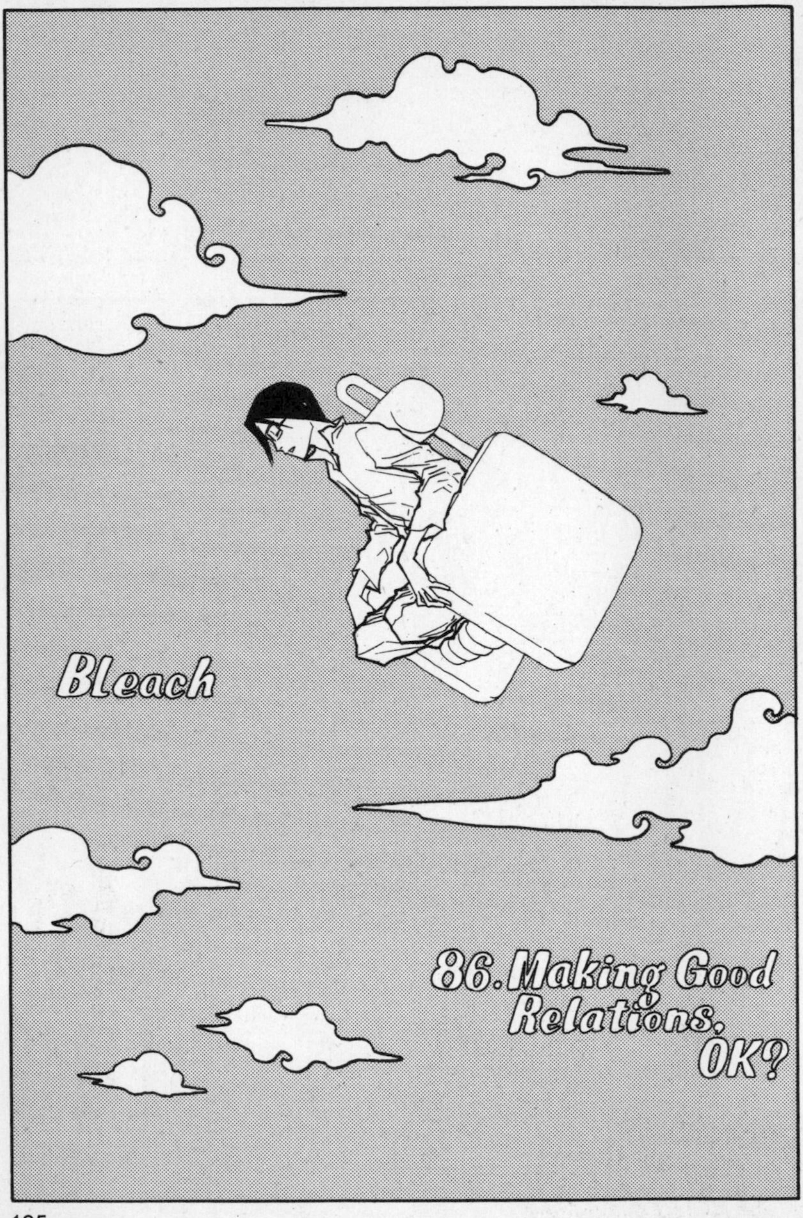
Bleach
86. Making Good Relations, OK?

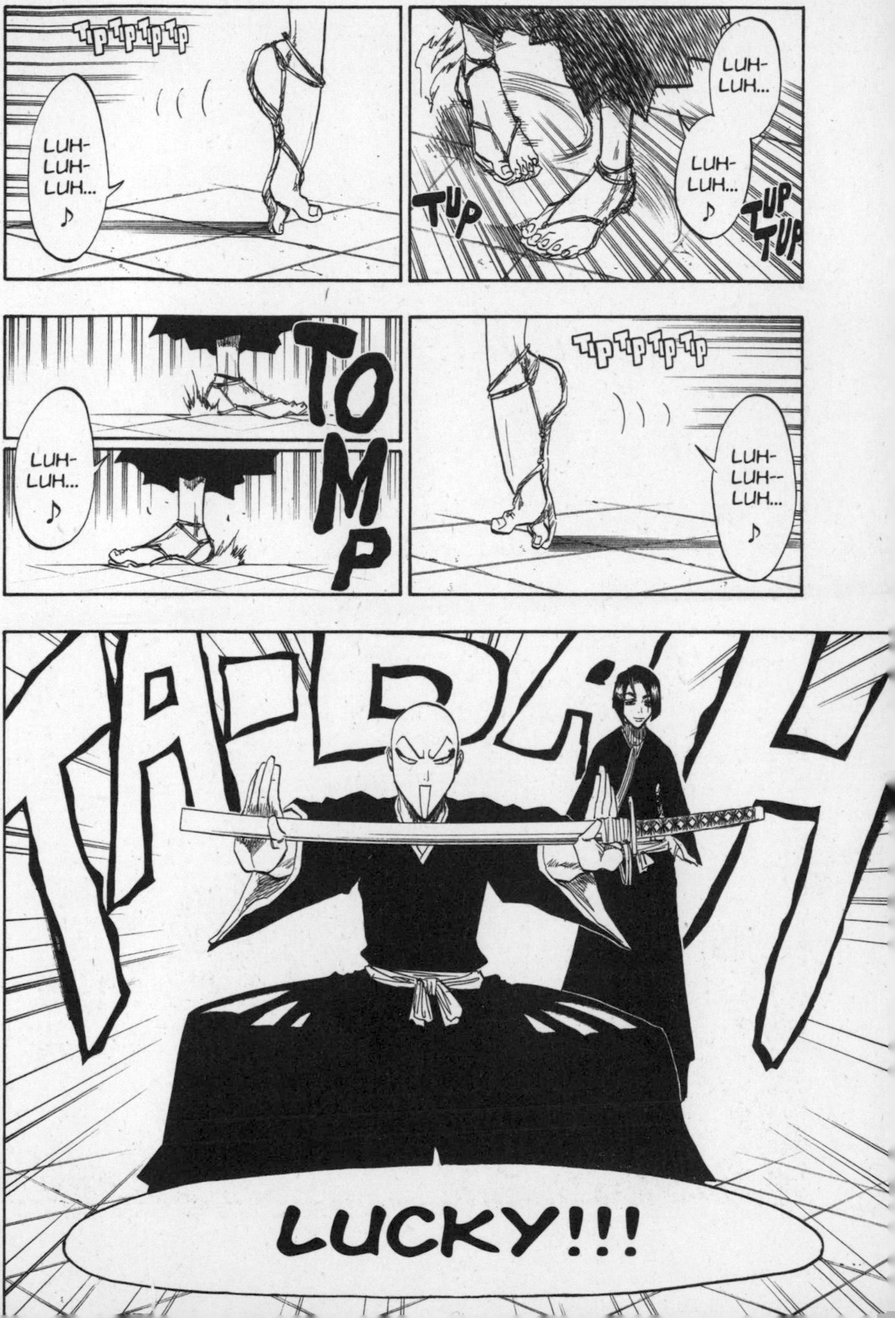
LUH-LUH...
LUH-LUH... ♪
TUP TUP
TUP
TIPTIPTIPTIP
LUH-LUH-LUH... ♪
TIPTIPTIPTIP
LUH-LUH--LUH... ♪
TOMP
LUH-LUH... ♪
LUCKY!!!

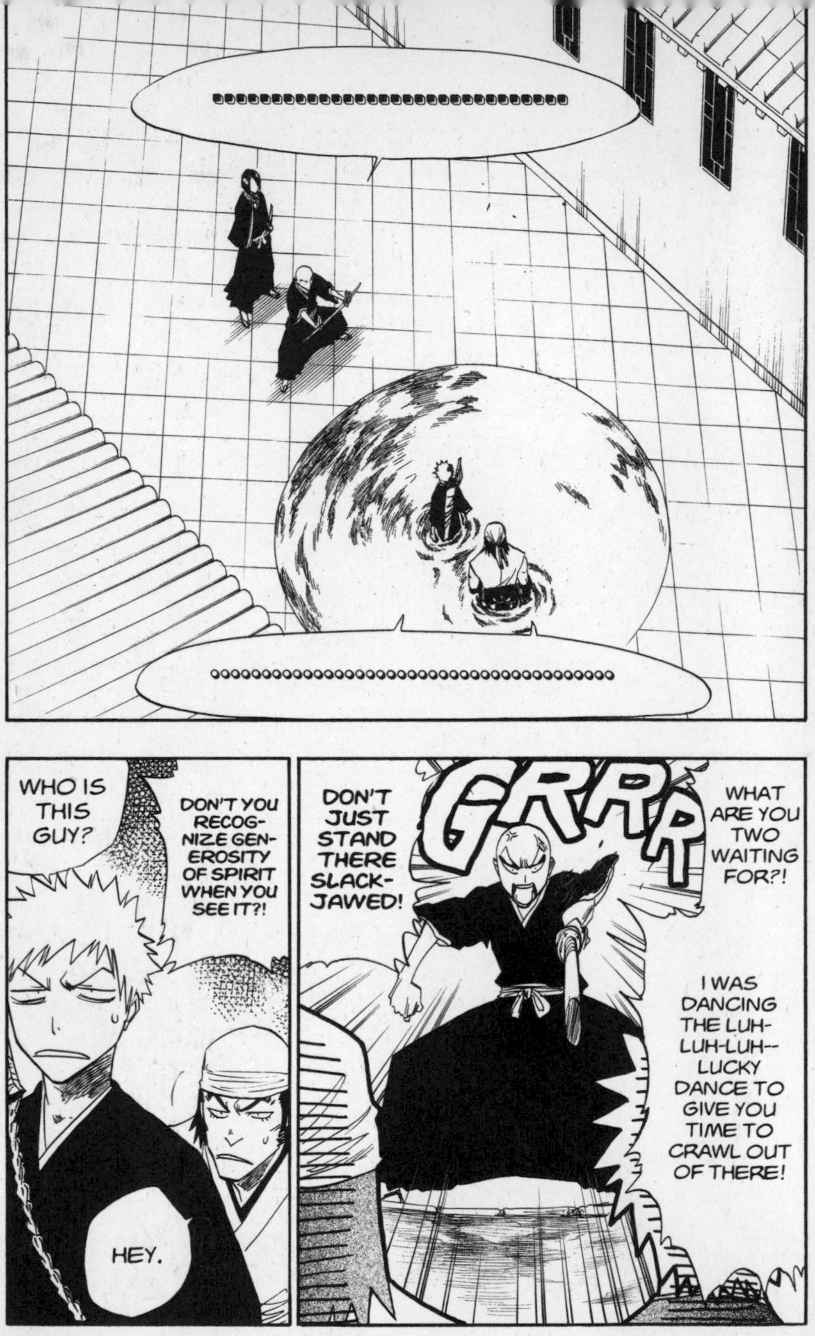
GRRR
WHAT ARE YOU TWO WAITING FOR?!
I WAS DANCING THE LUH-LUH-LUH--LUCKY DANCE TO GIVE YOU TIME TO CRAWL OUT OF THERE!
DON'T JUST STAND THERE SLACK-JAWED!
DON'T YOU RECOG-NIZE GEN-EROSITY OF SPIRIT WHEN YOU SEE IT?!
WHO IS THIS GUY?
HEY.

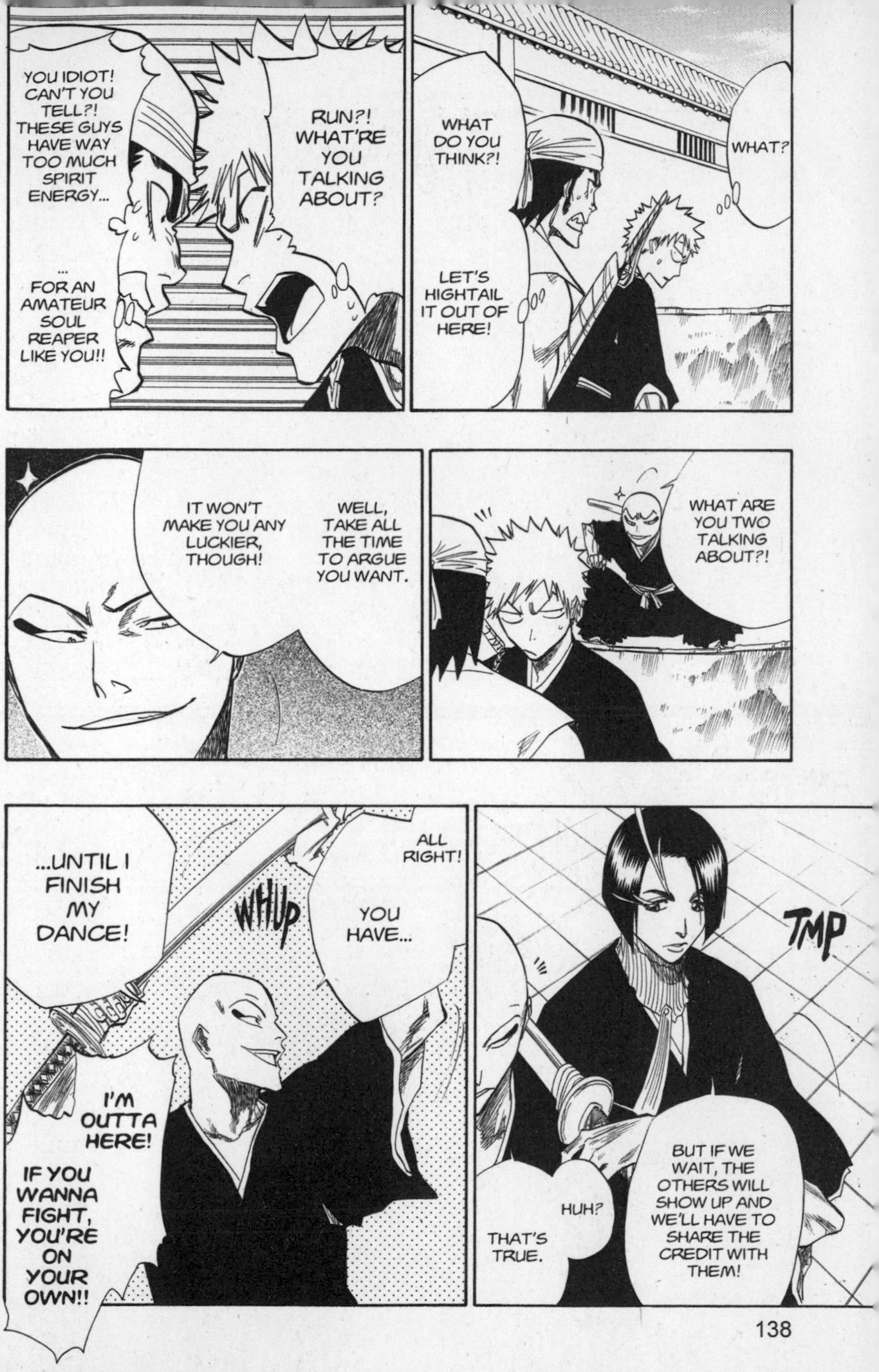
WHAT?
WHAT DO YOU THINK?!
LET'S HIGHTAIL IT OUT OF HERE!
RUN?! WHAT'RE YOU TALKING ABOUT?
YOU IDIOT! CAN'T YOU TELL?! THESE GUYS HAVE WAY TOO MUCH SPIRIT ENERGY...
...FOR AN AMATEUR SOUL REAPER LIKE YOU!!
WHAT ARE YOU TWO TALKING ABOUT?!
WELL, TAKE ALL THE TIME TO ARGUE YOU WANT.
IT WON'T MAKE YOU ANY LUCKIER, THOUGH!
TMP
BUT IF WE WAIT, THE OTHERS WILL SHOW UP AND WE'LL HAVE TO SHARE THE CREDIT WITH THEM!
HUH?
THAT'S TRUE.
ALL RIGHT!
YOU HAVE...
...UNTIL I FINISH MY DANCE!
WHUP
I'M OUTTA HERE!
IF YOU WANNA FIGHT, YOU'RE ON YOUR OWN!!

READ THIS WAY

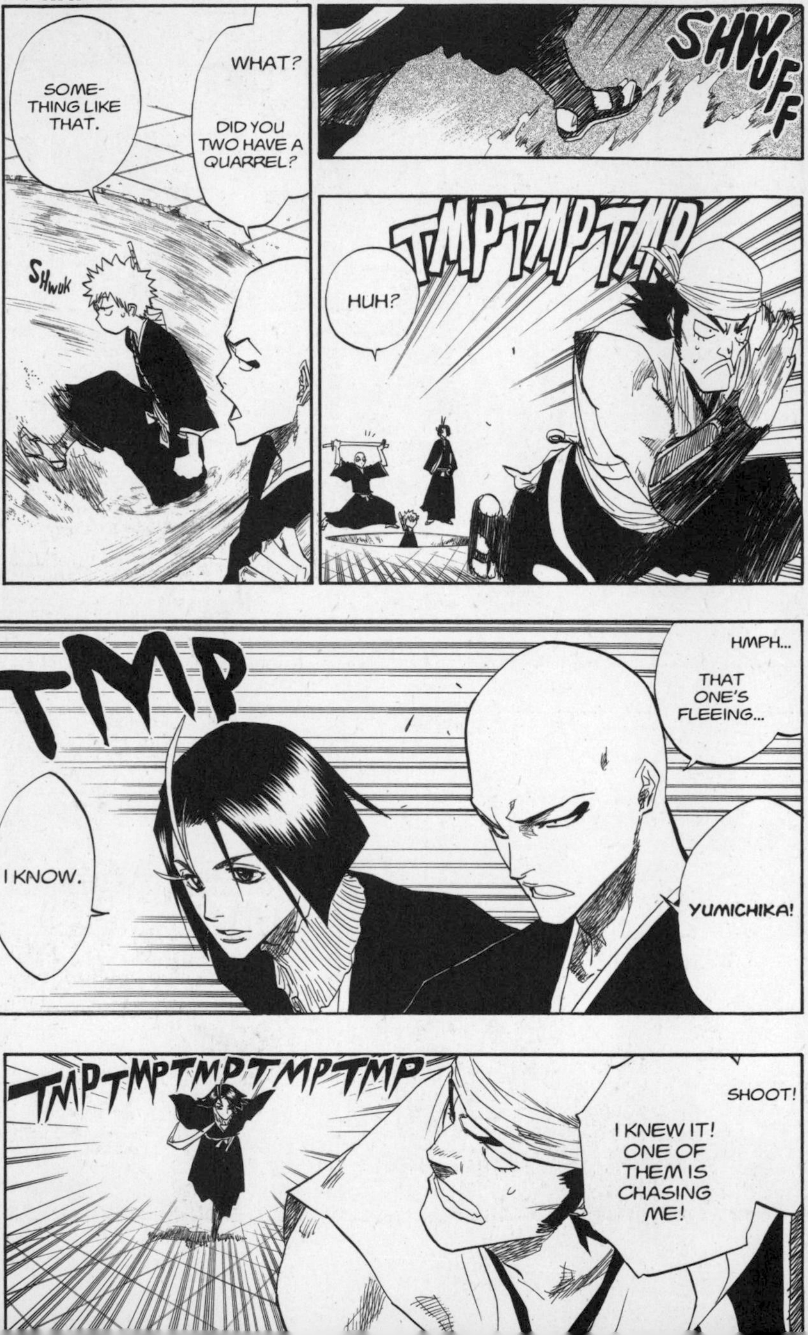
SHWUFF
TMPTMPTMP
HUH?
WHAT?
DID YOU TWO HAVE A QUARREL?
SOME-THING LIKE THAT.
SHWUK
HMPH...
THAT ONE'S FLEEING...
YUMICHIKA!
TMP
I KNOW.
SHOOT!
I KNEW IT! ONE OF THEM IS CHASING ME!
TMPTMPTMPTMPTMP

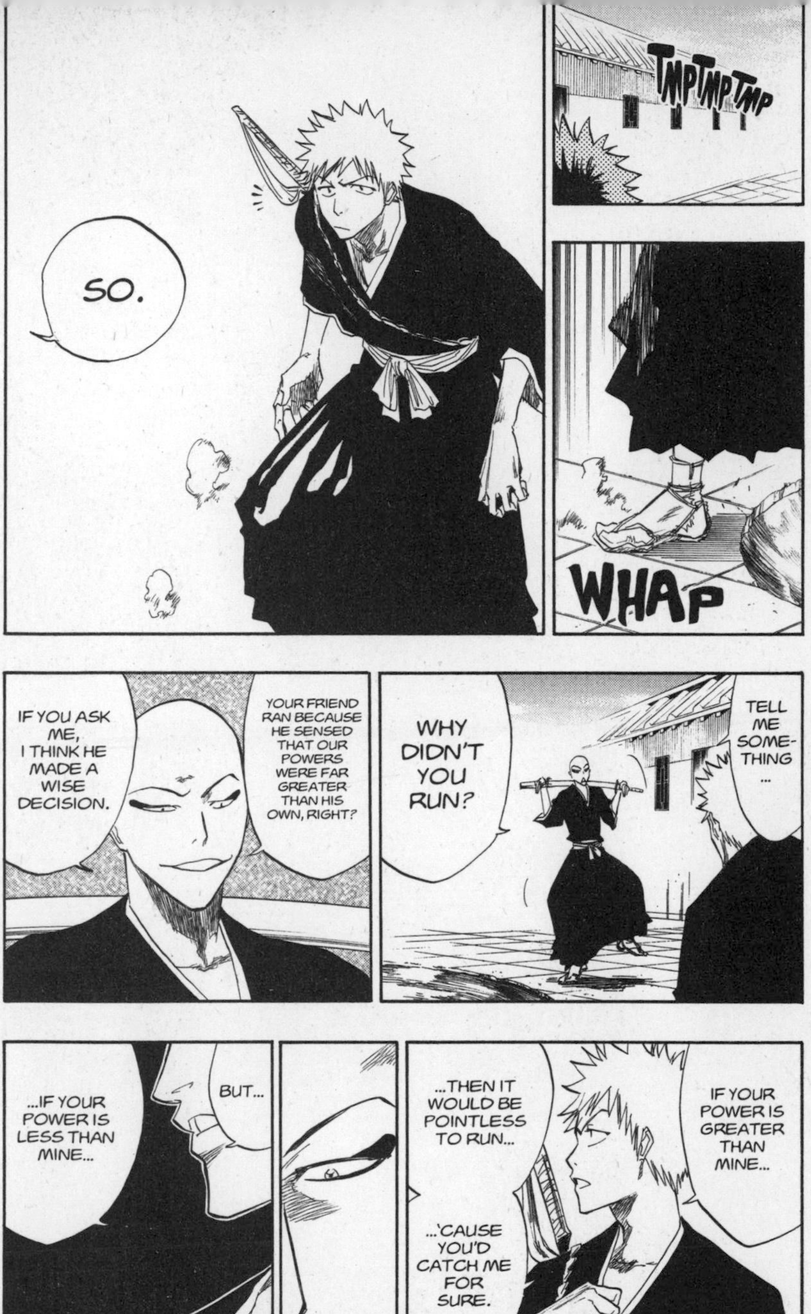
TMPTMPTMP
WHAP
SO.
TELL ME SOME-THING ...
WHY DIDN'T YOU RUN?
YOUR FRIEND RAN BECAUSE HE SENSED THAT OUR POWERS WERE FAR GREATER THAN HIS OWN, RIGHT?
IF YOU ASK ME, I THINK HE MADE A WISE DECISION.
IF YOUR POWER IS GREATER THAN MINE...
...THEN IT WOULD BE POINTLESS TO RUN...
...'CAUSE YOU'D CATCH ME FOR SURE.
BUT...
...IF YOUR POWER IS LESS THAN MINE...

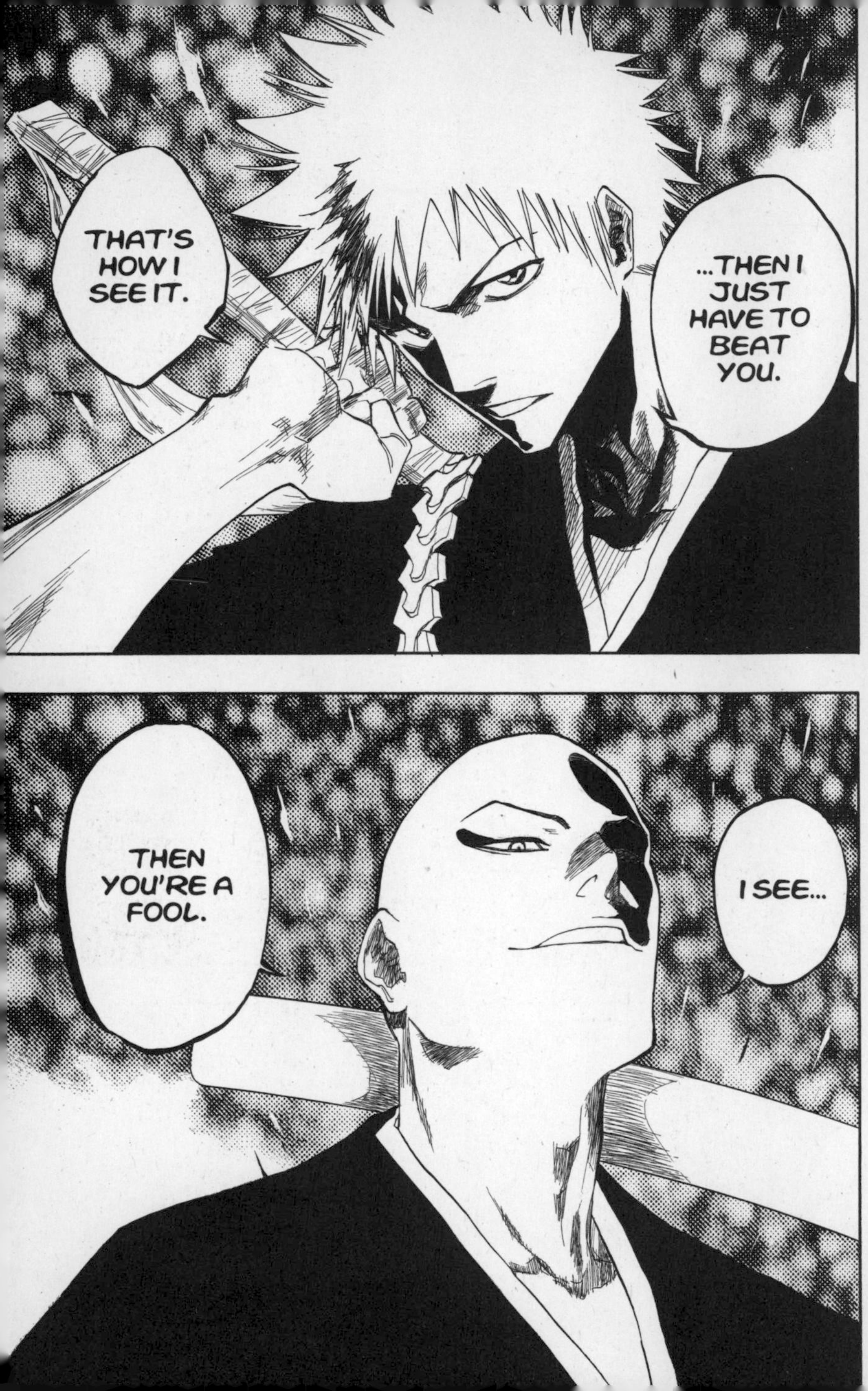
...THEN I JUST HAVE TO BEAT YOU.
THAT'S HOW I SEE IT.
I SEE...
THEN YOU'RE A FOOL.

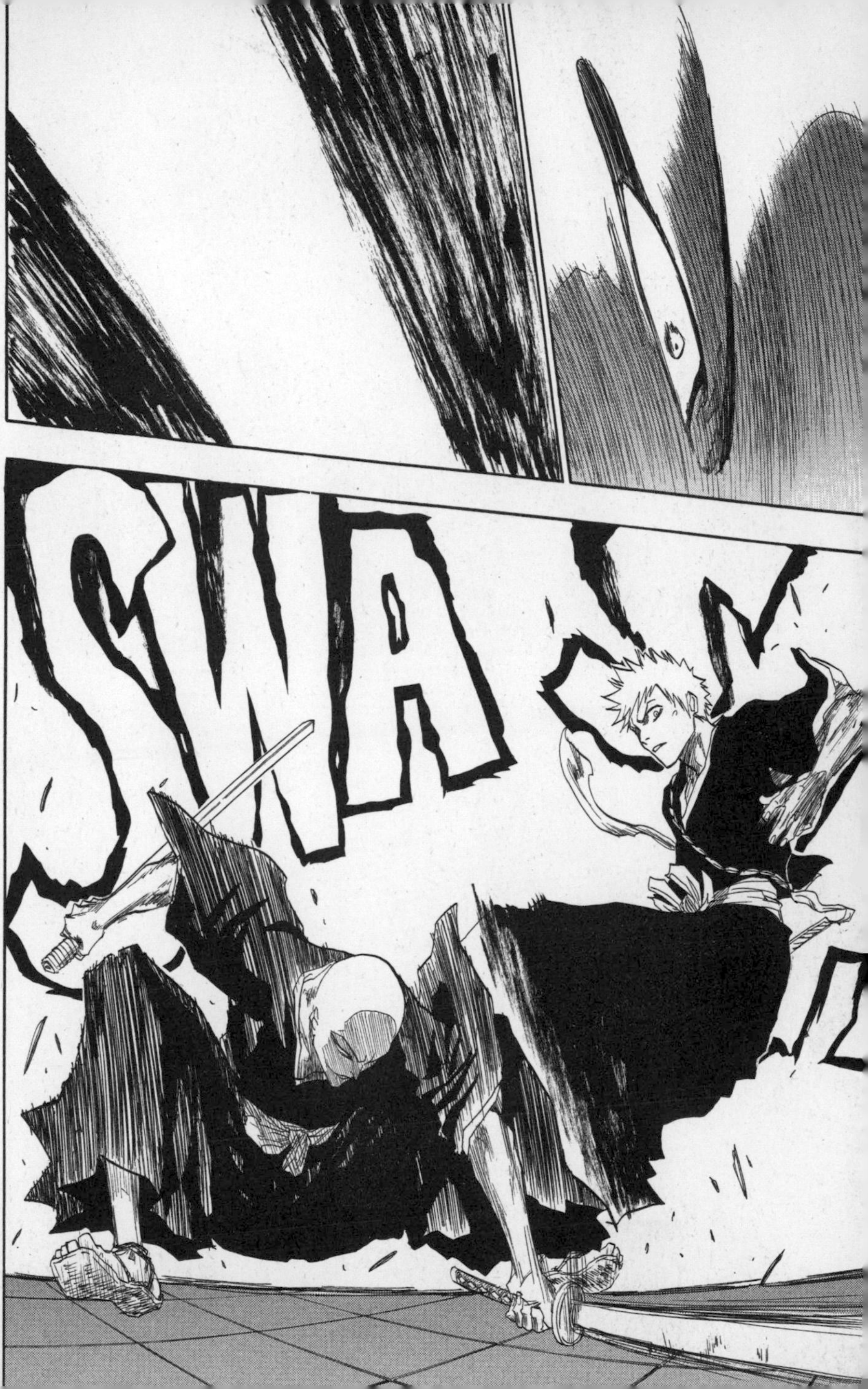
SWA

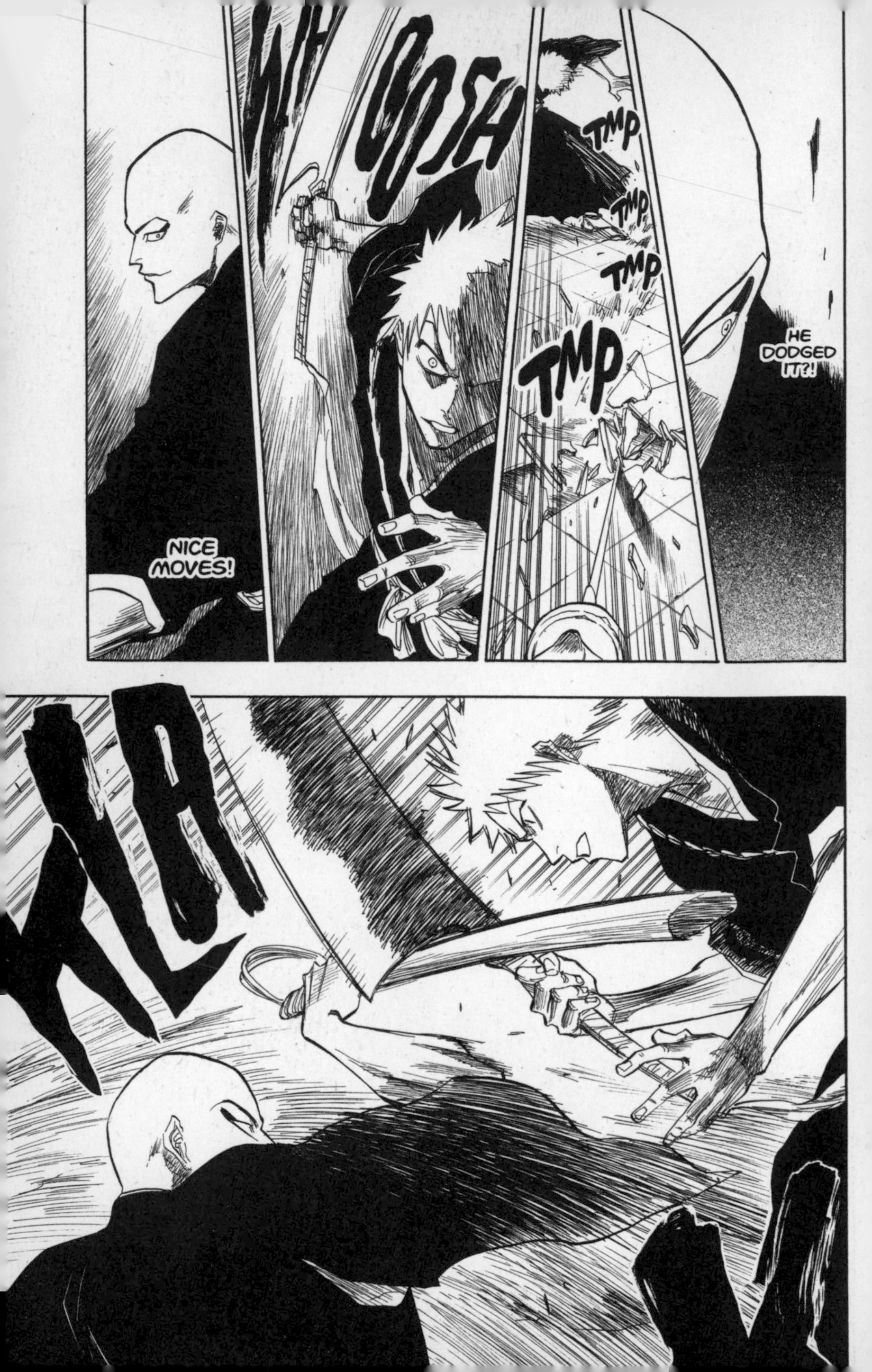
HE DODGED IT?!
TMP
TMP
TMP
TMP
WHOOSH
NICE MOVES!

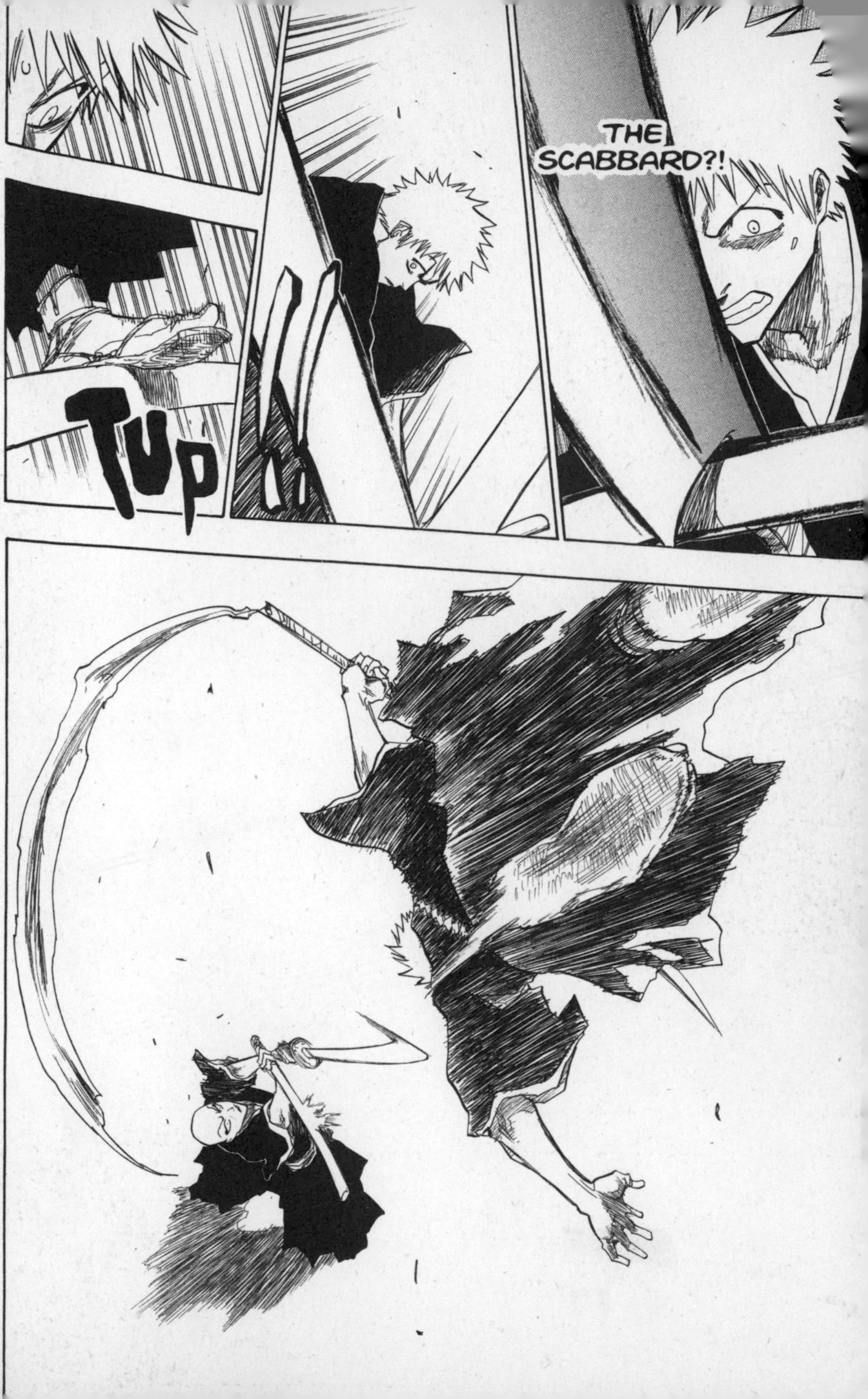
THE SCABBARD?!
TUP

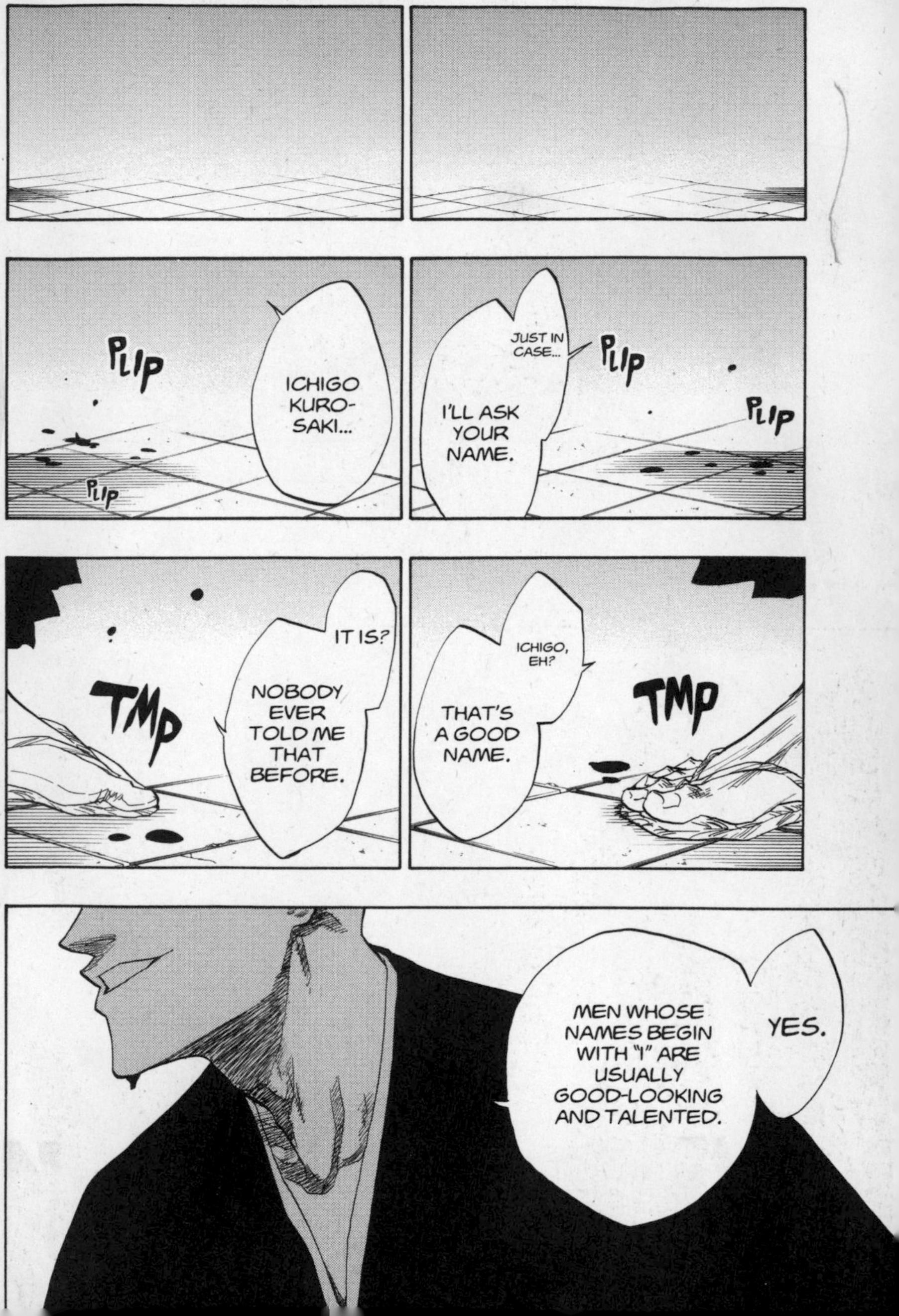
JUST IN CASE...
I'LL ASK YOUR NAME.
PLIP
PLIP
ICHIGO KURO-SAKI...
PLIP
PLIP
ICHIGO, EH?
THAT'S A GOOD NAME.
TMP
IT IS?
NOBODY EVER TOLD ME THAT BEFORE.
TMP
YES.
MEN WHOSE NAMES BEGIN WITH "I" ARE USUALLY GOOD-LOOKING AND TALENTED.

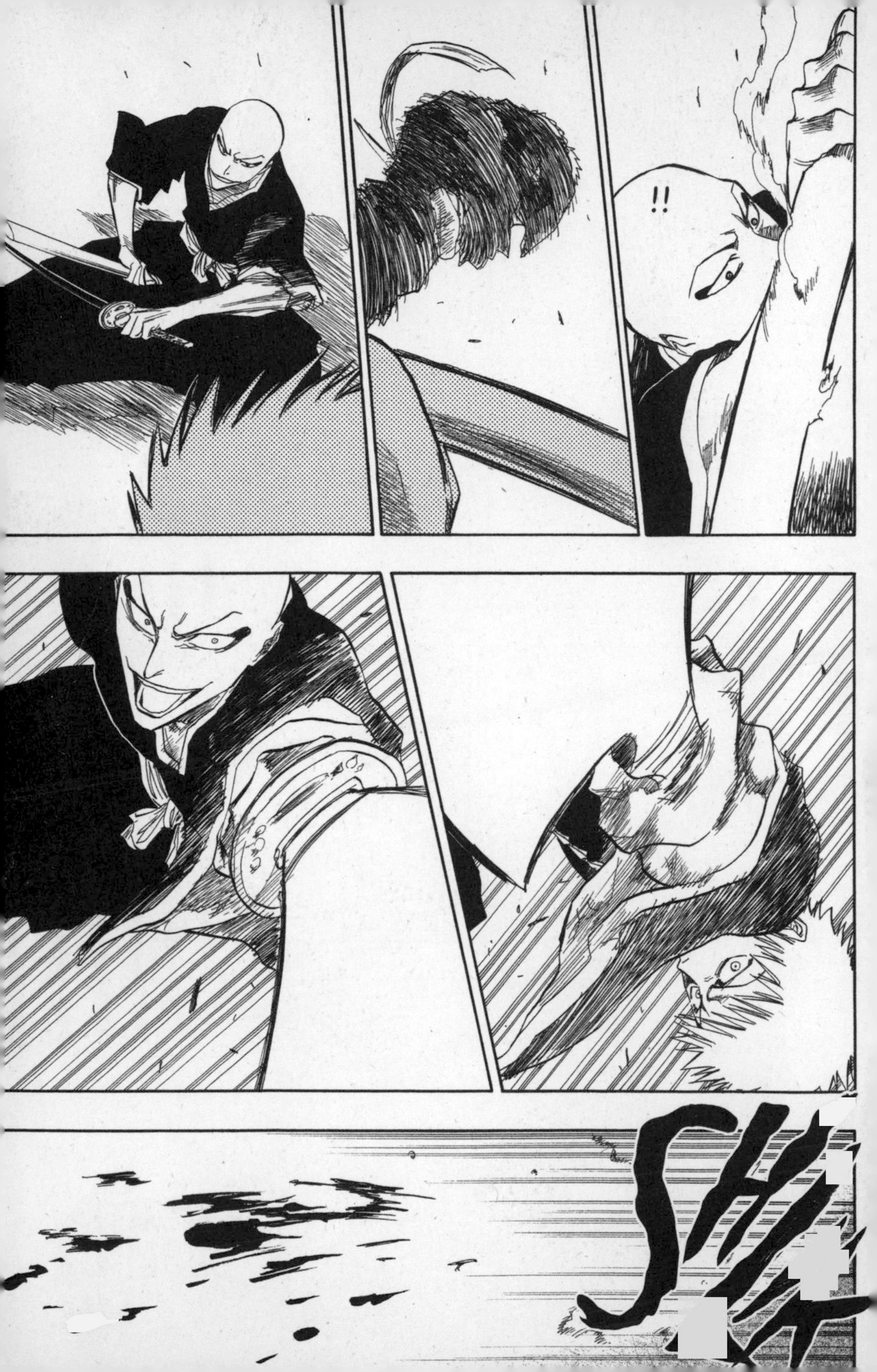
!!

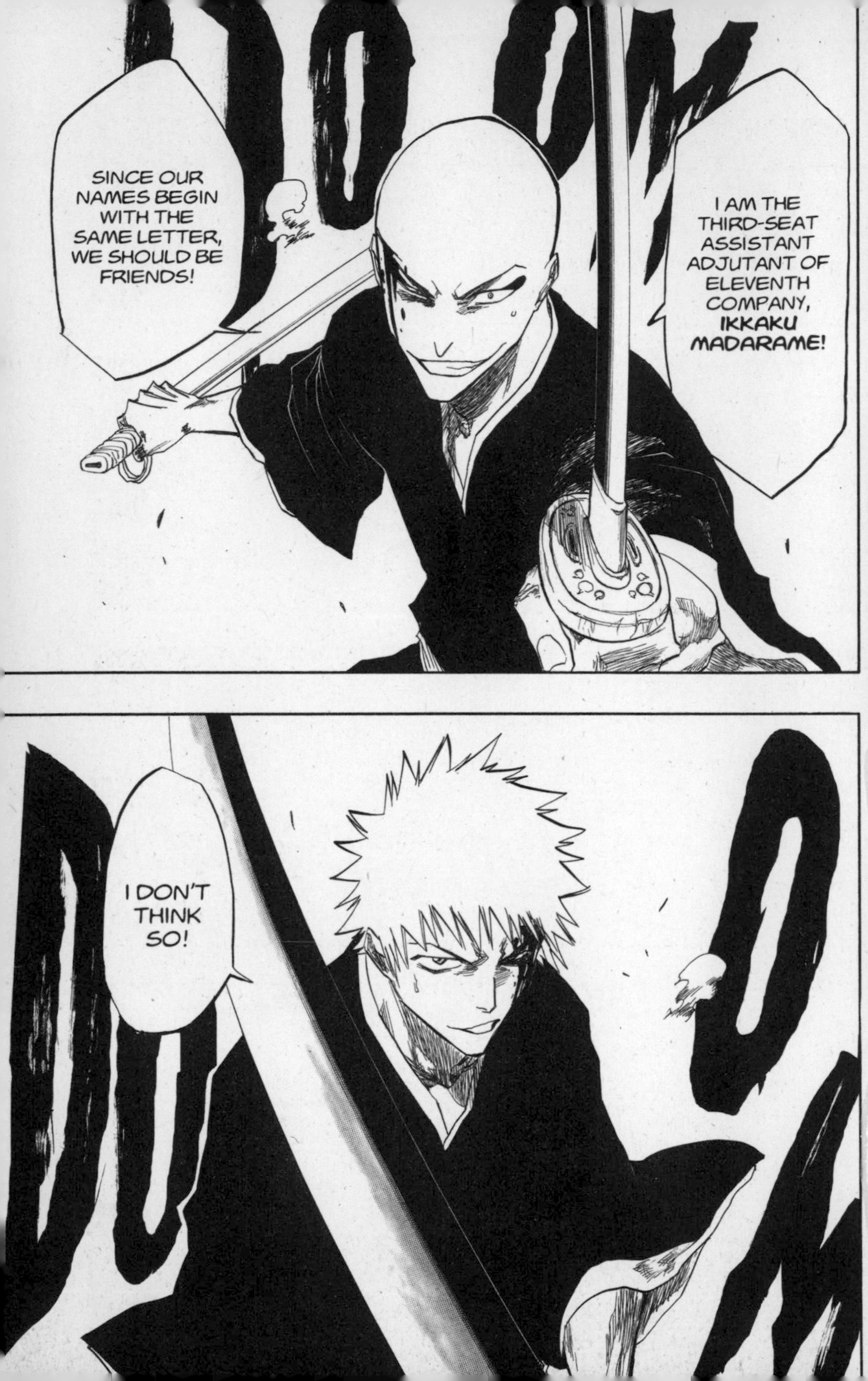
I AM THE THIRD-SEAT ASSISTANT ADJUTANT OF ELEVENTH COMPANY, **IKKAKU MADARAME!**
SINCE OUR NAMES BEGIN WITH THE SAME LETTER, WE SHOULD BE FRIENDS!
I DON'T THINK SO!

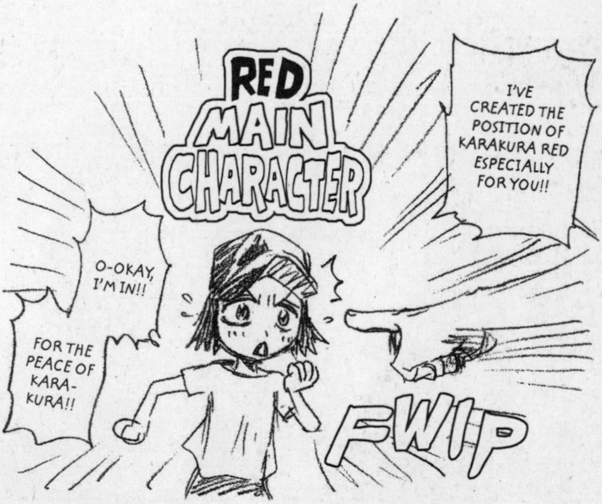
I'VE CREATED THE POSITION OF KARAKURA RED ESPECIALLY FOR YOU!!
RED MAIN CHARACTER
O-OKAY, I'M IN!!
FOR THE PEACE OF KARA-KURA!!
FWIP

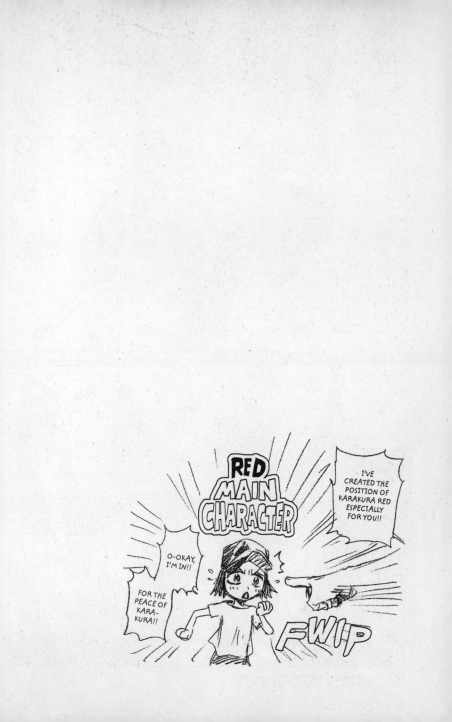

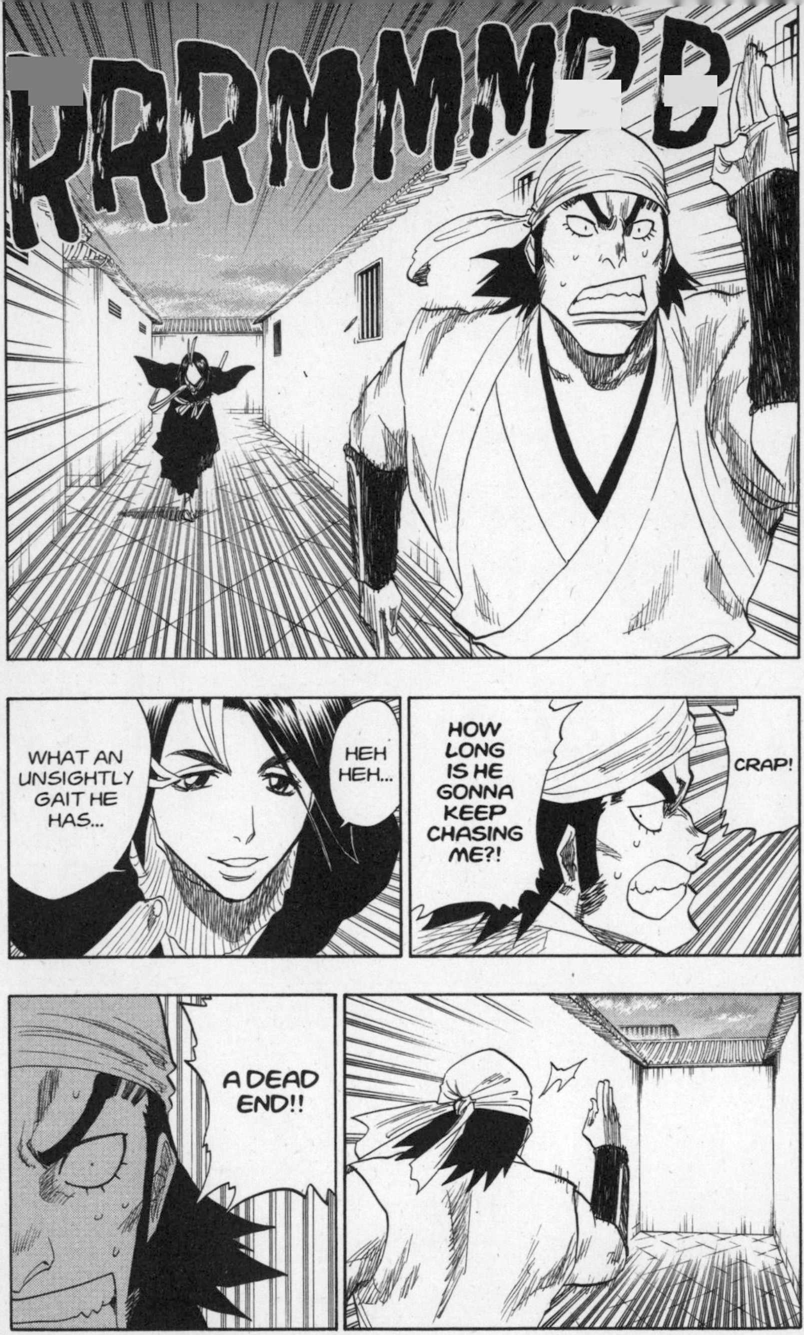
RRRMMM
CRAP!
HOW LONG IS HE GONNA KEEP CHASING ME?!
HEH HEH...
WHAT AN UNSIGHTLY GAIT HE HAS...
A DEAD END!!

87. Dancing With Spears

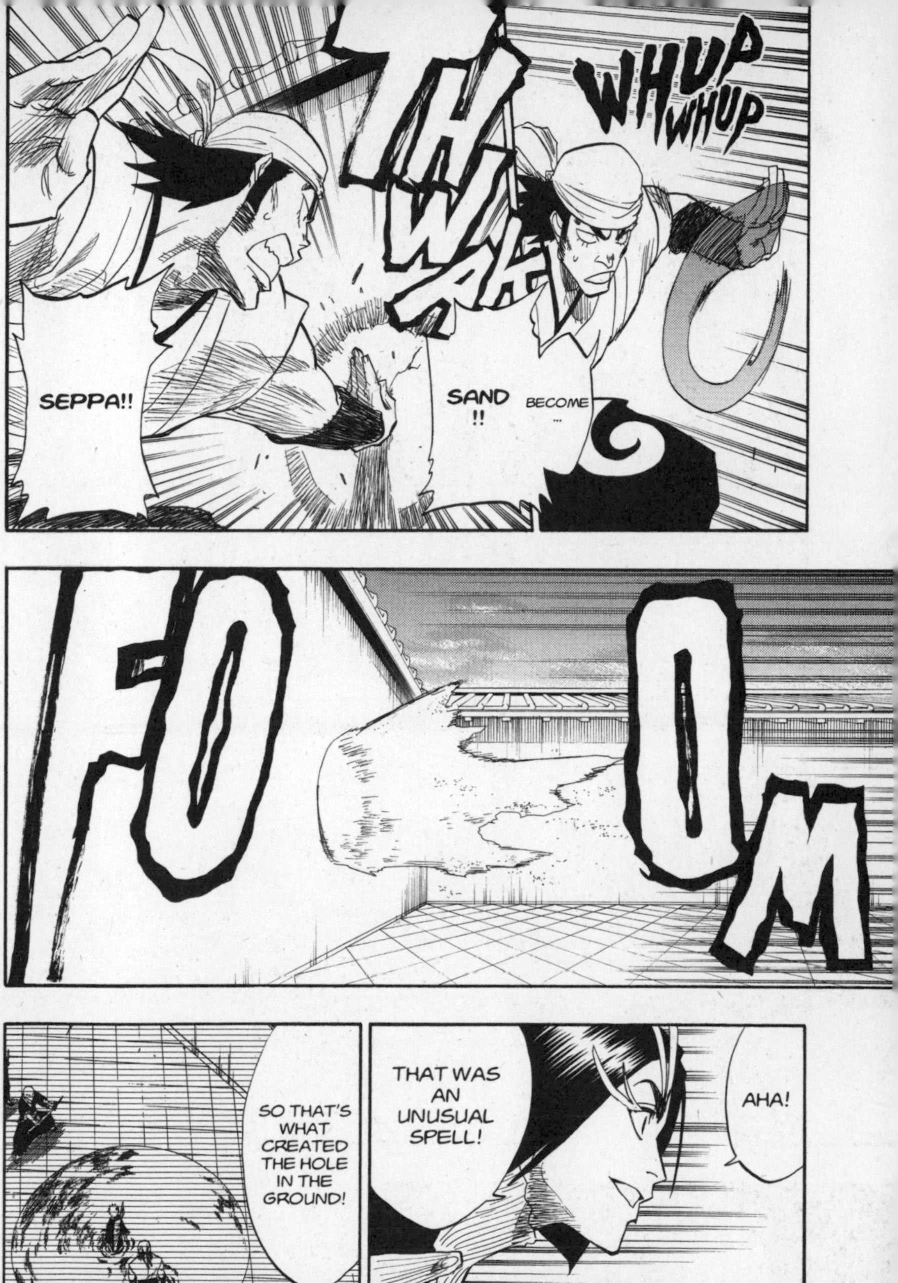
WHUP WHUP
CHWAK
BECOME...
SAND!!
SEPPA!!
FOOM
AHA!
THAT WAS AN UNUSUAL SPELL!
SO THAT'S WHAT CREATED THE HOLE IN THE GROUND!

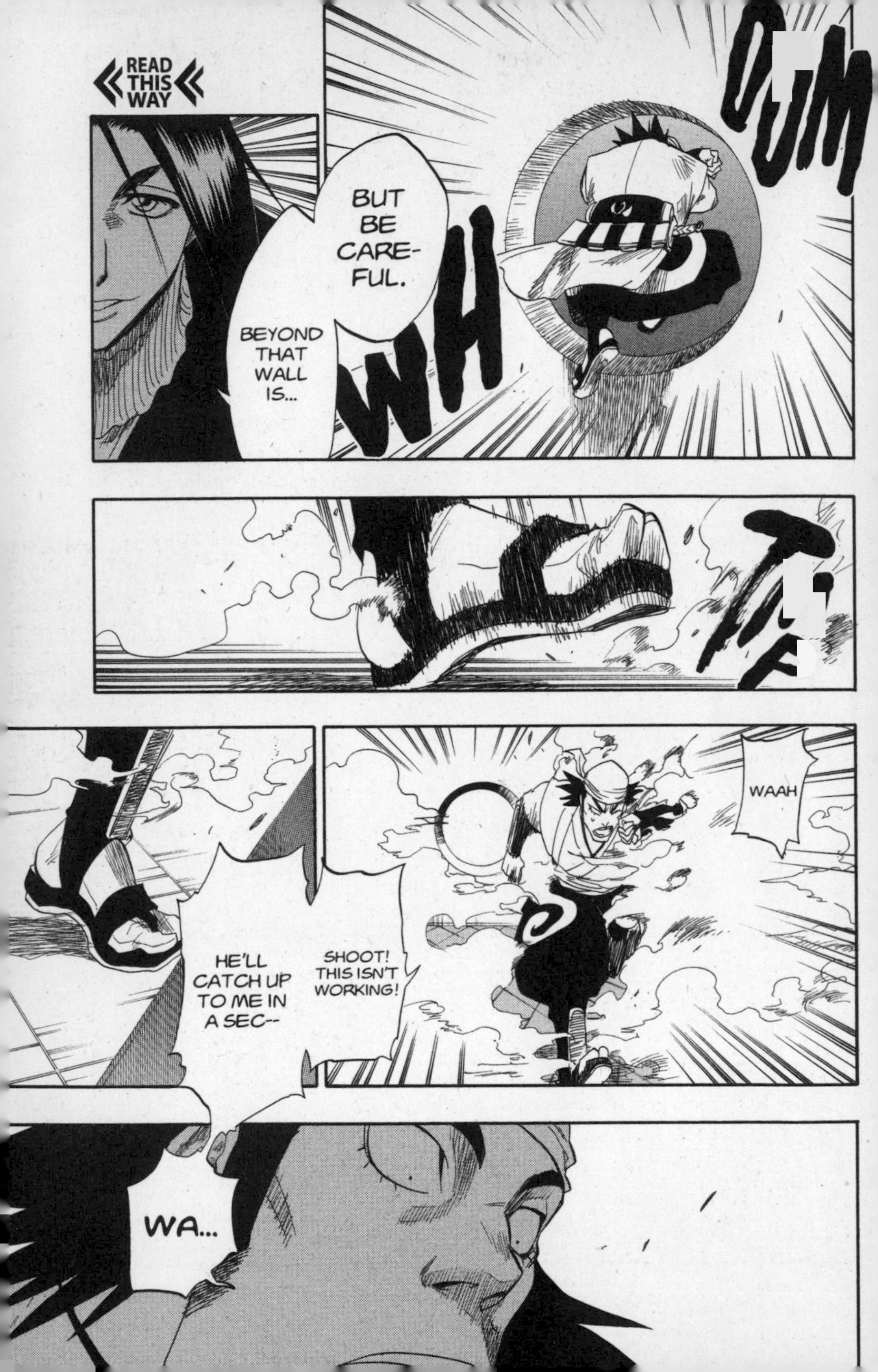
READ THIS WAY
OOM
WH
BUT BE CARE-FUL.
BEYOND THAT WALL IS...
TA
WAAH
SHOOT! THIS ISN'T WORKING!
HE'LL CATCH UP TO ME IN A SEC--
WA...

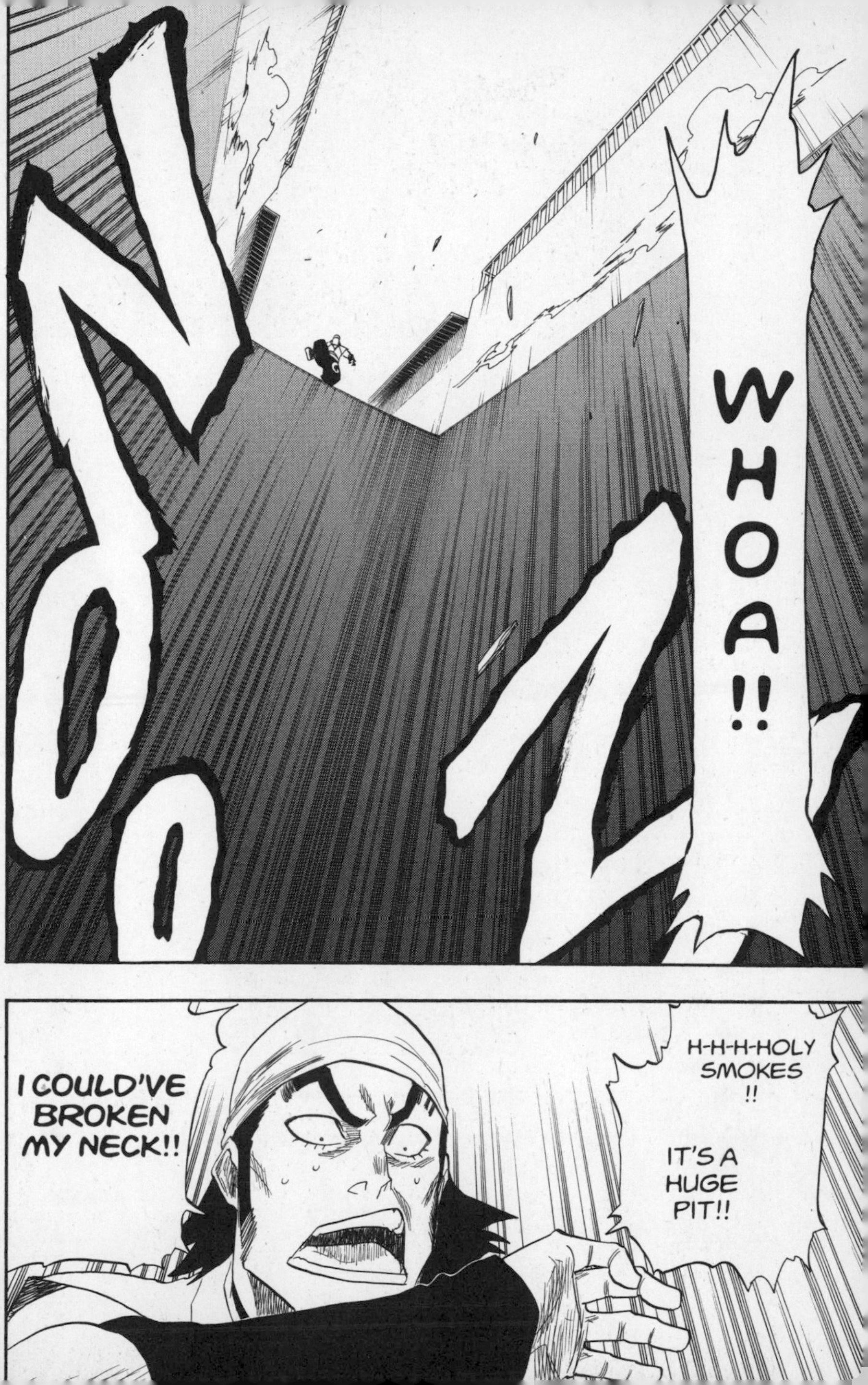
WHOA!!
H-H-H-HOLY SMOKES !!
IT'S A HUGE PIT!!
I COULD'VE BROKEN MY NECK!!

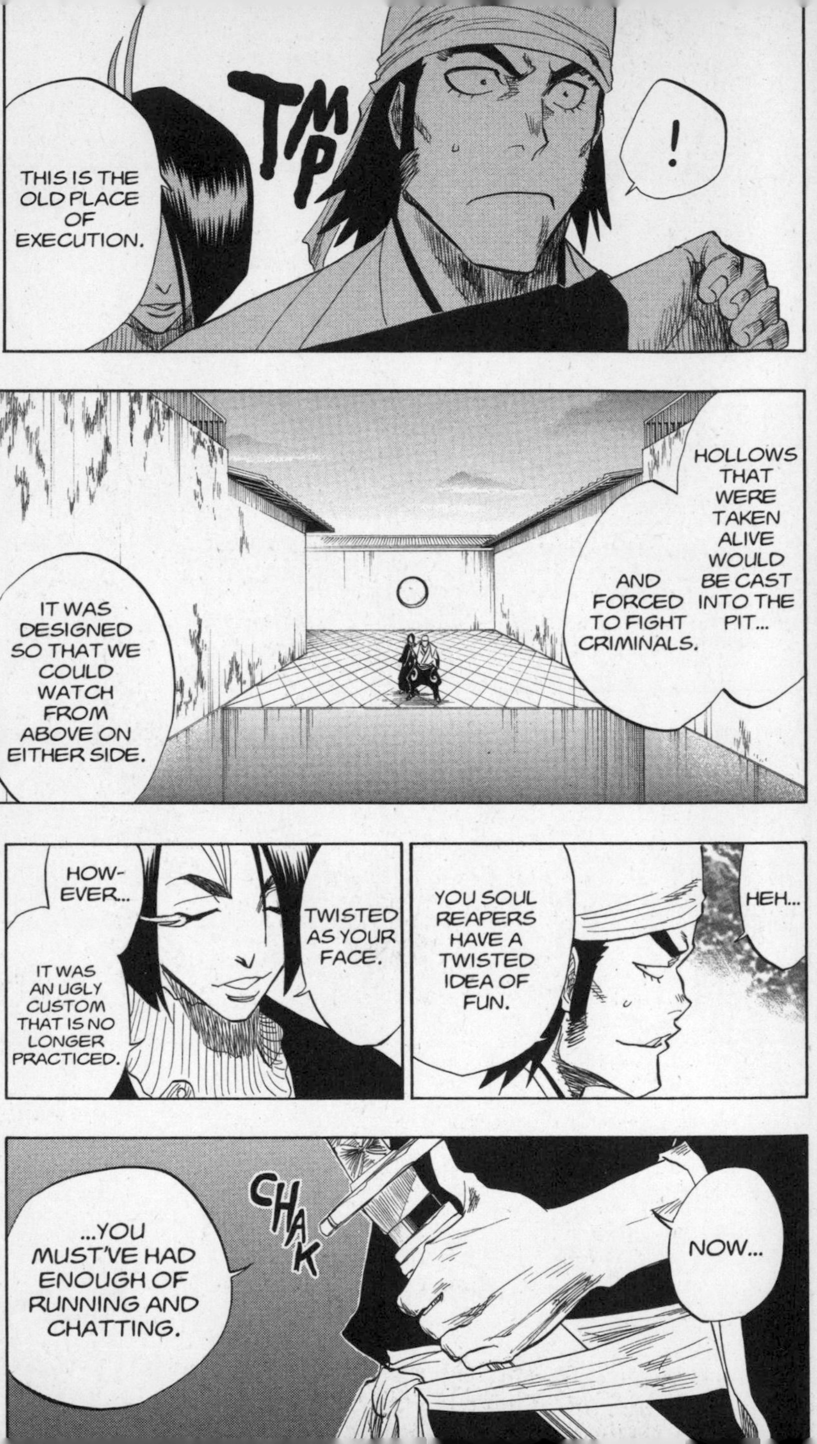
!
TMP
THIS IS THE OLD PLACE OF EXECUTION.
HOLLOWS THAT WERE TAKEN ALIVE WOULD BE CAST INTO THE PIT...
AND FORCED TO FIGHT CRIMINALS.
IT WAS DESIGNED SO THAT WE COULD WATCH FROM ABOVE ON EITHER SIDE.
HEH...
YOU SOUL REAPERS HAVE A TWISTED IDEA OF FUN.
TWISTED AS YOUR FACE.
HOW-EVER...
IT WAS AN UGLY CUSTOM THAT IS NO LONGER PRACTICED.
NOW...
CHAK
...YOU MUST'VE HAD ENOUGH OF RUNNING AND CHATTING.

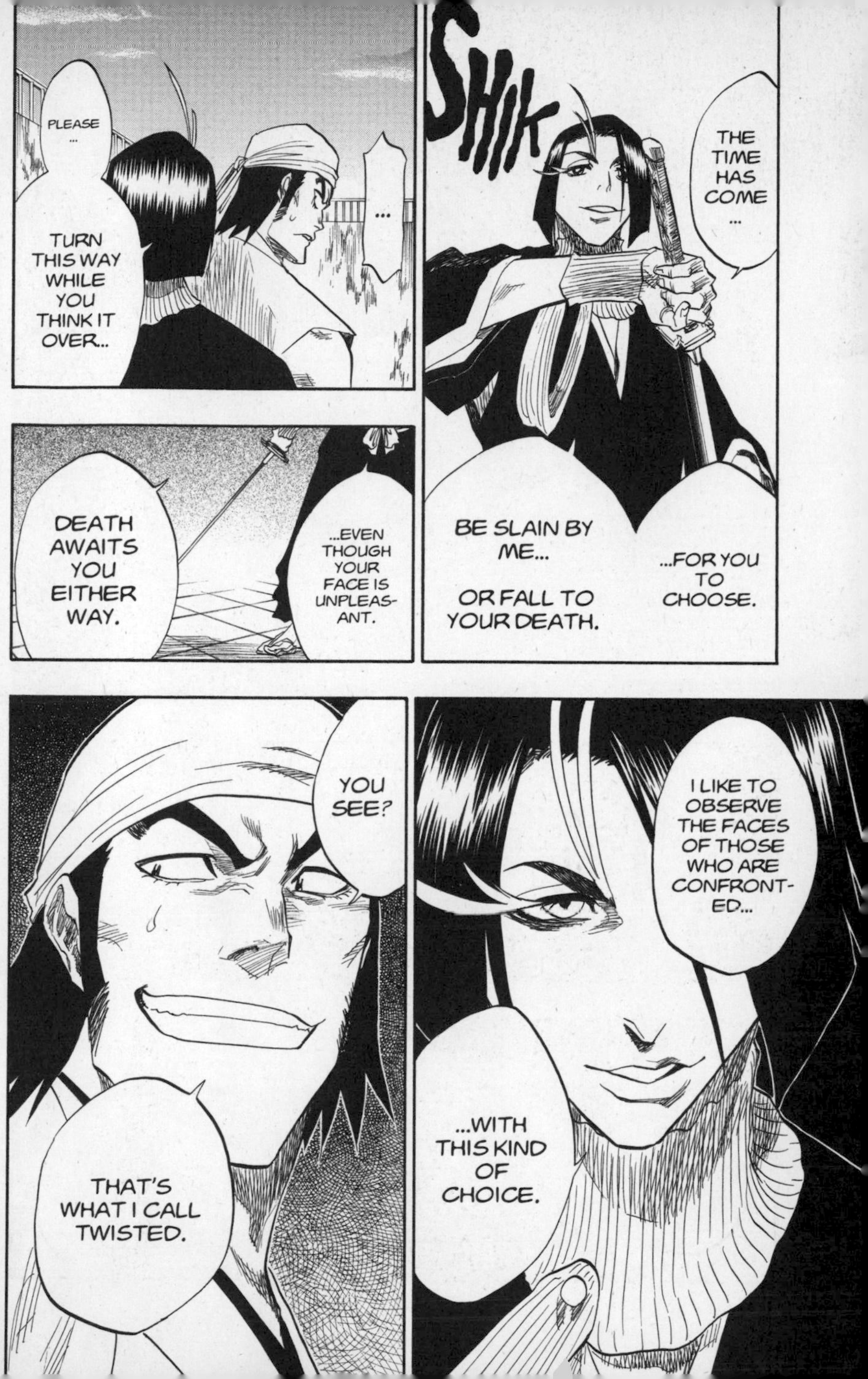
SHIK
THE TIME HAS COME...
BE SLAIN BY ME... OR FALL TO YOUR DEATH.
...FOR YOU TO CHOOSE.
...
PLEASE...
TURN THIS WAY WHILE YOU THINK IT OVER...
...EVEN THOUGH YOUR FACE IS UNPLEASANT.
DEATH AWAITS YOU EITHER WAY.
I LIKE TO OBSERVE THE FACES OF THOSE WHO ARE CONFRONTED...
...WITH THIS KIND OF CHOICE.
YOU SEE?
THAT'S WHAT I CALL TWISTED.

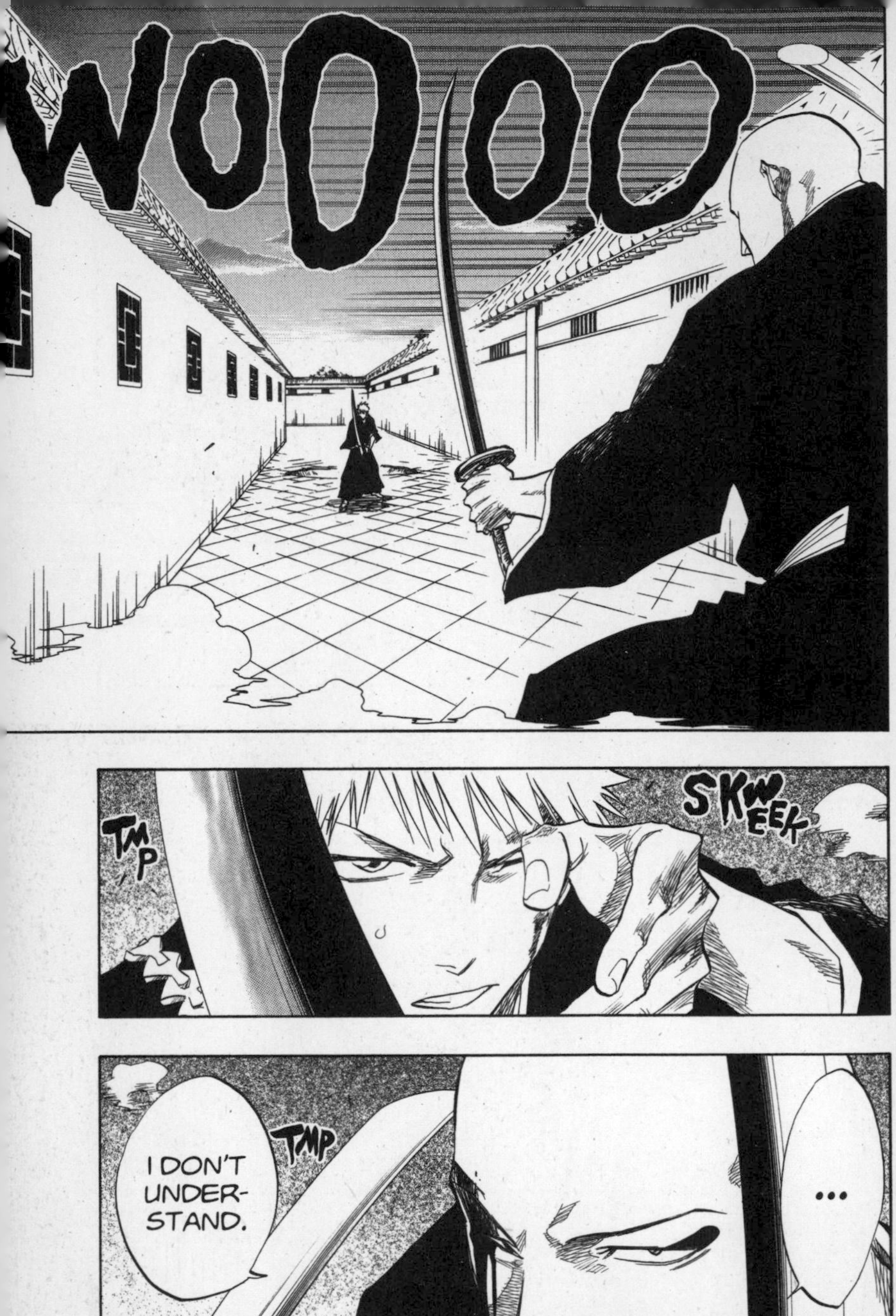
WOOOO
SKWEEK
TMP
...
TMP
I DON'T UNDER-STAND.

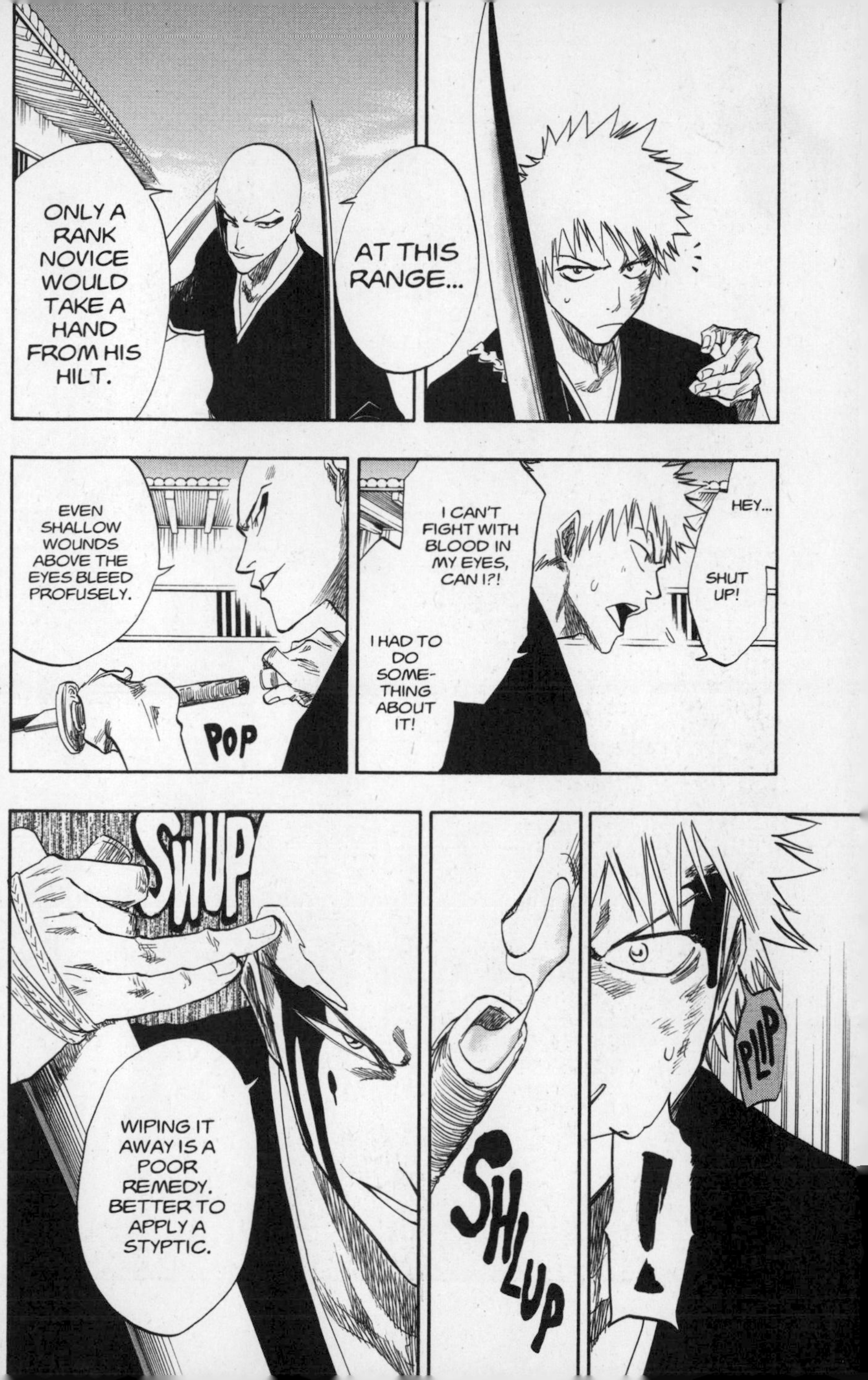
AT THIS RANGE...
ONLY A RANK NOVICE WOULD TAKE A HAND FROM HIS HILT.
HEY...
SHUT UP!
I CAN'T FIGHT WITH BLOOD IN MY EYES, CAN I?!
I HAD TO DO SOME-THING ABOUT IT!
EVEN SHALLOW WOUNDS ABOVE THE EYES BLEED PROFUSELY.
POP
PLIP
!
SHLUP
SWUP
WIPING IT AWAY IS A POOR REMEDY. BETTER TO APPLY A STYPTIC.

READ THIS WAY

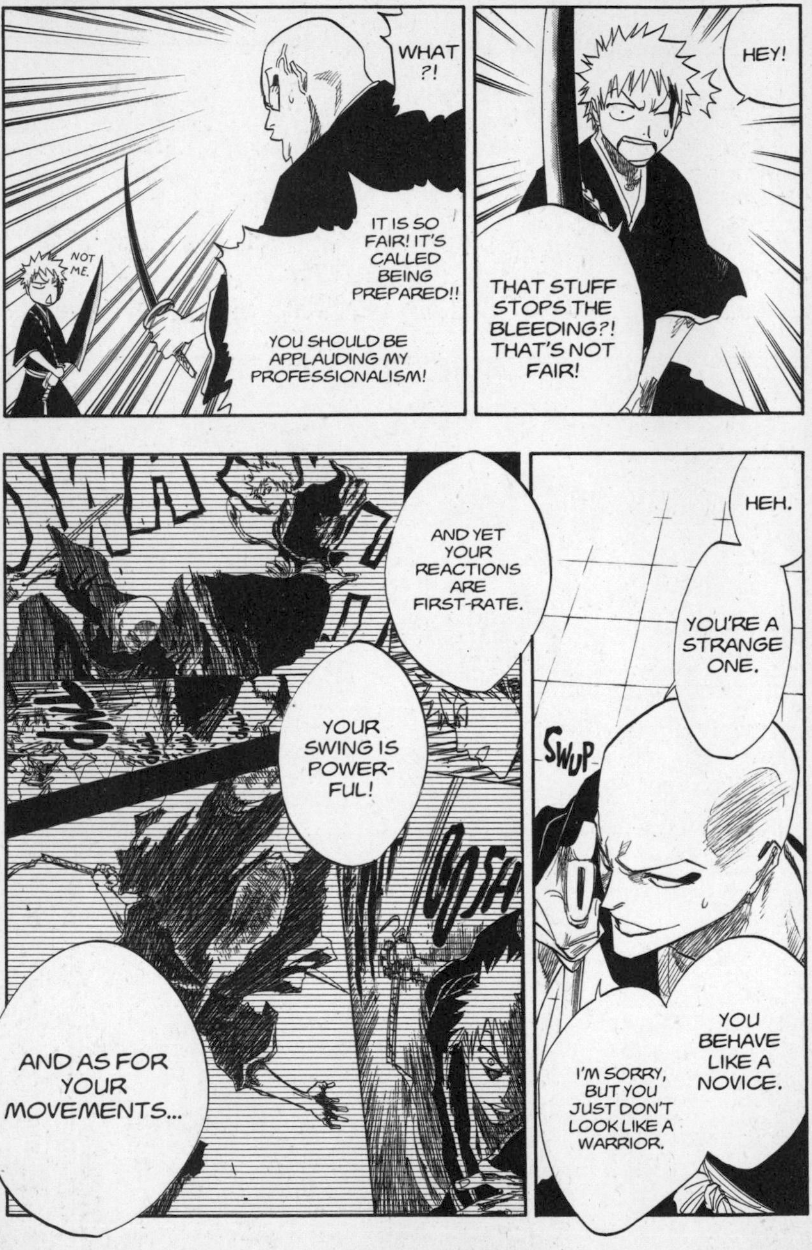
HEY!
THAT STUFF STOPS THE BLEEDING?! THAT'S NOT FAIR!
WHAT ?!
IT IS SO FAIR! IT'S CALLED BEING PREPARED!!
YOU SHOULD BE APPLAUDING MY PROFESSIONALISM!
NOT ME.
HEH.
YOU'RE A STRANGE ONE.
SWUP
YOU BEHAVE LIKE A NOVICE.
I'M SORRY, BUT YOU JUST DON'T LOOK LIKE A WARRIOR.
AND YET YOUR REACTIONS ARE FIRST-RATE.
YOUR SWING IS POWER-FUL!
AND AS FOR YOUR MOVEMENTS...

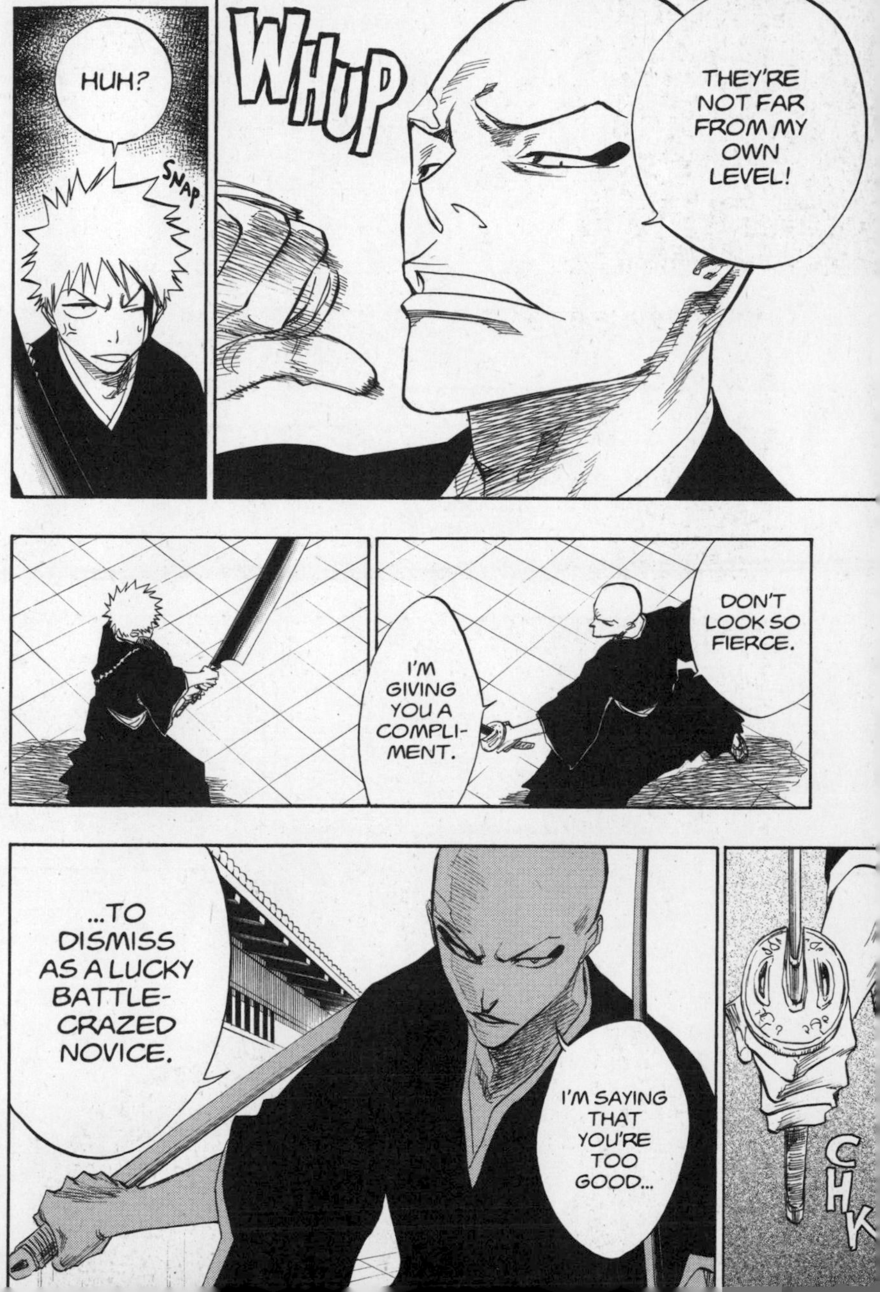
WHUP
THEY'RE NOT FAR FROM MY OWN LEVEL!
SNAP
HUH?
DON'T LOOK SO FIERCE.
I'M GIVING YOU A COMPLIMENT.
CHK
I'M SAYING THAT YOU'RE TOO GOOD...
...TO DISMISS AS A LUCKY BATTLE-CRAZED NOVICE.

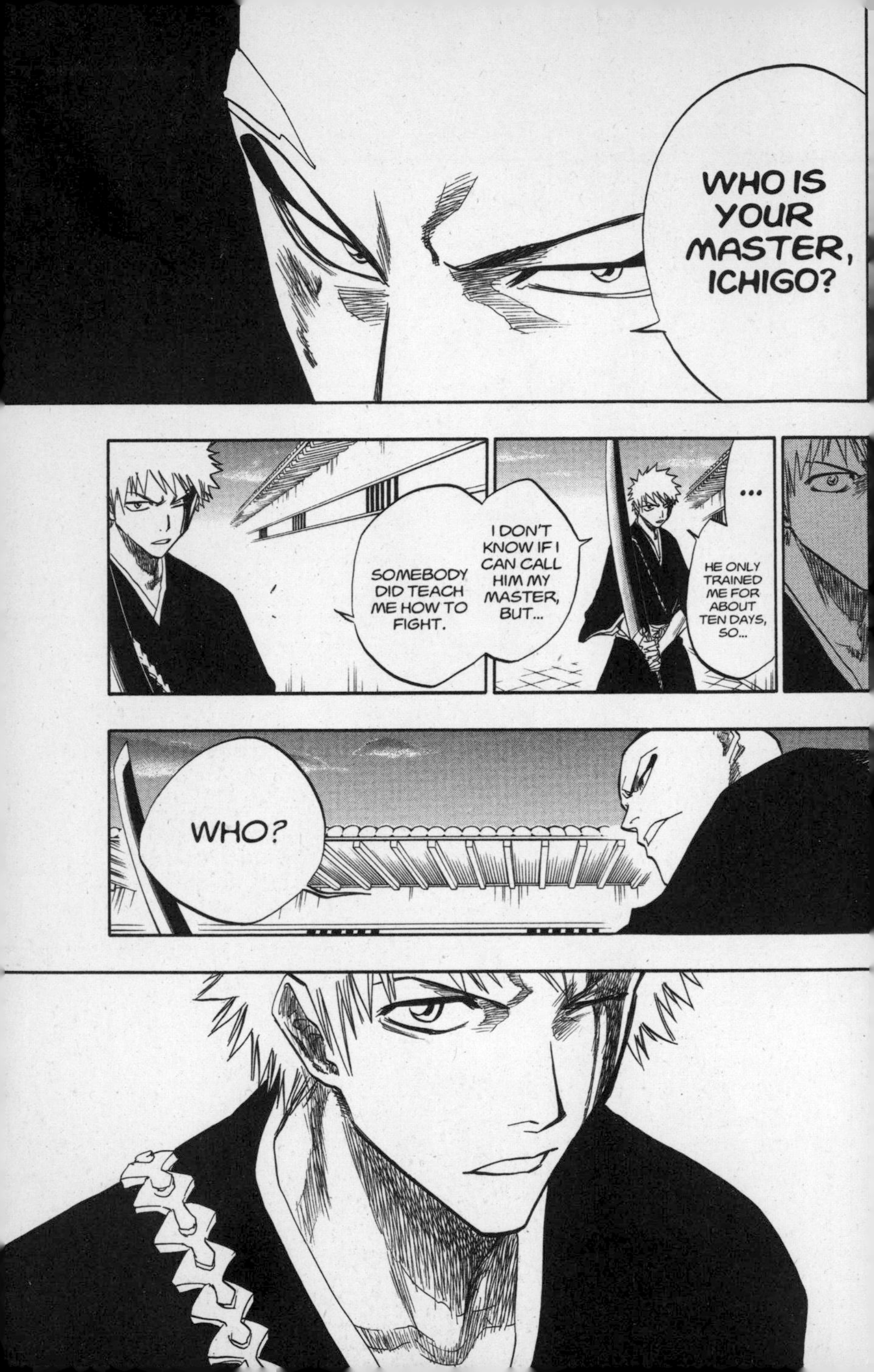
WHO IS YOUR MASTER, ICHIGO?
...
HE ONLY TRAINED ME FOR ABOUT TEN DAYS, SO...
I DON'T KNOW IF I CAN CALL HIM MY MASTER, BUT...
SOMEBODY DID TEACH ME HOW TO FIGHT.
WHO?

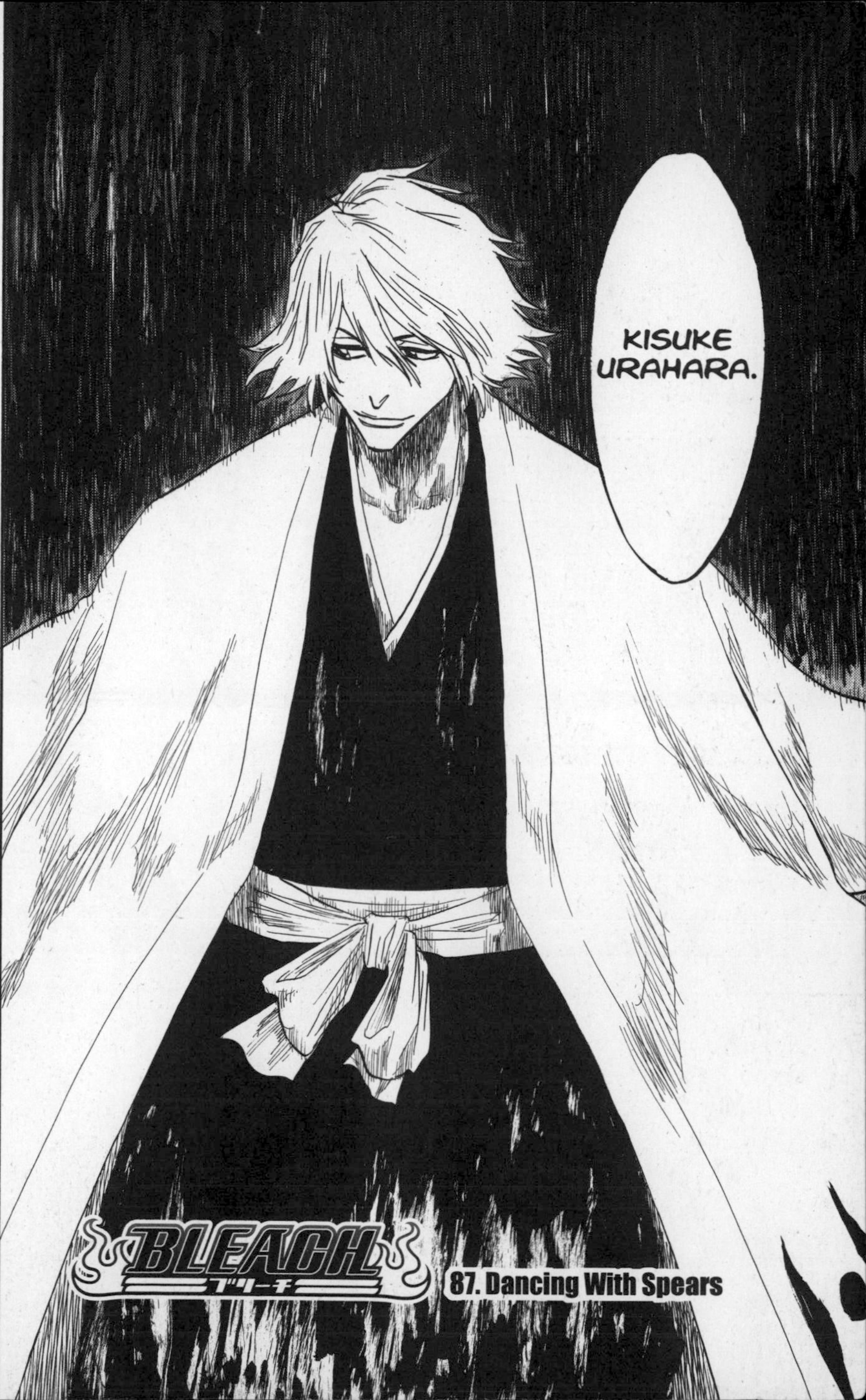
KISUKE URAHARA.
BLEACH
ブリーチ
87. Dancing With Spears

READ THIS WAY

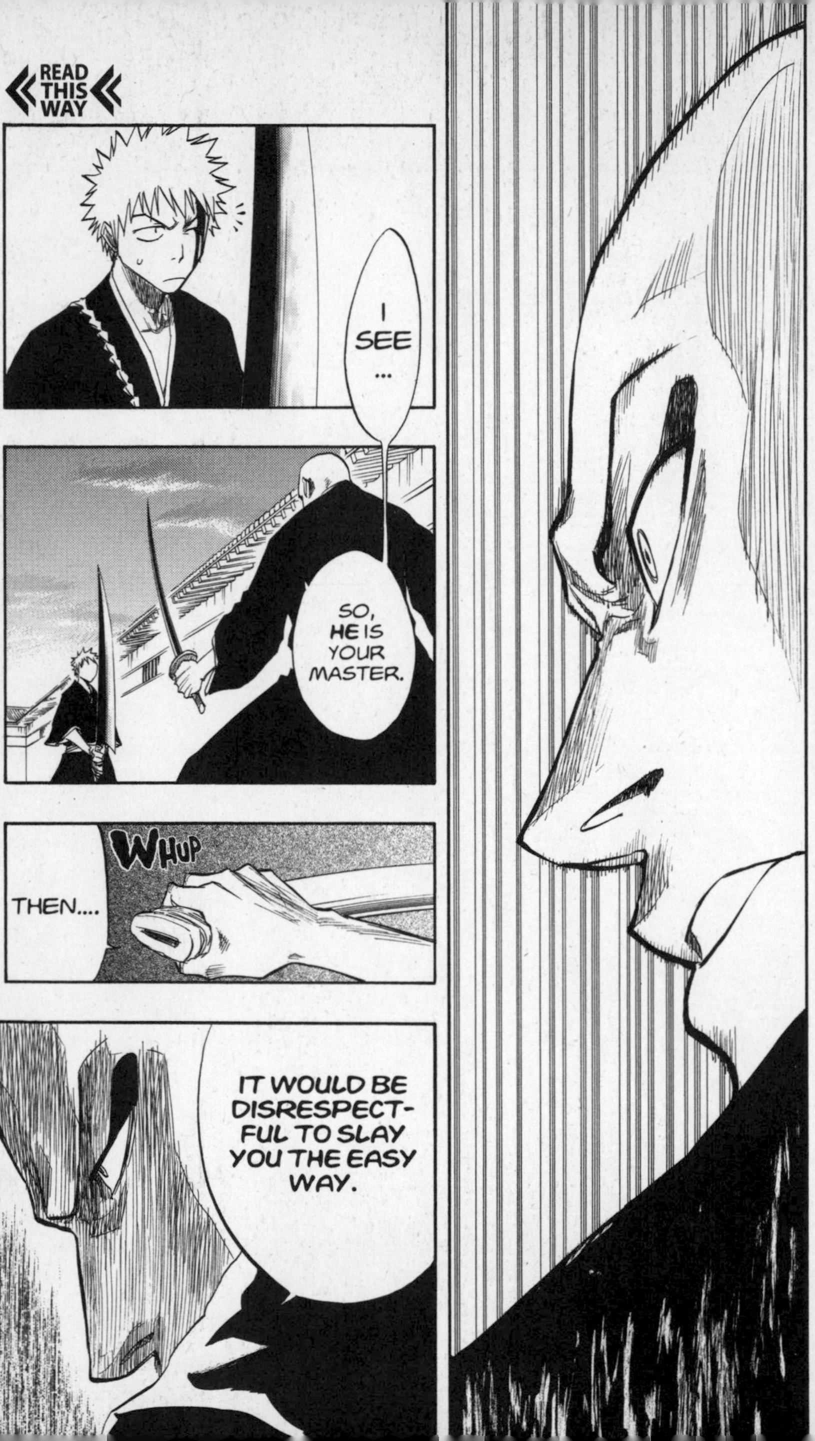
I SEE...
SO, HE IS YOUR MASTER.
WHUP
THEN....
IT WOULD BE DISRESPECTFUL TO SLAY YOU THE EASY WAY.

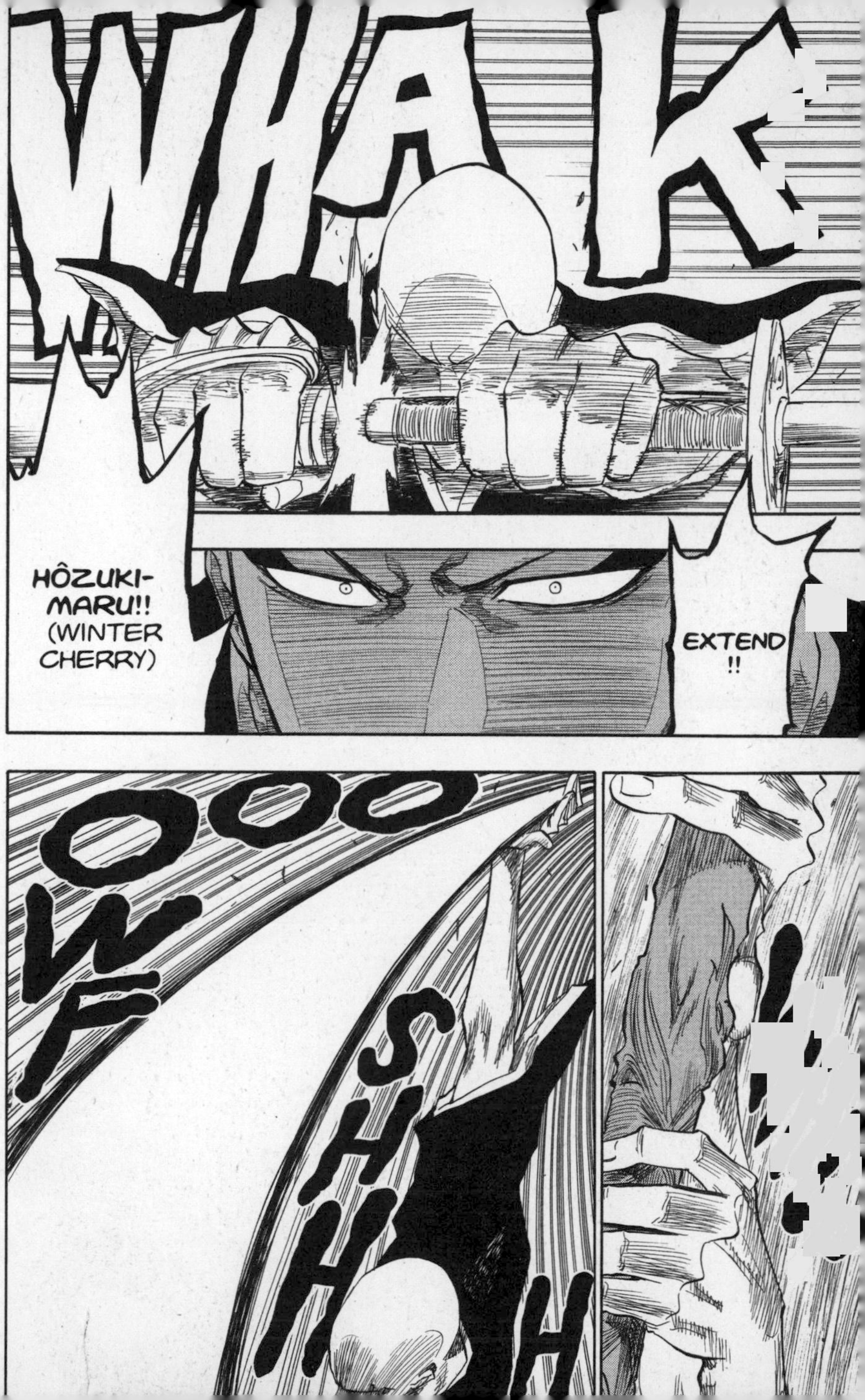
WHAK!
EXTEND!!
HÔZUKI-MARU!! (WINTER CHERRY)
FWOOOO
SHHHH

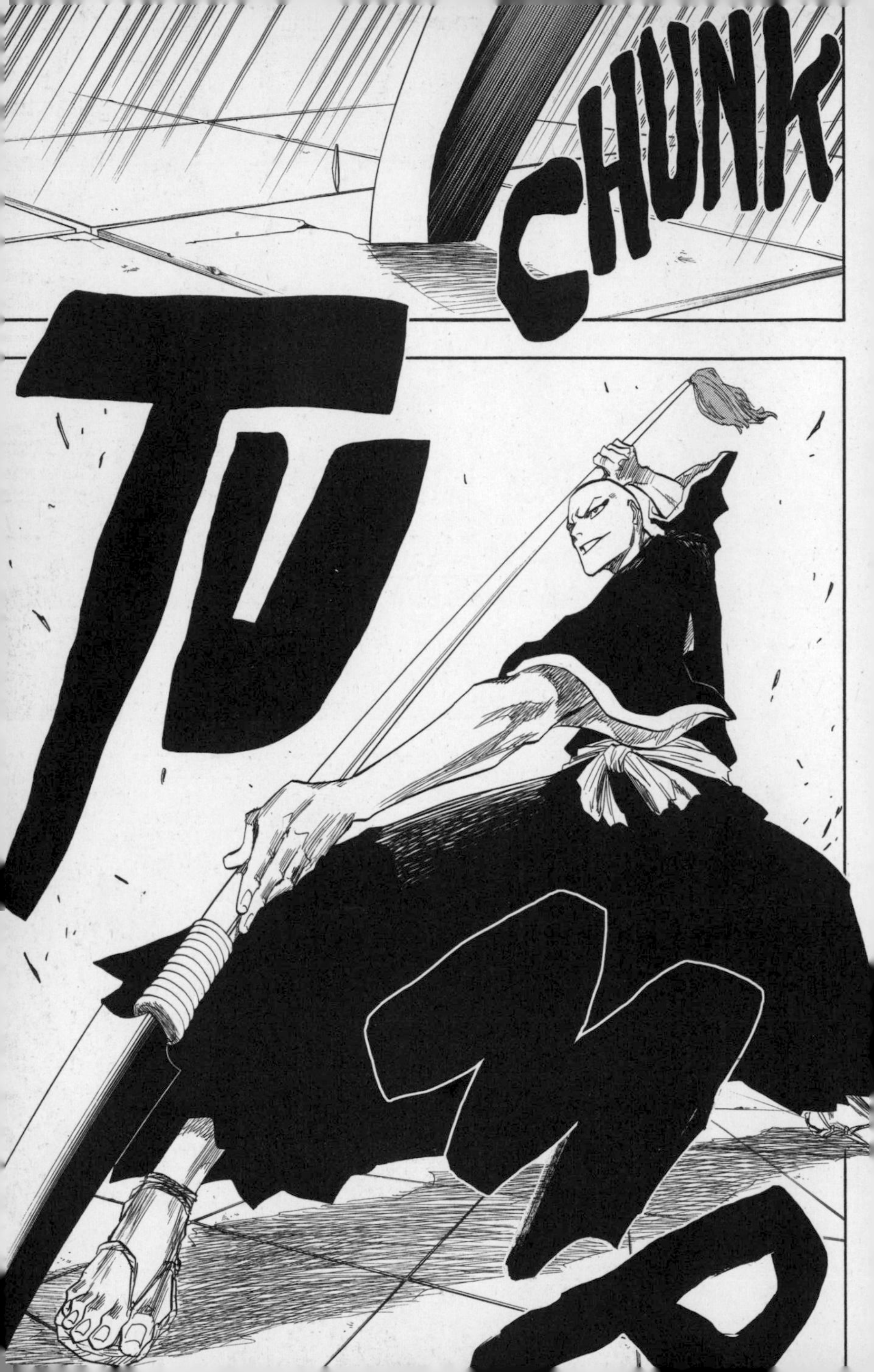
CHUNK

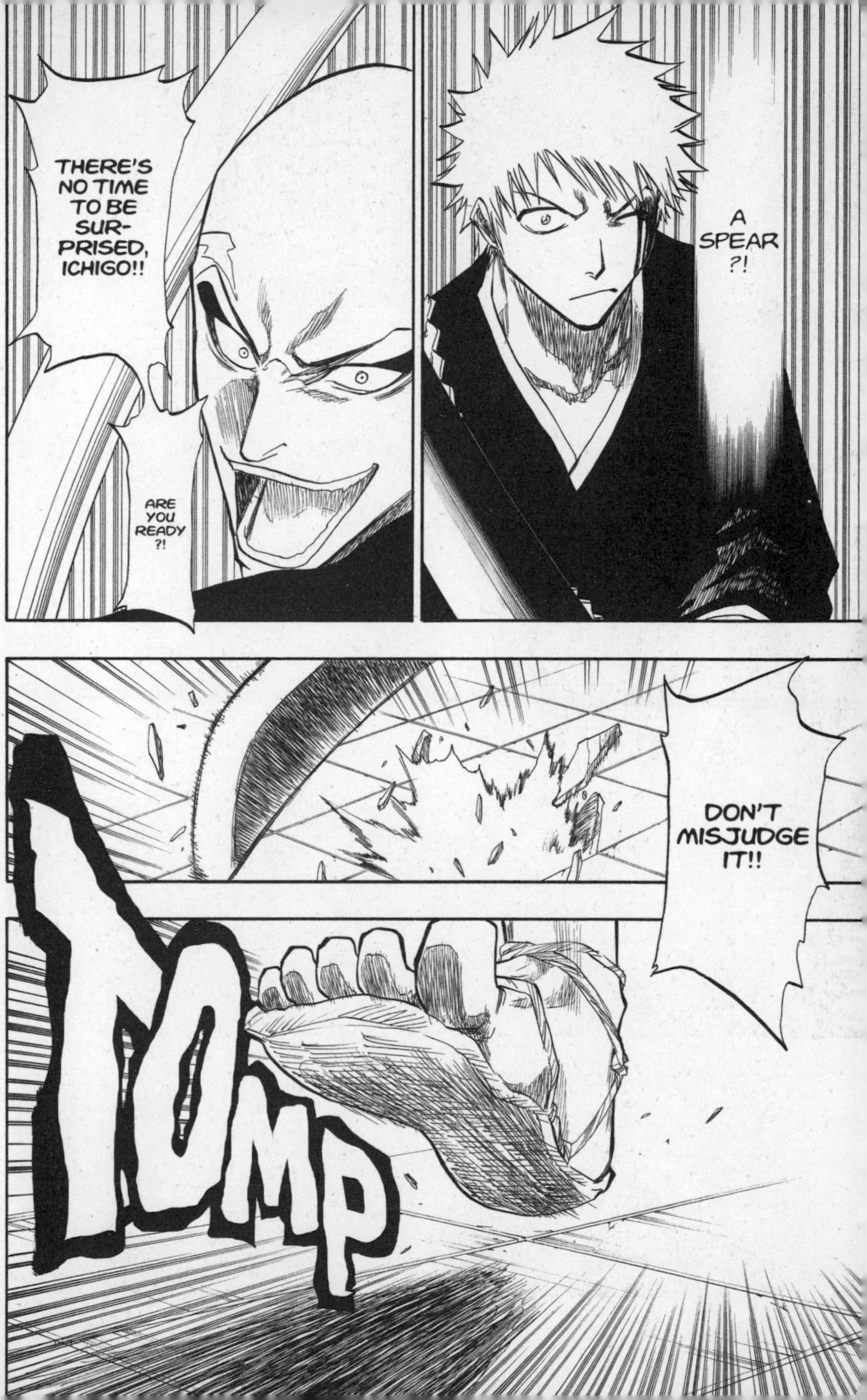
A SPEAR ?!
THERE'S NO TIME TO BE SUR-PRISED, ICHIGO!!
ARE YOU READY ?!
DON'T MISJUDGE IT!!
TOMP

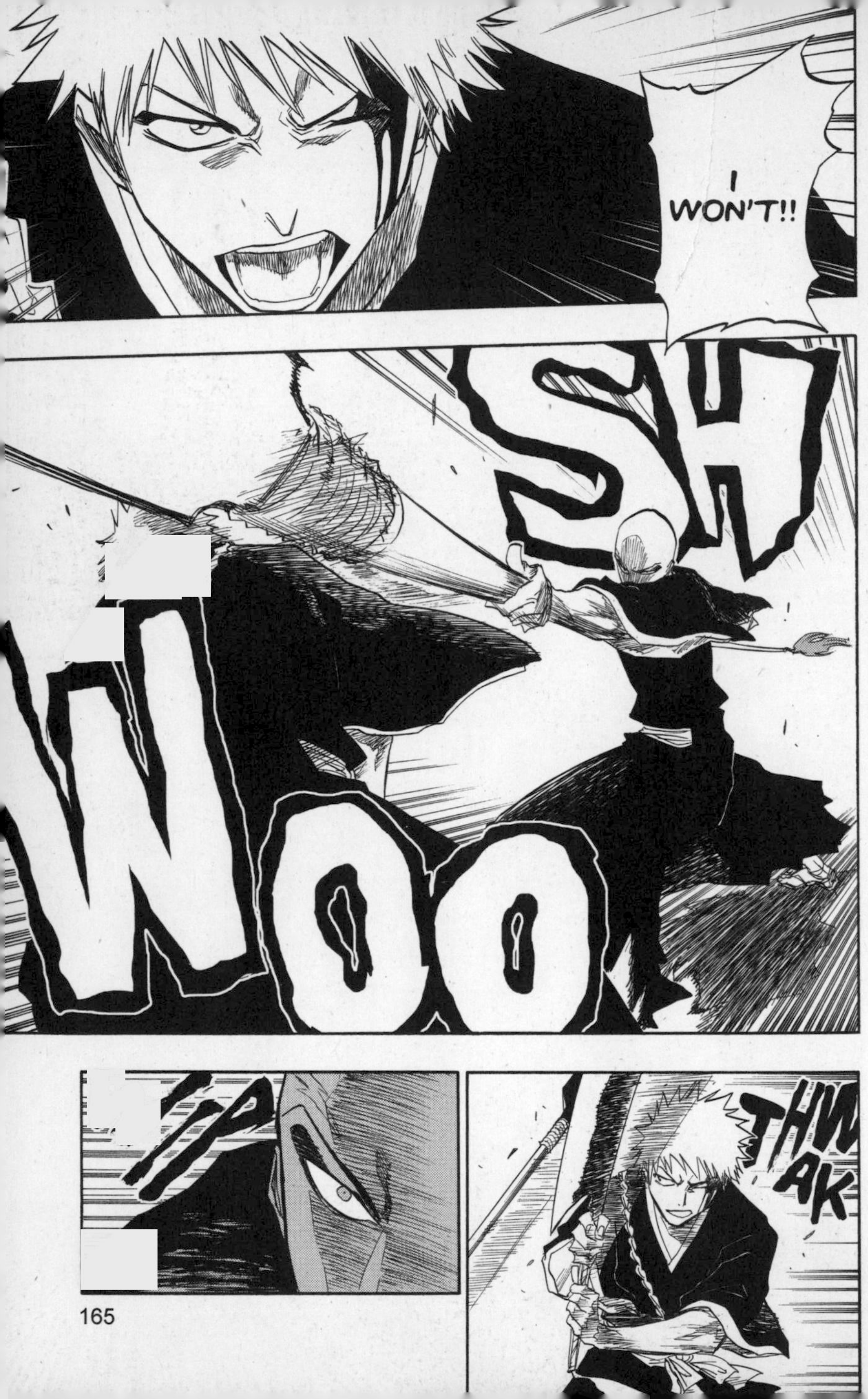
I WON'T!!
SHWOOO
THWAK

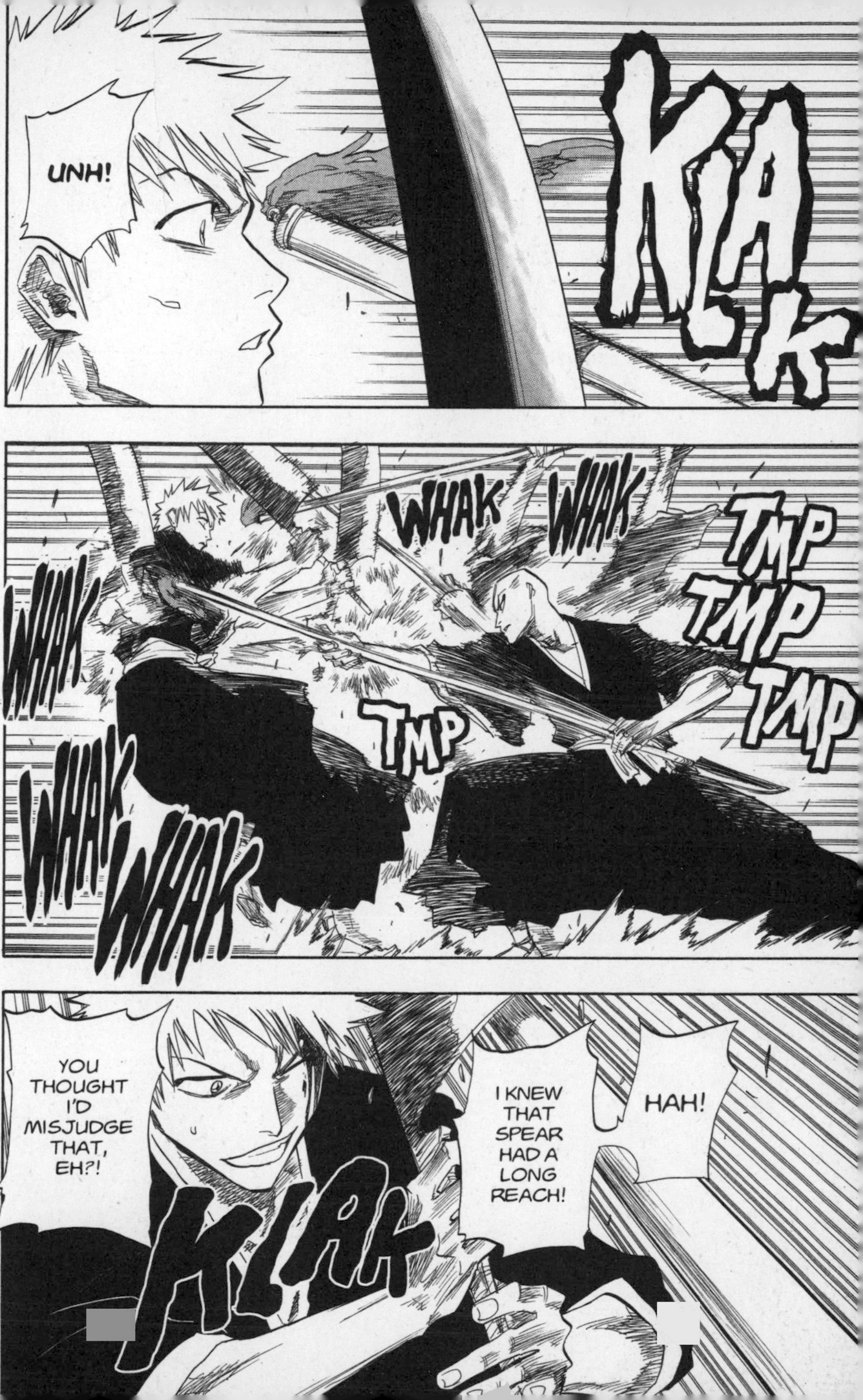
UNH!
WHAK
WHAK
TMP
TMP
TMP
WHAK
TMP
WHAK
WHAK
HAH!
I KNEW THAT SPEAR HAD A LONG REACH!
YOU THOUGHT I'D MISJUDGE THAT, EH?!
KLAK

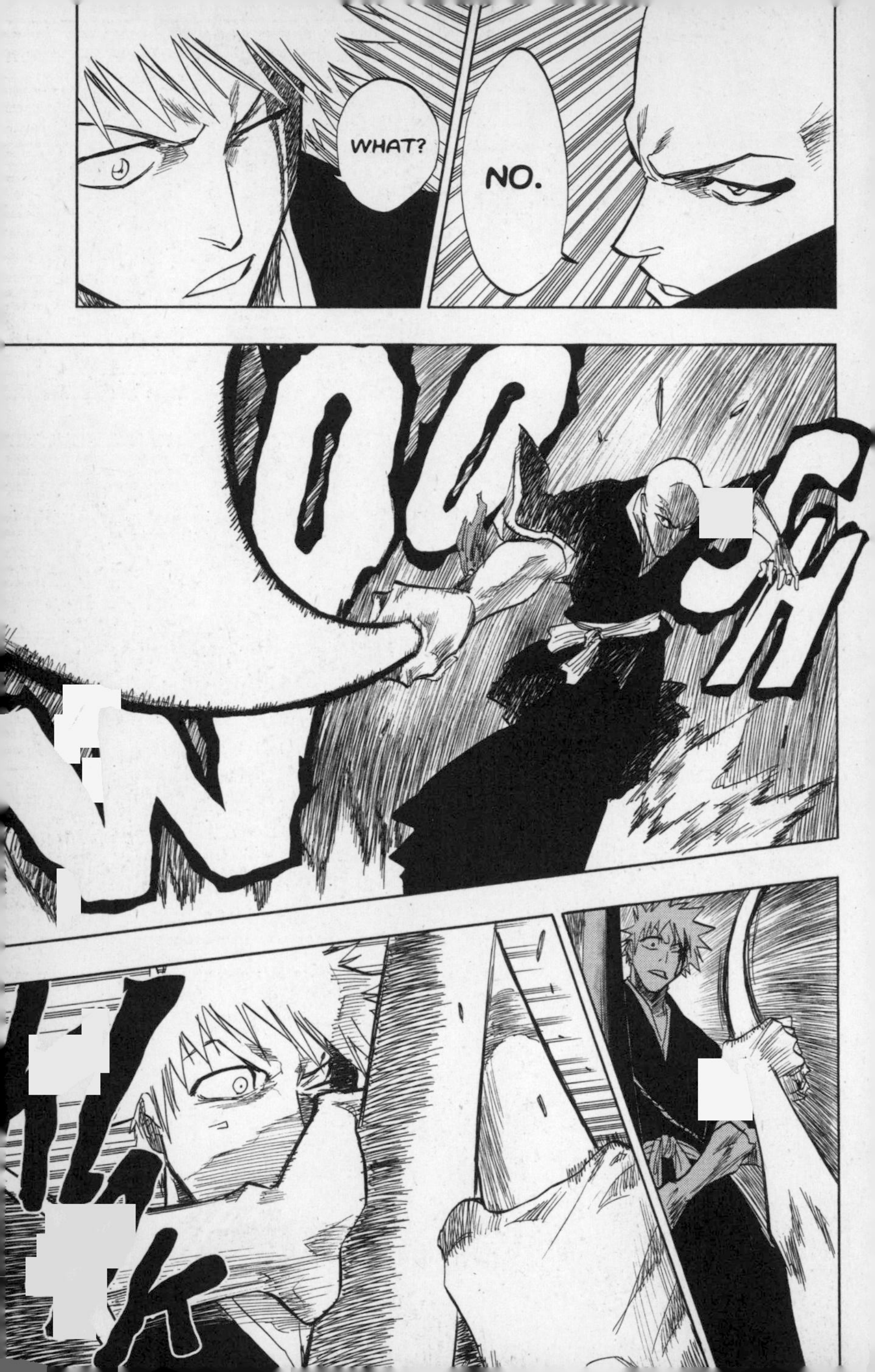
NO.
WHAT?

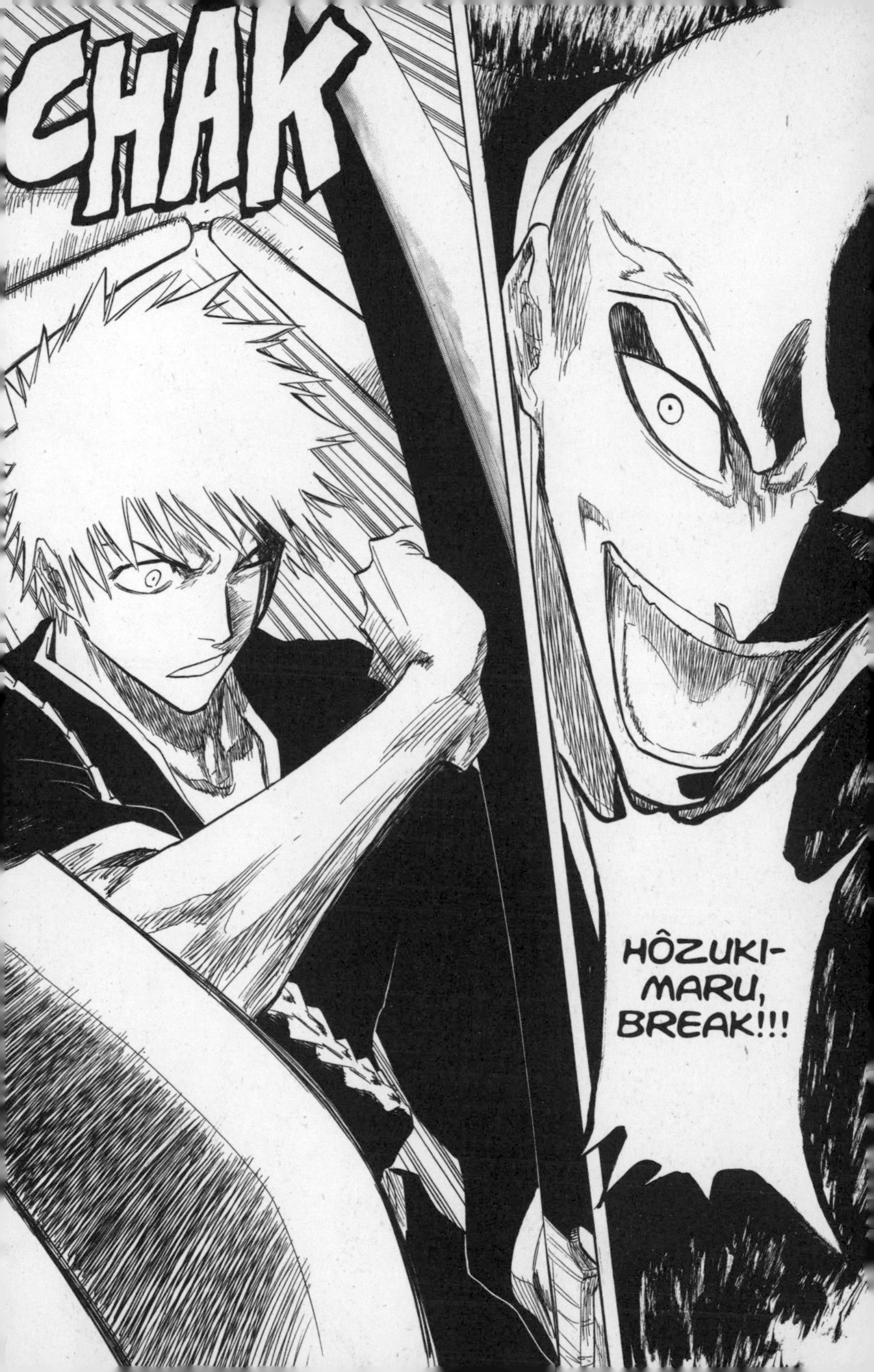
CHAK
HÔZUKI-MARU, BREAK!!!

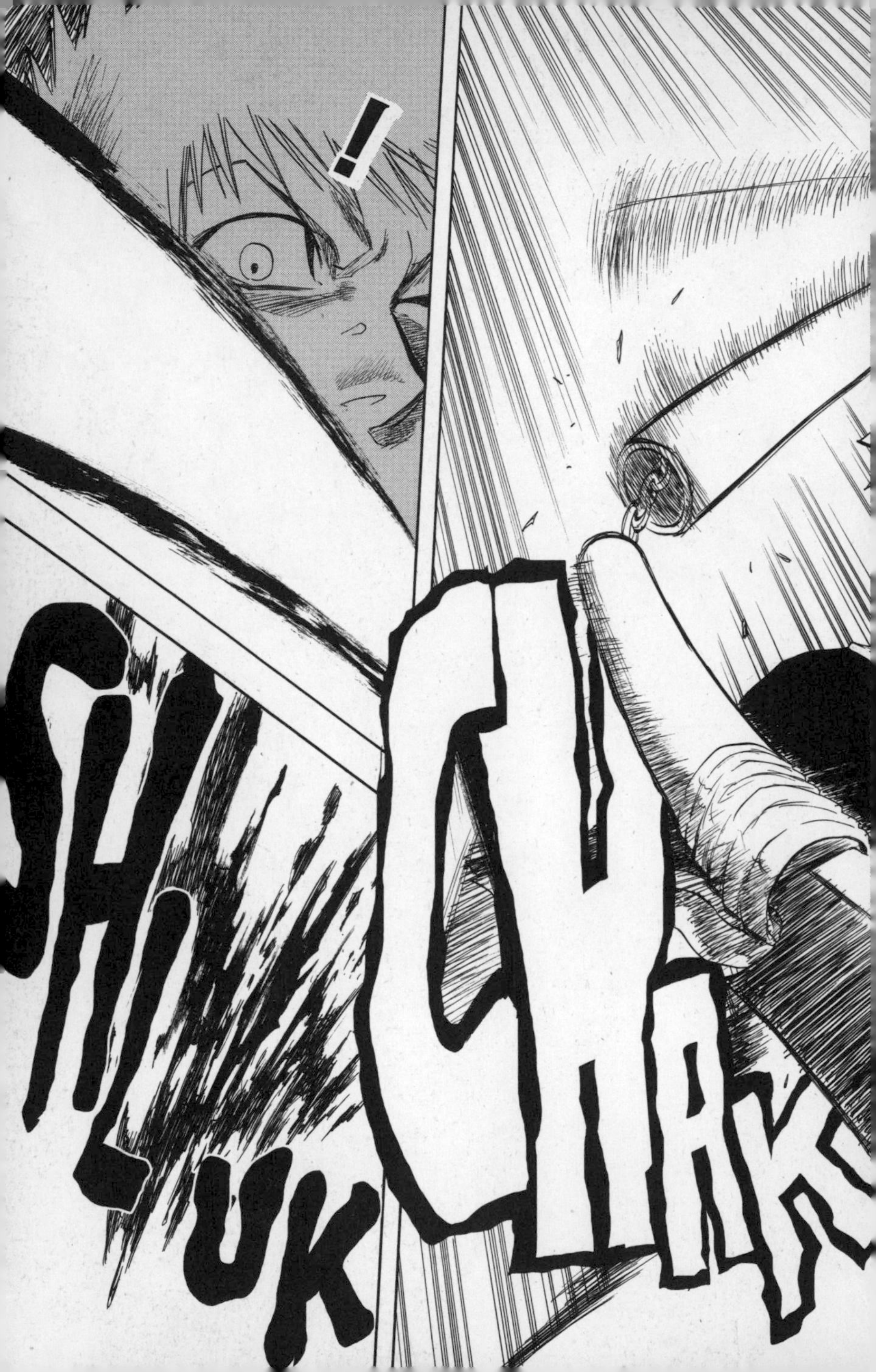
CHAK
!
SHUK

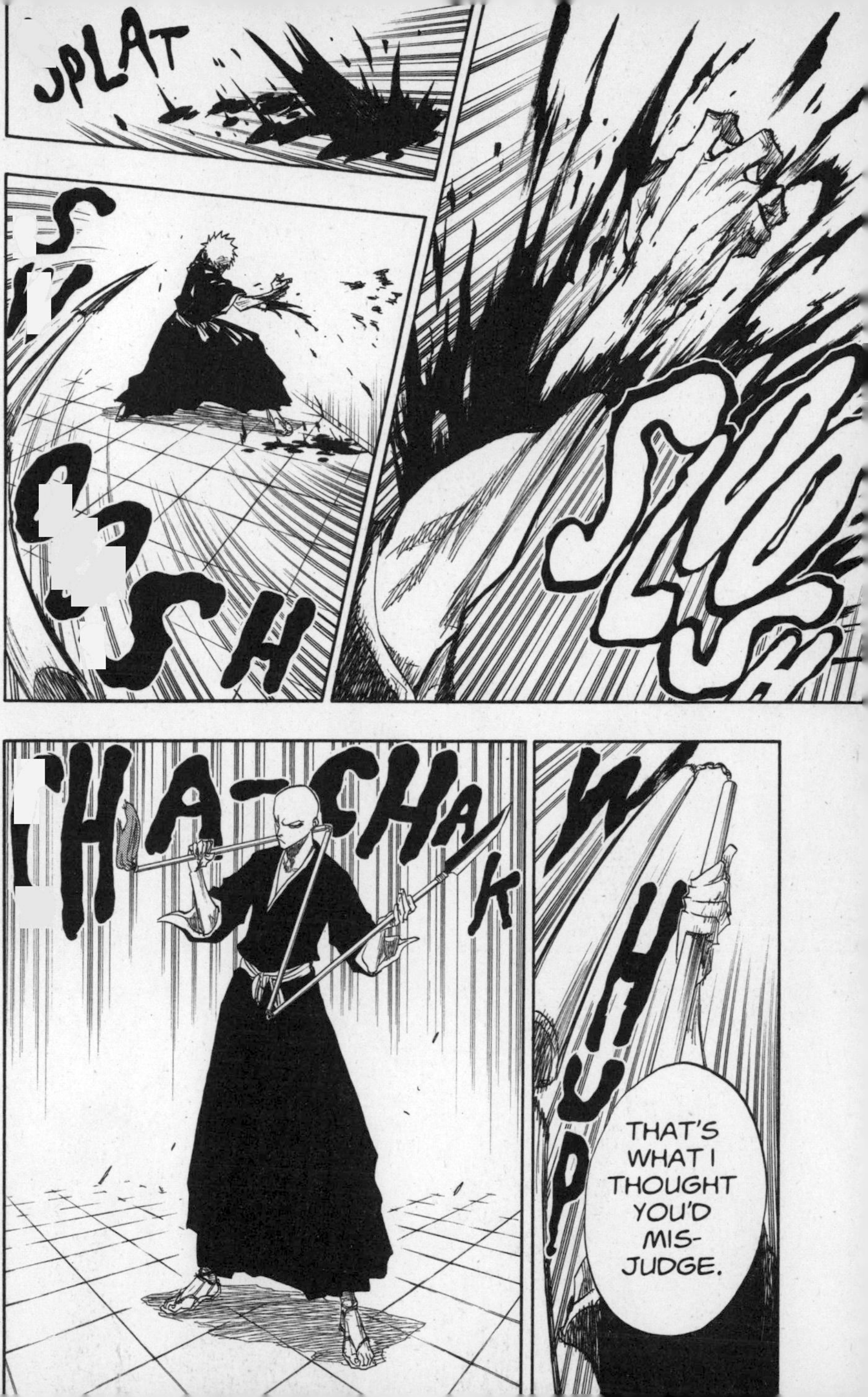
WHUP!
THAT'S WHAT I THOUGHT YOU'D MIS-JUDGE.

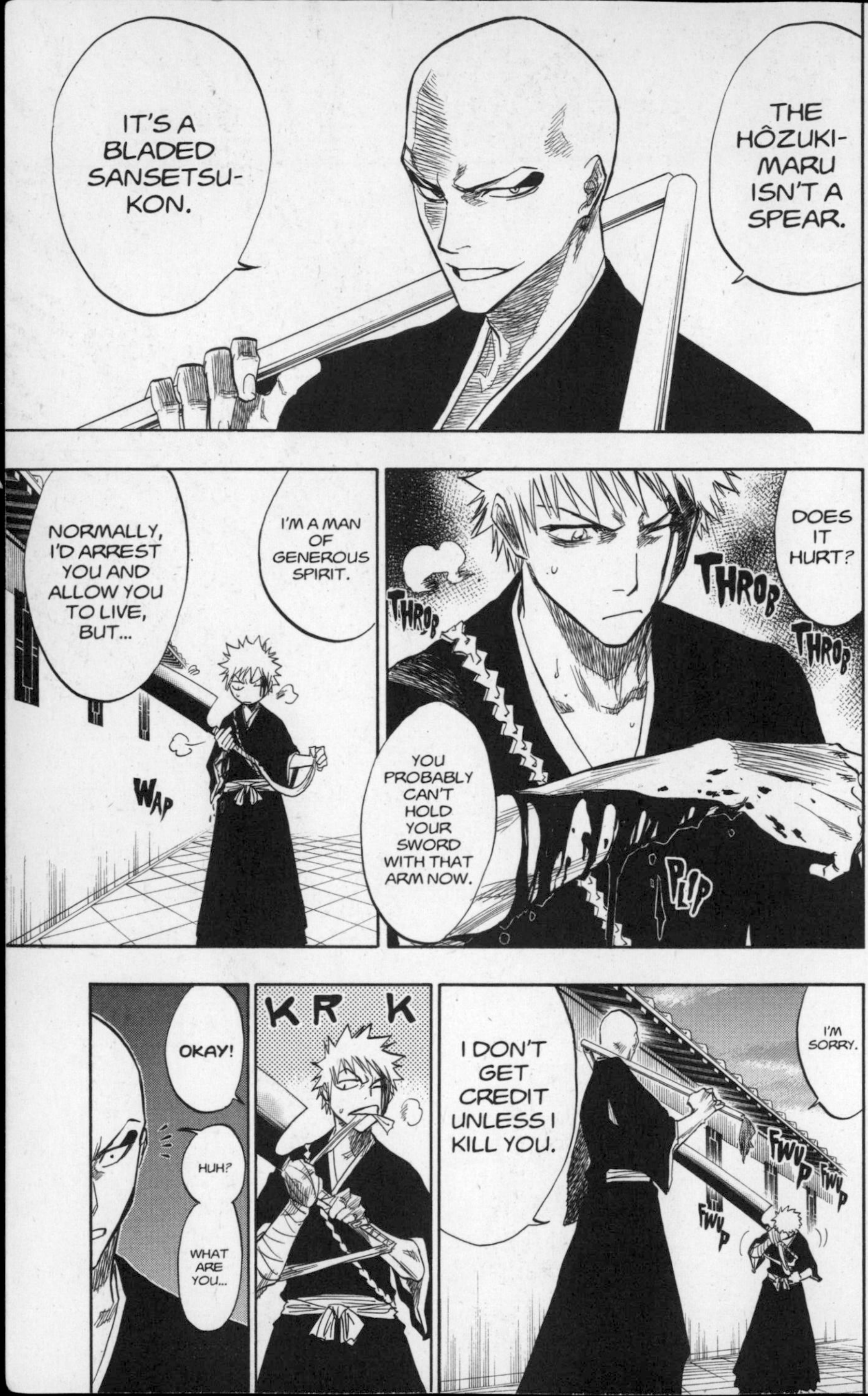
THE HÔZUKI-MARU ISN'T A SPEAR.
IT'S A BLADED SANSETSU-KON.
DOES IT HURT?
THROB
THROB
THROB
YOU PROBABLY CAN'T HOLD YOUR SWORD WITH THAT ARM NOW.
PLIP
I'M A MAN OF GENEROUS SPIRIT.
NORMALLY, I'D ARREST YOU AND ALLOW YOU TO LIVE, BUT...
WAP
I'M SORRY.
I DON'T GET CREDIT UNLESS I KILL YOU.
FWUP
FWUP
FWUP
KR K
OKAY!
HUH?
WHAT ARE YOU...

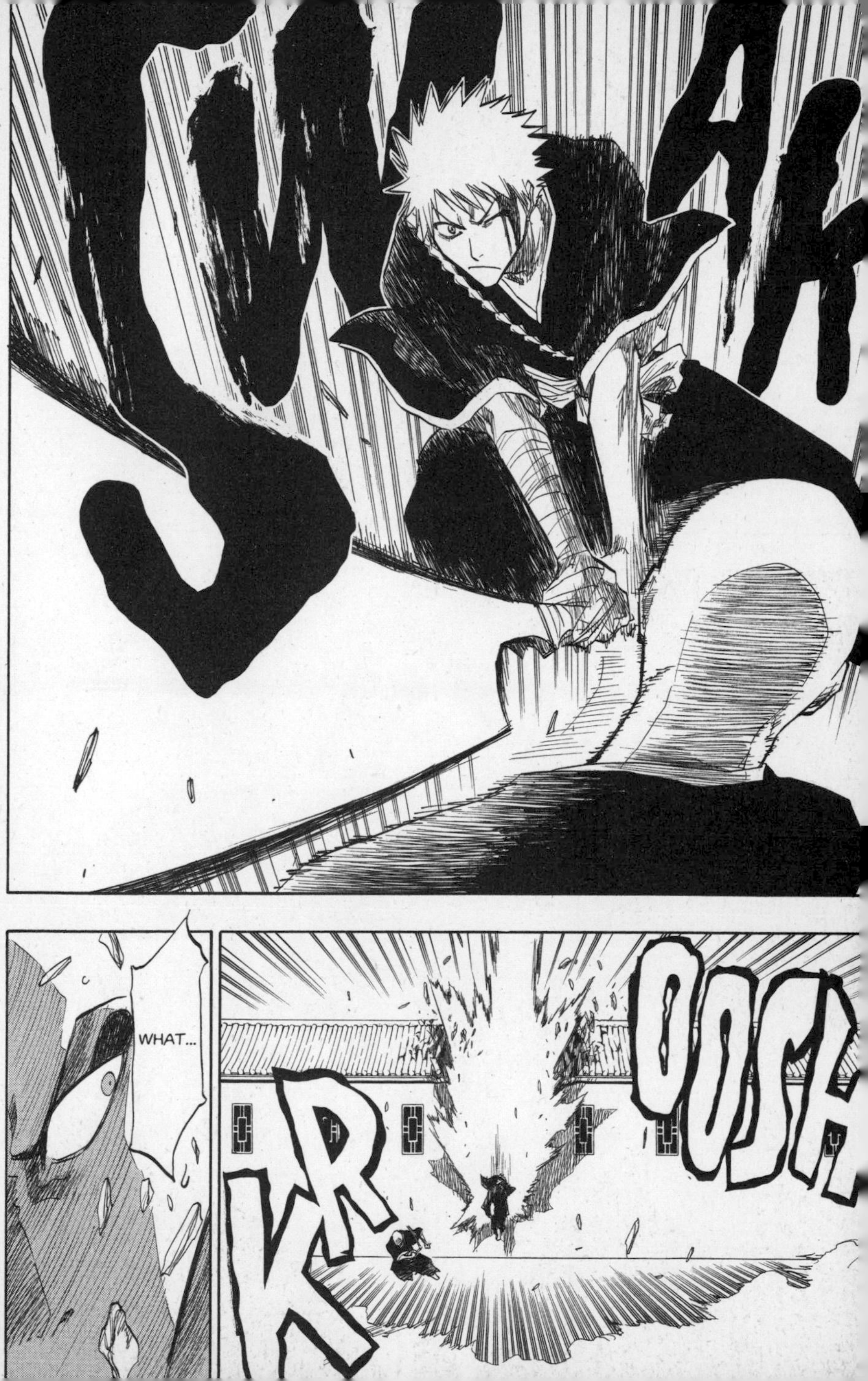
KR
OOSH
WHAT...

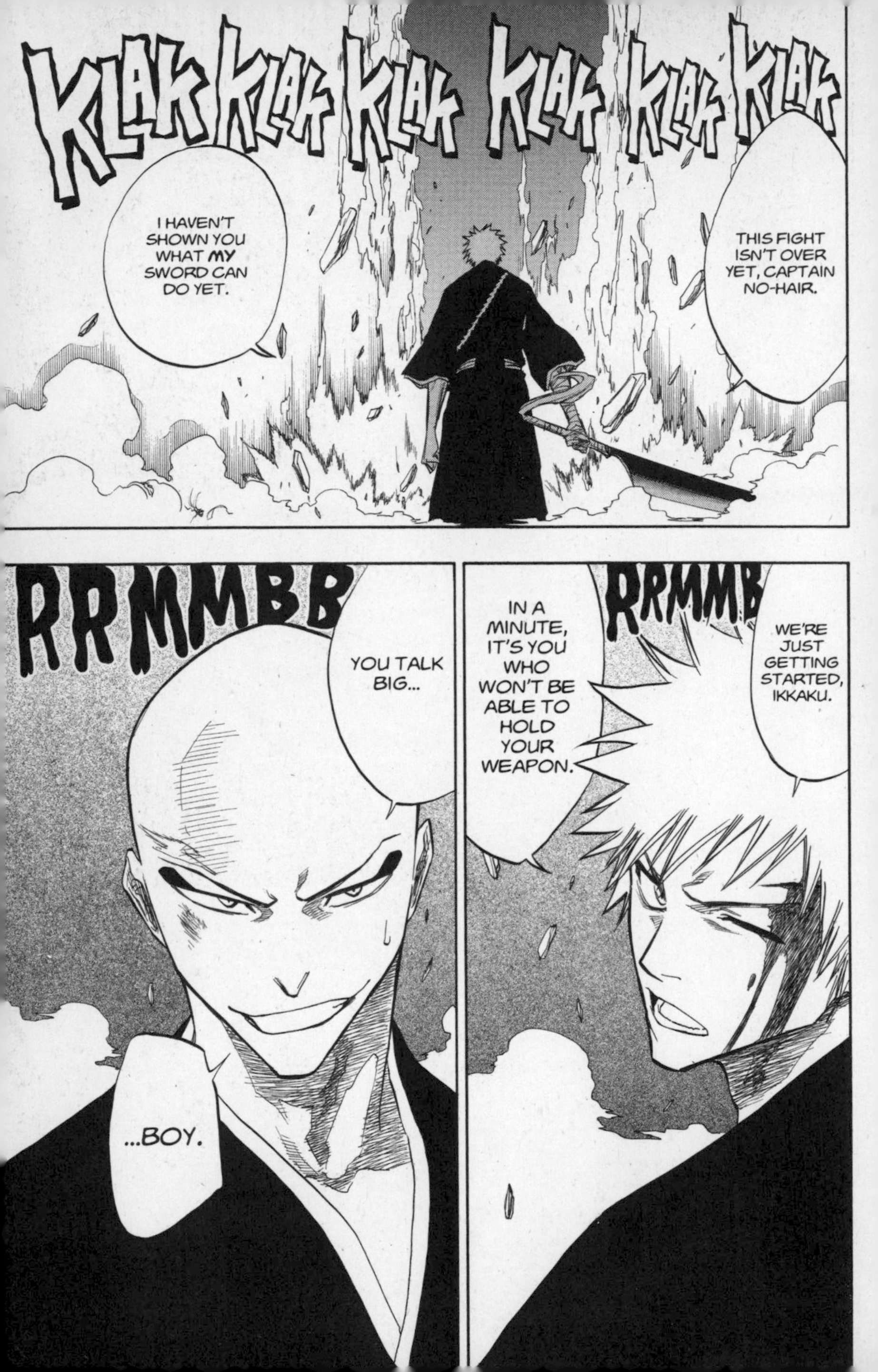
KLAK KLAK KLAK KLAK KLAK KLAK
THIS FIGHT ISN'T OVER YET, CAPTAIN NO-HAIR.
I HAVEN'T SHOWN YOU WHAT MY SWORD CAN DO YET.
RRMMB
WE'RE JUST GETTING STARTED, IKKAKU.
IN A MINUTE, IT'S YOU WHO WON'T BE ABLE TO HOLD YOUR WEAPON.
RRMMBB
YOU TALK BIG...
...BOY.

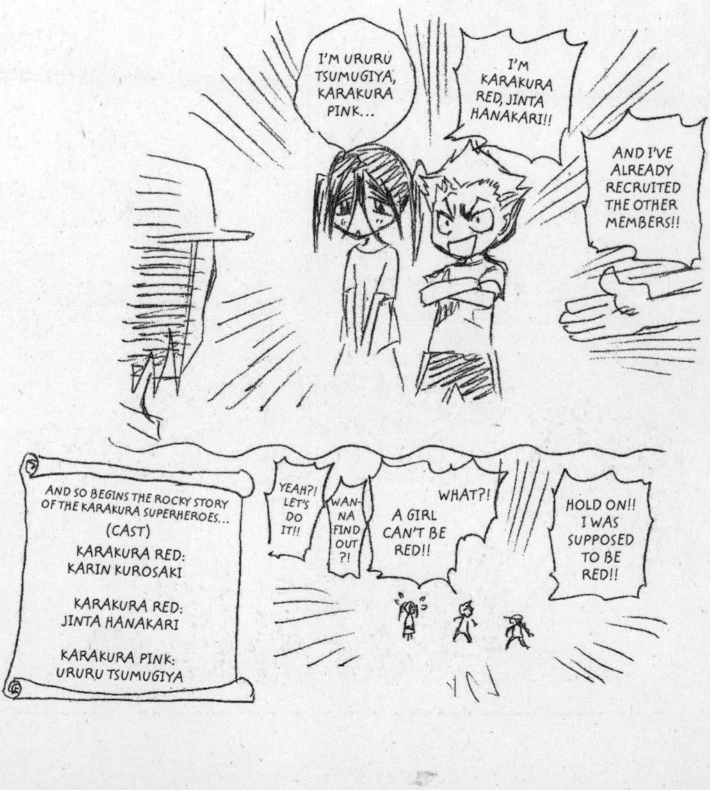
I'M KARAKURA RED, JINTA HANAKARI!!
AND I'VE ALREADY RECRUITED THE OTHER MEMBERS!!
I'M URURU TSUMUGIYA, KARAKURA PINK...
HOLD ON!! I WAS SUPPOSED TO BE RED!!
WHAT?!
A GIRL CAN'T BE RED!!
WANNA FIND OUT?!
YEAH?! LET'S DO IT!!
AND SO BEGINS THE ROCKY STORY OF THE KARAKURA SUPERHEROES...
(CAST)
KARAKURA RED: KARIN KUROSAKI
KARAKURA RED: JINTA HANAKARI
KARAKURA PINK: URURU TSUMUGIYA

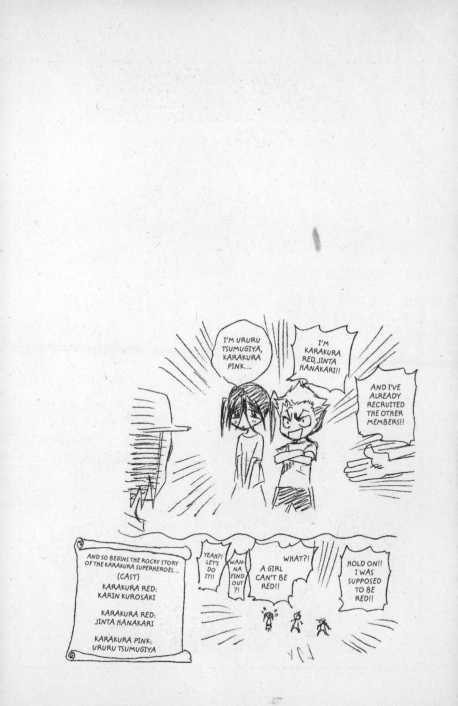

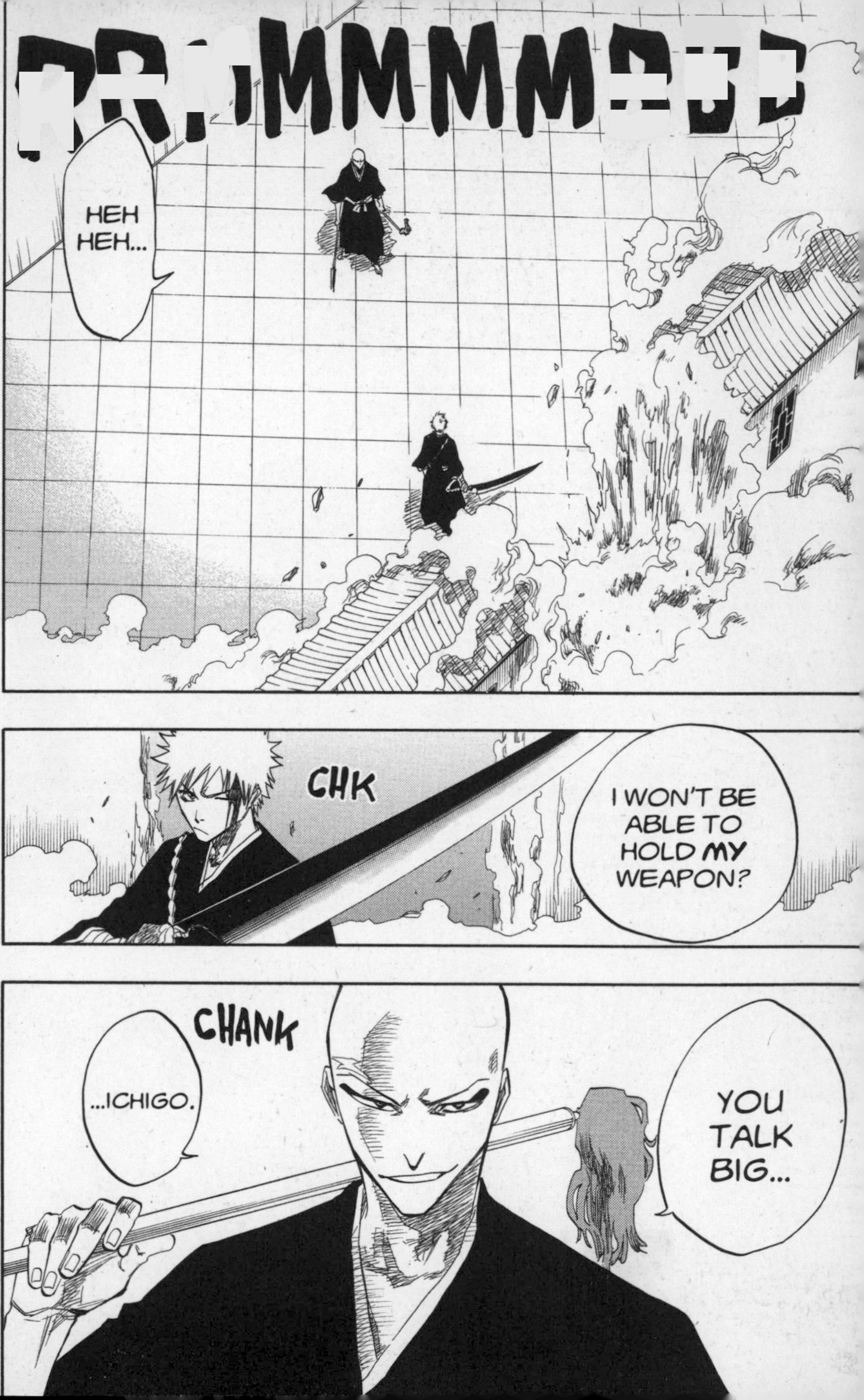
HEH HEH...
I WON'T BE ABLE TO HOLD MY WEAPON?
CHK
YOU TALK BIG...
CHANK
...ICHIGO.

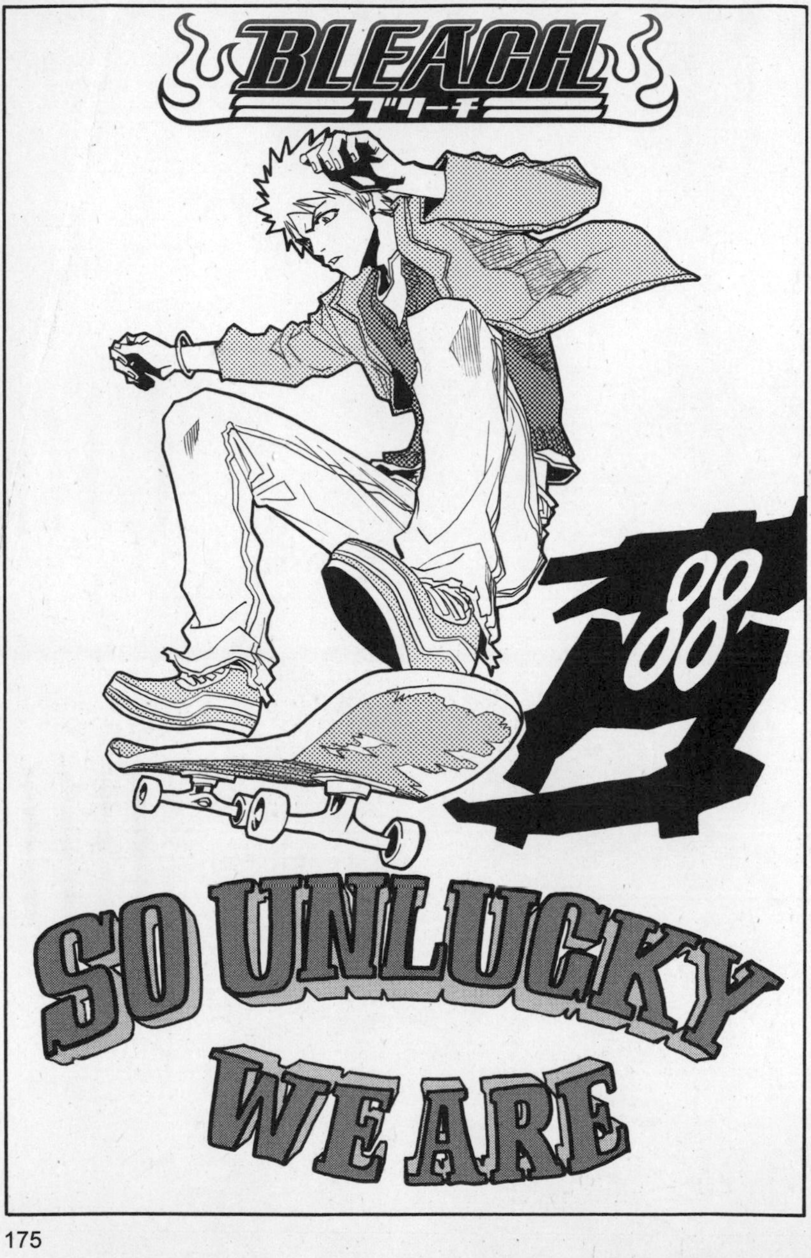
BLEACH
ブリーチ
-88-
SO UNLUCKY
WE ARE

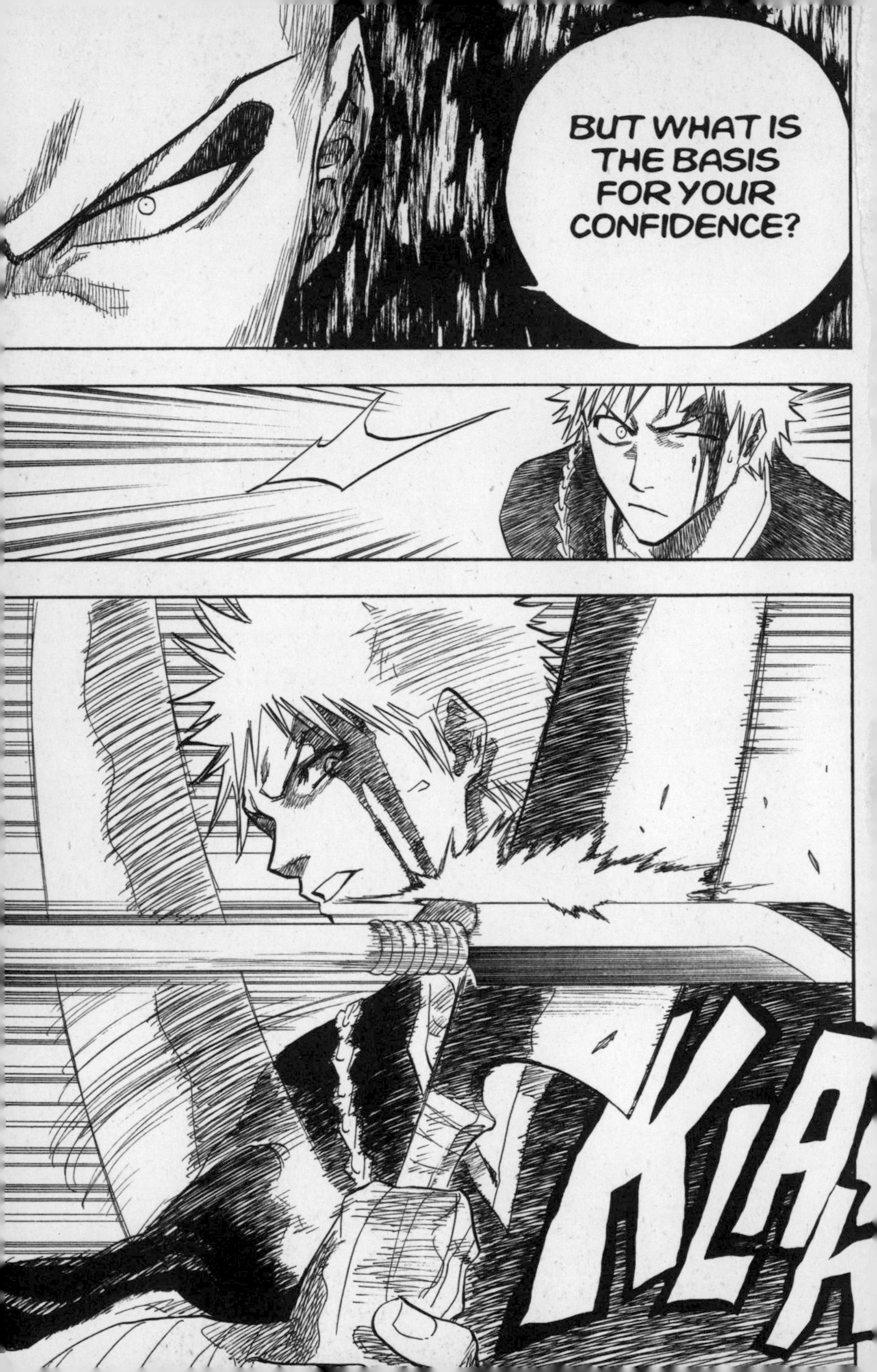
BUT WHAT IS THE BASIS FOR YOUR CONFIDENCE?
KLA

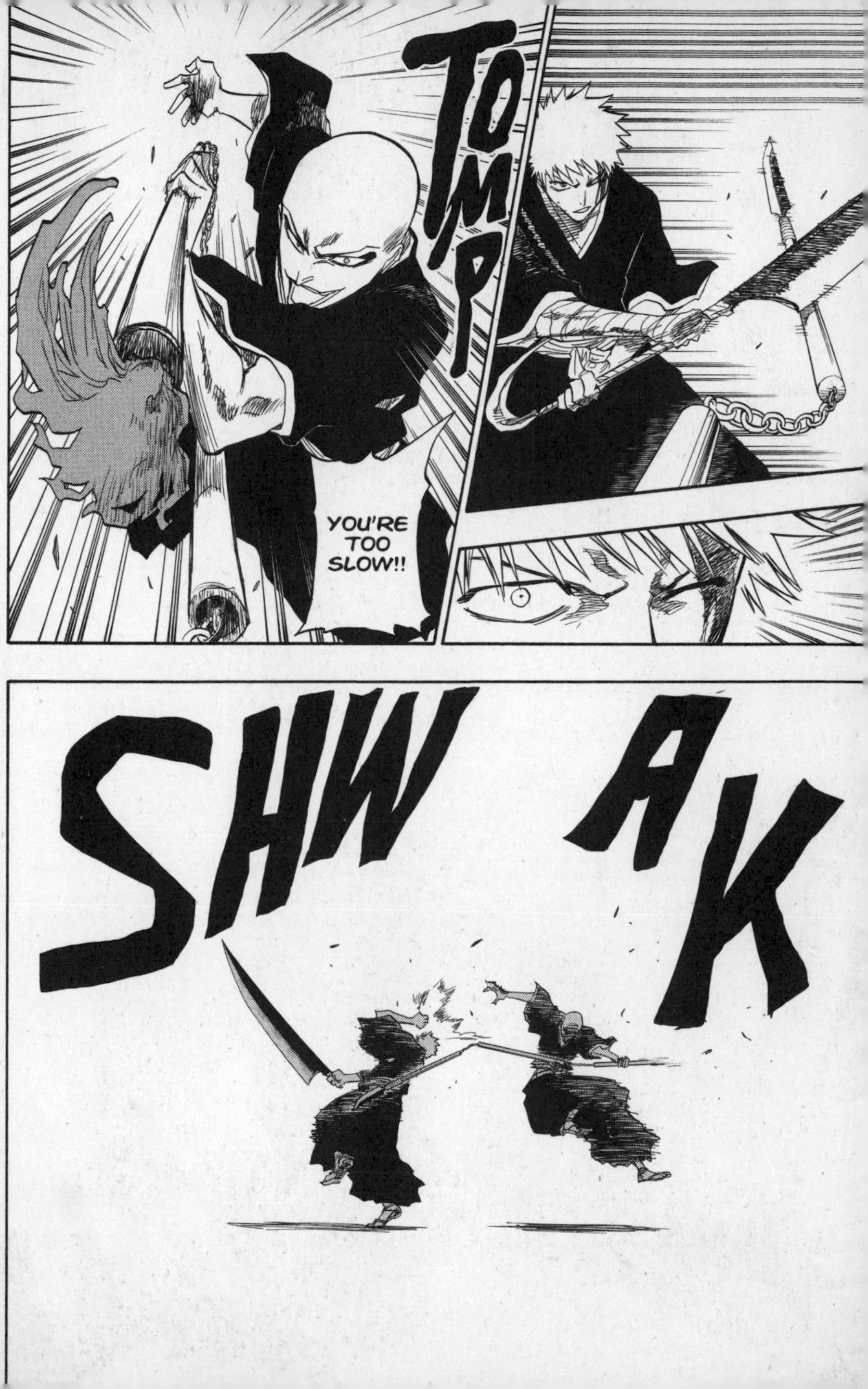
TOMP
YOU'RE TOO SLOW!!
SHWAK

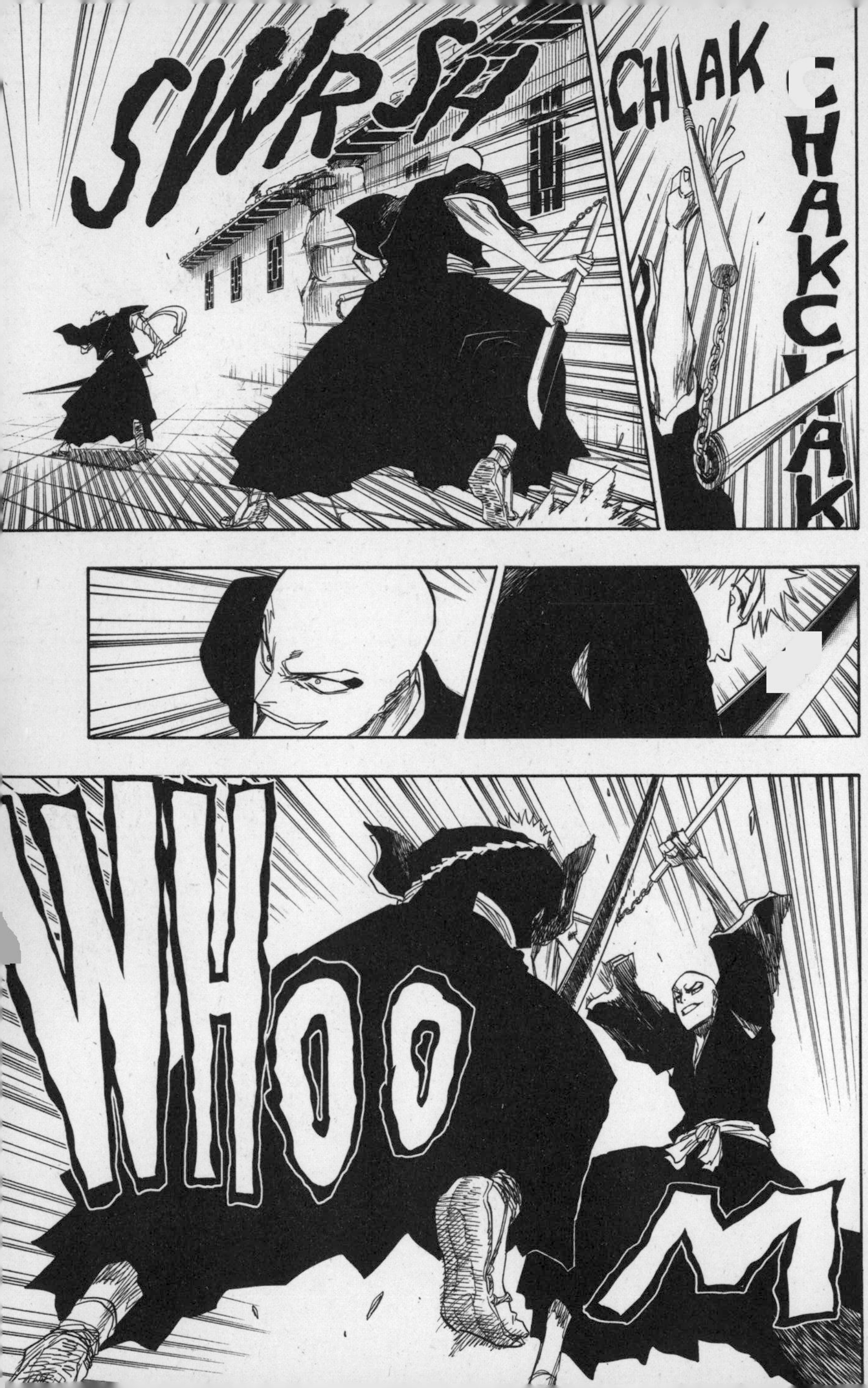
CHAK
CHAKCHAK
SWISH
WHOOM

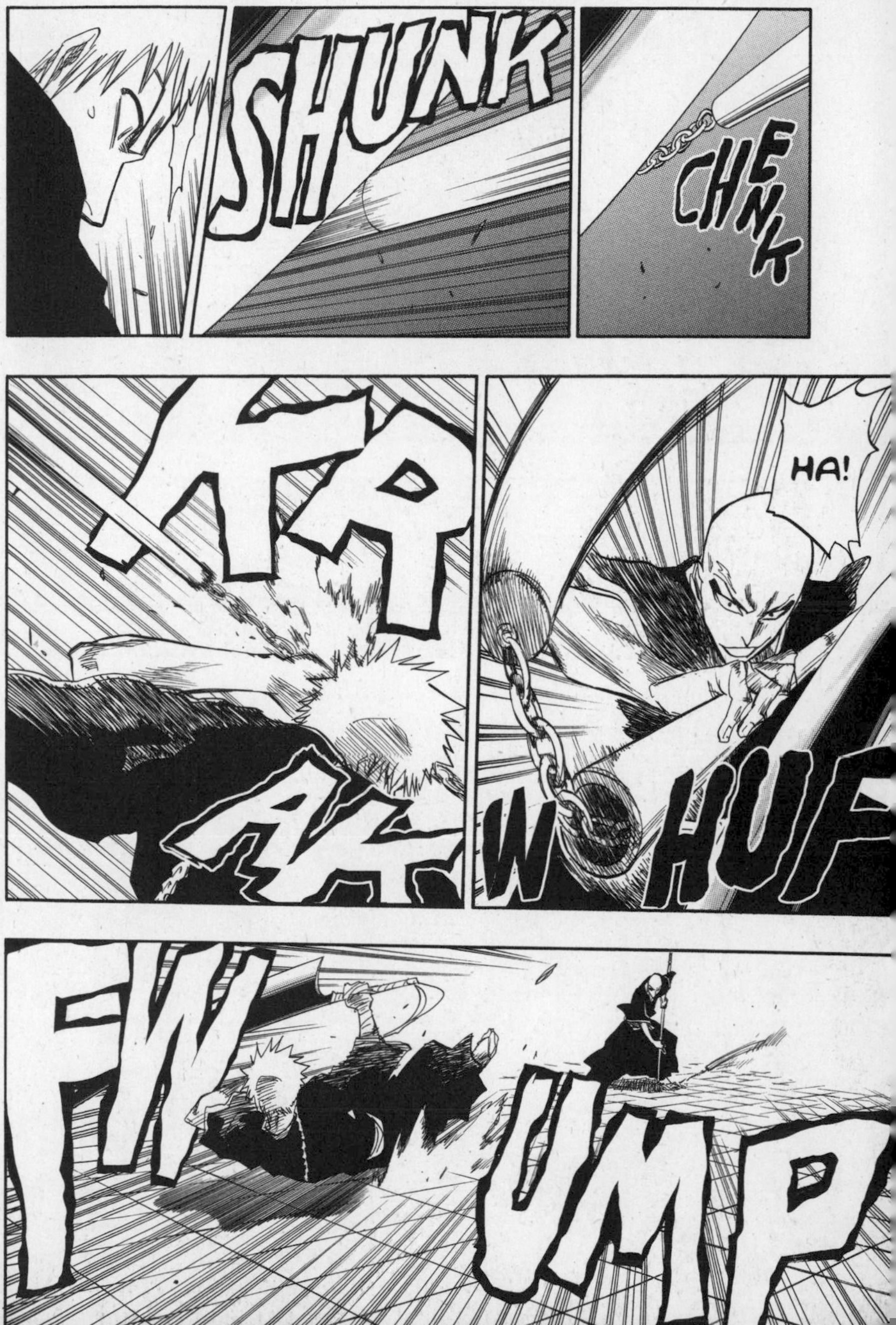
CHENK
SHUNK
HA!
WHUF
FWUMP

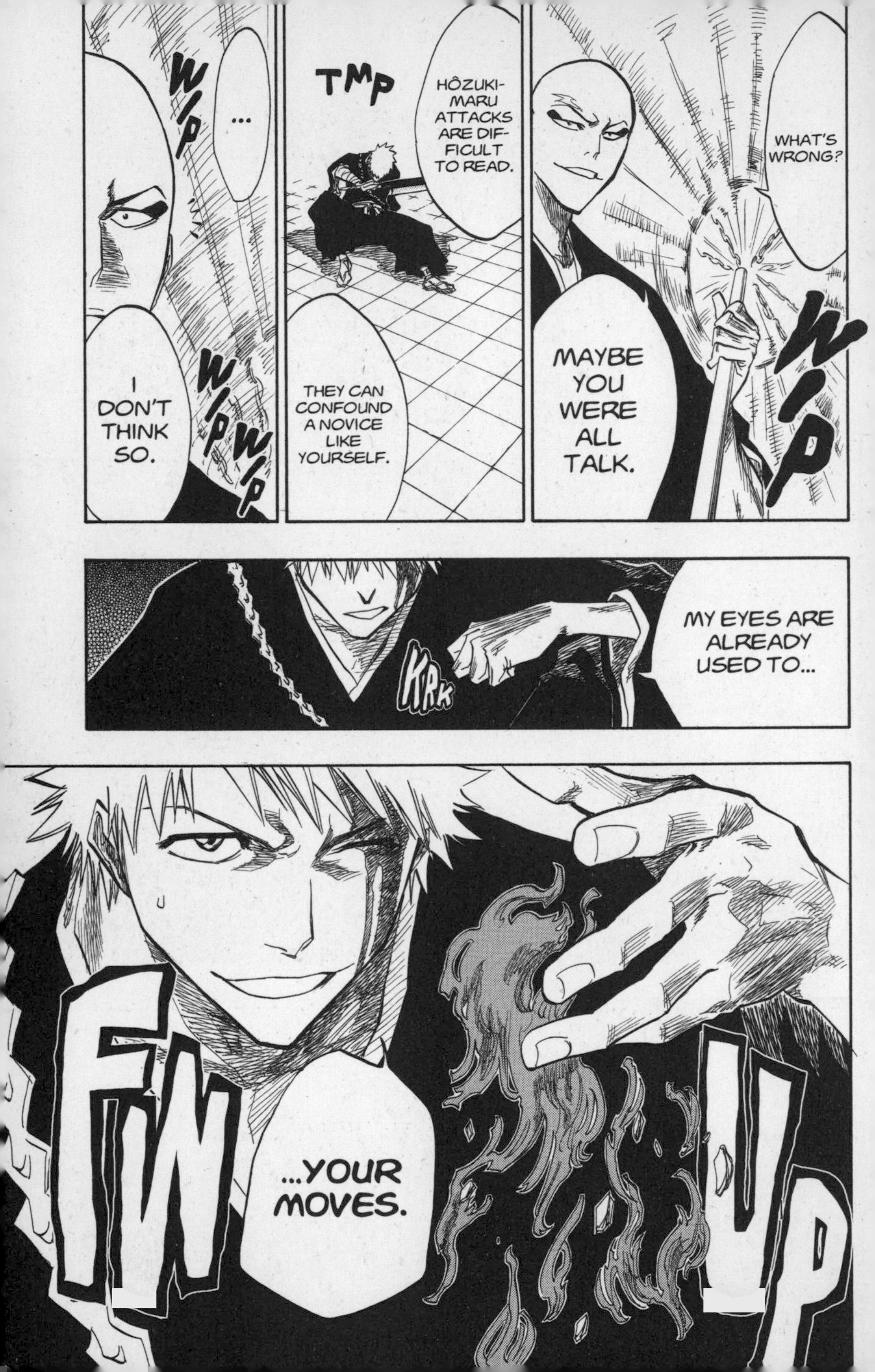
WHAT'S WRONG?
WIP
MAYBE YOU WERE ALL TALK.
TMP
HÔZUKI-MARU ATTACKS ARE DIFFICULT TO READ.
THEY CAN CONFOUND A NOVICE LIKE YOURSELF.
WIP
...
WIP WIP WIP
I DON'T THINK SO.
MY EYES ARE ALREADY USED TO...
KRK
FWUP
...YOUR MOVES.

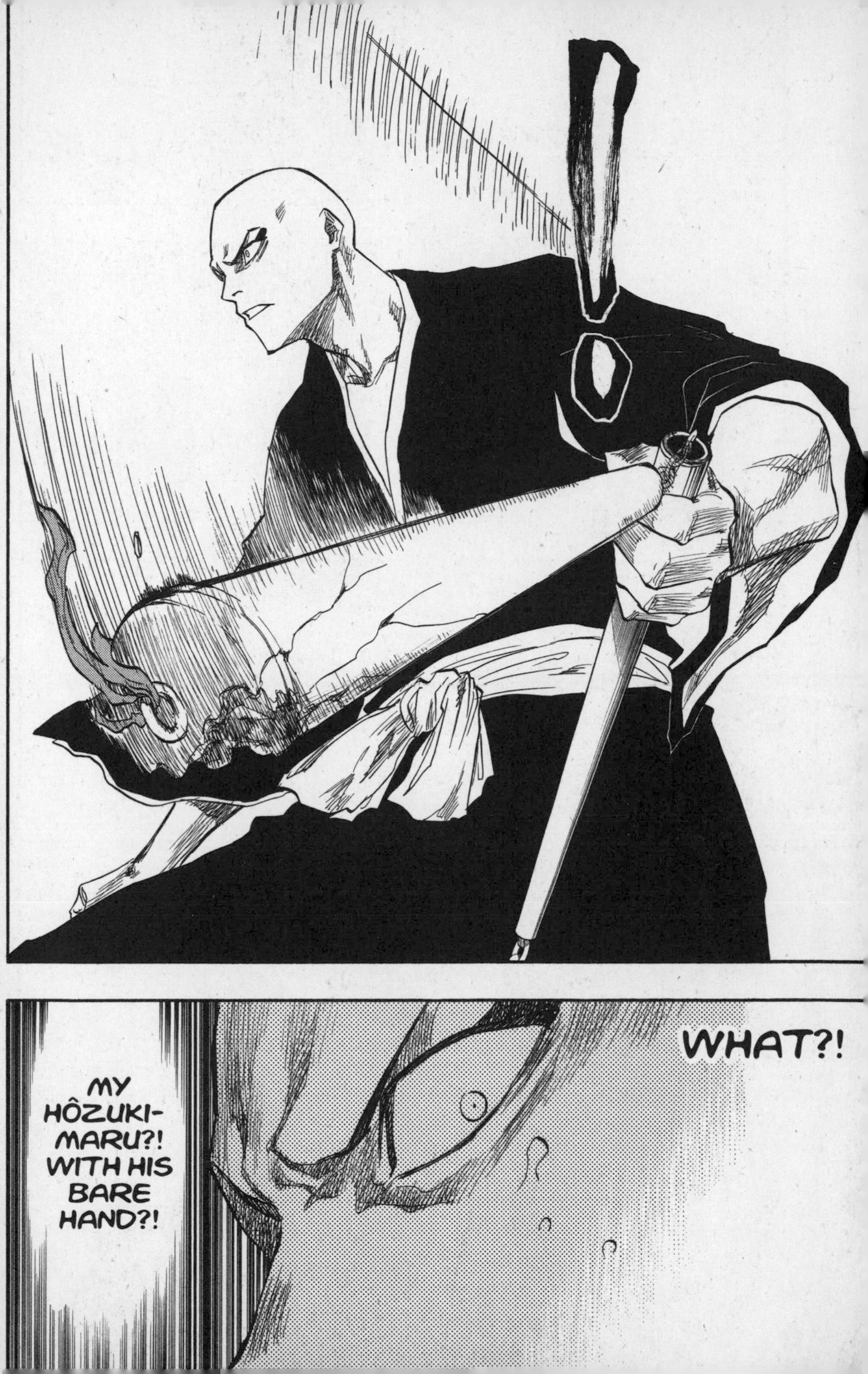
WHAT?!
MY HÔZUKI-MARU?! WITH HIS BARE HAND?!

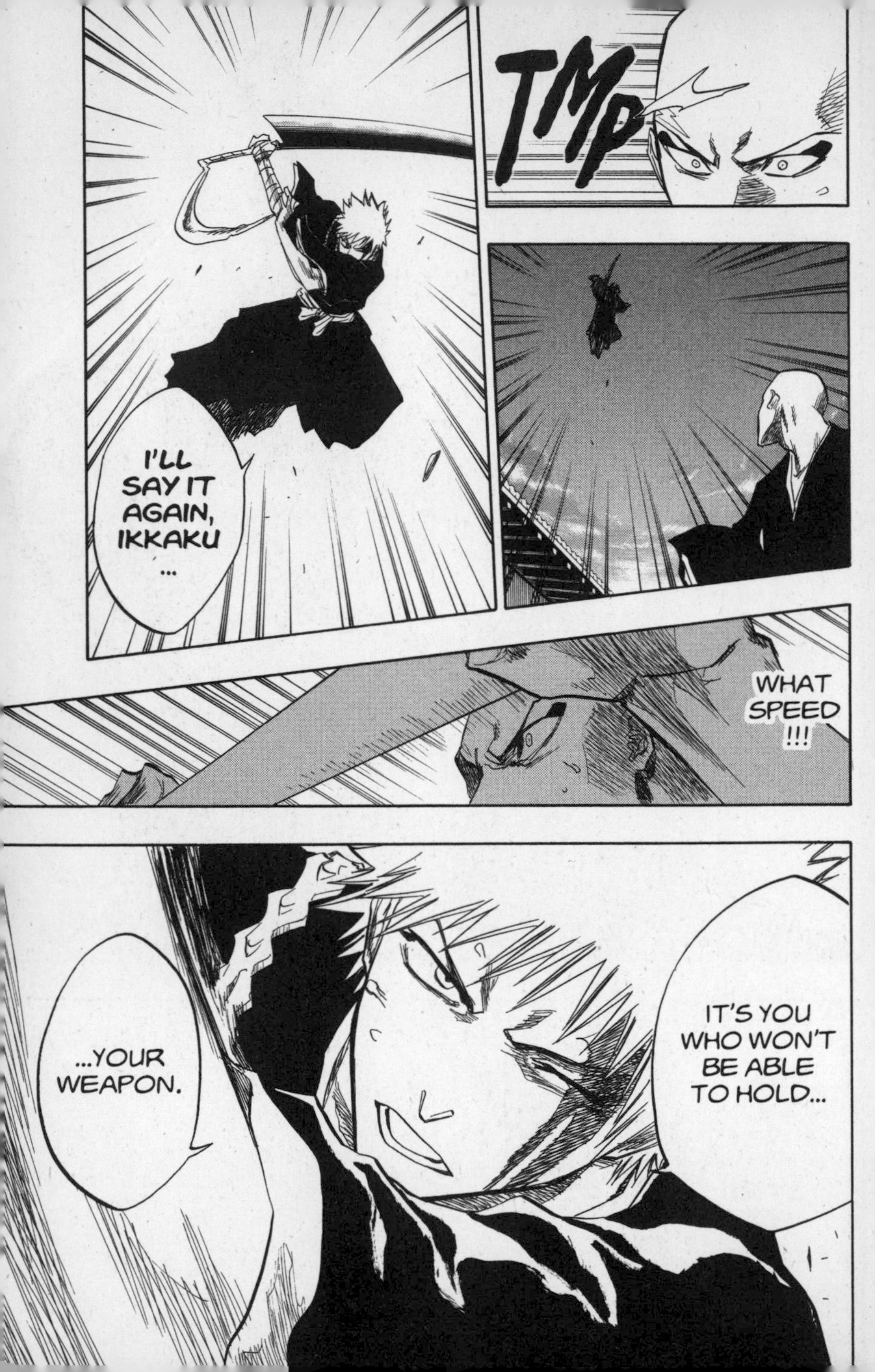
TMP
I'LL SAY IT AGAIN, IKKAKU...
WHAT SPEED!!!
IT'S YOU WHO WON'T BE ABLE TO HOLD...
...YOUR WEAPON.

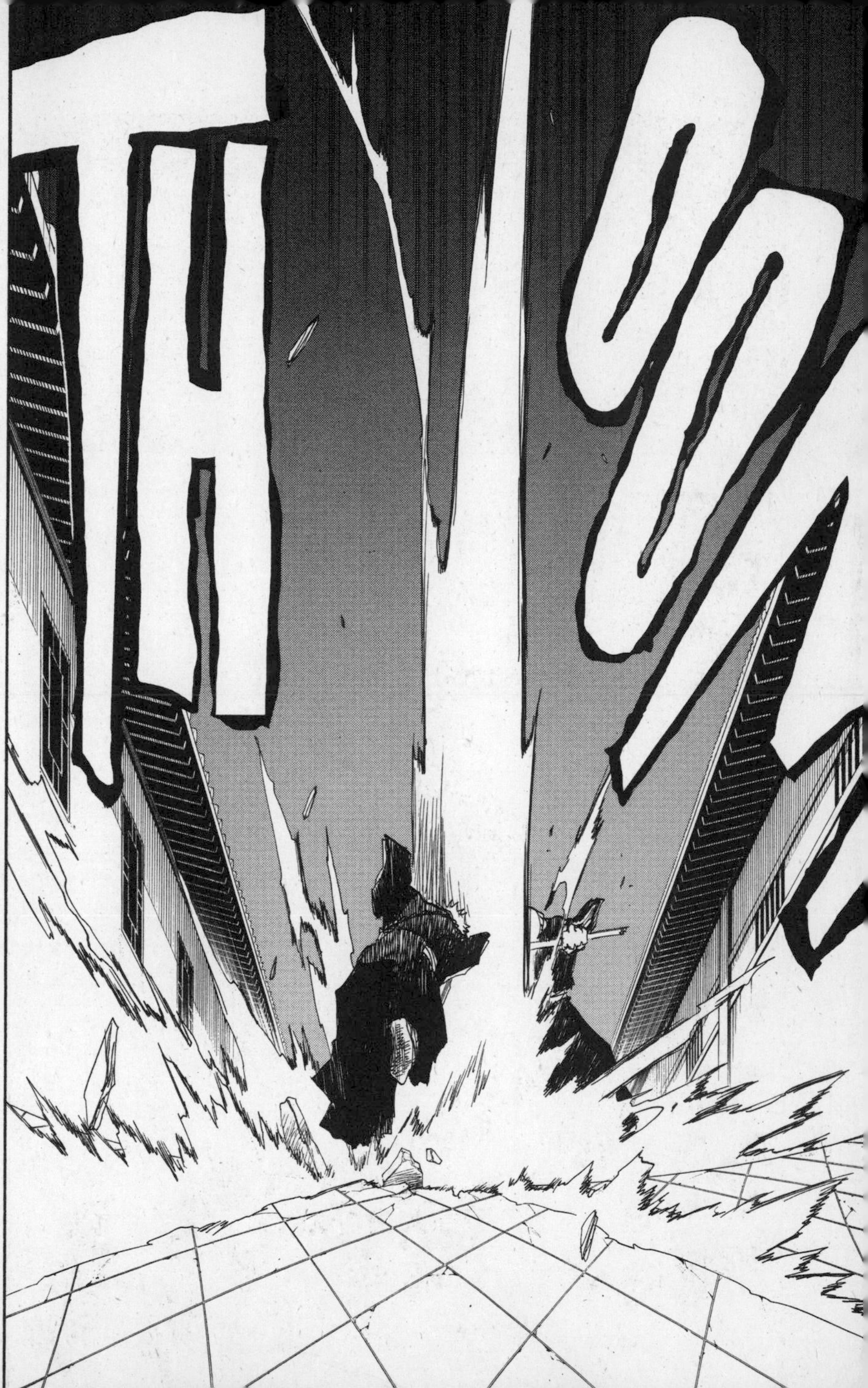

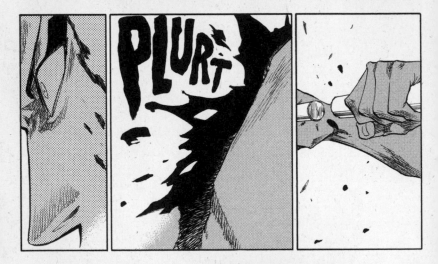

PLURT

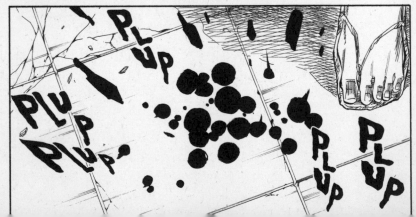

PLUP

PLUP
P

PLUP

PLUP

PLUP

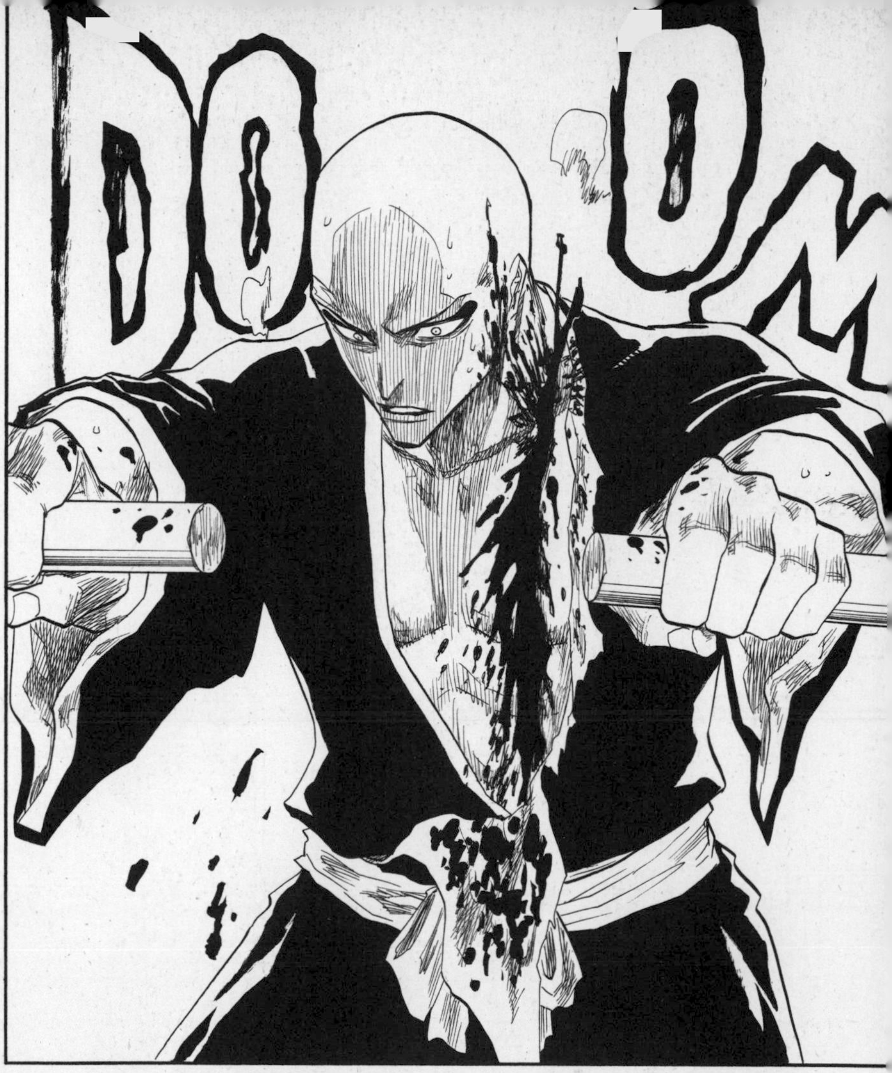
DOOM

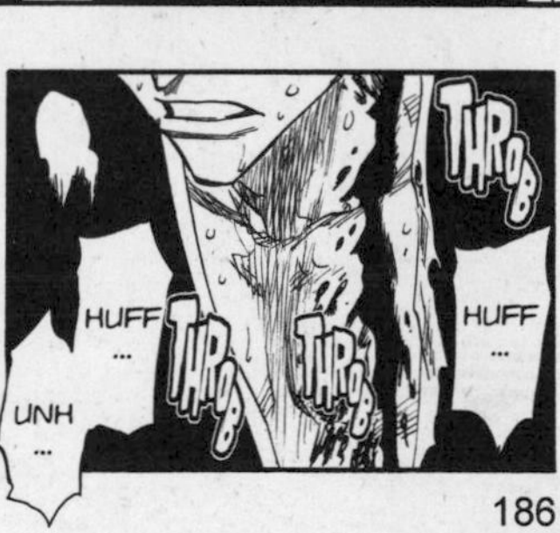
THROB
HUFF ...
THROB
THROB
HUFF ...
UNH ...

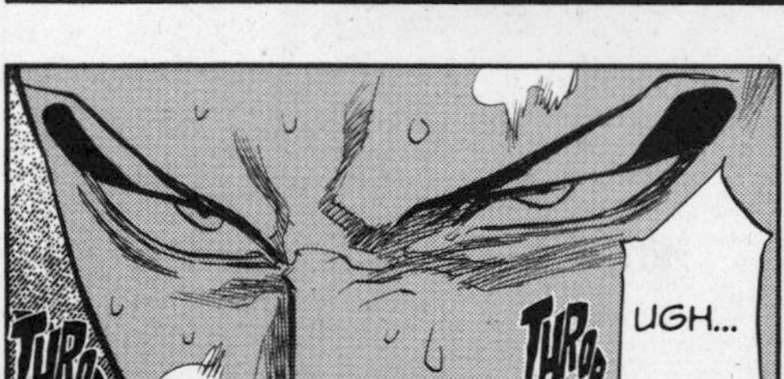
UGH...
THROB
THROB

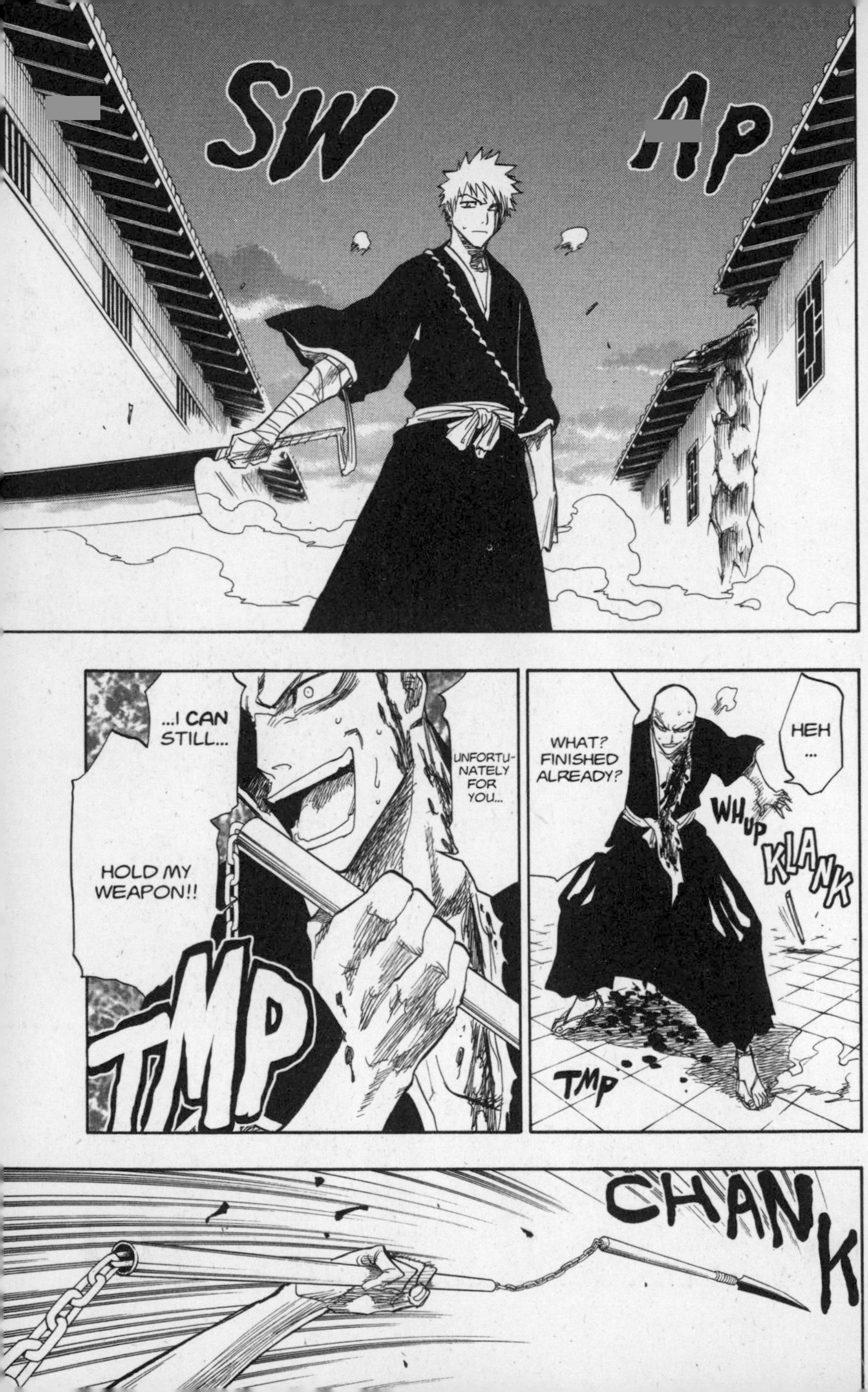
SW AP
HEH ...
WHAT? FINISHED ALREADY?
WHUP
KLANK
TMP
UNFORTU-NATELY FOR YOU...
...I CAN STILL...
HOLD MY WEAPON!!
TMP
CHANK

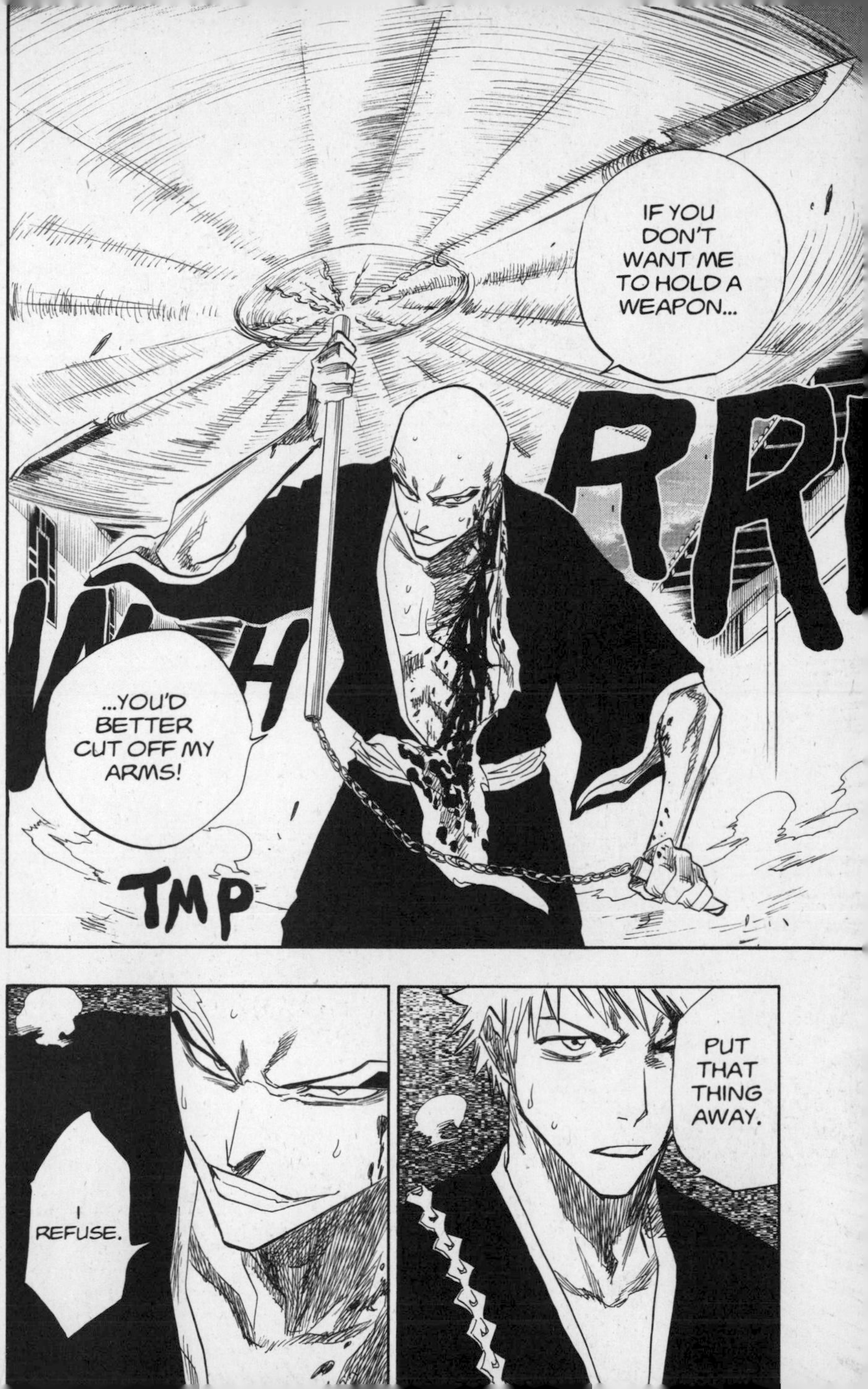
IF YOU DON'T WANT ME TO HOLD A WEAPON...
RRR
WH
...YOU'D BETTER CUT OFF MY ARMS!
TMP
PUT THAT THING AWAY.
I REFUSE.

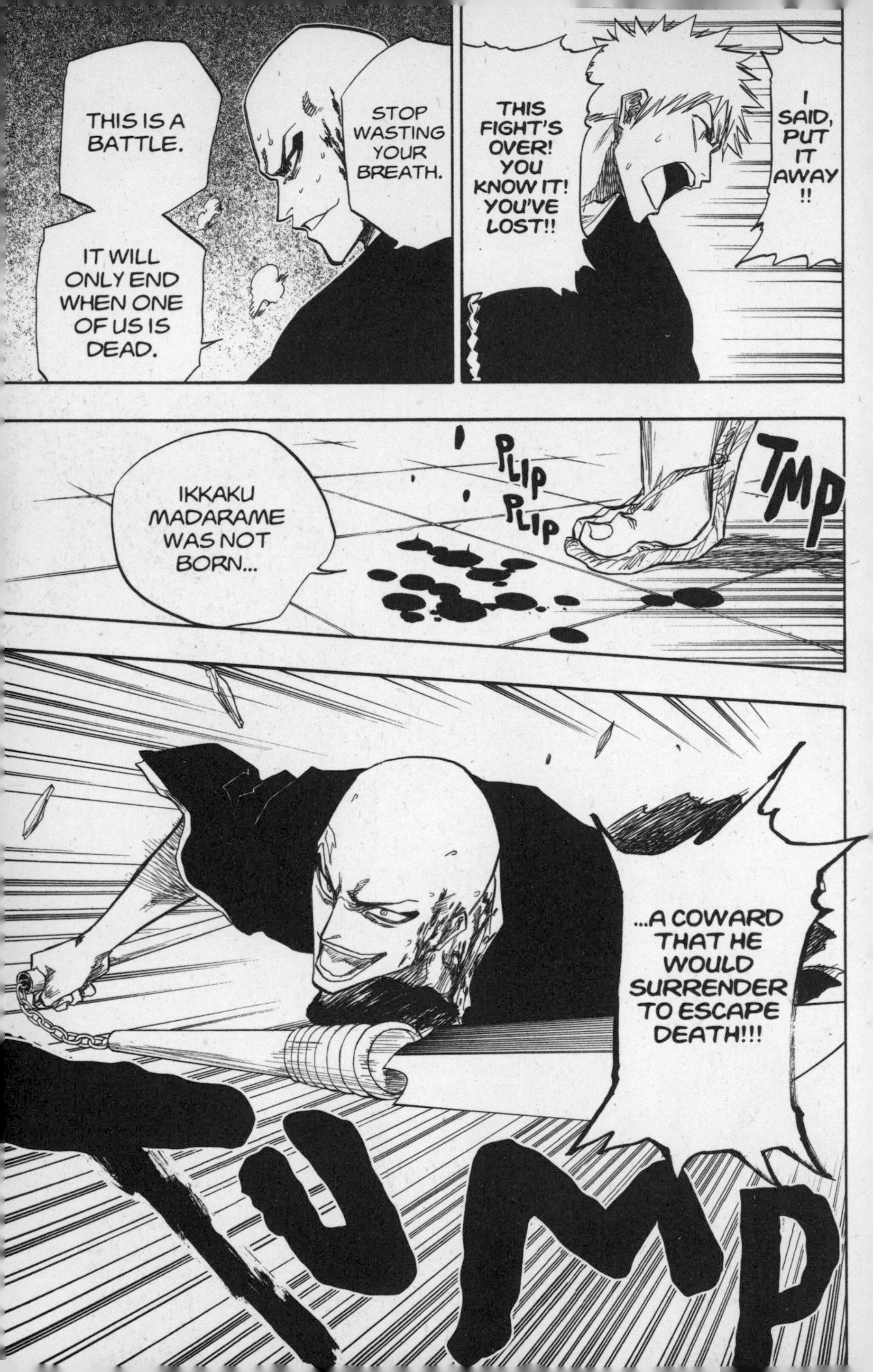
I SAID, PUT IT AWAY!!
THIS FIGHT'S OVER! YOU KNOW IT! YOU'VE LOST!!
STOP WASTING YOUR BREATH.
THIS IS A BATTLE.
IT WILL ONLY END WHEN ONE OF US IS DEAD.
TMP
PLIP PLIP
IKKAKU MADARAME WAS NOT BORN...
...A COWARD THAT HE WOULD SURRENDER TO ESCAPE DEATH!!!

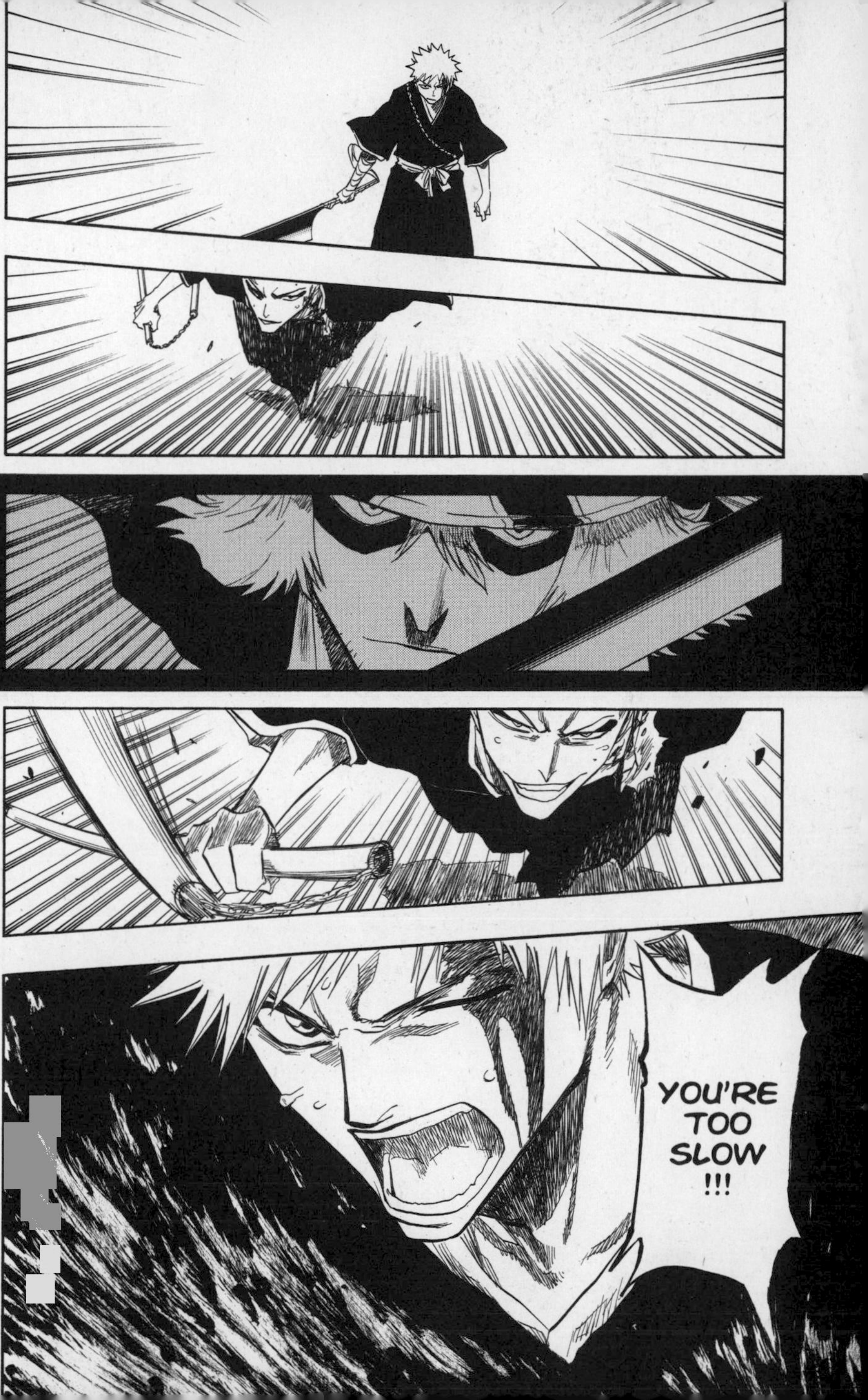
YOU'RE TOO SLOW !!!

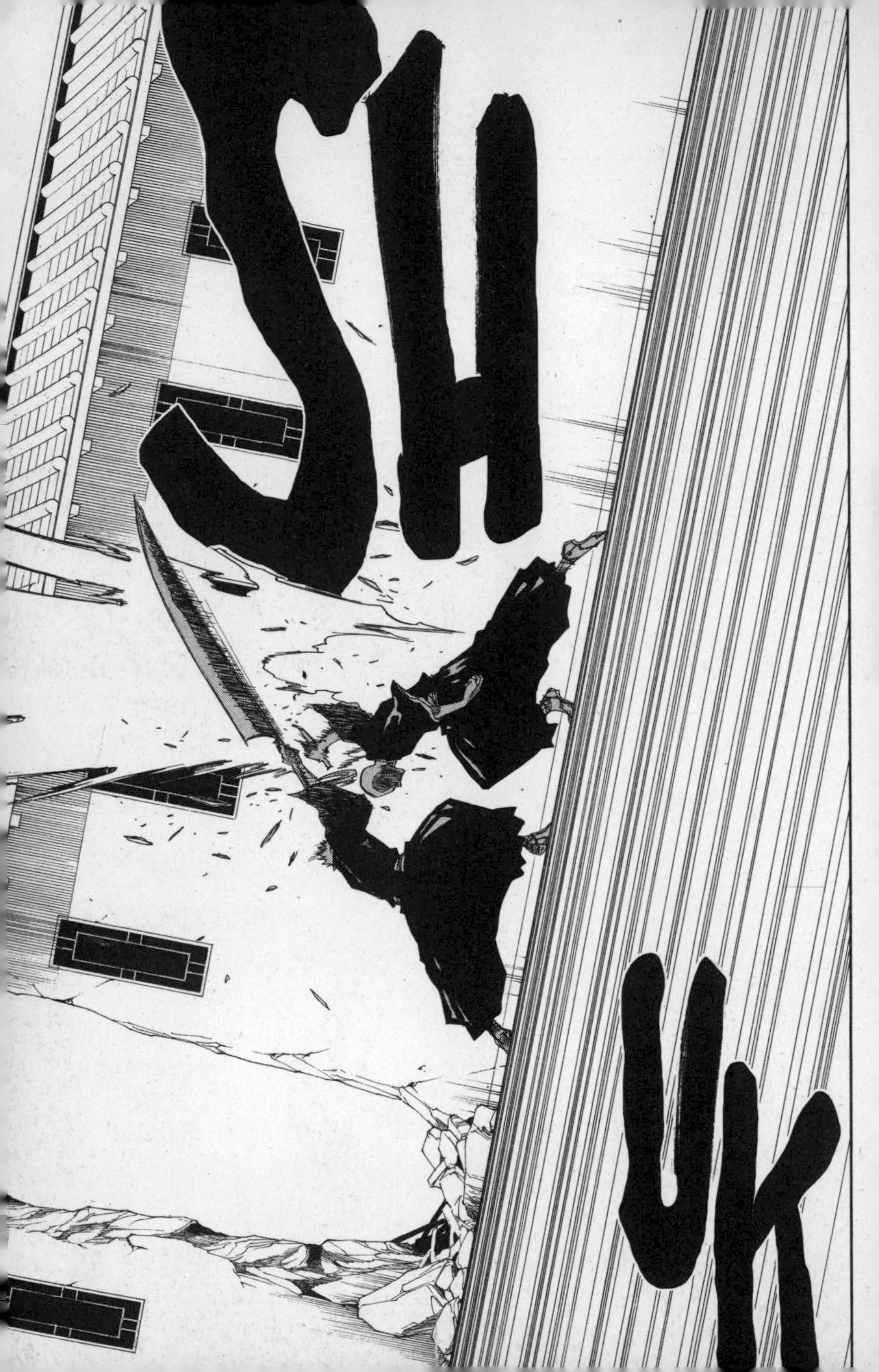
SHUK

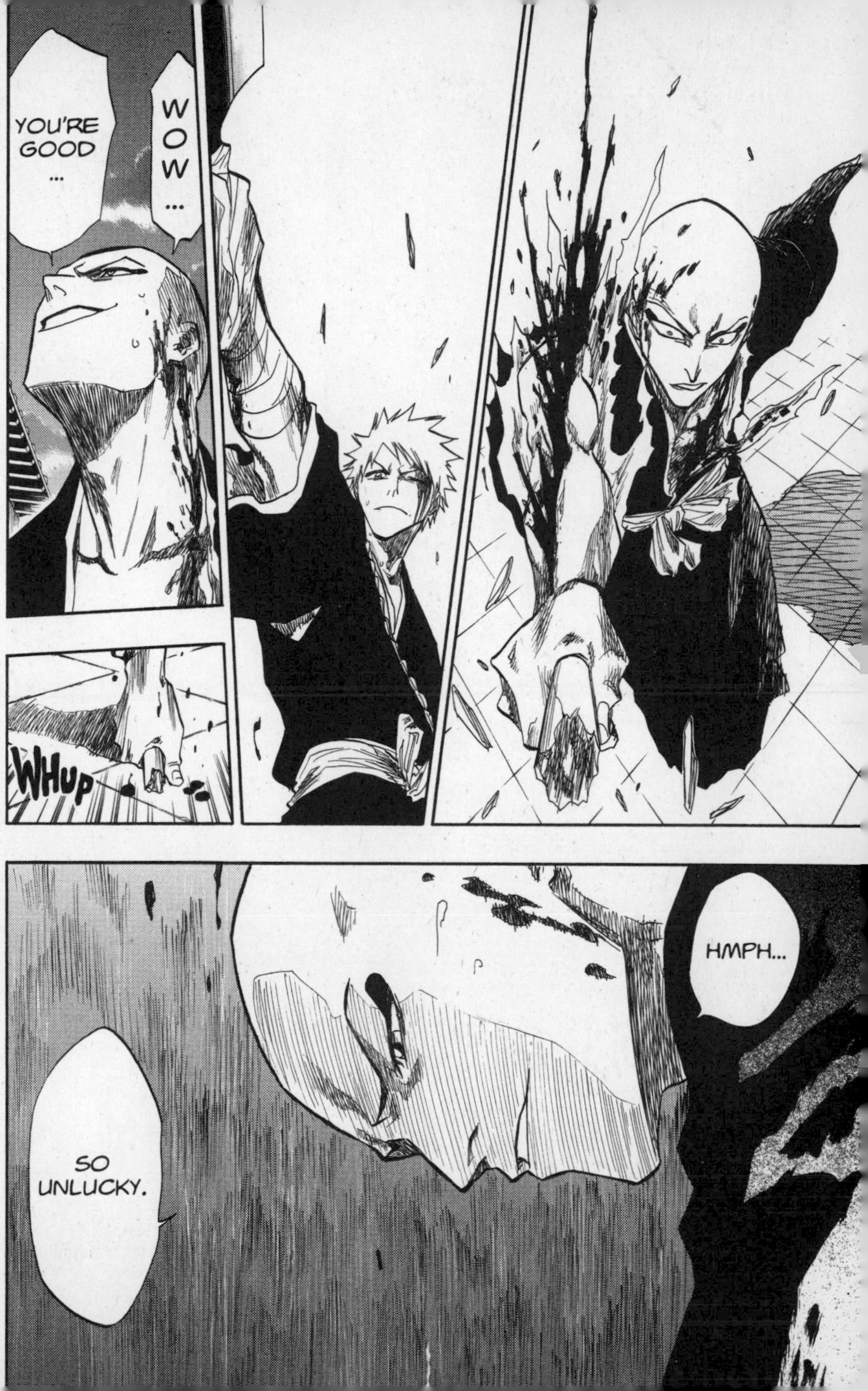
WOW...
YOU'RE GOOD...
WHUP
HMPH...
SO UNLUCKY.

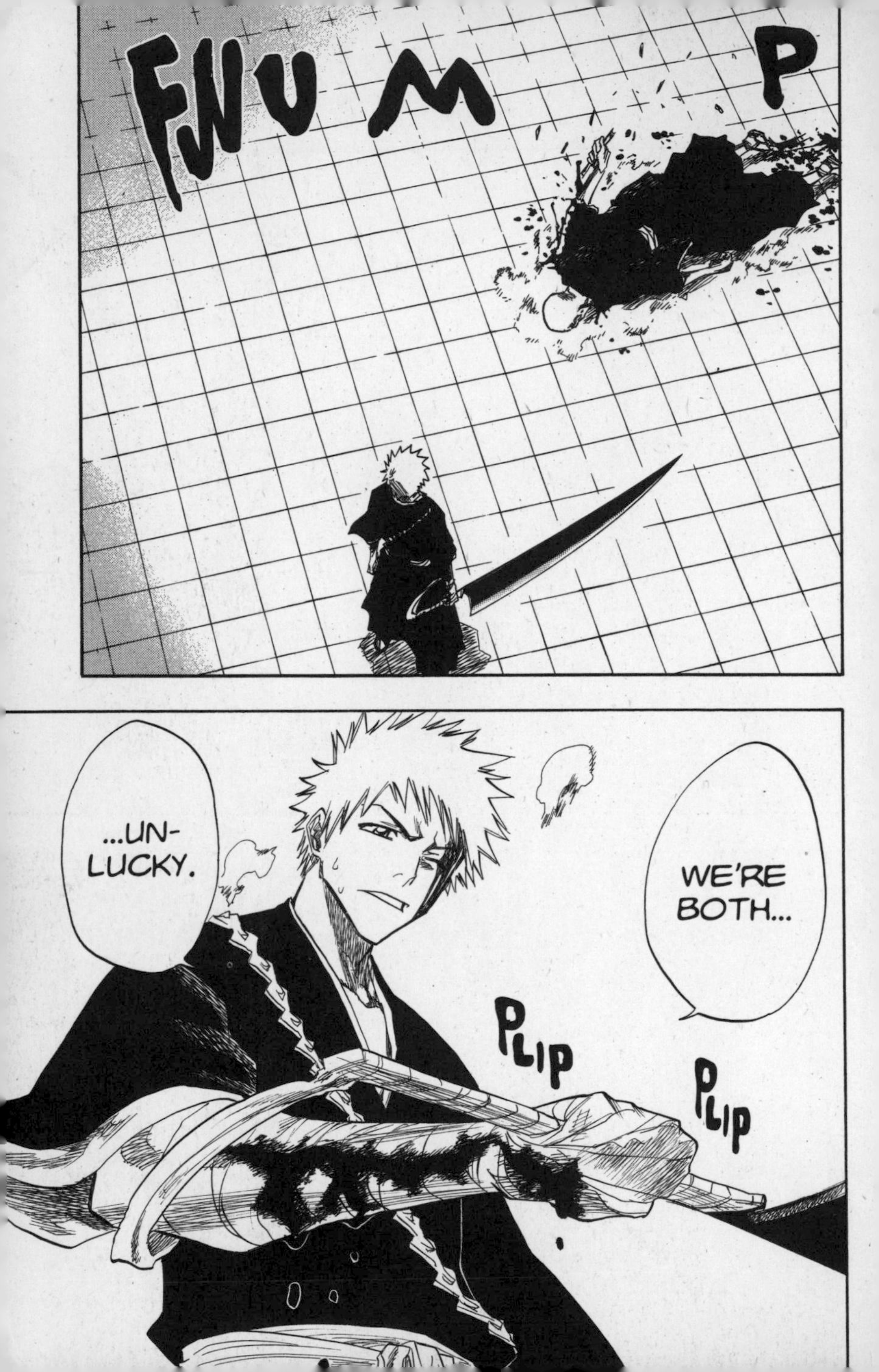
FWUMP
WE'RE BOTH...
...UN-LUCKY.
PLIP
PLIP

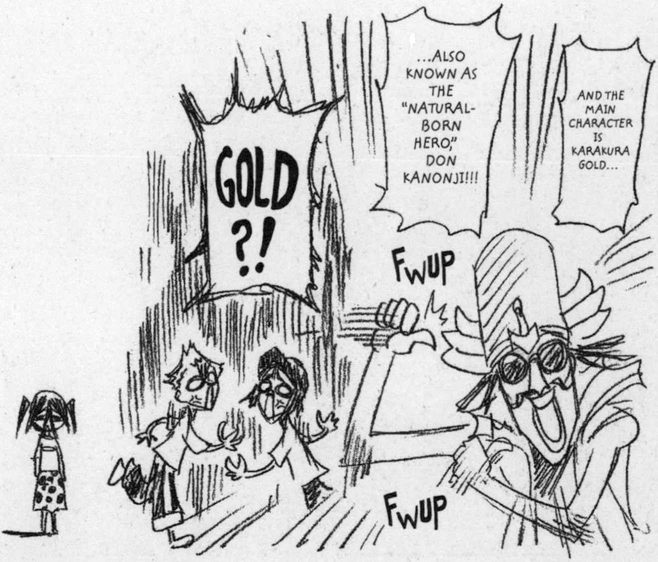
AND THE MAIN CHARACTER IS KARAKURA GOLD...
...ALSO KNOWN AS THE "NATURAL-BORN HERO," DON KANONJI!!!
FWUP
FWUP
GOLD ?!

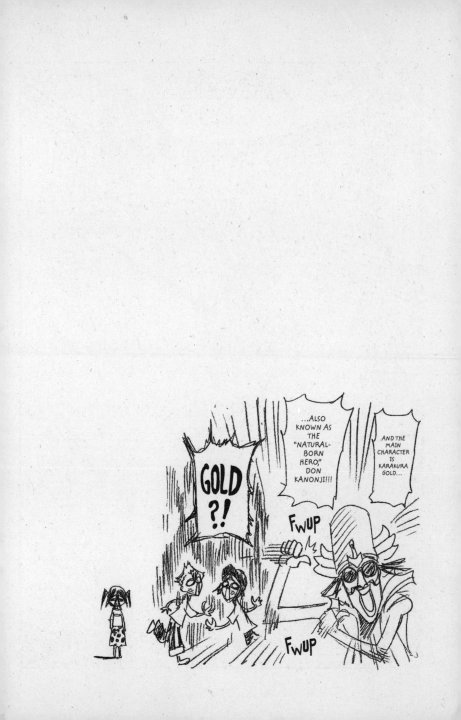

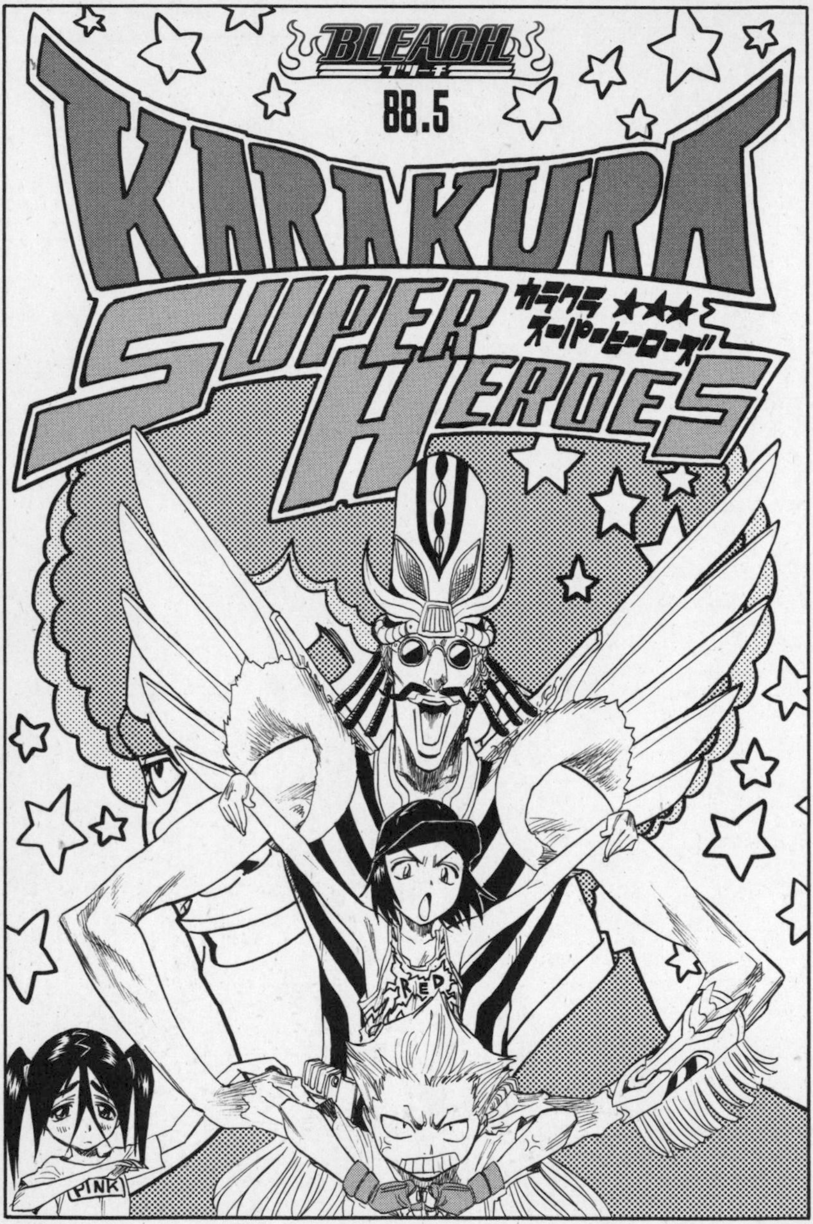
BLEACH
ブリーチ
88.5
KARAKURA SUPER HEROES
カラクラ★★★スーパーヒーローズ
RED
PINK

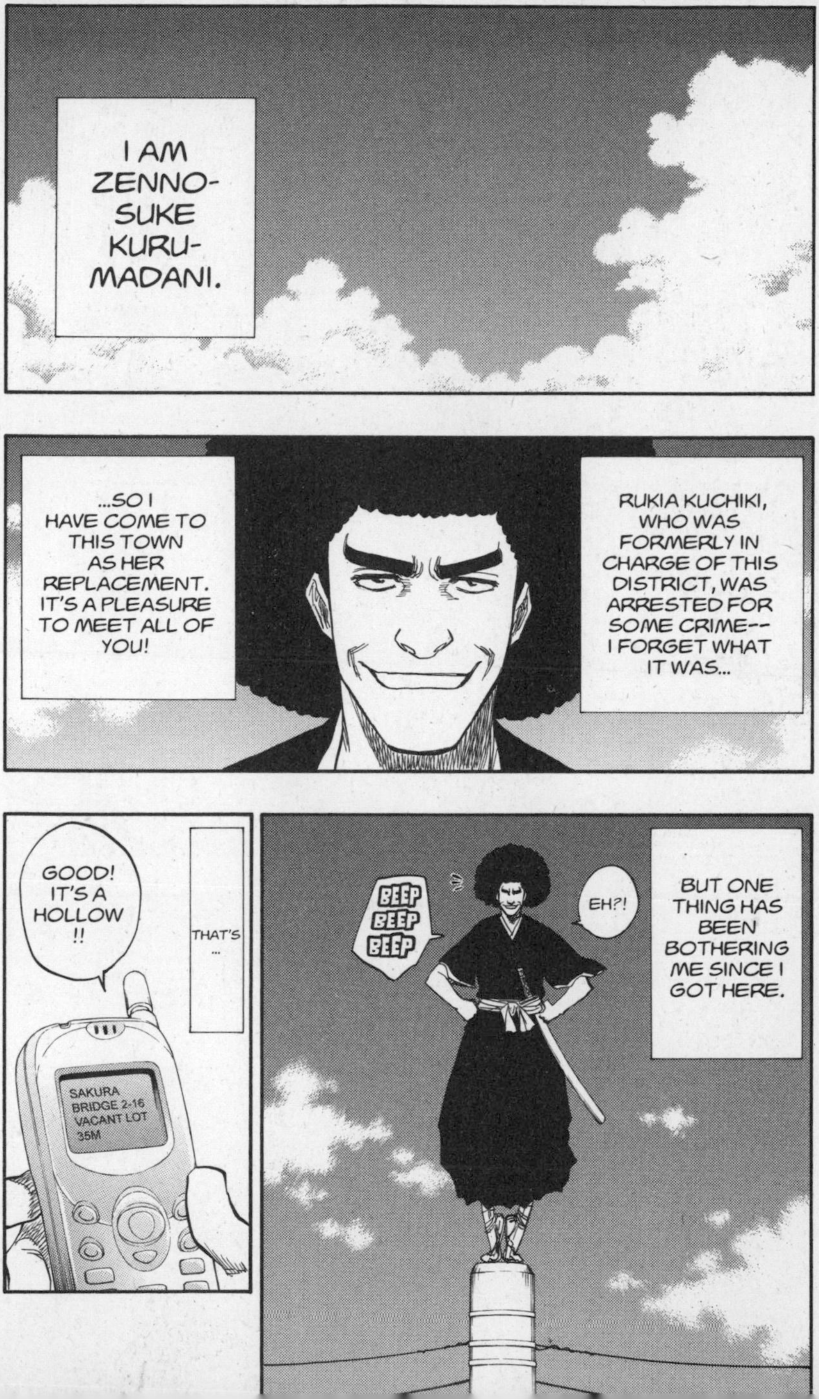
I AM ZENNO-SUKE KURU-MADANI.
RUKIA KUCHIKI, WHO WAS FORMERLY IN CHARGE OF THIS DISTRICT, WAS ARRESTED FOR SOME CRIME-- I FORGET WHAT IT WAS...
...SO I HAVE COME TO THIS TOWN AS HER REPLACEMENT. IT'S A PLEASURE TO MEET ALL OF YOU!
BUT ONE THING HAS BEEN BOTHERING ME SINCE I GOT HERE.
EH?!
BEEP BEEP BEEP
THAT'S ...
GOOD! IT'S A HOLLOW !!
SAKURA BRIDGE 2-16 VACANT LOT 35M

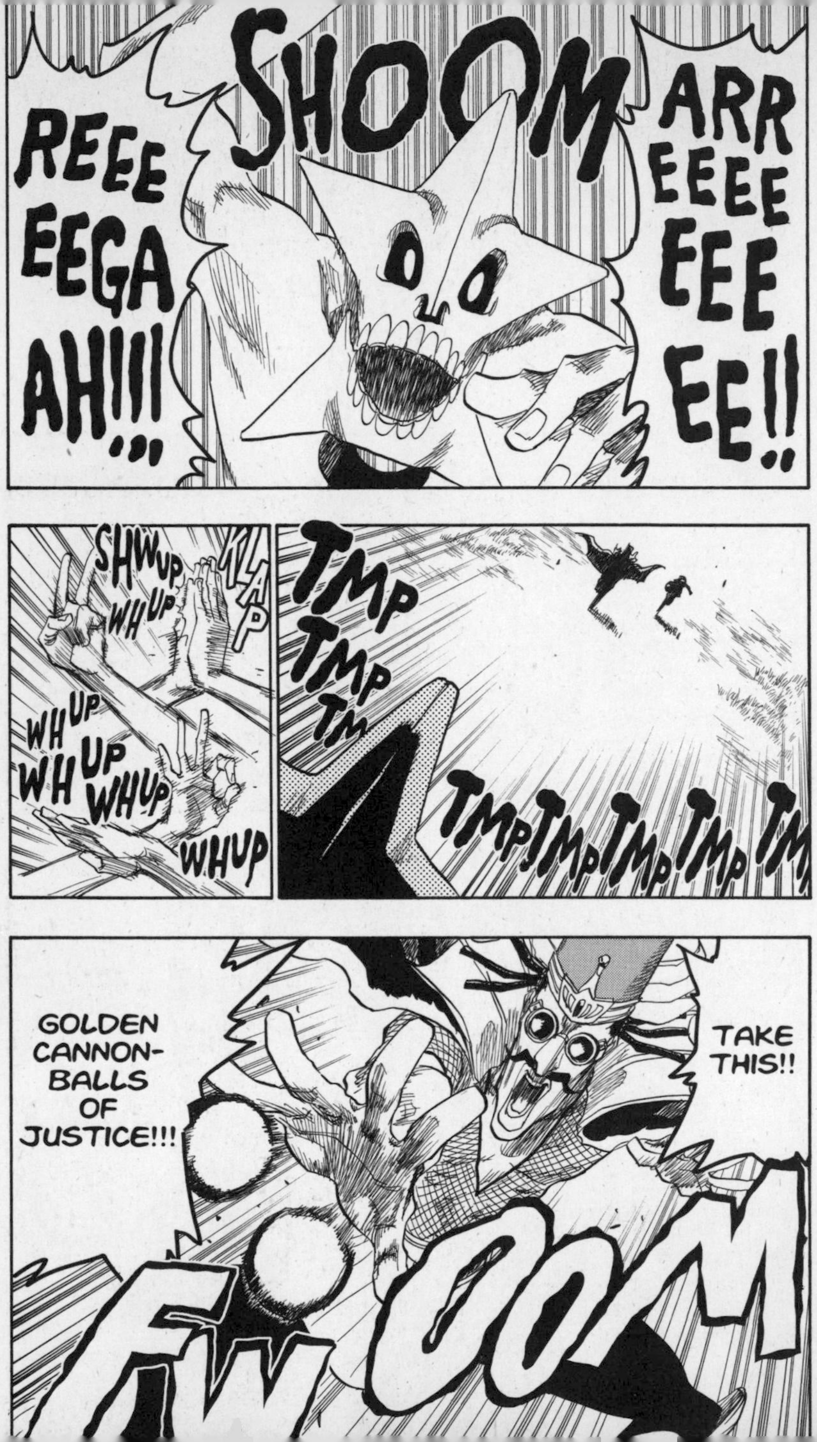
SHOOM
ARREEEEEEEEE!!
REEEEEGAAH!!!
TMP TMP TM
TMP TMP TMP TMP TM
SHWUP
KLAP
WHUP
WHUP
WHUP
WHUP
WHUP
TAKE THIS!!
GOLDEN CANNON-BALLS OF JUSTICE!!!
FWOOM

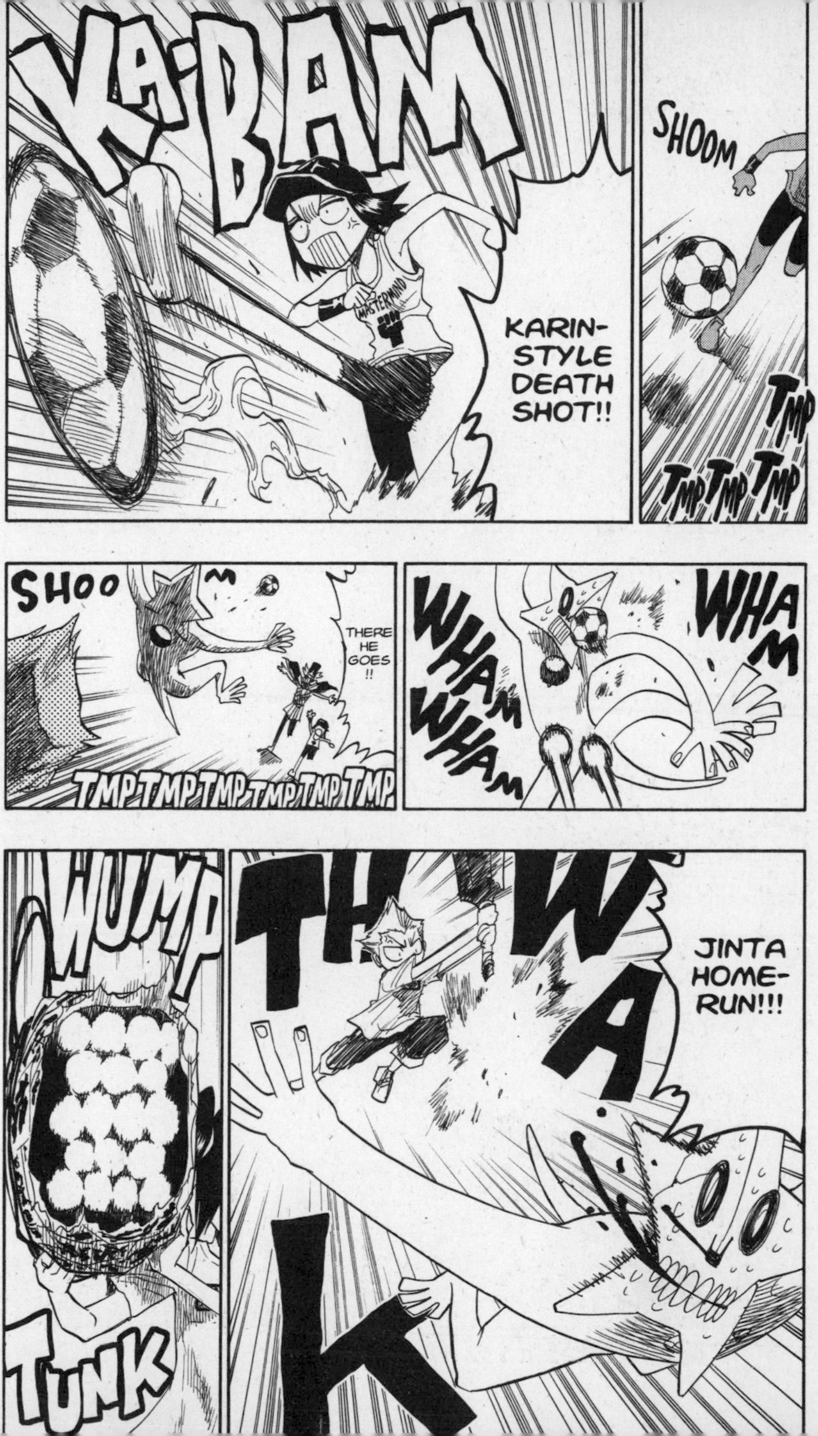
SHOOM
TMP
TMP TMP TMP
KA-BAM
MASTERMIND
KARIN-STYLE DEATH SHOT!!
WHAM
WHAM WHAM
WHAM
SHOOM
THERE HE GOES!!
TMP TMP TMP TMP TMP TMP
THWAK
JINTA HOME-RUN!!!
WHUMP
TUNK

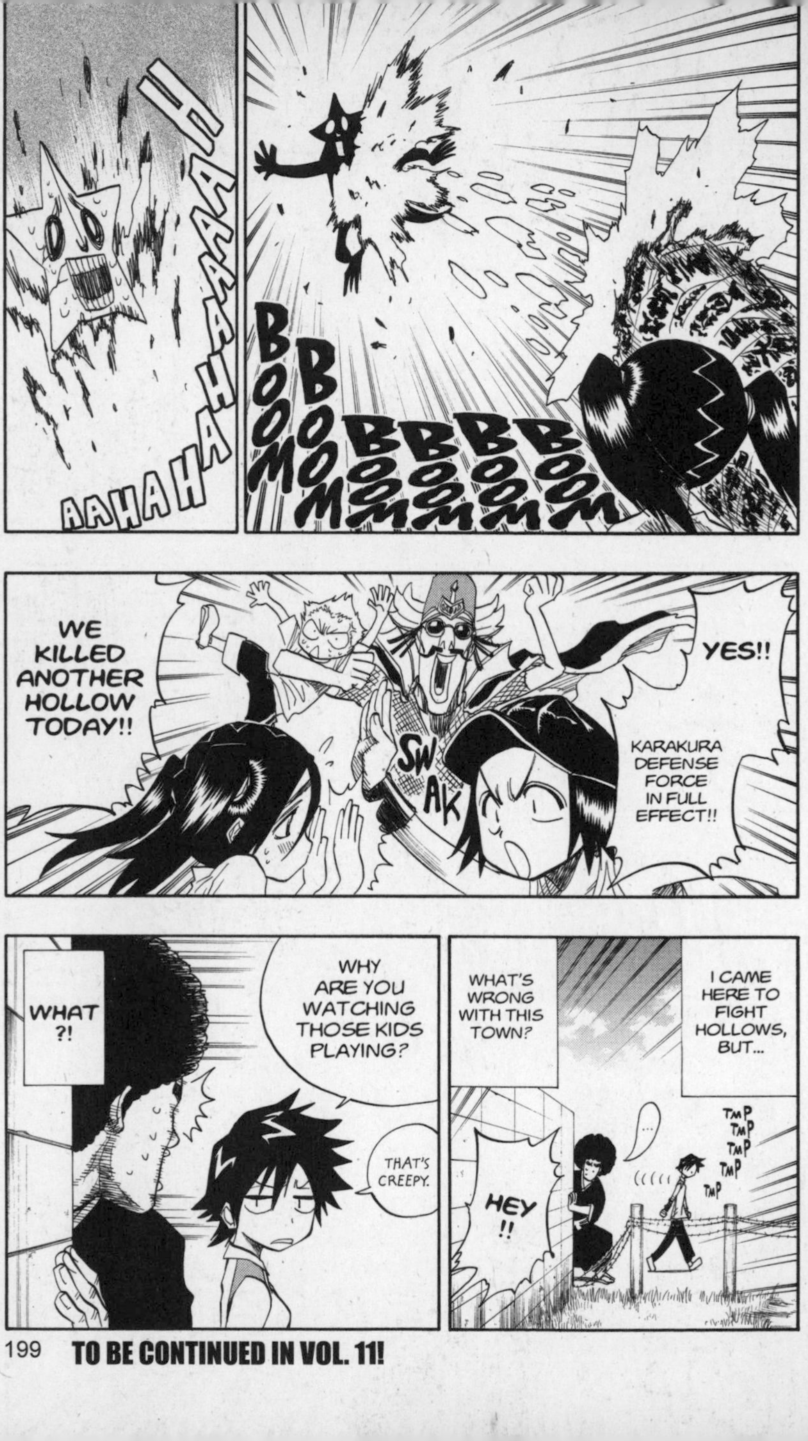
BOOOM BOOOM BOOOM BOOOM BOOOM BOOOM
AAHAHAHAHAAAAH
YES!!
KARAKURA DEFENSE FORCE IN FULL EFFECT!!
SWAK
WE KILLED ANOTHER HOLLOW TODAY!!
I CAME HERE TO FIGHT HOLLOWS, BUT...
WHAT'S WRONG WITH THIS TOWN?
...
TMP TMP TMP TMP TMP
HEY!!
WHY ARE YOU WATCHING THOSE KIDS PLAYING?
THAT'S CREEPY.
WHAT?!

TO BE CONTINUED IN VOL. 11!

Next Volume Preview

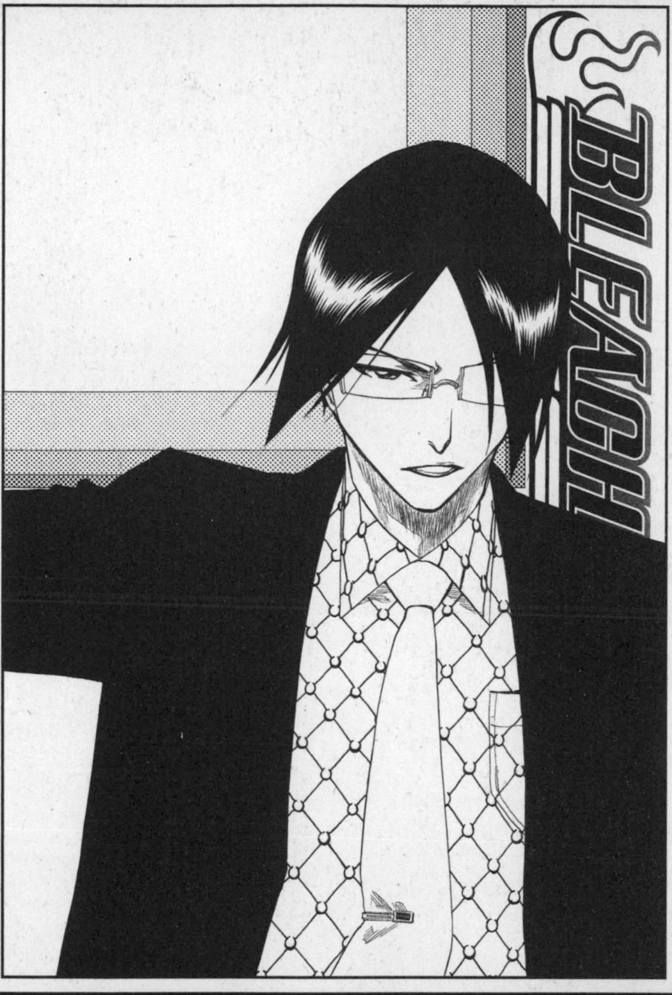
BLEACH

Ichigo's hard-fought battle with Ikkaku of the Eleventh Company provides our surly Soul Reaper with a valuable piece of information: the location of where his friend Rukia is being held while she awaits execution. However, knowing where she is, and actually being able to free her, are two completely different things. Also, Uryû and Orihime run up against Jirôbô, the younger brother of the giant Jidanbô, who they tangled with a little while back. Will Uryû's intensive training pay off, or will he and Orihime need Ichigo to bail them out of trouble?

Available Now

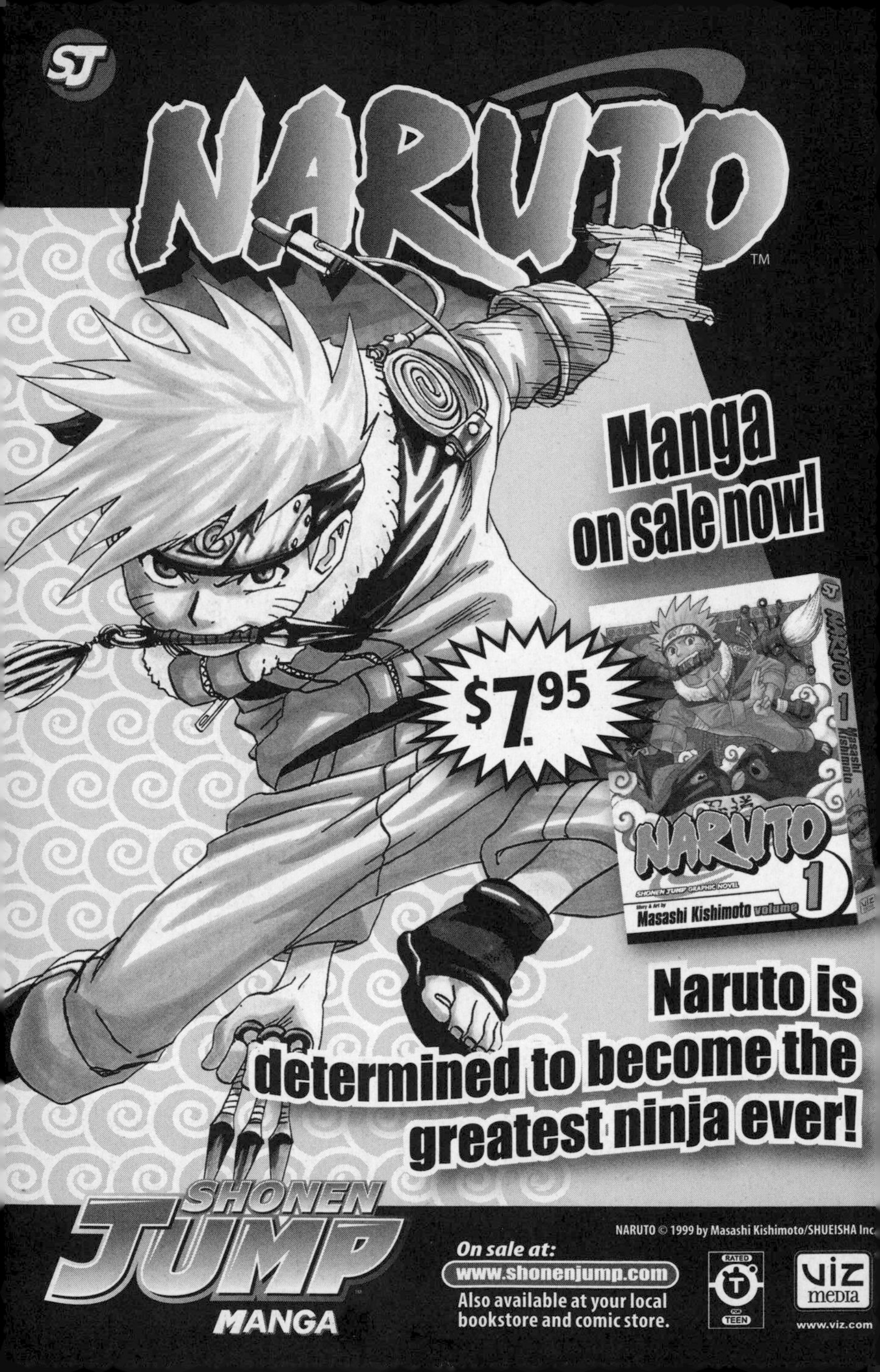
SJ
NARUTO™
Manga on sale now!
$7.95
SJ NARUTO 1 Masashi Kishimoto
NARUTO 1
SHONEN JUMP GRAPHIC NOVEL
Story & Art by Masashi Kishimoto volume 1
Naruto is determined to become the greatest ninja ever!
SHONEN JUMP MANGA
NARUTO © 1999 by Masashi Kishimoto/SHUEISHA Inc.
On sale at:
www.shonenjump.com
Also available at your local bookstore and comic store.
RATED T FOR TEEN
viz media
www.viz.com

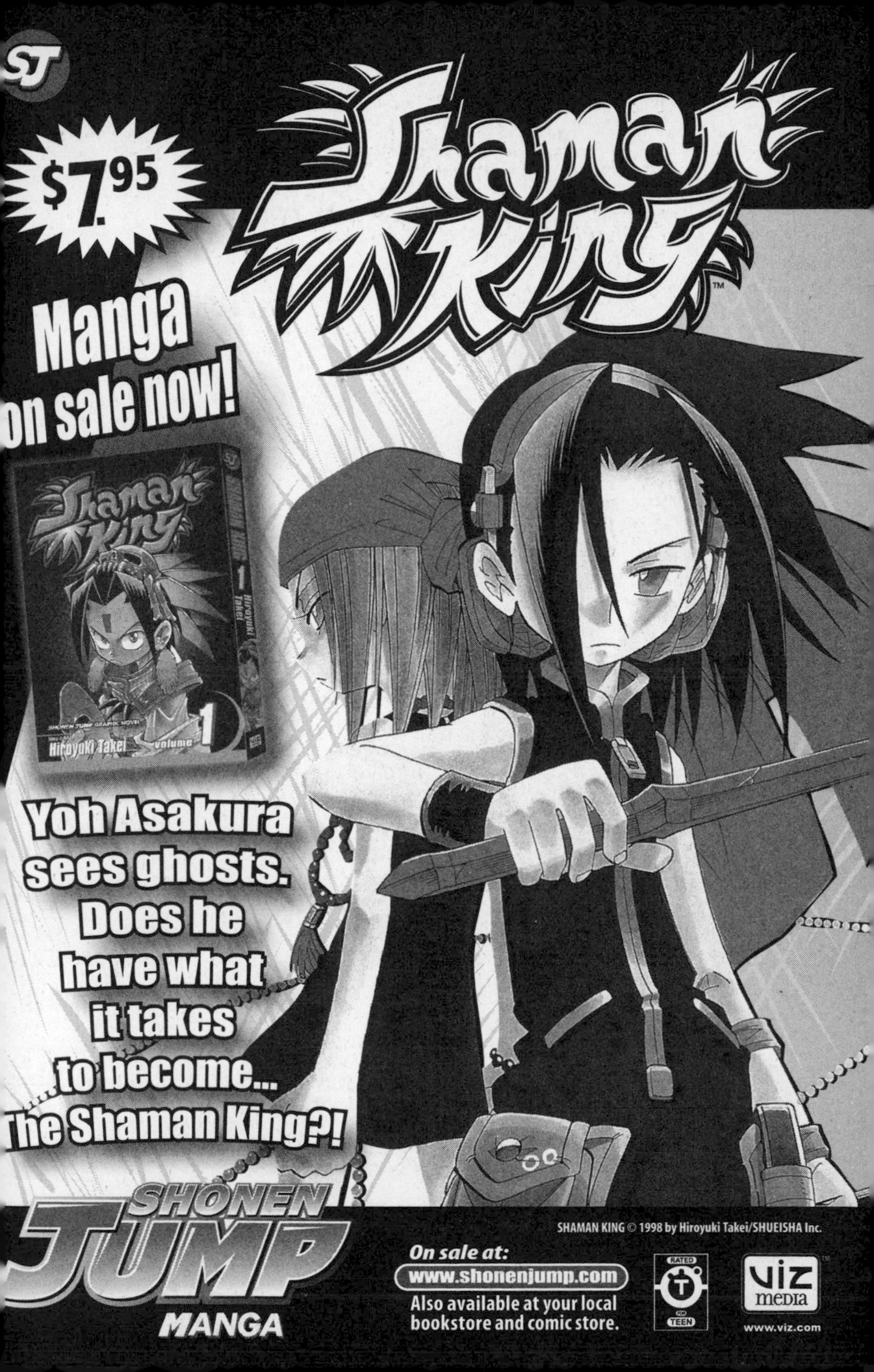
SJ
$7.95
Shaman King™
Manga on sale now!
Shaman King
1
Hiroyuki Takei
volume 1
Yoh Asakura sees ghosts. Does he have what it takes to become... The Shaman King?!
SHONEN JUMP MANGA
SHAMAN KING © 1998 by Hiroyuki Takei/SHUEISHA Inc.
On sale at:
www.shonenjump.com
Also available at your local bookstore and comic store.
RATED T FOR TEEN
viz media
www.viz.com

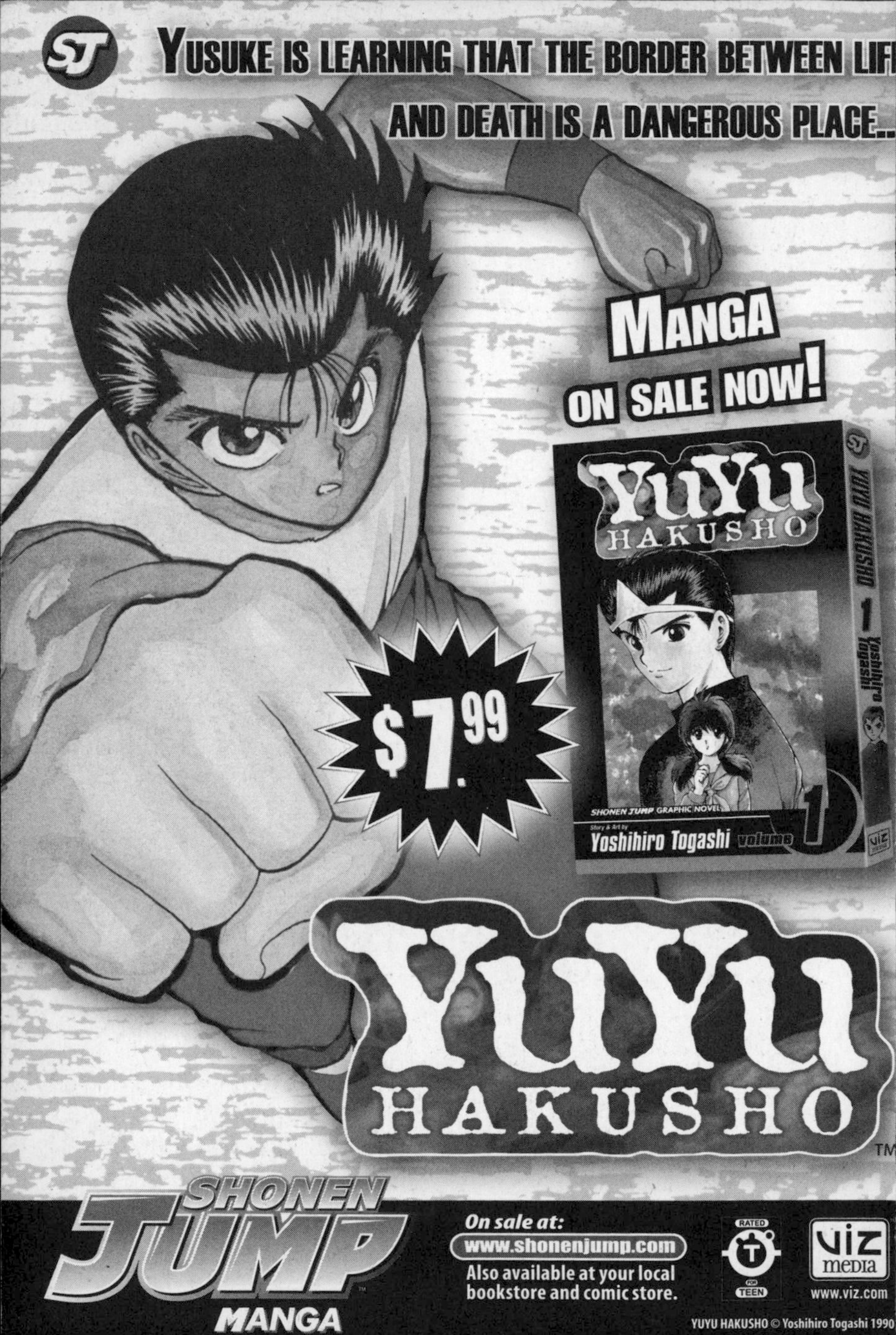

SJ
YUSUKE IS LEARNING THAT THE BORDER BETWEEN LIFE AND DEATH IS A DANGEROUS PLACE...
MANGA ON SALE NOW!
$7.99
YUYU HAKUSHO
SHONEN JUMP GRAPHIC NOVEL
Story & Art by
Yoshihiro Togashi volume 1
YUYU HAKUSHO
HAKUSHO
TM
SHONEN JUMP MANGA
On sale at:
www.shonenjump.com
Also available at your local bookstore and comic store.
RATED T FOR TEEN
viz media
www.viz.com
YUYU HAKUSHO © Yoshihiro Togashi 1990

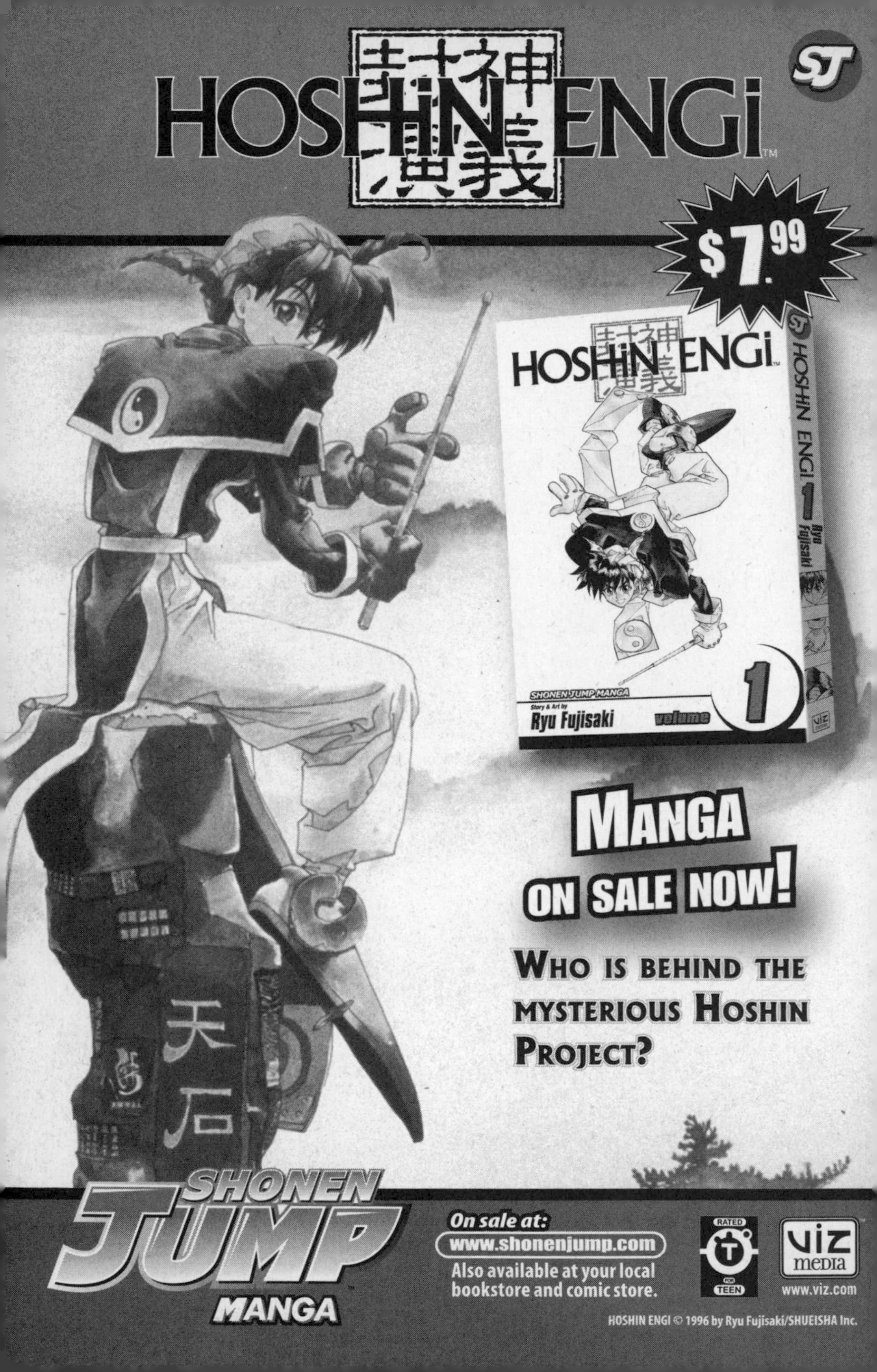

封神演義
HOSHIN ENGI™
SJ
$7.99
HOSHIN ENGI
SHONEN JUMP MANGA
Story & Art by
Ryu Fujisaki
volume 1
MANGA
ON SALE NOW!
WHO IS BEHIND THE MYSTERIOUS HOSHIN PROJECT?
天
SHONEN JUMP MANGA
On sale at:
www.shonenjump.com
Also available at your local bookstore and comic store.
RATED T FOR TEEN
VIZ media
www.viz.com
HOSHIN ENGI © 1996 by Ryu Fujisaki/SHUEISHA Inc.

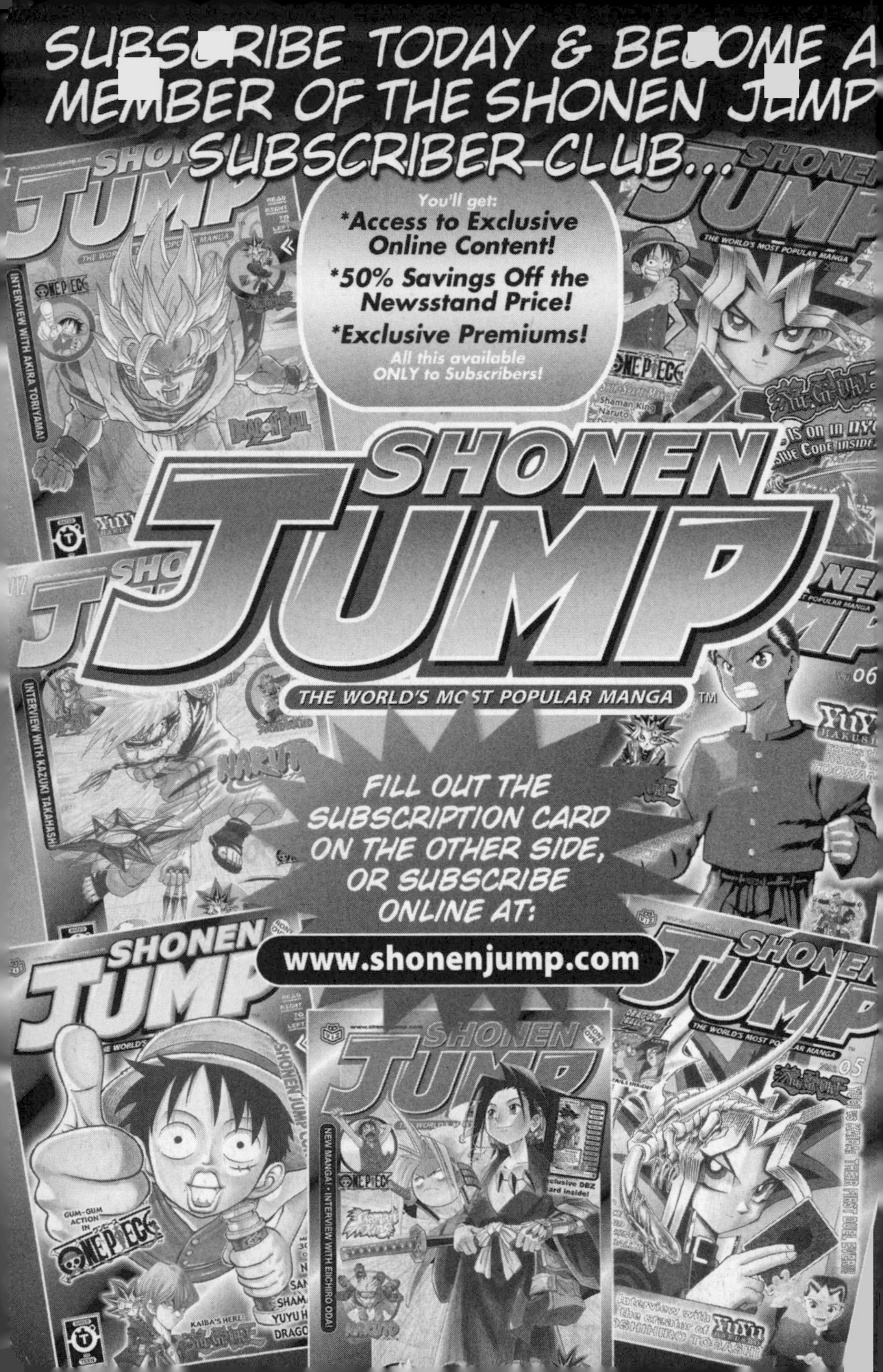
SUBSCRIBE TODAY & BECOME A MEMBER OF THE SHONEN JUMP SUBSCRIBER CLUB...
You'll get:
*Access to Exclusive Online Content!
*50% Savings Off the Newsstand Price!
*Exclusive Premiums!
All this available ONLY to Subscribers!
SHONEN JUMP
THE WORLD'S MOST POPULAR MANGA
FILL OUT THE SUBSCRIPTION CARD ON THE OTHER SIDE, OR SUBSCRIBE ONLINE AT:
www.shonenjump.com